THE MAKING OF INDIA AND INDIAN TRADITIONS

The Making of India and Indian Traditions

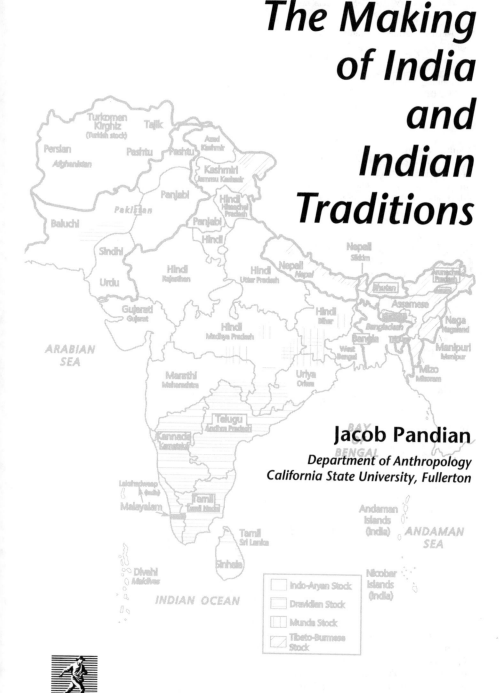

Jacob Pandian

Department of Anthropology
California State University, Fullerton

	Indo-Aryan Stock
	Dravidian Stock
	Munda Stock
	Tibeto-Burmese Stock

Prentice Hall, Englewood Cliffs, New Jersey 07632

Library of Congress Cataloging-in-Publication Data

PANDIAN, JACOB.
   The making of India and Indian traditions / by Jacob Pandian.
p.cm.
      Includes bibliographical references and index.
      ISBN 0-13-124421-3
      1. India   I. Title.
   DS407.P26   1995
    954 dc20   94-16912

Acquisitions editor: *Nancy Roberts*
Project manager: *Joanne Riker*
Cover design: *Tom Nery*
Buyer: *Mary Ann Gloriande*
Editorial assistant: *Pat Naturale*

©1995 by Prentice-Hall, Inc.
A Simon & Schuster Company
Englewood Cliffs, New Jersey 07632

Printed in the United States of America

10 9   8   7   6   5   4   3   2   1

ISBN   0-13-124421-3

Prentice-Hall International (UK) Limited, *London*
Prentice-Hall of Australia Pty. Limited, *Sydney*
Prentice-Hall Canada Inc., *Toronto*
Prentice-Hall Hispanoamericana, S.A., *Mexico*
Prentice-Hall of India Private Limited, *New Delhi*
Prentice-Hall of Japan, Inc., *Tokyo*
Simon & Schuster Asia Pte. Ltd., *Singapore*
Editora Prentice-Hall do Brasil, Ltda., *Rio de Janeiro*

Dedicated to my daughter
Georgina Pandian
who may one day discover and create
a different configuration of India
than the one
that I have created in this book.

 # CONTENTS

PREFACE   xv

Map: Language Families of South Asia   1
Map: Languages of South Asia   3

INTRODUCTION   4

    i.   Objectives and Scope of This Study   4
    ii.   The Melting Pot of Indus Culture and the Ethnic Salad Bowl of India   5
    iii. A Note on the Organization of This Book   *10*
    iv. A Note on the Semiotic Perspective of This Book   *11*
    v.   A Note on Writing Textbooks and Survey Books on India   *16*

PART 1
THE MELTING POT OF INDUS CULTURE AND THE ETHNIC SALAD BOWL OF INDIA   19

Map: Indus Valley Civilization in Northwestern India 3000–1500 B.C.E.   19
Map: India's Trade Links with West Asia and Central Asia B.C.E.   20
Map: Languages of India   21

CHAPTER 1
THE SEMIOTICS OF INDIA AND INDIAN IDENTITY   *23*

i.   Indus River and Indus River-Dwellers: Persian and Greek
      Significations of India   *23*
ii.   The Signification of Northern and Southern India   *26*
iii. Pan-Indian Linguistic Dominance: Sanskrit, Persian, English,
      and Hindi   *27*
iv.   The Persianization of Khari Boli Dialect of India and the
      Development of the Hindi-Urdu Language   *29*
v.   The Invention of Indian Nationality and the Hindi-ization
      of India   *31*
vi.   Colonialism, Racism, and Colorism in India   *34*

CHAPTER 2
THE SEMIOTICS OF HINDUISM   *49*

i.   Hinduism and Religious Freedom:
      There Are No Hindu Heretics   *49*
ii.   The Semantics of Hindu Pluratheism   *54*
iii. The Cultural Formulations of Metaphysical, Biopsychological,
      and Sociological Hinduism   *57*
iv.   Hinduization   *58*
v.   Sanskritic and Brahmanical Rituals of Hinduism   *61*
vi.   The Sacred Symbol of the Mother Goddess in Hinduism   *63*

CHAPTER 3
THE SEMIOTICS OF CASTE IN INDIA   *66*

i.   The Nature of Caste and the Caste System of India   *66*
ii.   Caste Emblems: Jati Names, Jati Titles, and Varna Symbols   *69*
iii. Transformation of Caste Identity and Social Mobility   *71*
iv.   Caste and Hindu Sectarianism   *75*
v.   Caste and the Tribal Frontier   *77*

CHAPTER 4
THE SEMIOTICS OF ALIEN ETHNIC IDENTITIES IN INDIA 80

i.   Caste and Alien Ethnic Identities   *80*
ii.   Symbols of Islamic Ethnicity and Muslim Identities in India   *81*
iii. Persianization of Muslim Identity in India   *83*
iv.   Arabization of Muslim Identity in India   *87*
v.   Caste, Ethnicity, and Islamic Nationalism Among
      the Muslims of India   *90*
vi.   Symbols of Jewish Identity in India   *93*
vii. Symbols of Syrian-Christian Identity in India   *96*
viii. Symbols of Parsi Identity in India   *97*
ix.   Symbols of Anglo-Indian Identity   *99*

CHAPTER 5
THE SEMIOTICS OF COLORISM IN INDIA *103*

i.   Ethnic Symbols of Physical Beauty   *103*
ii.   Symbols of Wheatish and Fair Skin Color in India   *105*
iii. Pre-Islamic Symbols of Skin Color in India   *107*
iv.   Post-13th Century Symbols of Skin Color in India   *108*
v.   Aryanism and Colorism in Modern India   *110*
vi.   The Pragmatics of Colorism in Modern India   *113*

PART II
STATE SYSTEMS AND NATIONAL TRADITIONS OF INDIA *117*

Map: India under Emperor Asoka circa 240 B.C.E.   117
*Map: India in the 19th Century C. E. with British Territories
    and the Native Princely Kingdoms   118*
Map: Contemporary Linguistic State Boundaries in India   119

CHAPTER 6
THE DEVELOPMENT OF EMPIRE-STATES AND THE FORMATION OF THE BRITISH-INDIAN EMPIRE IN INDIA   *120*

i.   Empire-States and Nation-States   *120*
ii.   Pre-British Empire-States and Kingdoms   *124*
iii. The Emergence of British Rule in India   *126*
iv.   Company Raj and the British Empire-State of India   *129*
v.   The Constitution of Rational Political and Legal Institutions in India   *131*
vi.   The Introduction of the Politics of Racial Hierarchy in India   *135*

CHAPTER 7
HINDI RAJ AND THE CREATION OF THE INDIAN EMPIRE-STATE   *139*

i.   Crown Raj of the British-Indian Empire   *139*
ii.   The Emergence of the Dominions of India and Pakistan   *140*
iii. Hindi Raj and the Indian Empire-State   *142*
iv.   The Constitution of the Linguistic States in India   *145*
v.   India and Western Democracy   *148*

CHAPTER 8
THE ETHNOLINGUISTIC STATES AND NATIONAL TRADITIONS OF INDIA   *153*

i.   The Linguistic States of Hindistan, or the Land of the Hindi Speakers   *153*
ii.   The Linguistic States of Panjab and Kashmir: The Land of Panjabi and Kashmiri Speakers   *155*
iii. The Linguistic States of Gujarat and Maharashtra: The Land of Gurajati and Marathi Speakers   *159*
iv.   The Linguistic States of Bengal, Orissa, and Assam: The Land of Bengali, Oriya, and Assamese Speakers   *160*
v.   Austro-Asiatic and Tibeto-Burman Linguistic States of India   *162*
vi.   The Linguistic States of Karnataka and Andhra Pradesh: The Land of Kannada and Telugu Speakers   *163*
vii. The Linguistic States of Tamil Nadu and Kerala: The Land of Tamil and Malayali Speakers   *164*

CHAPTER 9
LINGUISTIC NATIONALISM AND THE QUEST FOR DRAVIDASTAN (THE LAND OF DRAVIDIAN SPEAKERS): THE TAMILS *169*

i.   National Autonomy and the Quest for Statehood   *169*
ii.   Dravidian-Speakers of India and the Linguistic-Cultural Distinctiveness of the Tamils of India   *171*
iii. Ancient Tamil Kingdoms and Tamil Polity   *173*
iv.   Ancient Tamil Social Organization and Religion   *175*
v.   Brahmanical Priesthood and State Temples in the Tamil Territory   *177*
vi.   The Symbol of Chenthamil or Pure Tamil   *178*
vii. Tamil Poets and Tamil Literary Academies   *179*
viii. Naturalism and Supernaturalism in the Tamil Literary Tradition   *180*
ix.   The Symbol of Karppu: The Tamil Theme of Female Chastity-Spirituality   *181*
x.   Kannagi: The Representation and Interpretation of Chastity in the Tamil Epic *Silapathikaram*   *183*
xi.   The Symbol of Tamilakam: The Home of Tamils   *185*
xii. The Politics of Linguistic Nationalism   *186*
xiii. The Quest for Dravidastan   *188*

CHAPTER 10
RELIGIOUS NATIONALISM AND THE QUEST FOR KHALISTAN (THE LAND OF THE PURE): THE SIKHS *192*

i.   Religious Nationalism and the Quest for Statehood   *192*
ii.   The Socioreligious and Political Contexts of 15th-Century Northern India   *196*
iii. The Sant Tradition of Hinduism and Sikhism   *198*
iv.   Guru Nanak Panth and the Sikh Panth of Nanak's Successors   *199*
v.   Guru Gobind Singh and the Khalsa Panth   *200*
vi.   The Quest for Khalistan   *201*

PART III
VILLAGE TRADITIONS OF INDIA   203

Map: Tamil Nadu, India   203
Map: Pulicat Village and Its Vicinity   204
Map: Pulicat Lake Showing Territory of Pulicat Revenue Village   205

CHAPTER 11
THE STUDY OF VILLAGE TRADITIONS   206

i.   The Village Communities of India   *206*
ii.   Anthropological Studies of Indian Village Communities   *208*

CHAPTER 12
PULICAT: AN ESTUARINE VILLAGE
OF EASTERN INDIA   215

i.   A Note on the Physical Structure of Pulicat Village   *215*
ii.   Pulicat and Its Hamlets   *217*
iii. The Kuppams (Hamlets or Subvillages)   *222*

CHAPTER 13
A BRIEF HISTORY OF PULICAT VILLAGE   226

i.   Political History of Pulicat   *226*
ii.   Recent Economic and Social History of Pulicat   *230*
iii. Recent Religious History of Pulicat   *232*

CHAPTER 14
ECONOMIC AND SOCIOPOLITICAL TRADITIONS OF PULICAT
VILLAGE   236

i.   Patrons and Clients in the Economic Structure of Pulicat   *236*
ii.   Sociopolitical Structure of Pulicat Village   *240*
iii. Corporate Authority in Pulicat Village   242

CHAPTER 15
RELIGIOUS TRADITIONS OF PULICAT VILLAGE AND THE
PAROCHIAL MODELS OF VILLAGE HINDUISM   *245*

i.   Brahmanic Rituals and Jati Identity   *245*
ii.   Non-Brahmanical Shamanism and Group/Individual Rituals in
      Pulicat Village   *249*
iii. Household Rituals and Religious Integration of the Cultural
      Hindu Self   *254*
iv.   Pulicat Hindu Religious Tradition, and the All-India Parochial
      Models of Village Hinduism   *256*

CONCLUSION   *259*

i.   The Making of India and Indian Traditions   *259*
ii.   India and Discourse on History   *263*
iii. India and Western Discourse on Civilization   *266*
iv.   India and Discourse on Ethnicity and Nationalism   *268*
v.   Some Final Thoughts   *274*

BIBLIOGRAPHY   *283*

INDEX   *295*

THE MAKING OF INDIA AND INDIAN TRADITIONS

Language Families of South Asia

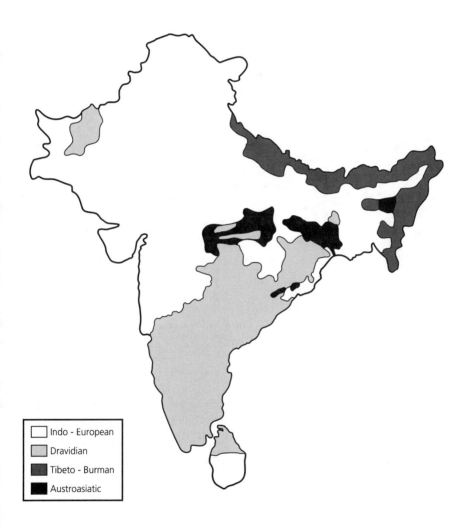

Indo - European
Dravidian
Tibeto - Burman
Austroasiatic

Languages of South Asia

☞ INTRODUCTION

i. Objectives and Scope of This Study

Is India an empire-state, an artifact of British colonialism, which will sooner or later collapse like the Soviet Union? Or is India the home of a dynamic Hindu civilizational system that integrates various ethnic and linguistic groups, castes, and nationalities? Is India the prototype of a polyethnic, pluralistic society with viable democratic institutions? Or is India a conglomeration of unequal, quasi-religious, and antagonistic political entities that are regulated by a Hindi-speaking elite (successors of the English-speaking elite of the British empire and the Persian-speaking elite of the Mughal empire) who have greater access than the speakers of other Indian languages to the all-India bureaucratic, industrial, and military organizations? In this study I address these and other related questions in a number of different ways. The following paragraph identifies briefly the theoretical perspective of this study.

This book offers a semiotic discourse on how certain symbols of India and Indian traditions (and identities) have been constituted. I describe and interpret the origins and maintenance of various representations or symbols of Indian cultural boundaries, ethnolinguistic national identities, and village traditions and analyze their meanings and uses in diverse sociopolitical contexts. A semiotic or symbolic-interactional analysis of this kind is generally associated with humanistic approaches of history, sociology, and anthropology. I present interpretations and conclusions that are based on anthropological, historical, and sociological studies of worldviews, values, conceptions of ethnic and religious identities, and political configurations. Therefore, the theoretical/methodological framework of this book overlaps the disciplinary boundaries of history, sociology, and cultural anthropology and may simply be identified as a cultural analysis of India and Indian traditions. I provide a historical overview of India, focusing on the cultural developments that occurred in relation to the migrations of central and west Asian ethnic groups, such as Aryans, Scythians, Arabs, Huns, Turks, Persians, and Mongols into India, and discuss briefly the factors that fostered the emergence of Turkish, Mughal, British, and Indian empire-states in India. Also, I delineate certain religious, social, and cultural categories of India, focusing on Hinduism, caste, colorism, and nationalism, and offer an in-depth historical, sociological, and cultural analysis of Sikh religious nationalism and Tamil linguistic nationalism. And I present a discussion of village traditions as well as an analysis of a particular village—its physical features, history, and socioeconomic and religious traditions—based on my ethnographic study.

This book sheds light on a wide variety of features about India. How did the indigenous and Aryan cultural traditions blend to foster the continuation of beliefs and practices that probably began in the Indus Valley Civilization between 3000 and 1700 B.C.E.? Why does Hinduism not have an ecclesiastical orientation? How did Indians acquire color prejudice? How does Indian colorism differ from racism? What is the nature of caste? How does caste mobility occur? How do west Asian ethnic groups become castelike groups and coexist with caste groups? How did empire-states evolve in India? How did the British succeed in establishing politico-economic dominance in India? How did the Turks and Mughals shape the creation of modern India? How and why did the British introduce Western institutions in India? Is contemporary India an extension of British India? How are the linguistic states and ethnonational traditions formed? What are the factors that make the Tamil and Sikh traditions very distinctive despite their foundations in Hindu culture? Beyond the answers to the foregoing questions about India, this book presents a model of India that should enable the reader to understand why and how there is cultural and racial unity of India despite the existence of multifarious cultural, religious, and ethnic traditions. It is my hope that the reader will also understand, from reading this book, why there is so much violence and bloodshed in India when the ideal image of India is that it is a country of spirituality, nonviolence, and tolerance.

ii. The Melting Pot of Indus Culture and the Ethnic Salad Bowl of India

The title of Part I, "The Melting Pot of Indus Culture and the Ethnic Salad Bowl of India," captures a significant fact about India. On the one hand, there is an Indus or Hindu cultural unity of India; on the other hand, India is composed of thousands of culturally, religiously, and linguistically distinctive ethnic groups that make India ethnographically more heterogeneous than the European ethnographic area. India has populations that are linguistically members of four language families. In 1990 it was estimated that about 630 million people spoke Indo-European languages such as Hindi (about 360 million), Marathi (about 77 million), Bengali (about 66 million), Gujarati (about 42 million), Uriya (about 30 million), Assamese (about 27 million), Panjabi (about 20 million), Kashmiri (about 7 million), and Konkani (about 1 million). Two hundred and one million people spoke Dravidian languages such as Telugu (about 66 million), Tamil (about 59 million), Kannada (about 46 million), and Malayalam (about 30 million). About 8 million people spoke

Tibeto-Burman languages and 1 million people spoke Austro-Asiatic languages. Although over 80 percent of the estimated 840 million were Hindus, India had about 130 million Muslims, which made Indian Muslims the second largest Muslim population in the world (next to Indonesian Muslims), and there were about 15 million Christians and about 15 million Sikhs.

The nation-state boundary of India, incorporating such diverse populations, evolved out of the *empire concept*. Such a concept was introduced in India by the Persian Achaemenid Empire of 550–330 B.C.E. and was continued at different times by other empires. If the Islamic and British Empires (i.e., Turkish sultanates from the 12th to 16th centuries, the Mughal Empire from early 16th to early 19th centuries, and the British Empire from the early 19th to mid-20th centuries) had not been established in India, there would be no single nation-state called India today. Instead, India would be like Europe. And just as we identify a group of people as "European," we would probably identify a group of people as "Indian," but there would be several monarchical-states or linguistic nation-states such as Gujarat (Gujarati language), Tamil Nadu (Tamil language) and Maharashtra (Marathi language), comparable to France (French), Denmark (Danish), and Italy (Italian). It should be pointed out that there is a greater difference between Gujarati and Marathi than between French and Italian, and a greater difference between Tamil and Marathi than between French and Hungarian. I have made these contrasts mainly to sensitize the reader to the facts pertaining to the heterogeneity of the people who are lumped together as "Indians." In Chapters 1, 2, 3, 4, and 5 (Part I) I will discuss the ethnic diversity of the Indians with reference to their Dravidian, Aryan, Persian, Scythian, Hunnish, Greek, Afghan, Turkish, and Mongol heritages. From an ethnic perspective of identification, a large number of people in India could have labels that refer to their non-Indian ancestry, and the variations in the physical characteristics of the Indians are largely due to the waves of migrations of peoples from central and western Asia from the 7th century B.C.E. to the 17th century C.E. rather than to the ancient (1700-1500 B.C.E.) migrations of Aryans. To illustrate this fact, I will give two well-known Indian names as examples. Salman Rushdie, who is identified as an "India-born British writer," is Turkish-Persian-Indian. Rajiv Gandhi, the deceased Indian leader, was part Kashmiri-Indian and part Persian-Indian (Parsi). His great-grandfather was from Kashmir (which was ethnically linked with Turkestan) and his father was Parsi (Persian). It would be as absurd to wonder why most Indians do not look like either Salman Rushdie or Rajiv Gandhi as it would be to wonder why Africans do not look like Europeans.

Had the empire concept not taken hold in the imagination of the "Indian" political leaders who became active during the British Empire in opposing both the British and the native princes or kings of their kingdoms in India, there would be no such nation-state called India or a nation-state called Pakistan today. As Maloney (1991:3) correctly points out,

Europe arranged itself through a process of wars into countries largely following linguistic boundaries; so did East and Southeast Asia. But by historical accident, India arranged itself into linguistic states within a central government. Had it not been for the Mughal and British concept of empire, perhaps India too would have arranged itself by war into a number of linguistic modern nations.

The metaphors of melting pot and salad bowl are apt, in many ways, to comprehend the cultural, social, and political landscape of India. The Aryan invaders and immigrants of the period 1700-1500 B.C.E. became culturally, socially, and politically Indian in the sense that they gradually discarded Aryan customs and adopted Hindu, Indus, or Dravidian traditions. In other words, the Aryans were Dravidianized or Hinduized and melted or blended into the *Indus cultural pot*. The Dravidianized Aryans and the indigenous populations participated in the maintenance of the Hindu or Indus traditions such as the caste system, the principles of ritual purity and impurity, the yoga system, the worship of Siva and the mother goddess, and the doctrines of reincarnation in a number of varying, complementary, contradictory, and creative ways. The Dravidian-Aryan synthesis was remarkable in reaffirming and elaborating upon the Indus cultural heritage.

The invasion-migration of Scythians and Iranians (Persians) from the 7th century B.C.E. created major political upheavals and cultural crises in northwestern and northern India. And, there arose several socioreligious cults during the 7th and 6th centuries (B.C.E.). It is a well-known fact that in situations of cultural stress and social-political unrest, religious movements arise, with prophetic leaders promising hope and salvation for their followers. In the 6th century B.C.E. Jainism and Buddhism became popular, but several other religious movements also developed during that period.

The rise of the Achaemenid Persian Empire (550–330 B.C.E.) established some stability in northwestern and northern India, but the Persian Empire also fostered and facilitated more invasions and immigrations. The Greeks entered northwestern India in the 4th century B.C.E. and established political dominance in parts of northwestern (Panjab) and northern (Kashmir) India. Scythian invasions and migrations continued until the 4th century C.E., and large numbers of Huns entered India during the 5th and 6th centuries C.E. The Persians, Greeks, Scythians, and Huns who settled down in northwestern and northern India between the 7th century B.C.E. and the 7th century C.E. were, for the most part, co-opted into the Hindu society (caste system) as warrior class (Kshatriyas), and many acquired the status symbols of princes with titles such as Rajputs (sons of kings). Thus, although these ethnic groups introduced a new type of ethnicity, linking the Kshatriyas of northwestern and northern India with physical features that we often associate with Persians, Greeks, Scythians, and Huns, these groups also blended or melted in the Indus cultural pot.

The significant impact of the period between the 7th century B.C.E. and the 7th century C.E. was that in northwestern and northern India, the ruling families (both the Kshatriyas and in some regions the Brahmins) often had the physical features of west and central Asians. This fact created a profound misunderstanding in the interpretation and explanations of Hindu culture and Hindu ethnicity in the 19th century. European and Indian scholars began to equate light-brown skin color and upper- caste status, identified people of light-brown skin color as Aryans and the people of dark-brown skin color as Dravidians, and theorized that Aryans (i.e., the light-brown peoples) created Hindu civilization. As I have pointed out, the Aryans who entered India between 1700 and 1500 B.C.E. merged or blended with the indigenous populations. This was similar to what happened to the Aryans who entered Europe: The light-brown skinned (and dark-haired) Aryans merged with the pre-Aryan populations of Europe who were, for the most part in northern Europe, blondes with white skin color.

The invasions and migrations that took place after the 10th century C.E. created an entirely new dimension in the political-economic landscape of northwestern and northern India. The new immigrants and invaders did not fit or melt in the Hindu cultural pot. These populations fostered the making of modern India into a salad bowl, with several alien ethnic, religious, and linguistic factors shaping modern India:

1. Islam was introduced in the 10th century C.E., and it acquired importance as the religion of the ruling class in certain parts of northwestern and northern India and ultimately provided the cultural foundation for Muslim intellectuals to propound the *two-nation* theory (Islamic and Hindu nations of India) in the early 20th century, and to form the country of Pakistan (partitioning British India into the Muslim state of Pakistan and the secular state of India in 1947);
2. as large numbers of Turks and Persians entered India and occupied important political positions, Turko-Persian physical features acquired importance as the physical characteristics of the ruling class;
3. Turkish and Persian languages acquired importance in northwestern and northern India, and such an importance gave rise to the emergence of the Urdu-Hindi language by the 12th century, a fact that had a major political consequence in the 20th century with Urdu becoming the national language of Pakistan and Hindi becoming the national language of India;
4. Persian language and customs acquired importance as vehicles of high civilization, replacing Sanskrit language and customs in northwestern and northern India; and
5. a self-conscious Arab identity was cultivated by many Muslim communities in the western and eastern coasts of India. (See Chapter 4 for a comprehensive discussion, and also refer to Chapters 13 and 14 for an analysis of how Muslim communities exist in the village tradition.)

about a hundred years; in contemporary India, there is a strong sentiment, although not explicitly supported by all the Sikhs, for the creation of a separate Sikh nation-state called *Khalistan* (the land of the pure). The Tamils live about two thousand miles south of the Panjab and speak a Dravidian language in contrast to an Aryan language (Panjabi) spoken by the Sikhs; for about three thousand years, the Tamils have sought to protect the "purity" of their language, and linguistic nationalism has been an important component of Tamil culture for over two thousand years. In the past century, there has been a strong sentiment against the Hindi speakers of northern India and the Sanskritic (Aryan language) scriptures, and a large number of Tamils have favored the creation of a separate Tamil nation-state called *Dravidastan* (the land of Dravidian speakers).

An ironic though tragic fact is that Sikhs and Tamils have played a significant role in the collapse of the Nehru dynasty of the Indian empire. Indira Gandhi (daughter of Jawaharlal Nehru, the first prime minister of India) authorized, as the prime minister of India, the Indian military assault on the Sikhs who had barricaded themselves in the building complex of the holiest temple of the Sikhs (the Golden Temple in Amritsar) and, in retaliation, she was assassinated by her Sikh bodyguards. Rajiv Gandhi, who succeeded his mother as the prime minister of India, authorized military action against the Tamils of Sri Lanka (Ceylon) and, in retaliation, a Tamil woman assassinated him on a suicidal mission. The press has shown a tendency to demonize and dehumanize the Sikhs and Tamils as "terrorists" and "assassins." Although no one can defend—and indeed it is necessary to denounce—terrorism and political murders by individuals who are identified as Sikhs or Tamils, it is important to affirm the humanity of Sikhs and Tamils and to try to understand or fathom the depths of their despair and agony, their real and imagined fears of oppression and tyranny, and their willingness to die and be tortured for defending what they believe to be their rightful heritage.

iv. A Note on the Semiotic Perspective of This Book

The India I present in the following pages is beautiful and ugly, a land of great tolerance and great bigotry, a region of remarkable spiritual insights and social injustice, and a tapestry of cultural diversity with the enactment of a wide range of human possibilities. I have created this book on India for an understanding of what it means to be an Indian and what it means to be a Hindu, a Muslim, a Sikh, a Christian, or a Tamil in India. I have tried not to distort the facts, but there are many aspects of India that cannot be objectively stated as this or that because there are different versions of and perspectives on the significance of the dates, events, ideas, languages, religious beliefs, rituals, social arrangements, or national politics. For well over three thousand years, there has been a continuous process of inventing and rein-venting India and group identities of Indians by scholars and nonscholars alike. It is best to identify the cultural principles and mechanisms that have been used to create and re-create India and Indian identities rather than to assert any one version of Indian and Indian identities as true. India is like a puzzle whose pieces can be arranged and rearranged to produce different cultural configurations. I present to the reader one cultural configuration, and the reader may wish to create another configuration or accept mine.

The cultural configuration that I present in this book is constructed with theoretical assumptions about how and why human beings create and use symbols, and by using the hermeneutic methodology to identify and re-veal the structures and meanings of these symbols. Such an approach to the understanding of sociocultural reality can be characterized as the *semiotic per-spective*. Semiotic analysis of culture entails the interpretation of symbols at multiple levels of their construction and use in terms of their connectedness and meaning. As Geertz (1973:3-30) has eloquently argued, cultures are so-cially established structures of meaning and significations; once a researcher understands or comprehends these "structures of significations," it should en-able him or her to construct models of the sociocultural reality that are em-pirically verifiable and are adequate to generate appropriate behaviors and interpretations (just like the "natives"). Semiotics, in a broad and general sense, is the study of the life of signs in a society. The researcher analyzes or decodes the sign systems through the methodology of structural linguistics and hermeneutics.

We can use the characteristics and nature of language as an analog to illustrate the nature of culture. Language is created collectively by human minds; but once created, a language acquires coherence, structure, and meaning that are external to the human mind. A language is a symbolic sys-tem of communication that an infant acquires as a member of a group. Acqui-sition of a language involves the child's internalizing the significant sounds (phonemes) of a language, learning to constitute phonemes as meaningful representations or words (morphemes), and using the words in an arrange-ment (syntax) to convey information in sentences. Once a child has acquired linguistic competence, he or she can generate new sentences or engage in speech (*parole*) through the deployment of the same or recurring linguistic structure (*langue*). The operation of these mechanisms of communication is unique to the human species, and it is through the operation of linguistic communication that the creation, maintenance, and recreation of culture occurs. Culture corresponds to language in several ways. Just as language is a creation of human minds, culture is a creation of human minds; and just as linguistic coherence, structure, and meaning are external to the human mind, cultural coherence, structure, and meaning are external to the human mind. A child acquires the culture of a symbolic tradition that explains how to function as a human being in a group, and once an individual has acquired tion. Depending on how we define the term *textbook*, there are either thousands of them or dozens of them on India. As there are sociocultural features that dramatize the unity of India as a particular type of civilization and as there are so many regional variations that make the conceptualization of India's unity problematic, Western and non-Western scholars have been churning out textbooks on India that attempt to capture the essence or genius of India as well as textbooks on the history and sociology of regional civilizations of India. My book is an attempt to capture certain central or core symbols of India to reveal the symbolic nature of all-India cultural uniformities, the symbolic nature of the regional-national civilizations, and the symbolic nature of the village traditions.

Survey textbooks on countries or civilizations usually provide or enumerate demographic and statistical information or data that serve the needs of policy makers, administrators, and tourists as well as students who look for specific facts. Thus there are several kinds of survey textbooks that cater to the political, social, and intellectual needs of the time, and survey textbooks range from those that focus on the bizarre and exotic to those that serve as encyclopedias of a given area or region. The writing of survey textbooks on India has a long history; they were primarily written by Western travelers, merchants, adventurers, missionaries, and administrators, dating back to the Western Middle Ages. However, the largest and most influential collection of survey textbooks began to appear with the establishment of British political-economic dominance in the 18th century in Madras and Bengal, and this trend has continued, with an ideological link or connection with the discipline of anthropology. Although the stated objective of many of these survey textbooks is to enhance knowledge about the variations and similarities of cultures and races of India, they have invariably served the goals and needs of the dominant ruling class and the governments. Hundreds of survey textbooks were written on the castes and tribes of India by government administrators, often within the racist-anthropological framework of what was called the *Census of India* or the *Anthropological Survey of India*. The British administrators had the support of the British government for their racist-anthropological research because of two factors: (1) Anthropological knowledge could be used to assert political dominance and intellectual superiority, and (2) anthropological knowledge could be used to regulate and govern the subordinated peoples within a "native" framework, thus preempting protest or revolt against the British. The government of India has continued the British policy, and hundreds of reports, gazettes, and surveys on the tribes of India have been produced either indirectly (through fundings or universities) or directly by the government. Some of the survey books of the 19th and early 20th century are classics, containing a wealth of information that can be used for various purposes even today. Often undertaken by scholar-administrators, many projects that were initiated to describe the "peoples of India" had the help of many scholar-research collaborators and native government employees; as a result, the survey textbooks were comprehensive and accurate in many ways, and many of them have appeared as reprints or have been summarized in abridged volumes. The two excellent survey textbooks of recent times, written by Western Indologists with a commitment to intellectual honesty, are *India: An Anthropological Perspective* (Tyler 1973) and *Peoples of South Asia* (Maloney 1974).

My book is not a survey textbook. Although I provide brief descriptions of the different regions of India and discuss Hindu and caste practices, my main concern in this book is to identify historical processes, sociological principles, and cultural themes that constitute (or make up) the united India and regional civilizations or traditions. Therefore, I do not present a detailed discussion of the tribes of India. A coherent discussion of the tribes of India would take a book by itself because we must have a theoretical understanding of what is meant by *tribes,* and we must recognize the existence of major differences in the tribal traditions that derive from their Austro-Asiatic, Dravidian, or Tibeto-Burman linguistic/cultural foundations. As the tribes have been isolated to some extent from the historical processes, sociological principles, and cultural themes that I have attempted to delineate in this book, and as the tribes have had different kinds of political relationship with the governments of India, it is necessary to have a separate study of tribal traditions of south and southeast Asia rather than to combine such a study haphazardly with the study of Indian culture, ethnonational civilizations, and village traditions. It is also debatable whether the tribes can even be identified as "Indian" tribes.

As I noted in the beginning of this introduction, this book is an introduction to the history, sociology, and anthropology of India, focusing on the analysis and interpretation of the symbols of India and Indian traditions, and I hope I have succeeded in my effort to present a semiotic understanding of India and Indian traditions.

conceptualized as politically linked with northern India before the Arabs conceptualized such a linkage after the 6th century C.E.; the ports of Malabar Coast were referred to by Greek and Roman writers as the commercial centers of India without any reference to northern India. It should be noted that at a later period the term Malabar Coast became associated only with the coastline of southwestern India (from Cannanore to Cape Comarin) and the term Coromandel Coast was introduced by the European traders to identify the southeastern coastline of India (from Pulicat to Tutucorin).

Miller (1988:609) notes,

> Goods from South India had reached the Middle East as early as the third millennium B.C.E. But the discovery of monsoon winds by Greek soldiers about C.E. 45 made it possible for ships serving Rome to sail from the Horn of Africa to Kerala [Malabar Coast] in only 40 days. This shifted the focus of the spice trade from north Indian ports to Muziris [Kodungallur on the Malabar Coast], which Pliny called the "first commercial center of India."
>
> Stimulated by the Roman demand for exotic goods, Indian and Malayan merchants also pushed east during this period, collecting silk cloth and cinnamon from China and pearls, precious stones, and tortoise shells from Indonesia. These they brought to Muziris and other south Indian ports to be loaded onto Greek and Arab ships. Positioned midway along the spice route between Rome and China, Kerala thrived as an international meeting place.

The existence of the sea-trade routes, connecting Europe, India, Southeast Asia, and China, facilitated the travels of men like the Italian merchant Marco Polo (in the 13th century) and the Moroccan jurist Ibn Battuta (in the 14th century) in India. Incidentally, both Marco Polo and Ibn Battuta knew of the land route that connected Europe and Asia. Marco Polo entered China by land through central Asia and served as an administrator of Kubilai Khan, the Mongol emperor of China, before embarking on the sea voyage back to Italy that included sojourns in various towns of southern India. Ibn Battuta entered India through Afghanistan (north of northwestern India) and served as an administrator of the Turkish emperor of northwestern and northern India, Sultan Muhammad Ibn Tughlug, before journeying to China through the seaports of southern India.

iii. Pan-Indian Linguistic Dominance: Sanskrit, Persian, English, and Hindi

India has never been a culturally or linguistically homogenous geographical region. Within the territory we identify as India, there have been several national or ethnolinguistic traditions that are quite different from each other. Cross-cultural communication in India (i.e., communication across the linguistic groups) has been facilitated by the development and use of a common pan-Indian religious or political language among the literati. Sanskrit, which became the sacerdotal language by 1000 B.C.E., served as the unifying, intercultural religious language of the literati from about the 7th century B.C.E. Persian became the political and court language of the literati from about the 11th century C.E. in northwestern and northern India. English became an important intercultural language of India from about the 18th century and acquired significance as the official administrative language of India in the 19th century.

From the early 20th century, many Indian nationalist leaders promoted Hindi as the pan-Indian political and administrative language of India. When the British left and the constitution of independent India was adopted in 1950, the constitution included the statement that "The official language of the Union [of India] shall be Hindi in Devanagari script and that Hindi will replace English (as the official language) by the year 1965." With widespread opposition to the elimination of English in 1965 in the regions where Hindi was not the national-cultural language, an Official Language Bill was approved in 1965 by the Indian (federal) Parliament to permit the continued use of English indefinitely.

It is necessary to examine the cultural, religious, and political assumptions that led to the creation of Sanskrit, Persian, English, and Hindi as pan-Indian official languages in order to understand the reasons for making Hindi *the* pan-Indian official (political and administrative) language.

Sanskrit acquired its present grammatical form in the 4th century B.C.E. when the great Hindu grammarian-semiotician Panini standardized and refined the scriptural language of the Vedas as the sacred language. Sanskrit, which literally means *perfected,* was contrasted with the *imperfect* or *unrefined* colloquial Aryan dialects. Sanskrit had always been a sacerdotal language, and it was never a language of the "folk." It was the language of the religious scholars, most of whom were Brahmins, and it was the language of the Brahmanical priesthood. Thus, when Sanskrit was spoken, it was spoken among members of a religious community or for ritual activities. However, some Hindu kings and emperors patronized Sanskritic scholarship, and Sanskrit became the official court language and was used to write religious commentaries and formulations of arts (*sahitya*) and sciences (*sastras*). As a result, Sanskrit acquired a functional similarity to Latin (as Latin functioned in Europe during the medieval period) and scholars all over India could communicate through the medium of Sanskrit although they spoke only the local or regional languages of the national-cultural traditions in their homes and other social domains. Some of the major Sanskritic treatises were composed or written in southern India where Dravidian languages were spoken, and the religious or scriptural orientation of Hinduism that was conveyed through Sanskrit had long ago (perhaps by 1000 B.C.E.) ceased to be that of the central Asian Aryans who had settled down in India c. 1500 B.C.E.

When the Turkish Muslims established kingdoms and empires in India after the 11th century C.E., they introduced Persian as the court language, and by the time the Mughals came to power in the 16th century, Persian had become the official political and administrative language in most of northern and central India. There were quite a few differences between how Sanskrit and Persian were used as intercultural languages. Persian was not a sacerdotal language, and it was spoken by a majority of people in Iran; it was the native or adopted language of the Turkish and Mongol nobles who had immigrated into India in large numbers. Many of these Persians, Turks, and Mongols served as administrative officers in India from the 11th to the 19th centuries. Upper-class Indians studied Persian if they desired to serve the Turkish sultans or the Mughal emperors (or the governors of the sultans or emperors), and these Indians often emulated Persian customs to secure recognition as elites.

When English replaced Persian in the early part of the 19th century, "universal" education in English was promoted, as opposed to the restricted entry into the category or class of *religious elite* (Sanskrit) or into the category or class of *political elite* (Persian). The British did not have the manpower for native-born English speakers to be in charge of all the British activities, and the British had no desire to establish permanent British settlements in India as the Turks and the Mughals did before them. Thus, universal education in English served a very important function of producing English-educated Indian workers to serve as employees of the British crown. Consequently, there came into being a class of Indians (who were recruited from different linguistic or cultural groups) who were united in speaking English and, in some ways, sharing a commitment to British norms and laws. Also, there emerged a wealthy class of Indians who made their fortunes through the practical use of English (for intercultural trade or industrialization) and through the application of British laws (for accumulation of wealth in banking and/or real estate). English also became a window to the world, and wealthy Indians acquired education in Europe or the United States from the late 19th century.

iv. The Persianization of the Khari Boli Dialect of India and the Development of the Hindi-Urdu Language

The origin and development of the Urdu/Hindi language correspond to the entry and expansion of Persianized Turks and Mughals in India. In other words, Urdu/Hindi began to develop in relation to the invasion of India by the Persianized Turks in the 10th century C.E. and the language acquired many of its characteristics in the period of 800 years, roughly from the 11th to the 19th centuries. Stephen Tyler, an authority on the languages and linguistics of India, notes,

When the Islamic invaders came into contact with the Indo-Aryans of north India, they learned a regional dialect (Khari Boli) which was first a soldier's and trader's patois, but gradually became a *lingua franca* in the north. This language, though derived from an Indo-Aryan dialect, contained a large number of Persian loan words and eventually came to be written in the Arabic script. Subsequently, it developed a highly stylized literary form and eventually replaced Persian as the official language in lower administrative levels. This "Persianized" language, known as Urdu, was also written in Devanagari derived from Sanskrit, and in the nineteenth century developed a "Sanskritized" literature. This "Sanskritized" version came to be known as Hindi.

—Tyler (1973:174)

Tyler's interpretation of the origin and development of Urdu/Hindi correctly identifies the influence of Persian in the development of Urdu/Hindi. It is accurate to state that the Urdu/Hindi language is a *Persianized Indian dialect*. The development of Urdu/Hindi coincides with the emergence of many of the essential differences in cultures and the physical appearances of the peoples of northern and southern India which began after the 10th century C.E. with the migration of Persianized Turks into India. The Aryans who entered India around 1500 B.C.E. were few in number, and although they succeeded in establishing political and linguistic dominance, they merged with the preexisting populations (Dravidians) of the Indus Valley Civilization. Aryan dialects were Dravidianized, and Aryan cultures underwent Dravidianization, and as a result the linguistic, cultural, and racial characteristics of the north and the south were not markedly very different. But the Turks, Mongols, and Persians who entered India after the 10th century C.E. maintained their distinctiveness (largely because of their Islamic religious identity) and contributed to the emergence of ethnic pluralism in India. After the 10th century, there was a progressive separation of northern and southern India, with the north acquiring many Persian/Turkish/Mongol cultural, religious, linguistic, and racial characteristics.

From the 11th century C.E., Persians and Persianized Turks called the dialects of central-northern India such as Khari Boli collectively as Hindavi, meaning *language of Hindia (India)*, or as Hindustani, meaning *language of the land of Hindus*. (As noted earlier, the word Hindu was originally used by the pre-5th-century Persians to signify the people who lived near the river; the ancient Aryan word for river was *sindhu* and the people who lived near the river were called *sindhavan* or river dwellers; Greeks borrowed the word Hindu and modified it as Indu, and since the 4th century B.C.E. terms such as Indus, Indu, Intu, and Hindu have been used to denote or connote India or facts about India; the word *stan* is Turkish for *land of*.)

As the Turks interacted extensively with the Persianized Khari Boli-speaking merchants and soldiers, Persianized Khari Boli was viewed as the language of the marketplace and military camps; and as the Turkish sultans and governors were successful in their military campaigns, Persianized Khari Boli (which was identified as Hindavi or Hindustani) spread rapidly throughout northwestern, northern, and northeastern India, acquiring Persian, Turkish, and Arabic vocabulary as well as the vocabularies of different Prakrit or Apabhramsha dialects of northern India. The establishment of Turkish and Mughal empires gave Hindavi a status as the medium of mass communication in the different regions of the empire. Although Hindavi was the language used for mass communication, there was no standardized, or officially recognized, Hindavi or Hindustani until the 18th century. Prior to the 18th century, various Hindavi or Hindustani dialects were often cultivated and propagated by Hindu and Muslim saints, as well as by military commanders in the military camps which had soldiers and officers from different communities and regions. From the 18th century, the Turkish term *Urdu*, which means camp, was used to identify Hindustani's link with Persian. Historically, there evolved Hindustani literature which was modeled after Persian literary idiom and written in Perso-Arabic script from about the 16th century. But the label Urdu was used to identify this literature only in the 18th century when Hindustani literature based on Sanskrit idiom and written in Devanagari script was identified or labeled as Hindi. (It is debatable whether there were distinguishable Urdu and Hindi literary forms prior to the 16th century. Hindustani has continued to be the colloquial version of Urdu and Hindi with closer identification with northern Indian Muslims.)

The identification of Urdu as a separate language, that is, different from Hindi, became increasingly important *after* the 18th century when Urdu was used largely to create a separate national identity for the Muslims of India and to distinguish the linguistic and cultural heritage of Muslims as different from that of Hindus. Despite the fact that Urdu written in Perso-Arabic script has the connotation of sacerdotal legitimacy, Hindi and Urdu have not separated structurally and are the same for practical communication purposes. Hindu intellectuals, who cultivate Hindi, use the Sanskrit idiom and style and more Sanskrit words; Muslim (and non-Muslim) intellectuals, who cultivate Urdu, have borrowed Persian literary style or rules as well as Persian and Arabic vocabulary. (Urdu is currently the official language of Pakistan just as Hindi is the official language of India; Urdu is also an official language of the Kashmir state of India.)

v. The Invention of Indian Nationality and the Hindi-ization of India

The conception of India as a single geographic unit and the conception of Indians as the peoples of this area have existed for a long time. But until the 19th century when the British established economic and political control over India, there was no conception of Indian nationality. Even when the Mughals ruled most of India from the middle of the 16th century to the middle of the 18th century (with a centralized government based in Delhi), only regional, religious, and caste loyalties and identities prevailed. There was *no* native conception of Indian nation or Indian nationality before the British introduced such a political orientation in the consciousness of the peoples of the Indian territory that came under the economic and political control of the British. Perhaps, the reader should be reminded of the fact that three nation-states emerged in India (Pakistan, India, and Bangladesh) after the departure of the British. The emergence of Pakistan and Bangladesh present an interesting case study of nationalism. At the time of the departure of the British, Pakistan was created based on a theory of the existence of two religious nations in India, with a Muslim majority in northwestern and northeastern India and a Hindu majority in the rest of India. The Panjabi speakers of the northwest were divided as Muslims and Hindus, with the Muslim Panjabi speakers joining Islamic Pakistan; likewise, the Bengali speakers of the northeast were divided as Muslims and Hindus, with the Muslim Bengali speakers joining Islamic Pakistan. The Urdu language acquired significance as the Islamic national language of Pakistan, and when the nation-state of Pakistan was created in 1947, it had a western region known as West Pakistan with a majority of Panjabi speakers and an eastern region known as East Pakistan with a majority of Bengali speakers. East Pakistan became a separate nation-state about three decades later, with a name Bangladesh signifying it was the land of Bengali speakers, and Urdu ceased to be the national language of Bangladesh. Urdu has continued to be the Islamic national language of West Pakistan (later named Pakistan). As the nation-state of India had Panjabi-speaking Hindus and Bengali-speaking Hindus, their regions became linguistic states of India known as Panjab and West Bengal. The Hindi language, which is the same as Urdu, except for the fact that Urdu has had more Persian, Arabic, and Turkish influence than Hindi and is written in Persianized Arabic script, acquired significance as the national official language of the republic of India. The republic of India was also officially labeled Bharat, named after a mythical Hindu kingdom (of the mythical king Bharat) of ancient times.

The above-mentioned nationalisms were all the creations and inventions of the British, who had introduced European models of state nationalism that became politically significant institutions and beliefs in India during the 19th century. The British involved themselves in Westernizing (and in that process *nationalismizing*) India with social reforms and political, legal, and educational norms that, while undermining certain primordial loyalties, promoted a kind of territorial unity of India with overlapping assumptions of peoplehood that included Indianness as well as religious and linguistic nationalism. The British initiated the nationalism-building process to protect their own economic and political interests, but this process created a force, like the genie out of a bottle, that made it inevitable for the British to leave India. The empire-state of the British was opposed by the claim by Indians for a nation-state of India with the political slogan of native rule (*swarajya*).

Many Indian nationalist leaders perceived the use of English by the literati in India to signify a lower or slavish status for Indians. In the early 20th century, Mahatma Gandhi, among others, voiced the concern that using the colonial language (English) was tantamount to accepting colonial dominance and he began to use Hindi/Urdu as a substitute for nationalist discourse and debate. Mahatma Gandhi favored the colloquial version of Hindi/Urdu because he realized intuitively that the colloquial version (Hindustani) could neutralize the Muslim opposition to India's independence from British colonial rule. (Many Muslim leaders were afraid that the departure of the British could result in the domination of Muslims by the Hindu majority, and Hindu leaders of the 20th century tried to provide guarantees to protect the religious and linguistic distinctiveness of Muslims.) Mahatma Gandhi was right in assuming that the use of Hindustani would appeal to Muslims not only because Muslims, as a community, were the least influenced by English education, but also because they were less educated in any literary idiom.

In their animosity toward English, the Indian nationalist leaders failed to recognize the fact that the use of Hindi/Urdu as the nationalist language was not different from how Persian was used by the Mughals. Just as it was easier for northwestern, northern, and northeastern Indians to learn Persian (because Persian and the languages spoken in those regions belonged to the same language family) than for southern Indians (who spoke languages of a different language family), it was easier for the non-Hindi-speaking peoples of northwestern, northern, and northeastern India to learn Hindi/Urdu than for southern Indians. But, the learning of Hindi/Urdu was promoted as a *nationalist imperative*, and the use of Hindi/Urdu was identified as signifying opposition to British rule. This approach to nationalism was, no doubt, predicated upon the assumption that there was and ought to be a political entity called India (which was essentially created by the British) and that this empire-state should be continued after the departure of the British.

A logical approach would have been to promote all the Indian languages of India as *nationalist* languages; ideally, the use of all the Indian languages (not simply Hindi/Urdu) could have been presented as opposition to the English language and British rule. Instead, one of the Indian languages (Hindi/Urdu) acquired a political status as the nationalist language and its use was valued as affirming the pan-Indian national unity. Nationalist leaders were afraid that unless Hindi/Urdu was legitimized as a pan-Indian language, the different regions of India with distinctive national/cultural traditions and civilizations would secede from the union of India and that it would result in the disintegration of India. Disintegration of India was contrasted with the *national integration* of India, and national integration of India meant *Hindi-ization* or *Urdization* of India. Hindi-ization of India began earnestly in the

1930s, and when the British left in 1947 efforts were made to replace English with Hindi as the official language, and the constitution of India which came into being in 1950 proclaimed that "the official language of the Union shall be Hindi in Devanagari script." Thus, Devanagari script acquired recognition as the pan-Indian national script of India, as opposed to the Perso-Arabic script which was used in the writing of Urdu (and became the national script of Pakistan).

The identification of the official language of the Union as *Hindi in Devanagari script* marked the conceptual separation of Urdization and Hindi-ization. It is important that we recognize the implications and consequences of Hindi-ization. When Sanskrit was the pan-Indian language of the literati, the process of Sanskritization provided the Brahmin community and Brahmanical priesthood (who served as the custodians of Sanskritic learning and rituals) with high ritual status and great economic and political power (disproportionate to their numbers). When Persian was made the pan-Indian language of the elites, it provided the Persians, Turks, Mongols, and the Persianized Indians with great wealth and power for about eight hundred years. When English was made the official language, it helped to create an upper-class Indian community linked with Westernization and produced the racial dichotomy of a superior British race and inferior Indian races. Hindi-ization has created a similar intellectual, social, economic, and political orientation. In modern India it is politically necessary, economically advantageous, and socially prestigious to speak Hindi if a person desires to establish political, economic, and social networks across India beyond one's own national boundary. Such an orientation has favored the peoples of middle-north India composed of regions or areas identified as Rajasthan, Haryana, Himachal Pradesh, Madhya Pradesh, Uttar Pradesh, and Bihar where Hindi is spoken as the mother tongue (with minor dialectical variations). Hindi speakers, who constitute about 40 percent of the total population of India, have been granted by the constitution of India a built-in linguistic advantage to succeed in and secure high-level bureaucratic positions in all the federal agencies of the union government such as the Indian Civil or Administrative Service, Indian Foreign Service, Indian Police Service, and the Indian Military Service. There has, as a result, emerged Hindi linguistic elitism: Hindi-speaking government officials and businessmen use Hindi in non-Hindi-speaking regions and seldom learn the languages of these regions, and government officials and businessmen from non-Hindi-speaking regions have to learn and use Hindi in Hindi-speaking regions of India.

vi. Colonialism, Racism, and Colorism in India

From the early 19th century, the British cultivated, self-consciously, their cultural and racial separation from India. The dichotomy, distinguishing colonial masters and colonial subjects, became more and more pronounced with the creation of exclusive housing areas, social clubs, travel facilities, and so on by the middle of the 19th century. This dichotomy united all the native populations of India in opposition to the British. Thus, the term Indian acquired new meaning as a colonized people who were conceptualized as a racially inferior people. Colonialism and racism complemented each other, and the British Empire used the wealth and manpower of India in its quest for world dominance.

Initially, the concept of race acquired significance in Western civilization with the enslavement of native Americans and Africans. Europeans propagated scientifically spurious theories that related or linked intellectual and moral characteristics with physical characteristics. The European conception of slavery, which was colorblind until the 16th century, gradually became an institution for the enslavement of nonwhite or racially non-European peoples. It should be noted that the Muslim conception of slavery contrasted with that of the Europeans. Religion rather than race provided justification for the enslavement of peoples. Thus, Muslim Turks, Arabs, and Persians enslaved people who were not Muslims; it was the Arab search for non-Islamic peoples to serve as slaves and soldiers that provided the opportunity for Turks to expand out of central Asia and to eventually establish slave (*mamluk*) dynasties and empires in places like Egypt and India.

I noted earlier that the Aryans, who had entered India between 1700 and 1500 B.C.E., had merged with the indigenous populations and had culturally been Dravidianized. Between the 7th century B.C.E. and the 7th century C.E. various Persian, Scythian, Greek, and Hunnish groups settled in northwestern and northern India, adopted the status of warrior classes (*kshatriya*) and fit in the caste system and the Hindu social order. Persian, Arab, Turkish, and Mongol migrations to India after the 10th century C.E. (which continued until the 18th century) resulted in the creation of large settlements of Islamic groups that did not fit in the caste system, although in most instances they acquired the status of nobility with links to the Persianized Turkish rulers.

The new migrations resulted in some populations of northwestern and northern India having physical features of the populations of western and central Asia, and because these populations had acquired high economic-political status (as nobles linked with the Turkish sultans and Mughal emperors), an association was made between upper-class membership and light-brown skin color. Gradually, a cultural orientation of *colorism* emerged in India, with wealthy men seeking women with western or central Asian physical features as their wives or concubines. But there was no racism, a fact that is evident in the practice of Ethiopian slaves (*mamluks*) in the Turkish sultanates acquiring high political status. (I discuss this phenomenon of colorism, in detail, in Chapter 5.)

The discipline of anthropology was adapted or co-opted into the service of the British cultural structure of colonialism-racism. Scientific racism in

India occurred through the combined efforts of anthropologists and anthropologically oriented administrators who were stationed in India. Through institutions such as the Census Bureau of India and the Anthropological Survey of India, thousands of Indian clerks, enumerators, and field staff were deployed in the collection of information about the races, castes, customs, and tribes of India. Hundreds of volumes were published in the 19th and early 20th centuries that were devoted to the compilation of ethnological facts about India.

Most geneticists today do not use the concept of race or racial classifications because racial classifications measure mostly culturally significant characteristics rather than scientifically significant characteristics. Particularly, the type of anthropometric studies that were undertaken to classify the races of India are rejected in contemporary genetic anthropology as totally worthless. However, I provide below some information on the 19th- and early 20th-century anthropometric studies because it has historic value and also highlights the complexities of delineating human groups of India as Indian.

Risley (1915), a British census commissioner of India, offered the following classification of the "races of India":

1. *The Turko-Iranian* type, represented by the Baloch, Brahui, and Afghans of Baluchistan and northwestern India. Skin color is light and stature is above mean. Hair on face plentiful. Indices: Cephalic—80 to 85; nasal—68 to 80.
2. *The Indo-Aryan* type, occupying the Punjab, Rajputana and Kashmir. Skin color is light brown and stature is above mean. Hair on face plentiful. Indices: Cephalic—72 to 86; nasal—70 to 75.
3. *The Scytho-Dravidian* type of western India, comprising the Maratha Brahmins, the Kunbis, and the Coorgs. Skin color is light brown, stature medium; hair on face scanty. Indices: Cephalic—77 to 80; nasal—72 to 76; orbito nasal—113-132.
4. *The Aryo-Dravidian* type found in the United Provinces of Agra and Oudh, Rajputana, Bihar, and Ceylon. Skin color brown. Stature medium; hair on face plentiful. Indices: Cephalic—72 to 90; nasal—73 to 88.
5. *The Mongolo-Dravidian* type found in Bengal and Orissa. Skin color is dark brown and the stature is medium. Hair on face plentiful. Indices: Cephalic—79 to 83; nasal—70 to 85.
6. *The Mongoloid* type of the Himalayas, Nepal, Assam, and surrounding areas. Skin color is brown with a yellowish tinge. Stature is short; hair on face is scanty. Indices: Cephalic—72 to 80; nasal—67 to 85.
7. *The Dravidian* type extends from Ceylon, the island south of India, to southern India, central India, and eastern India. Skin color is brown to dark brown. Stature varies from short to medium. Hair on face is plentiful.

To see the regional differences in indices at a glance, I provide a table based on Risley's anthropometric data:

	M. Ceph. Index	M. Nasal Index
Northwest India		
Rajput	72.4	71.6
Sikh	72.7	86.8
Northeast India		
Santhal	76.1	88.8
Brahman	73.1	74.6
Central India		
Bhil	76.5	84.1
Tharu	73.9	79.5
Southern India		
Nayar	73.2	76.7
Malayali	74.4	77.8

Hutton (1935), another census commissioner of India, suggests the following classification of the populations of India. He includes the population of the Andaman islands with the populations of India:

1. *Negrito* type is the first inhabitant of South East Asia. Traces of Negrito race are found in the populations of northeast India and the hill tribes of southern India. Andaman population is of "virtually pure Negrito stock." Skin color is black. Stature is small.
2. *Proto-Australoid* type came from East Mediterranean area, that is, they migrated to India from the West. They are represented by the Veddah, Malavedans, and so on of Ceylon and southern India, and the tribal population of central, eastern and northeastern India. Skin color is dark brown. Stature is small.
3. *Early Mediterranean* type, also immigrants from the West, brought earlier forms of Austro-Asiatic languages. They are spread all over India. Skin color is dark brown. Stature is small.
4. *Civilized Mediterranean* type occupying parts of northern, northwestern, northeastern India and the whole of southern India. They are known as the Dravidians of India. Skin color varies from light brown to dark brown. Stature medium.
5. *Alpine* type is represented by Banias and Brahmans spread over the whole of India. Skin color is light brown. Stature medium.
6. *Armenoid* type is the "true descendent of the Alpine type."
7. *Nordic* type seen in northern, northwestern, and central India. They are supposed to have brought the Sanskrit language to India (cf. the earlier discussion of how some anthropologists infer that since Sanskrit language is an Aryan language, those speaking Sanskrit would be Aryans

and so Nordic). Skin color varies from fair to light brown. Stature medium to tall.

8. *Mongoloid* type entered India from Northeast territory of India. They are represented in parts of central, northern, and eastern India, and the whole of northeastern India. Skin color is yellowish brown. Stature small.

Guha (1935), who assisted Hutton in census enumeration of the population of India, has derived six principal groups and subdivided them into thirteen races:

1. *Negrito*: Kadars, numbering about 300 in all, who live on the mountain belt of southern India, are regarded as true representatives of this race. The stature is short. Frizzy hair is noted in some. Skin color is dark brown to black.
2. *Proto-Australoid*: Represented by Mundas, Kols, and other tribes. Stature is short. Skin color is dark brown to black.
3. *Mongoloid*: (a) Palae Mongoloid—color dark to brown or nearly black, nose medium, eye slits oblique, and prominent cheek bones; (b) Tibeto-Mongoloid—broad-headed people with dark skin color, oblique eye slits, and broad nose. These types are represented by the Naga tribes of eastern India and the Bhutanese of northeastern India.
4. *The Mediterranean*: (a) Palae Mediterranean—represented by the population in southern India; (b) Mediterranean—represented by the population in Kashmir, western, central, and northwestern India; and (c) Oriental type—distributed in northern India.
5. *The Nordic*: Stature is tall; skin color fair; long head, and narrow nose. Represented by Bengalis. (Note that whereas Guha has located the Nordics in northeastern India, other classifiers locate them in northern or northwestern India—a distance of about 1500 miles.)
6. *Alpo-Denaric*: (a) Alpinoid—confined to western and eastern India.

Guha's map showing the distribution of brachycephalic and dolichocephalic populations of India serves no useful purpose.

According to Hooton (1946), the Indo-Dravidian population is a composite race which is predominantly white. It is a combination of Classic Mediterranean, Australoid (Veddoid), Negrito, Armenoid, Nordic, and Mongoloid subraces. Hooton (1946:593-616) describes the physical characteristics as follows:

1. Hair form: Straight to frizzy, but predominantly wavy.
2. Hair color: Usually black.
3. Skin color: Varies from light brown to dark brown.

4. Eye color: Nearly always dark brown.
5. Hair quantity: Beard and body hair, usually medium to pronounced.
6. Nose form: Nasal index prevailingly mesorrhine (over 70); nose somewhat depressed at root; root and bridge of moderate height and breadth; profile commonly straight; tip of medium thickness, also somewhat flaring.
7. Face form: Usually narrow, medium length, leptoprosopic, little or no prognathism.
8. Head form: Cephalic index generally under 80; most group means dolichocephalic; moderate brow ridges, rounded foreheads.
9. Stature: Variable, but usually medium to small.
10. Body build: Usually slender, linear; non-Negroid legs.

Hooton classifies the population of India into five morphological types:

1. *Classic Indo-Dravidian* type predominates in north Indian population, including to some extent the Punjab (this type approaches the Classic Mediterranean).
   a. Hair form: In general straight but inclined to waviness
   b. Head form: Usually dolichocephalic, average 74.3
   c. Nasal index: Mesorrhine, averaging 73
   d. Stature: Short, averaging 163.4 cm
2. *Armenoid-Iranian Plateau* type is found in the western littoral of northeastern India.
   a. Hair form: Generally straight
   b. Skin color: Pale white to tawny brown
   c. Head form: Subbrachycephalic, averaging 81.8; high head with flattened occiput and often receding forehead
   d. Face form: Short face of medium breadth; total facial index averaging 69.8
   e. Nose form: Long, high-pitched, often convex; average nasal index 69.8
   f. Body hair: Beard and body hair well developed
   g. Stature: Medium, average 165.8 cm
3. *Indo-Nordic* type in its purest form is seen in northwest Himalayan tribes among Kaffirs, Pathans, and so on. Darker variants among Sikhs of the Punjab.
   a. Hair form: Generally straight
   b. Hair color: Usually black, sometimes dark brown
   c. Skin color: From rosy white to light brown
   d. Eye color: Minority with gray blue or mixed eyes
   e. Body hair: Well developed
   f. Head form: Dolichocephalic, cephalic index averaging 73.1
   g. Nasal index: Averaging 67.1, leptorrhine

    h. Stature: Above medium, averaging 168.6 cm

4. *Australoid* (*Veddoid*) type is the predominant element in central and southern India.

    a. Hair form: Wavy to curly

    b. Skin color: Dark brown, approaching black

    c. Nose form: Almost chamarrhine, averaging 81.4; root of nose broad and low

    d. Head form: Dolichocephalic with a mean of 72.9; prominent brow-ridges

    e. Face form: Short, narrow; moderately prognathous

    f. Hair quantity: Beard and body hair very sparse

    g. Stature: Medium, average 165 cm.

5. *Negritoid* type: Distribution—Kadars and Pulayans of the Perambiculam Hills.

    a. Hair form: Frizzy, or short spirals

    b. Skin color: Very dark

    c. Head form: Dolichocephalic, but with index rising as frizzy hair short ens into spirals

    d. Nose form: Nasal index averaging 86.5, chamarrhine

    e. Lips: Thick, everted

    f. Stature: Short, under 160 cm

Hooton's classification is both elaborate and comprehensive. But since it rests primarily upon Guha's postulates that are mere speculations, its usefulness as a scientific source of information is greatly undermined.

Coon (1965) states that greater India was "the meeting point of the three Eurasiatic subspecies: the Caucasoid, the Australoid, and the Mongoloid." He distinguishes five categories of people in India (Coon 1965:186-206):

1. *Indo-European speaking peoples of India, Pakistan and Ceylon*: Nearly 80 percent of the whole may be treated as a unit from a linguistic point of view and to a large extent in terms of race. The majority are Hindus in religion; others Muslims and Christians. Most of them are descended in part or wholly from Western Asia or more remotely, even from Europe. The mean stature of males ranges from 5 ft. 4.5 in. to 5 ft. 8 in. Cephalic indices range from 72 to 80. For the most part, hair form is straight or wavy, body hair variable. Most have glossy black hair, although brown hair is not uncommon. Almost all have brown eyes of various shades. Skin color is variable: Pinkish white skins are extremely rare and brunette white skins are also in a minority. Most of the light skins have a yellowish or reddish cast. Light brown skins are commonest in the western part of northern India and dark brown skins in the east and south where climate is both hot and damp.

2. *The Northern Mongoloids*: The skeletal material from the Indus Valley shows that some of them were in parts of greater India before the arrival of Aryan invaders. These peoples are found all the way from Afghanistan to Burma, in Pakistan, Nepal, Sikkim, Bhutan and India. They are divided into (a) the Bhotias and (b) the Hill tribes. The Bhotias are Tibetans living at an altitude of over 9000 feet. They are generally of short or medium stature, with long trunks and have large mesocephalic or brachycephalic heads and broad faces. They show an incidence of 60 percent or more of mongolian eye fold.

3. *Dravidians*: About 150 million people, speaking four languages—Tamil, Telugu, Kannara, and Malayalam—are grouped in this category. These people, whether Hindus, Muslims, or Christians, follow severe endogamous marital rules. The presence of Dravidian-speaking Brahui in Baluchistan, northwestern India, suggests that they came from the Indus Valley. Both the Brahuis and Baluchis bear some physical resemblance to the Dravidians of southern India.

4. *The Austro-Asiatic speaking tribes*: They are concentrated in Bihar state, northern India. Physically they resemble Cambodians. Men have a mean stature of 5 ft. 2.5 in.; they are dolicocephalic, have small heads, and are generally dark brown in skin color. Their hair form ranges from straight to very curly. They have broad nasal roots and alveolar prognathism is present. Beards are scanty and a minority have epicanthic folds and shovel-shaped incisors. They are a blend of Australoid and Mongoloid, with only a few Mongoloid elements visible.

5. *Veddoid*: Mean stature is 5 ft. 1.5 in. Racially they are primarily Caucasoid, but some of them have a partly Australoid appearance, particularly in the upper nasal region. Seen in parts of southern India and Ceylon.

There is no way of telling which classification describes the populations of India correctly. We can only point to certain gross discrepancies found in the data in comparison with data collected by others. Also, in most cases the local races differ markedly in physical characteristics among themselves. Almost any index used by the morphologist is bound to show great differences among the members of the same family. It is most common, especially in southern India, to find dolichocephals and brachycephals, leptorrhines and platyrrhines, light-brown skin color and dark-brown skin color, and tall and short individuals in the same family.

As the recent edition of the *Cambridge Encyclopedia of India* notes:

Except in special cases of extremely isolated primitive groups (themselves now largely extinct or assimilated) such as the Andaman Islanders or the Veddas of Sri Lanka, the present existence of radically distinct racial types may therefore be discounted. The internal groupings within the immensely complex societies of the region stem far more from cultural factors rather than from the facial or bodily appearance with which these may be associated in popular imagination.

—Robinson (1989:42)

The following photographs of men and women exhibit enormous variation in physical appearance. In many of the sources cited above, these portraits might have been used to illustrate racial types of India. However, all of the people shown here come from the same village. The variation in their appearance is due largely to cultural differences determined by markers of caste identity and religious affiliation.

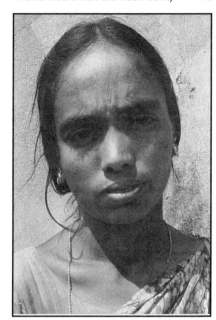

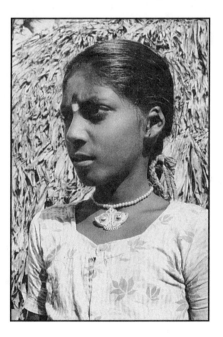

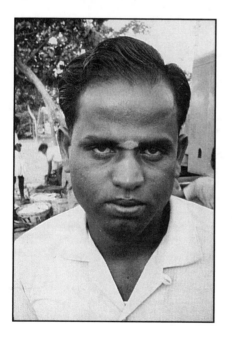

CHAPTER TWO

✿ THE SEMIOTICS OF HINDUISM

i. Hinduism and Religious Freedom: There Are No Hindu Heretics

In the Hindu view the various religions are understood as different and sometimes conflicting perspectives on the one divine reality. In fact divinity is sometimes described as "that in which opposites coexist." According to this logic Hinduism should be tolerant and open to other religions because the more aspects of the divine we can perceive, the more complete our understanding will be. ... Each of these is true within its own perspective; that is, each viewpoint is a logical conclusion based on the presuppositions of its own perspective.

—Harold Coward (1985:64-65)

Western minds, used to thinking in terms of this *or* that, but not this *as well as* that, may find in the wide latitude and moral relativism of Hinduism a deviousness or downright lack of principle. ... Yet one great merit of the Hindu way is its freedom from dogmatism and pretentions of an exclusive "revealed" Truth. Historically, Hinduism has been capable of generating new interpretations in the interest of social reform.

—Sara S. Mitter (1991:3)

Unlike most faiths, Hinduism is based on personal experience and spiritual practice more than on belief. To be a good Hindu it is not imperative that you adopt a particular doctrine, and thus *there are no heretics or apostates in our religion.*

—*Rev. Swami Siva Siva Palani (1991:13) [Emphasis mine]*

Logically and theologically, Hindu "fundamentalism" is a contradiction in terms. Hindus have many gods; they have scores of religious books, but no agreement on a "bible"; they have no organized church only temples with regional and local influence. Sects with competing deities and ideologies flourish; it is quite possible to be an atheist or an agnostic, observe no rituals, eat beef or be a vegetarian, and still be a good Hindu.

—*Professor Veena Talwar Oldenberg (1990:M7)*

Hinduism by definition is secular. It embraces all religions.

—*Anonymous Indian Leader (1990:A12)*

Taken as a whole, Hinduism has neither dogma, nor founder, and nobody—not even Gandhi, who tried his hand at it—was ever able to define it. ... It rejects all kinds of proselytism ... and accepts within its fold only those who are born in it. ... Hinduism has an enormous and ever-increasing number of sects, cults and philosophic systems; but their diversity raises no doctrinal difficulty because the Hindus view them as mutually complementary facts of one truth. ...

—*Professor Jean Herbert (1968:67-68)*

[Hindu] belief systems are personal, subdued, flexible, and subordinated to practical expressions of faith in vows, devotions, prayers, life-cycle rituals, festivals and pilgrimages. While these traditional family and community stepping-stones dominate, their importance fluctuates according to the period of life and specific challenges of that period.

—*Professor David M. Knipe (1991:144)*

Several years ago, while I was in India, I encountered a young man who was creating an idol of Ganesha (the deity with the elephant head, son of the deity Siva) and building a shrine for Ganesha. He told me that he wanted to worship Ganesha in his own way, emphasizing the attributes of the deity which were meaningful to him; he was not satisfied with worshipping Ganesha in the temple that existed near where he lived. No one bothered him or called him a heretic, and he did not try to attract anyone to worship his creation of Ganesha (although there were a few curious onlookers). I do not know what happened to the young man and the Ganesha shrine, but my encounter with him has remained as a parable or allegory, revealing an important truth about Hinduism. Two possible developments could have occurred: The young man could have continued as a solitary worshipper with Ganesha as his personal deity (*Ishta Devta*), or the young man could have started a local Ganesha cult. The occurrence of both possibilities is acceptable in the Hindu perspective.

Hindus may (and are within their religious right) to create deities or adapt deities with attributes that are suitable to comprehend their own social, emotional, intellectual, and metaphysical needs but do not have the religious right to impose on anyone the worship of their deities or the worship of the attributes of the deities that are important for them. Hindus have the right to worship any deity (or emphasize certain attributes of the deities in the worship) but do not have the right to demand that they should be allowed to worship the deity who is created by an individual or group for exclusive worship. On the one hand, deities belong to all; on the other, individuals and groups establish special, exclusive relationships with deities. Just as there are personal deities (*Ishta devta*), there are family deities, group deities, and local village deities, and permission to worship in these family and group shrines can be denied.

As a result of this approach to worship, there is a proliferation of shrines and temples and there are multitudinous forms of worship with each person striving to establish a unique kind of relationship with his or her deity. Changes in the techniques of worship as well as variations in the nuances of worship and differences in the interpretations of myths and ritual occur all the time. The affirmation of the integrity and uniqueness of the individual along with his or her right to establish a particular kind of relationship with the deity is an important aspect of Hindu religiosity.

Ideally, there are no heretics in Hinduism, and the only heresy is the identification or denotation of a belief or ritual as heretical. *The Hindu perspective affirms such an ideal and permits the freedom to choose a religious path that is suitable to an individual's social, intellectual, emotional, and spiritual needs. As a result, Hindu traditions maintain and promote religious freedom for the individual as well as free and critical inquiry of all Hindu beliefs and rituals.* Ideally, no one should be condemned or burned at the stake for heresy, and no one should try to impose his or her beliefs and rituals on another person. An essential feature of the Hindu perspective is religious freedom which translates as affirmation of personal freedom to engage in any type of religiosity.

If the foregoing statements are valid, why does India have a long history of religious violence? Historically, religious violence has been associated with the conflict between prophetic, ethically dogmatic religions and Hinduism.

There have been numerous prophetic, ethically dogmatic religious movements that have arisen as offshoots of Hinduism. The most successful and widely known Hindu religious movements were Jainism and Buddhism. Jainism and Buddhism were established in the 6th century B.C.E., based on the teachings of the prophets Mahavira and Siddhartha, with several varieties and sectarian divisions. There is considerable recorded evidence pointing to the violent conflicts among the followers of Hinduism, Jainism, and Buddhism.

The conflict between the followers of Hinduism and Jainism ceased when Jainism developed into a Hindu sect and into a castelike (endogamous) group. This pattern of initial conflict between the followers of a Hindu prophet and the followers of traditional Hinduism and the gradual formation of a caste group composed of the followers of the Hindu prophet has been repeated time and again for over 3000 years.

The conflict between Hindus and the proselytizing religious groups such as Bahais, Muslims, and Christians must be understood through a historic analysis of the types of conversions to Bahaiism, Islam, and Christianity and the lack of conversion to Hinduism from these religious groups. Traditionally, there have been two types of conversion of Hindus to other religions: In one type, the conversion occurs because the Hindus who convert come from poor, low-caste communities, seeking better economic conditions, protection from upper-caste members, and higher social status; the other type is forced conversion to Islam, which was common at the time when the Turkish and Mughal sultans, emperors, or chiefs ruled most of India for about 800 years (11th to 19th centuries).

Hindus seldom protest individual conversions that occur when a Hindu finds in Buddhist, Bahai, Islamic, or Christian religious perspectives certain factors that are socially, intellectually, emotionally, and metaphysically more appealing. Such conversions are viewed as the essence of Hindu religiosity, which promotes the personal freedom to choose a deity and the attributes of a deity that correspond to one's personal needs.

In contrast, when Hindu group conversions occur for monetary reasons or because of fear of physical violence, Hindu protest movements come into being. And, when Hindus imagine or perceive threats to their religious beliefs and practices, protest movements arise. Hindu protest movements are of two types: those that protest against mass conversions of Hindus and those that protest against destruction or degradation of Hindu beliefs and practices. In both instances, the protest is for the protection of religious freedom, and conversely for personal freedom to pursue one's own spiritual goals. Mass conversions pose a threat to the Hindu perspective because such conversions take away the personal right to choose any deity or any kind of divine attribute. Destruction and degradation of Hindu beliefs and practices undermine an individual's freedom and the personal dignity to be associated with *any* form or belief or ritual.

As Danielou (1991:9) points out, "Persecution or proselytization of other religious groups, however strange their beliefs may seem to him, can never be a defensible attitude from the point of view of the Hindu." Despite the fact that Hindu beliefs and practices have been denounced by many Muslim and Christian missionaries, Hindu priests and gurus have seldom indulged or engaged in denouncing or ridiculing other religious beliefs and practices. Religious debate and discourse in Hinduism were seldom conducted to discredit other religious truths but were encouraged to understand and learn about the multiple or plural conceptions of divinity. As Coward (1985:80) notes;

> Throughout its long history, Hinduism's attitude toward other religions has remained constant. There is one divine reality that manifests itself in many forms. The various religions are simply different revelations of the one divine reality. In this recognition of other religions as being different revelations of the One and as providing different paths by which devotees may attain release from *karma-samsara*, Hinduism sees itself as being a very open and tolerant religion.

Coward (1985:80), however, raises the question of whether Hinduism is not like other religions in asserting the validity of the Vedas (Hindu scriptures). He is of the view that

> once one steps back from Hindu metaphysics, Hinduism no longer appears so open and tolerant in its view of other religions. The Hindu approach to other religions is to absolutize the relativism implied in the viewpoint that the various religions are simply different manifestations of the one Divine. The Hindu refusal to recognize claims of exclusive truth (e.g., Christianity or Buddhism) that differ from the revelation of the Veda indicates the limited nature of Hindu tolerance. In this, of course, Hindus are no different from the believers of other religions who believe they have the true revelation and seek to impose their truth upon others.
>
> —*Coward (1985:80)*

I suggest that the rejection of the claims of exclusive truth is a central, core principle of the Hindu perspective, and as I pointed out earlier, there are no Hindu heretics because there is no Hindu orthodoxy which claims to possess exclusive revealed truth. Hindu intolerance is directed toward claims of exclusive revealed truth whether such claims are made by non-Hindus, or by Hindus themselves. Any individual may seek personal self-realization of spirituality and may attain his or her revealed (*sruti*) truth. Revelation (sruti) of the Vedas mainly refers to the seeing or hearing of truth by the *rishis* (seers), and the Vedas provide the epistemological authority and methodological principles for learning to accept revelation to "see or hear truth."

The Hindu perspective does not absolutize the relativistic view of respecting different religions but relativizes the absolutist religious dogmas.

Perhaps the above interpretations can be illustrated with a brief discussion of why Hindus incorporated Buddhism as one of the several relevant religious paths within Hinduism but became very antagonistic toward the Buddhist order and monks when it became clear that Buddhists promoted dogmas of exclusive revealed truth and engaged in doctrinaire polemics.

Although Buddhism arose in the Hindu civilization and shared with Hinduism certain principles such as the belief in reincarnation and the focus on the self, its development in the two centuries that followed the Buddha's death created major divisions in dogma (i.e., schisms stemming from disputes on which teachings and interpretations were orthodox or heretical) and gradually three types of Buddhism emerged, with their own types of clergy and dogmatic canons of exclusive truths. None of these types of Buddhism have many followers in India today, although in the 3rd century B.C.E. emperor Asoka became a Buddhist convert and sent several missionaries to proselytize Hindus to Buddhism.

The reasons for the lack of success on the part of Buddhist missionaries were many. Although there were kings in India who supported Buddhist monks at different periods of Indian history, the persecution of Buddhists was also rampant at different periods of Indian history. The primary reason for the persecution was the fear that Buddhist proselytization undermined personal religious freedom and blocked the path of personal or individual realization of spirituality. Buddhism could easily have become a sect of Hinduism (like the Jains or the Lingayats) and the Buddhists could have become castes with their own brand of Hindu perspective, but instead the Buddhist orders became prophetic religions that sought to proselytize and teach special brands of exclusive revealed truth, thus separating themselves from Hinduism.

ii. The Semantics of Hindu Pluratheism

The Hindu, whether he be a worshiper of the Pervader (visnu), the Destroyer (Siva), Energy (Sakti), or the Sun (Surya), is always ready to acknowledge the equivalence of these deities as the manifestations of distinctive powers springing from an unknowable "Immensity."

Since he realizes that other deities are but other aspects of the one he worships, he is basically tolerant and must be ready to accept every form of knowledge or belief as potentially valid.

At every step he finds within the multiplicity a lesser degree of differentiation suitable to his stage of development. ... The seeker chooses at each stage the deities and rites which are within his reach as he progresses on the path that leads toward liberation.

During the pilgrimage of life he goes from one temple to another, adopts different forms of ritual, different modes of living, and various means of self-development. He is constantly aware of the coexistence of different approaches to divinity, suitable for people at stages of realization different from his own.

—*Danielou (1991:9)*

Danielou (1991) identifies the above Hindu orientation as "polytheistic." While I agree fully with his interpretation of Hindu polytheistic orientation, I prefer to substitute *pluratheism* for polytheism because the concept of pluratheism is better able to identify the nature of the Hindu orientation toward divinity. The Greek Olympic pantheon of gods and goddesses would be a typical example of the polytheistic religious orientation. Although polytheism is similar to pluratheism, polytheism does not convey the meaning of divinity manifesting in multiple forms or in plurality of attributes. As Danielou (1991) has correctly pointed out, the attributes of divinity selected for Hindu worship or meditation correspond to the different stages of an individual's self-development.

There are multitudinous and multivarious conceptions of divinity (supernatural beings, power, or sacred others) in Hinduism, but it is possible to identify two distinctive types (with variations) of conceptions. In one type of Hindu perspective, divinity is conceptualized as without qualities or attributes; the second type of conception signifies divinity as having pluralities of qualities or attributes that correspond to the pluralities of individual selves.

In the first type, divinity is viewed as the supreme or the absolute or the ultimate reality which is both transcendent and immanent at the same time, thus emphasizing the internalness or interiority of god. *Taittriya Upanisad* (one of the philosophical treatises of the *Vedas*—the religious texts of Hindus) states that "the Supreme in its inner being is the one self-subsistent reality that cannot be defined by logical categories or linguistic symbols. It is the incomprehensible *nirguna* (qualities) *Brahman*, the pure Absolute" (Radhakrishnan and Moore 1957:38).

The second type of conception relates divinity and self in innumerable ways, conceptualizing divinity as an immanent (interior or internal) supernatural reality that acquires multiple forms. In the Upanisadic expositions, the second type of conceptualizing the divinity (as having multiple forms or qualities) is reflected in the following quote: "It is envisaged as *saguna* (with qualities) *Brahman* or Isvara, a personal god, when It is viewed as the constitutive reality of the many or the cause of the world, as the source, ground, and dwelling place of selves" (Radhakrishnan and Moore 1957:38).

To many Hindus, the three main deities (Brahma, the creator, Vishnu, the preserver, and Siva, the destroyer) embody in themselves or through their manifestations and complementary female counterparts the essence of Hindu divinity. Temples for Brahma are few, but for Siva and Vishnu there are thousands. Siva's two sons, Subramania (Muruga) and Ganesha (Pullaiyar-Vinayakar), and consort Parvati (who manifests as Shakti, Kali, Ammans, Durga, and so on) also have thousands of temples in combination with Siva or separately. Shakti-goddess worship is most common throughout India, and Shakti-Shakta cults are also popular in many regions. Vishnu temples dot every region of India (with or without his consort Lakshmi), and two of Vishnu incarnations (*avatars*), Rama and Krishna, have many temples. Krishna devotional (Bhakti) cults are very popular throughout India. And there are innumerable local and regional Hindu deities that have significance or importance only in particular localities or regions.

It is common for a Hindu to have a personal god (*ishta devta*), who may also serve as the family deity, and he or she may simultaneously be a devotee of a particular deity in a particular temple whose followers may worship another deity in the same temple or may worship in a different temple with the same or different deity. A Hindu may change the focus of worship, emphasizing the worship of different deities in relation to changes in his or her own intellectual/emotional growth, or may remain devoted to the worship of a particular deity. A Hindu may worship at a temple on a regular basis, make offerings (*puja*) to the deities of the temple, and perform rituals of purification and rituals of life passages. A Hindu may complement such worship and ritual performances with participation in sects or cults.

The two main Hindu sectarian traditions are Siva sectarianism and Vishnu sectarianism. There are regional centers of religious discourse with religious heads associated with these sectarian traditions, but the Siva and Vishnu temples and their officiating priests who have competence in the Sanskritic-Vedic knowledge (the Hindu scriptural tradition of over three thousand years) are not necessarily associated with the sectarian traditions and may exist as independent units. Priests belong to different caste groups and are often ranked as having a higher or lower status with reference to their ritual or scholastic functions.

There are innumerable cultic-esoteric ritual traditions; the two widely practiced traditions are the Krishna cults and the Shakti or Shakta cults. Krishna is both an object of devotional worship and philosophical-religious discourse on moral duty and action, and a theory of retributive justice (*karma*). In the Hindu epic *Mahabharatha*, Krishna (as the incarnation of Vishnu) establishes moral justice (dharma) and teaches the paths and goals of righteous action. In the epic *Ramayana*, Rama (as the incarnation of Vishnu) destroys evil and establishes righteous kingship. Shakta cults focus on the worship of energy as it manifests in female spirituality. For many Hindus, the centers of pilgrimage constitute vital components of Hinduism. Some centers of pilgrimage have associations with places where the nectars of the gods had fallen, and some have association with the sexual energy of Siva and his phallic emblem (*linga*), but there are others that have significance because of the special powers of a deity or temple or saint, and most hills and rivers are also viewed by many as endowed with supernatural powers. The river Ganges is conceptualized as goddess Ganga (whose locus is on the head of Siva), and a Hindu can free him- or herself from the cycle of birth and rebirth by performing rituals in the river or by his or her corpse being placed in the river.

As Mount Kailas in the Himalayas is the abode of Siva, pilgrimage to Kailas, or performing yoga rituals on the Himalayas, are believed to be spiritually ennobling.

iii. The Cultural Formulations of Metaphysical, Biopsychological, and Sociological Hinduism

In my book *Culture, Religion, and the Sacred Self* (1991), I interpreted the role of religion as providing sacred or supernatural qualities for the cultural for-mulations of the (symbolic) self, which in turn help to maintain cultural traditions. I pointed out that the supernaturalness or the sacred quality of the symbolic self is achieved and affirmed through two modalities: (1) through the emulation of divine beings (sacred other) or the adoption of certain standards of conduct that are believed to have divine sanctions and (2) through the merging of the symbolic self and the symbols of divine beings or divine powers. Whereas the first modality has greater significance for the biopsychological aspects of human life, the second modality has more relevance for the social aspects of human existence. I identified the two modalities as shamanistic and priestly self-orientations, and I pointed out that societies vary in their emphasis on one or the other orientation and that individuals differ in terms of their focus on one or the other, with the same individual emphasizing one orientation or the other in different contexts and in different stages of development.

As all the Upanisadic treatises propound and expound upon the nature of ultimate reality (*brahman*) and the nature of the relationship between the ultimate reality and the metaphysical self (*atman*), as well as offer extensive discourses on how to conceptualize the oneness or unity of brahman (conceptualized as universal self) and atman (conceptualized as individual self), scholars occasionally surmise that Hindu philosophy deals only with questions about the metaphysical, ontological existence or non-existence of self. While there may be some justification (although selective) for arriving at such a conclusion, it is very important, and indeed crucial, to keep in mind that this type of philosophical discourse is only one of the several types of discourse on the nature of divinity and self. We can recognize the existence of two other elaborate systems of discourse on divinity and self. One deals with the biopsychological processes (*jiva*) and the other with social processes (*varnashrama-dharma*).

We can safely say that these three elaborate discourse systems of Hinduism developed in the Indus traditions of ancient India. Because there is no evidence of Indo-European speakers developing such ideas elsewhere (in either Europe or Asia), it is improbable that the Aryan invaders of India introduced Hindu metaphysics, psychology, and sociology. As noted earlier, the preponderance of evidence suggests that most of the beliefs and practices that we associate with Hinduism developed in the Indus cultural tradition from about 4000 B.C.E. to 1500 B.C.E., and that these beliefs and practices continued after that period, transmitted through Dravidian and Dravidian-ized Aryan languages.

The Hindu metaphysical system (or metaphysical Hinduism) focuses on the study of the relationship between nirguna brahman (qualityless absolute) and the individual metaphysical self (atman); according to this system, an individual gradually becomes aware of the metaphysical self in him- or herself, and such an awareness leads to the realization that the individual metaphysical self (atman) and the absolute, universal self (brahman) are one. In such a formulation, self-realization or becoming aware of the unity of the individual metaphysical self and the universal self is viewed as the attainment of deliverance, release, or liberation (*moksa*) from the cycle of birth and rebirth (*samsara*). Brhad-aranyaka Upanisad captures the essence of the discourse on metaphysical self in the following aphorism: *Tat tvam asi* (That art thou). *Tat* (that) represents the brahman (the universal self or soul, also the ultimate reality) and *tvam* (thou) represents the atman (the individual metaphysical self). True knowledge of the metaphysical self (atman) is conceptualized as the realization of how not to make a distinction between the individual metaphysical self and the universal self (brahman). Attainment of such knowledge is the same as establishing a correspondence between the self and the internal sacred other, or as becoming conscious of the existence of a correspondence between the universal self or ultimate reality (brahman) and the individual self (atman).

In the Hindu biopsychological system (or biopsychological Hinduism), the focus is on the study of biological and psychological processes with reference to sexual energy, psychic powers, and so on. In the Hindu sociological system (or sociological Hinduism) there is an elaborate discourse on several significant Hindu religious conceptions such as *avatara* (divine incarnation), *karma* (law of cosmic retribution), *dharma* (righteous, moral conduct), *varna* (social class), caste (*jati*) endogamy, *samskara* (rituals and beliefs related to the initiation into different stages of life), *upanayana* (ritual for acquiring the sacred knowledge), *puja* (worship through ritual offering), and *samsara* (cycle of birth and rebirth through reincarnation). Sociological Hinduism explains the function of divine manifestations (saguna brahman) and offers interpretations of the various ritualistic forms of Hindu social life. It is sociological Hinduism that makes Hinduism into a way of life, making religion almost inseparable from other aspects of society and culture.

iv. Hinduization

Historically, human beings have created multitudinous models of supernatural reality, and these diverse models of supernatural reality have functioned as meaningful and relevant systems in different cultural settings. As the models of supernatural reality are true to the believers, they have the power to motivate the believers to act in certain ways, enabling them to cope with biopsychological contingencies such as sickness and death.

Models of supernatural reality may change in relation to changes in other aspects of culture. Contacts between peoples of different cultural traditions have often generated changes. During the past five thousand years, various historical changes occurred in the cultural traditions of India: Conquest, trade, and migrations created major changes. In some instances foreign and indigenous groups merged and alien cultures were absorbed by the indigenous cultures, and in some instances the invading or migrating groups succeeded in imposing their language and/or religion on the preexisting populations. In some cases, a synthesis of diverse cultures occurred, but in other instances violent conflicts occurred in defense of language and religion; in some instances, a kind of stabilized cultural pluralism emerged in which distinctive groups coexisted within the same political state boundary.

Despite the great many changes that occurred in the cultural traditions of India (during the past five thousand years), most of the core features of Hindu civilization and Hinduism have prevailed. These core features developed in the Indus Valley Civilization (c. 3000–1500 B.C.E.), and during the subsequent periods, the various invading groups borrowed these features and became assimilated into the Hindu civilization. Such a process of assimilation may be identified as Hinduization. As Tyler points out,

> Many of the themes and motifs of later Indian civilization are already present in the Indus civilization. Phallic worship, mother-goddess cults, ritual lustration, sacred plants such as the pipal, hieratic symbols such as swastika, and theriomorphic deities all attest to a set of religious themes and motifs as characteristic of contemporary Hinduism as of Indus civilization itself ... the Indus civilization with its fertility cults, castelike subdivisions of society, and centralized agricultural economy represents in its earliest form the essential paradigm of all subsequent Indian civilization, and behind the diversity of modern India it is still possible to discern this ancient form, elaborated but never destroyed in the turmoil of Indian History. ... The great granaries of Mohenjo-Daro and Harappa are the enduring symbols of a civilization whose essential characteristics have always centered on the grain heap. ... Each division of society played an essential role in the formation of the heap and each received a share of it in return. ... Participation in this system of production transforms the peasant from agricultural laborer to ritual specialist. ... When we come to the realization that the Indus civilization was organized around the notion of society as a ritual organization, then we can understand why it was so uniform and conservative, and possibly why it disappeared only to live on.
>
> —*Tyler (1973:38-39)*

The entry of Aryans introduced the institution of warrior-king in the Hindu civilization. Originally, the tribal chieftain or king (*raja*) among the pastoral Aryans was one who was skillful in leading the people in battle; the king performed sacrifices for victory in battle and propitiated the god *Soma* in whose honor the hallucinogenic or narcotic drink called soma was consumed before and after battle. The king probably rode the horse-drawn chariot in a half-dazed and inebriated abandonment with his axe and bow and arrow to do battle. This type of behavior and the use of horse and chariot were unknown to the Indians of Indus Valley Civilization, and the behavior of the Aryan warrior must have struck fear among them. Aryan warriors were victorious in battles, and the Aryan establishment of political and linguistic dominance occurred swiftly.

The Aryan warrior or king was not culturally endowed with divine or supernatural qualities, except possibly when he was possessed by Soma and doing battle. But at a later period, with the emergence of kingdoms, the king was referred to as *deva* and occasionally worshipped as god. But this kind of reference was not different from how men of great quality and achievement were often viewed as devas, gods, or celestial beings. The path of the warrior-king was one of the several paths to become or to be considered a deva, and it is incorrect to assume that an inherent relationship existed (in Hindu conceptions) between divinity and kingship. However, in Hindu myths and legends we find divine incarnations (Rama, for example) becoming kings to save the moral-social order, and it was common for kings to claim that they had a divine duty to establish and uphold Hindu dharma (moral-social order).

In our interpretation of Hinduization, it is important to note that the Brahmanical priesthood existed in Indus Valley Civilization but not in the pre-Indus Aryan cultural tradition. Aryan tribes had shamans and family-lineage-clan priests; shamans and shamanistic orientations merged with Brahmanical priesthood, and very elaborate ritualism evolved as a result of the synthesis of the rituals/beliefs of both Indus and Aryan traditions. The Brahmanical priesthood in the Indus Valley Civilization was the institution that regulated the caste system. The position and caste status of the warrior-king acquired legitimacy from the Brahmanical priest who performed purificatory and other rituals to annoint the king and to affirm the king's status. The king, in turn, protected the caste system which provided the highest or most pure ritual status to the Brahmanical priests.

In his study of the adoption and maintenance of Hindu customs, Max Weber (1967) pointed out that the term Hinduization can be used as a concept to identify the process of various ethnic groups becoming Hindus through the adoption of caste statuses in the caste system. In other words, the transformation of groups from their non-Hindu orientation to caste orien-tation signified the Hinduization of groups. This process has been continuous in the history of India since the beginning of the Indus Valley Civilization. In many instances, the central and west Asian tribal groups who invaded and established settlements in India were Hinduized with their adoption of the caste-class status of warriors (*kshatriyas*). Tribal groups, with demonstrated superior political power, often acquired the kshatriya status because of the existence of a functional relationship between political dominance and kshatriya status. (I discuss this aspect of Hinduization in greater detail in Chapter 3.)

v. Sanskritic and Brahmanical Rituals of Hinduism

The well-known Indian sociologist Professor M.N. Srinivas introduced the concept of *Sanskritization* to identify and explain caste mobility in India. According to him, Sanskritization is the process through which low-caste groups discard their non-Sanskritic lifestyles in favor of Sanskritic lifestyles that include the performance of certain rituals officiated by Brahmin priests and the adoption of certain dietary rules. Professor Srinivas holds that this process gives India its unity, connecting the diverse regional Hindu traditions and thus universalizing certain core beliefs and practices of Hinduism. Implicit in the theoretical formulation of Sanskritization is the notion that Sanskritization is a superior civilizational system of India. The formulation of Sanskritization in this manner erroneously delineates the existence of superior and inferior forms of Hinduism. As I have pointed out in a paper on Sanskritization:

> Social anthropological studies of social change and caste mobility that use the paradigm of Sanskritization have essentially incorporated the Western epistemology of civilization and cultural evolutionism and have introduced a spurious dichotomy or distinction between the civilized/Sanskrit/universal/great tradition of India and the primitive/non-Sanskritic/parochial/little traditions of different regions and groups.
>
> The division of Hinduism into Sanskritic and non-Sanskritic Hinduism is peculiar not only because it is like dividing a whole religion into two incomplete religious perspectives, but also because scholars also disagree on the interpretation of certain traits as Sanskritic or non-Sanskritic. Most of all there is a fallacious, implicit assumption that Sanskritic tradition is largely Aryan, and that it is "supra-societal" and pure, influencing and transforming the indigenous and regional cultures and groups of India.
>
> —*Pandian (1984:65)*

Historically there developed a cultural orientation of identifying Brahmins as the custodians of the Sanskritic scriptures, and gradually the rituals performed by Brahmanical priesthood acquired significance as having the sacred authority of the Sanskritic Vedas. These factors resulted in Brahmin castes becoming a class that was culturally endowed with certain unique sacred or supernatural characteristics (not shared by other classes or varnas) and these characteristics were conceptualized as necessary components for the maintenance of political and social order. Although the political authority was vested in the king or the kshatriya class, Brahmins were necessary to legitimize the political authority; and, although the caste system could (and does) function without the Brahmins, the conception of Brahmin castes as the most pure (in religious or ritual terms) became a vital component of the Hindu social order.

A close identification was made between the Brahmanical priesthood and Sanskrit: The ancient Vedas (scriptures) were recited in Sanskrit, and such an association made Sanskrit a sacred language. As the custodians of the Sanskritic vedic knowledge were the Brahmins, only Brahmins could officiate over the performance of rituals that were viewed as valid in the Sanskritic-Vedic system. These factors could be identified as the *Sanskritization of Hinduism*, but we should be careful to note the fact that this kind of Sanskritization of Hinduism served as a vehicle to transmit, elaborate, and continue the religious tradition that had been in existence in the Indus Valley Civilization rather than to create new, superior religious traditions.

There have been several attempts (some very successful and others not successful) to repudiate and reject the Sanskritic authority or legitimacy of the Brahmanical priesthood, viewing it as a corrupt form of Hinduism. The well-known successful religious movements against the Brahmanical priesthood were Jainism and Buddhism, but there has been an ongoing process of protest movements against the Brahmanical priesthood that occasionally fostered major sociopolitical-religious transformations as in the case of the Lingayat movement of the 12th century or the Dravidian purity movement of the 20th century. There have been thousands of minor cults, sects, and religious movements that rejected the authority of the Brahmanical priesthood; also, the mystical and devotional sectarian traditions of Hinduism have frequently de-emphasized the use of Sanskritic Vedas and labeled the caste system a corrupt Brahmanical system.

The Arya Samaj religious movement of the 19th century opposed the Brahmanical priesthood and its association with Sanskritic-Vedic scholarship but affirmed the sanctity of ancient Vedas and Sanskrit and promoted the view that anyone, irrespective of his or her caste status, could *become* a Brahmin by acquiring knowledge of ancient Vedas and Sanskrit. The founder of the Arya Samaj (Dayanand Saraswati) was influenced by the various reform movements of the 19th century, but the goal of Arya Samaj was to revive a real or imagined past of Aryan Hinduism which he believed to be free of cultural orientations such as Brahmanical control of Vedas and Sanskrit, and corrupt practices such as widow-burning (*sati*), idol worship, and child marriage.

Perhaps it is useful to conceptualize Sanskritization as a process similar to the process of Latinization in Europe during the medieval period. Latin was the language of scholarship and religious ritual, and it was primarily cultivated by the Roman Catholic Church with its clergy serving as the custodians of Latin and Christianity. Sanskrit had a similar role; the people who had the knowledge of Sanskrit served as literary, religious, and cultural elites. The nonuse of Sanskrit to propagate religious beliefs, as in the case of Buddha who used Pali language or Sarawati who used Hindi, was a frequent expression of opposition to the Brahmanical priesthood. Also, several linguistic-national traditions of India have had very elaborate Hindu religious treatises in their languages, often coexisting with Sanskritic texts. Sanskrit and Brahmanical priesthood fostered a particular kind of *pan-Hindu* identity rather than a *pan-Hindu* unity. Non-Brahmanic Hindu *sanyasis* (ascetics), pilgrims, *gurus* (teachers), and priests from different regions of India held certain shared assumptions of Hinduism through the existence of Sanskritic as well as non-Sanskritic scholarship, and the use of Sanskrit should not be interpreted to mean that there are two kinds of Hinduism, namely, Sanskritic Hinduism and non-Sanskritic Hinduism.

It is also important to note the fact that Sanskritic religious elites often engaged in intercultural discourse within and outside India (e.g., Thailand, Cambodia, and Java). Just as Sanskrit was Indianized or Dravidianized in the early encounter of Aryans and indigenous populations, at a later period Sanskritic clergy often influenced (Sanskritized) the other Aryan languages (such as Hindi, Gujarati, and Bengali in northern India) and the Dravidian languages in southern India (such as Telugu and Malayalam), as well as the Austro-Asiatic and Austronesian languages of southeast Asia. In other words, Sanskritization of the languages of India and southeast Asia was an important factor in the existence of certain common words for the expression of religious ideas in India and southeast Asia. Sanskritization of languages was neither uniform nor progressive, leading to the emergence of certain predictable forms. The borrowing of Sanskrit varied, with some languages becoming heavily Sanskritized and others resisting such a process.

vi. The Sacred Symbol of Mother Goddess in Hinduism

For an in-depth understanding of applied or practical Hinduism, we should analyze the structures, meanings, and uses of the sacred symbols of Hinduism that have regional or caste-group significance. The dichotomy of Hinduism into Brahmanical/Sanskritic/Literary Hinduism and non-Brahmanical/non-Sanskritic/non-Literary Hinduism distorts the structural-functional unity of Hinduism. The Hindu sacred symbols are relevant to the believers because they are structurally and functionally meaningful to comprehend a variety of existential and experiential questions. Thus, it is reasonable to focus our attention on the study of particular regional or group-specific sacred symbols of Hinduism. These symbols include Vishnu and his human incarnations, Siva and his sons Ganesha and Muruga as well as a multitude of less widespread gods, demi-gods, and goblins. A sacred symbol of significance in many regions of India (as well as for many groups) is the mother goddess. Mother goddess is often identified with reference to particular characteristics that are appended with motherhood, but names such as Kali, Durga, and Sakti are frequently used in association with (or separate from) the god Siva who is conceptualized as her consort.

The conceptual category of the mother goddess enables a devotee to comprehend his or her experiences with reference to the immanence or presence of supernatural power which mediates between the known and the unknown. The concept is metaphorical in the sense that it facilitates cognition of the unknown through the association of phenomena from different experiential domains in which the goddess actively participates. The goddess is associated with prosperity, protection, fertility, and life as well as with decline, danger, disease, destruction, and death, and thus she combines various contradictory aspects of human experience. The concept of the mother goddess simultaneously denotes the positive and negative aspects of the phenomenal reality, and the believers conduct propitiatory ceremonies for her at both levels of experience. Divinatory rituals are frequently performed to seek answers about future events through her shamans (or priests), and the shamans divine the etiology of human calamities as well as render services to eliminate those calamities. Her blessing is sought at annual community ceremonies as well as at specific family ceremonies, and her presence is invoked at all times in one form or another to insure the continuation of the positive aspect of the phenomenal reality. She is also propitiated for the elimination of the negative aspect, as, for example, when there is a disease epidemic, famine, or other personal and group misfortunes. These two aspects are represented in the goddess's identification with two trees believed to be her sacred extensions. The neem tree (*melia India*), which in Indian pharmacology has curing qualities, and the poisonous oleander tree are viewed by the believers to be the dual expressions of her personality.

The dual attributes of the mother goddess—a benevolent, protecting deity and a malevolent, destroying deity—are rooted in experience and in the ethos surrounding femininity which is believed to be both good and evil. Just as the neem and oleander trees are perceived as the expressions of the mother goddess in having life-saving and life-destroying properties, women are perceived as manifestations of the mother goddess in having the dual benevolent and malevolent characteristics. If the death of a girl or woman that occurs under certain unusual circumstances is viewed as the result of the manifestation of the mother goddess, a shrine may be built to worship the manifestation. When a woman dies of smallpox, cholera, or some other virulent form of disease, a temple may be built in her honor and her name prefixed to the conceptual category of mother goddess; such a procedure constitutes one of the important channels by which mother goddess temples multiply. Devotees of mother goddesses know the history of their manifestations and their temples, and this knowledge is a vital component of the beliefs and rituals of applied or practical Hinduism. (In Chapter 15, I describe and discuss the significance of mother goddess worship and practical Hinduism in the village context and suggest that it is valid to conceptualize the village Hindu symbols as parochial models of Hinduism.)

Much of the distinctiveness and differential qualities of mother goddess worship can be traced historically to the context in which a temple was erected for a particular goddess. Often, conflict between caste groups (or between villages) leads to the building of new mother goddess temples that are maintained for the exclusive use of one or a few groups. The distinctiveness in the qualities of the goddesses are, in some instances, due to a particular group consciously attributing such qualities to distinguish itself from other groups and distinguish its goddess from other goddesses. When mother goddess temples proliferate, mother goddesses who are identified with particular diseases such as smallpox and cholera coexist with goddesses who are not directly identified with any particular disease.

Sacred symbols such as the mother goddess are part of the Hindu cosmological/mythological system which represents also the values of particular groups or regions. Thus, depending on the kinds of historical experiences and differences in the values of the different groups, distinctive kinds of deities or sacred symbols acquire greater or lesser significance and function to mediate between Hindu theodicy and the group or regional ethos. Leach (1972:304–305), in his reference to mother goddesses, indicates that they serve as mediators between man and supreme deities and equates them with Christian saints. As his aim is to show that "complicated facts of Indian religion are … reducible to an elementary structural pattern" and to compare the structure of Hinduism with other religions, it is perhaps legitimate to make an analogy between the goddesses and saints. But it appears to me that he minimizes the difference between religions such as Christianity which are essentially prophetic-ethical dogmas founded on the experience of an individual but imposed on alien cultural settings, thus necessitating the formulations of saint-symbols to represent the values of such settings, and religions such as Hinduism that are rooted in historical/social settings of their origins. Leach attributes the existence of Hindu tolerance for contradictions and ambiguities to a general Asian attitude according to which "religious dogmas are complementary rather than antagonistic." I would suggest that the Hindu tolerates contradictions and ambiguities, viewing religious dogmas as complementary due to a recognition that diverse sacred symbols, or diverse attributes of sacred symbols, are necessary and relevant for approximating the diverse social, intellectual, emotional, and spiritual needs of different regions, groups, and individuals.

CHAPTER THREE

℘ *THE SEMIOTICS OF CASTE IN INDIA*

i. The Nature of Caste and the Caste System of India

Caste systems are moral systems that differentiate and rank the whole population of a society in corporate units (castes) generally defined by descent, marriage, and occupation. Elaborately differentiated and ranked caste systems have developed especially in the regional societies of India and among adjacent Hindu and related populations in the territories of modern Pakistan, Bangladesh, Nepal, and Sri Lanka (Ceylon) over the past 2,000 years.

Caste systems resemble racial stratification in their biological concerns with differences of birth and marriage; they resemble stratified plural societies in their presumption of profound differences in group behaviour; they depart from both in conceiving of themselves simultaneously as unitary societies that are culturally integrated. Unlike racially or culturally plural societies, where prior intractable difference among groups is taken as a moral reason for the divided constitution of the society, established caste systems may differentiated into further, new units or they may reassemble their units into one.

—*McKim Marriott and Ronald B. Inden,*
New Encyclopaedia Britannica (1976)

The word caste is derived from the Portuguese term *casta* which means *breed*, a meaning that closely approximates how the Indians themselves perceive and conceptualize group distinctiveness. McKim Marriott and Ronald Inden have suggested (in their article on caste in the *New Encyclopaedia Britannica*, 1976) that this aspect of Hindu perception constitutes the single most important feature of social groupings in India. They correctly point out that "caste, understood as the institution of ranked, hereditary, endogamous occupational groups is a foreign conception. There is no indigenous word or idea that means that."

The study of caste has been extensively intellectualized, and as a result the interpretations and explanations that we have about caste, the caste system, caste hierarchy, and caste ranking are usually far removed from the actual operation of caste in India. Perhaps it is not possible to replicate a model of how caste operates for someone who does not participate in the use of caste. The structural or functional models that are used to interpret caste to Western readers are often caricatures of what occurs in India. And, for a long time a confusion in the study of caste existed because of two factors: (1) Students of caste did not make a clear distinction between *varna* and *jati*, and thus presented an idealized version of caste and (2) many Western and Indian scholars erroneously theorized that caste originated in the social context of conflict between the indigenous people of the Indus Valley Civilization and the Aryan-speaking immigrants who became assimilated into that civilization by about 1000 B.C.E.

Although the word *varna* is frequently used to denote *color*, varna connotes quality of life when used to identify categories of peoples. Varna is not a racial concept but is a class concept as well as model of normative order. Varna connotes that social characteristics of people can be delineated or conceptualized as different class categories, just as an individual's social characteristics can be conceptualized with reference to the different stages of life (*varnashrama-dharma*). The varna categories such as Brahmin, Kshatriya, Vaishya, and Shudra may be viewed as representations of characteristics that are believed to manifest in members of classes who pursue certain occupations and adopt a certain way of life. The term *jati*, on the other hand, refers to groups composed of members who are *one of a kind* and are in that social entity because of their being born into it. Jati groups are lumped together for their inclusion in the varna categories with reference to their occupations and ways of life. Thus, it is more appropriate to use the term caste to identify jati groups and the jati system rather than the varna categories.

The second factor that contributes to confusion in the study of caste comes from theories of the origin of caste. Recent scholarship on the study of the Indus Valley Civilization and of the ancient literary texts suggests that the institution of caste existed in the Indus Valley Civilization long before the Aryan speakers became part of that civilization. But because of the prevalence of racist theories of anthropology during the past two hundred years, many scholars assumed until recently that racial tensions must have existed between the light-brown Aryan speakers and dark-brown Dravidian speakers, and, as a result, the caste system of India was erroneously interpreted as an Aryan model that was imposed on the indigenous populations to safeguard or protect the racial purity of the Aryans. Modern scholarship suggests that Aryans were assimilated into the preexisting caste system of the Dravidian-speaking populations. It must be noted that physical features or skin color do not determine an individual's caste identity: People with light- and dark-brown skin color can be found in the same caste, just as diverse physical features can be found among members of an Indian family.

Ideally, the Indian caste system is based on the application of ritual or religious principles of endogamy, pollution, and hierarchy. An individual is born as a member of a particular jati group and is expected to marry within that group. The group is considered religiously polluting or not polluting in relation to its characteristic occupation (which is considered religiously defiling or nondefiling), and each group has a social status that is the social identity of all the members of the group. In other words, an individual is ascribed the status of the jati group. Jati groups are conceptually and socially located on a continuum of religious pollution and purity, with the groups that are religiously least defiling placed at the purity end of the scale (Brahmin quality) and the groups that are religiously most impure placed at the impurity end of the scale (untouchable quality), with all other groups in between. When this continuum is made vertical, we have a hierarchical model of the caste system. But, as ranking of jati groups is always in flux, there is very little consensus in terms of how different groups rank themselves and are ranked by others. In other words, members of a jati group may claim a high social-status rank but such a claim may not be validated by members of other jati groups. We must keep in mind the fact that the religious principles of endogamy, rank, heredity, and occupation which are identified as the distinguishing characteristics of the caste system do not constitute a coherent model for the users of the system. People use the principles selectively and in multiple combinations. Ranking of groups is always in relation to other groups, and groups move up and down in terms of their economic and political power which is represented in religious or ritual terms. Although the caste system is conceptualized with reference to pollution, it is maintained through the manipulation of the economic and political power of the groups. The caste system is distinguished from other systems of social stratification by the expression of politico-economic power in religious or ritual terms of relative pollution which is used to formulate a correspondence or congruence between high ritual or religious status and politico-economic dominance.

The study of the caste system is often linked with the study of the village economic system. In many parts of India certain caste groups function as patrons (*jajman*) and others as clients (*kamin*). This system of patron-client relationship, which is called the *jajmani* system, is not very common today. Where it exists, low-ranking and untouchable caste groups function as clients, and the dominant caste groups own most of the property within the village. The dominance of caste groups in the villages is derived from landownership, and landowning families receive services from members of client caste groups who receive produce of the land in return for their services. Mobility of low-caste groups in such a context is often thwarted by members of the dominant caste, but educational opportunities as well as opportunities for work in the urban centers have introduced major changes in the village economic system, alleviating the tyrannical suppression of the low-ranking and untouchable castes by the dominant, high-ranking castes.

ii. Caste Emblems: Jati Names, Jati Titles, and Varna Symbols

Researchers in India are well aware of the fact that if a person is asked a question about his caste identity, he may give one of several replies: (1) his caste name, which is not shared by other castes but may be shared by the subcastes of his caste; (2) his caste title(s), which may be shared by other castes and which could also be the caste name of some other caste; or (3) the varna category (Brahmin, Kshatriya, Vaisiya, and Shudra) within which he includes his caste. Occasionally, as Dumont (1970a:62) points out, an individual may identify his clan as the caste: "If one asks someone 'what is your caste?' (*jati*) he may indicate either which of the varna he belongs to ... or a caste title, or his caste, or his subcaste, or even the exogamous section (clan) to which he belongs." This is complicated by the fact that caste titles of some castes are also caste names of other groups, and that the caste titles occasionally correspond to varna categories.

I suggest that the confusion in the literature on caste may be cleared up if we realize that from the user's perspective, the conception of caste identity is not unidimensional. Caste identity is conceptualized with denotative and connotative symbols that have multiple referents and are multivocal. Therefore, a symbol that means or represents religious or ritual status in a certain context might represent political, economic, or kinship status in another context. There are, however, certain symbols of caste identity that we can identify as rooted in political and/or economic authority; others are rooted in sacred or ritual authority.

There are two structures that generate attributes associated with symbols of caste identity: (1) The structure of politico-economic dominance generates elements of meaning associated with caste titles; (2) the ritual or religious structure generates components of information that constitute caste names. The political and ritual aspects exist in a dialectical relationship; both are necessary for an individual to conceptualize his or her caste identity. In some instances the two are in close interplay, as when a single term serves as both caste name and title and thus acts as both a political and a ritual status or identity. In other instances the interplay is limited, as when some caste groups self-consciously distinguish their caste names and caste titles. But no matter how close the interplay, the political structure of caste identity is distinguishable from and cannot be subsumed under the ritual structure of caste identity.

An individual may use one or more caste labels (caste name, caste title, and/or varna category) to denote their caste identity. Unless an observer is familiar with the village and regional culture, it is not possible to know whether the labels signify ritual status or politico-economic dominance. The labels do not explicitly signify the difference in meaning but must be related to the meanings and definitions of the situations where they are deployed. In addition, there are differences in the use of the labels as terms of address or reference. Also, as Mandelbaum (1970:13) points out, "The answer a villager gives to the question, 'who are you?' depends, as it does everywhere in the world, on who is asking and on what the villager thinks the questioner wants or should know."

Caste titles are conceptually linked with village corporate authority and politico-economic dominance. Corporateness of village life, with everyone in the village being subjected to the adjudicative and penalizing power of the village or of the caste, is a significant part of the authority structure that every villager comprehends. Intra- and intercaste mechanisms of social control depend on the villager's accepting the authority of group action, which is regulated by the *panchayat,* or the council of elders. Various castes, and particularly the elders who have the authority to make decisions, use the symbols or labels of authority structure as their own caste identity. However, some castes that are neither politico-economically powerful nor ritually pure also use caste titles; thus it is necessary to interpret caste titles in terms of their link with the symbols of corporate authority within the village. It can be said that caste titles serve as vehicles of leadership and decision making within the caste, and that the titles serve as symbols of dominance and power when a caste is in reality politico-economically powerful in the village. The validation of titles has two contexts, one within the caste and the other in intercaste relationships. Any caste can adopt a locally relevant title, and the leaders will command within that caste the respect and authority associated with the title. When the caste is politico-economically dominant, the title is accepted also as a symbol of dominance of the caste in the village, and when the title is accepted as the caste name by other castes, it signifies high ritual and social status. The view of Dumont (1970a), Tyler (1973), and others that the Hindu village is a miniature kingdom, with the dominant patron caste functioning as the king, is correct, but we must add that every caste headman (irrespective of whether the caste is dominant in the region or not) is functionally a king in his caste. Just as it is legitimate to have caste titles for the dominant caste to represent its politico-economic role in intercaste relationships, it is legitimate to have caste titles for the headman of a caste group to discharge intracaste functions. Caste brethren adopt the same titles of their headman, and the proliferation of caste titles occurs. Some castes have multiple caste names and over a dozen caste titles.

High ritual status commonly corresponds to or is congruent with greater politico-economic power, and ritually low-ranking castes attempt to change their ritual status when their politico-economic conditions improve. Changes in status involve changes in caste names and caste titles. A good deal of theorizing in anthropology has focused on the dynamics of this process and as a result, scholars have neglected to examine the role of caste names and caste titles as distinguishable religious and political symbols of caste identity that have greater significance as models of caste behavior than the varna categories. For those who function and use the caste system, caste identity is not simply a matter of one's affiliation with his or her ritually pure or impure endogamous group (through a group's linkage with the symbols of varna hierarchy): Caste names and caste titles alternate in relation to status validation in the context of social interaction, and varna categories are invoked for inclusion or exclusion of caste groups in such categories as an affirmation of the dialectics and semiotics of the symbols of caste names and caste titles.

iii. Transformation of Caste Identity and Social Mobility

Until recently scholars failed to recognize the fact that social mobility of caste groups has been an ongoing process throughout India's history. There was an erroneous assumption that castes were fixed entities in the caste hierarchy and that there was no channel for castes to change their social status. During the past four decades there emerged a large body of data on caste that showed conclusively that social mobility of castes (or positional movement of castes) was, in fact, the norm of the Indian caste system. In an important historical study, the eminent scholar Burton Stein (1968) showed that social mobility occurred during the ancient times, comparable to (or more than) how such a mobility has occurred in recent times.

Stein (1968:78) points out,

Medieval Indian history appears to present widespread persistent examples of social mobility. It is known that members of lower rank ethnic units assumed roles and statuses which are usually reserved for higher units and with the consent of such higher units. It may be argued that this was one of the most, and as yet underrated, dynamic elements in medieval Indian history.

The reasons for our slow recognition of the fact or existence of social mobility are many. (1) Social mobility occurs at the level of the caste group and never at the level of the individual, and it is rare that such a mobility occurs in a single generation; (2) members of the caste group that has moved up will have a revised history of the past that would exclude any reference to their former inferior status, and the lack of scholarly historiography was a functional component of rewriting the past; (3) the continued existence of untouchability and untouchable caste groups has obscured the fact that the caste groups that are located in between untouchable (ritually most impure) and Brahmin (ritually most pure) caste groups have always moved up and down in relation to their politico-economic power; (4) there is little agreement over the ranking of the middle-level caste groups in the purity/pollution scale with many claims and counterclaims for superior ritual status, and these claims often do not reveal the true nature of caste status structure or social mobility.

The most widely noted phenomenon of caste mobility is how a ritually low-status caste group adopts new caste names, caste titles, and asserts a high ritual status in relation to its enhancement of politico-economic status. In other words, a new congruence between ritual and politico-economic statuses is established when social mobility occurs. It involves the caste group discarding its former lifestyle and adopting a lifestyle that is associated with ritually high-caste groups. This type of status emulation to achieve social mobility may be identified as Brahmanization or Sanskritization because it often involves the use of the services of Brahmin priests and the use of Sanskritic rituals. Low-ranking groups that seek recognition as high-ranking groups often abstain from performing ritually polluting occupations and from consuming meat and alcohol to signify their ritual purity. But caste mobility occurred frequently during the past two millennia through invasions. Often, the invading groups occupied high social status, and the low-caste indigenous groups moved up if they associated themselves with the invading groups (see Silverberg 1968).

As social mobility is always group-oriented, if an individual of a low caste is economically and politically successful and prosperous, he must seek to raise the economic/political status of his group to move up and must persuade his caste brethren to adopt a lifestyle that would be regarded as ritually pure. *The individual by himself cannot claim a ritually high caste status: It is the caste group identity that accords an individual a high or low ritual status.* Therefore, it is not uncommon for divisions in caste groups to occur, with successful members of the caste group forming a new caste group. In the following pages I present a discussion of a caste group whose social mobility has been recorded in detail. The social mobility of this group illustrates clearly the religious and nonreligious aspects of the caste system, shows how caste names and caste titles are used to signify power and status, and explains how caste identities change.

The Nadar caste has a high social and ritual status today. But about a hundred years ago it had a low status. The label Nadar is both a caste name and caste title. In the 20th century the label acquired significance as a caste name, replacing its 19th century caste name, Shanar. Along with this transformation, the ritually defiling caste occupation of collecting palm juice for making sugar and intoxicating beverages became a relatively unimportant activity, confined to only the poorest members of the caste. In the modern context, due to the numerical preponderance of the Nadar (estimated to be about five million) and the economic and educational advancement which began in the 19th century, the caste has a relatively high ritual, political, economic, and social position in Tamil Nadu. (See Thurston 1909, VI:365–78; Hardgrave, Jr. 1969; Rudolph and Rudolph 1967:36–49.)

The label Nadar is derived from the caste title Nadan which was traditionally used as the caste name by the upper-class members of the Shanar caste. The word Nadan means *landlord* or *ruler of the country*. In the southeastern tip of Tamil Nadu, the very hot, humid, and sandy region where the main vegetation is palm trees, and in the tropical southwestern tip of Tamil Nadu where most of the Shanar lived, upper-class Shanar owned the land where palm trees were cultivated and tapped for juice to make sugar and intoxicating beverages. In these areas, the upper-class Shanar, that is, the Nadans, distinguished themselves from the labor class of Shanars (identified as the "climber of palm trees") who were dependent on the Nadans for their livelihood.

The Nadan landlords were recognized traditionally as the retainers or tax collectors by the rulers of the deep south of southern India. This deep south, which at earlier times was ruled by different kings, today constitutes the two southern districts of Tamil Nadu. Many of the villages of the deep south were composed entirely or almost entirely of Shanars who had their own caste barbers and priests. Within these villages, the high ritual, social status, and the politico-economic power of the Nadan were never disputed. The class division cut across all the subcastes of the Shanar caste. The caste of Shanar as a whole was divided into five subcastes, each with several clans, and the clan temples were dedicated to Kali-Amman who was worshipped as the guardian of the Shanars. (See Hardgrave, Jr. 1969:12–42.)

In the villages and towns where Shanars did not constitute the majority, with no Nadan landlords, Shanars had a low ritual status and were ranked just above the untouchables. Their occupation was considered ritually polluting, and therefore they were prohibited from worshipping in the temples officiated by Brahmin priests. In parts of the deep south, as in the old kingdom of Travancore, Shanars were subjected to forced labor, or a kind of semiserfdom, and were prohibited from wearing upper garments (Hardgrave, Jr. 1969:56-70).

The transition from a caste of relatively low ritual status to a caste of high ritual status, and the transformation of caste name from Shanar to Nadar, have been documented in great detail in the missionary, court, and government documents of the 19th century. (See Hardgrave, Jr. 1969;

Rudolph and Rudolph 1967:36–49.) A large number of Shanar became Christians in the 19th century and many of them became professionals, merchants, and overseas traders, but their ritual status was linked with the traditional, ritually defiling occupation of making intoxicating beverages. Thus, despite their economic advancement, they were still not considered by the other castes to be a high caste.

About the caste titles of the Shanar, Thurston (1909, VI:377) notes:

> Some Tamil traders ... who returned themselves as Pandyan, were classified as Shanars, as Nadan was entered in their title. In Coimbatore, some Shanans, engaged as shop-keepers, have been known to adopt the name of Chetti. In Coimbatore, too, the title Muppan occurs. This title, meaning headman or elder, is also ... used by other castes.

In the 19th century, there was a self-conscious, organized effort to unify all the Shanars to affirm Nadar as the caste name and to include the caste in the Kshatriya varna category. Shanar caste historians claimed that Shanars were the descendants of the ancient Tamil ruling dynasties, and that the name Shanar was derived from the word *Shantror*, meaning nobility. Also, it was claimed that the caste title Nadan was indicative of *kingship* as the heritage of the Shanar caste. Bishop Robert Caldwell, one of the 19th century Christian missionaries who wrote extensively about the Shanar, theorized that the Shanars and other toddy tappers of South India had migrated from Ceylon (Sri Lanka), and pointed out that the label Shanar was in fact an honored caste title of the makers of intoxicant drinks in the Kerala state, such as the Ezhavas (Hardgrave, Jr. 1969:20).

The social mobility movement of the 19th century was resisted by the Maravar caste of southeast and the Nayar caste of the southwest. For about 50 years both the Maravar and the Nayar attempted to intimidate the Shanar with arson, assault, and murder. The Shanar, in presenting their claims for a higher ritual status, pointed out that their persecution by the Maravar (warrior caste of the Southeast) and the Nayar (warrior caste of the southwest) was itself proof that the Shanar were a conquered race of early Tamil royalty.

In the 20th century, the Shanar ceased to have their caste included in the Kshatriya category but by then their claims for a higher ritual status had gained implicit acceptance and recognition, and the political and social changes that had occurred in the 20th century throughout India had made it irrelevant whether they were known as Kshatriya or not (Rudolph and Rudolph 1967:49). But the label Nadar became important as the caste name, and the label Shanar was viewed as a derogatory term of reference and address.

The example of the Nadar shows how the title Nadan, a symbol of village corporate authority and politico-economic dominance and power, became the label of caste identity, and how the caste mobilization and regionalization of politico-economic dominance and power enabled all the members of the caste within the label of Nadar to be incorporated by the label. The existence of the Nadan upper class did not result in a permanent fission of the caste, but through the efforts of this class the entire group was elevated to participate in the politico-economic dominance and power under the caste label Nadar.

iv. Caste and Hindu Sectarianism

Caste groups and sectarian groups are similar and are also related in some ways in the Hindu cultural context. Castes may be viewed as religious minorities; they have distinguishable rituals or liturgies, and, in some instances, have particular temples, deities, and priests. But due to the fact that caste membership is inherited and caste ranking is symbolically validated by assumptions about differential purity or impurity (of caste groups), castes differ from sects that recruit their members by rejecting the rules of social heredity and purity or impurity.

The term *sect* is generally used by scholars to identify a division or group that has separated from an established ecclesiastical religion. Usually, sectarian leaders formulate distinguishable beliefs and practices to differentiate their sects from the parent ecclesia or church. Sects may transform into churches and, in turn, may face the possibility of further divisions. The history of world religions such as Buddhism, Christianity, and Islam illustrates such a relationship between church and sect. It is appropriate to state that today's sect is tomorrow's church because successful sects become churches.

Hinduism lacks an ecclesia except that castes may be viewed as ecclesiae. On the other hand, sectarianism is an integral, structural component of Hinduism. As noted in the last chapter, every Hindu has the freedom to create a sect and, as a result, there are no heretics in Hinduism. Although the Brahmanical priesthood is an important aspect of Hinduism, and although a Hindu is one who performs rituals that are associated with one's caste group (at least occasionally to mark the different stages of life such as birth, puberty, marriage, and death), Hindu sectarianism is an important aspect of Hinduism. *In fact, it is the existence of Hindu sectarianism as an integral aspect of Hinduism that enables Hinduism to remain an open and free inquiry into spirituality. Sects are viable components rather than divisive or heretical branches. Sectarian leaders are never denounced as heretics in the Hindu perspective.*

An important characteristic feature of Hindu sectarianism is that many sectarian leaders voice opposition to the Brahmanical priesthood as well as to the caste system. The followers of Hindu sects are generally recruited from *all* the castes with little or no commitment to the religious principles of purity and pollution. Many of the founders of the sects are from low-caste groups, and even when the founders of the sects are Brahmins (religiously the purest caste) there is a self-conscious attempt on the part of these leaders to renounce their caste identity. Some sects are formed as explicit revolts against the Brahmanical priesthood or the caste system, some are formed to promote new ways or paths to attain spiritual salvation, and others with a combination of social and spiritual goals.

Another important characteristic feature of Hindu sectarianism is that a significant number of the sects either develop into caste groups or become *ethnic* groups, that is, culturally distinguishable groups with boundaries which are internally differentiated into high- and low-ranking caste groups. In his insightful study of the sociology of Hinduism, Max Weber (1967) noted long ago the connection between Hindu sects and the caste system:

> When a principal anti-caste sect recruits former members of various Hindu castes and tears them from the context of their former ritualistic duties, the caste responds by excommunicating all the sect's proselytes. Unless the sect is able to abolish the caste system altogether instead of tearing away some of its members, it becomes, from the standpoint of the caste system, a quasi-guest folk, a kind of professional guest community in an ambiguous position in the prevailing Hindu order. Further definition of the situation by the remaining Hindus depends upon the style of life elaborated in the new community. If the sect permitted a way of life Hinduism considers ritually defiling (beef consumption), the Hindus treat it as a pariah people, and if this condition continues long enough, as an impure caste … if ritualistic defilement is not indicated, in time (particularly if the activities of the sect members are of a ritualistic nature—and such is usually the case), the sect may take its place among the surrounding castes as one with special ritualistic duties.
>
> —*Weber (1967:19)*

For an in-depth understanding of the relationship between caste and sect, it is necessary to make a distinction between sects that become castes and sects that become sectarian ethnic groups with their members divided into high- and low-ranking caste groups. In both instances, the ranking of these caste groups corresponds to the ranking of the Hindu caste groups from which conversion to the sect had occurred, but there are regional variations related to the politico-economic power of the sectarian ethnic group. In a summary of sectarian castes, Mandelbaum (1970:532) notes,

> Sectarian jatis are typically open to certain kinds of converts. In Ramkheri village, for example, there are three sect-based jatis. One centers on Shiva and is ranked with Rajput [Kshatriya] bloc; another focuses on Vishnu and is allied with the vegetarian jatis in the village. Both accept converts, but only those of equal or higher jati rank. The third sectarian jati is classed with Jarijans.

There are hundreds of other sectarian castes spread all over India. Sectarian ethnic groups are fewer, but some have acquired prominence in the economic and politcal domains of India through the acquisition of immense wealth and numerical preponderance. The widely known sectarian ethnic traditions such as Jainism, Lingayatism, and Sikhism arose in opposition to the Brahmanical priesthood and the caste system. Jainism was founded in the 6th century B.C.E. by Mahavira in northwestern India; Lingayatism was founded in the 12th century C.E. by Basna in southern India; and Sikhism was founded in the 16th century C.E. by Guru Nanak in northern India. The flowers of Jainism, known as Jains, are found mainly in northern and southern India; the Lingayats (bearers of lingam or Shiva's phallic symbol) are located in the southern Indian state of Karnataka, and the followers of Sikhism (known as Sikhs or disciples) constitute the majority of the population of the northern Indian state of Panjab.

There are about 60 Jain castes, most of whom have high- or low-status positions corresponding to the comparable Hindu castes. Historically, members of the Jain and Hindu castes of the same rank have intermarried, thus affirming caste endogamy rather than affirming sectarian ethnic group endogamy. Lingayats, who are divided into five distinctive hierarchically ranked castes (whose status positions correspond to status positions of comparable Hindu castes), have a hereditary priesthood (known as *Jangamas*), which is considered the most pure and important, and a group of untouchables who perform all the defiling or polluting occupations. The Sikhs are divided into two categories of castes: In one category are the high-ranking castes known as Khatri Sikhs, Jat Sikhs, and Arora Sikhs, and in the other category are the outcastes known as Ramdas Sikhs and Marzhabi Sikhs. Caste endogamy is important, but hypergamy is permitted along with the occasional marriage between a Sikh and a Hindu.

The foregoing discussion clearly illustrates the fact that the egalitarian ideals of the sectarian movements seldom operate beyond the early phases of the movement when recruitment into the sect from all the castes is encouraged. Egalitarianism is gradually replaced by caste hierarchy, and the sects become either castes with a particular status position, or they transform into a kind of sectarian ethnic group with internally stratified caste groups that have counterparts in the Hindu caste system.

v. Caste and the Tribal Frontier

Tribal groups in India are those who have a measure of political autonomy and who are not components of the Hindu social order (in which the groups are located in a system of hierarchical relationship based on their relative politico-economic power and religious purity). Technically, a tribe is a self-governing, culturally distinctive, endogamous unit with some internal stratification which facilitates the existence of a ruling stratum or chieftainship.

India has hundreds of small and large tribes, and some tribes constitute a numerical majority in certain isolated regions of central and northeastern India.

As noted in Chapter 1, India was invaded by several central Asian tribes. Groups such as the Aryans of the early period and the Scythians and Huns of later periods were nomadic tribes who were integrated into the Hindu caste system as Kshatriya castes, a process of adoption and integration which illustrates the fact that politically or militarily successful groups are accorded a high-status position in the Hindu caste system. The integration of powerful tribal groups is facilitated through the tribal groups adopting the style of life (or rituals) associated with the powerful caste groups. This process of tribal groups adopting Hindu ways of life and rituals may be characterized as Hinduization. The Aryan tribes were Hinduized, as were the Scythians and Huns.

Beyond the Hinduization of invading tribal groups, there has also been the Hinduization of indigenous tribal groups that have been located in isolated forested or mountainous regions where the members of the Hindu caste groups seldom visited. Some of these indigenous tribal groups participated in the Hindu civilization to a greater or lesser degree, and depending on the usefulness of adopting Hindu symbols of political validation, some tribal chiefs adopted Hindu titles and Hindu customs comparable to those of the Kshatriya rajas (kings) of the neighboring regions. Orans (1959:109) describes such a process:

> By the 16th century a Munda tribal in the Ranchi district established himself as a local Raja. By virtue of his wealth and power he attracted reputable Brahmans to his court who Sanskritized his rituals and manufactured for him a Rajput [son of king] genealogy. Eventually this status was accepted by other Rajputs [sons of kings].

Until the British established highways and railways that connected the urban centers and the forested and mountanous regions of India, the tribes of India remained largely as a frontier that was left alone. Hindus were afraid of the tribes who lived in the remote forested and mountainous regions not only because of the folklore about tribal warfare, witchcraft, and headhunting but also because of a common belief that evil spirits lived in those regions. The British favored the high-altitude regions with their cooler temperatures for summer residences and government bungalows, and the high-altitude regions became prime targets or valued property for the development of tea plantations and other cash crops. Hindu laborers were settled in these places to serve on the plantations, and many Hindu settlements began to emerge in the tribal regions.

From the 19th century, there was a progressive displacement of the tribal groups from their territory, and although the British made some effort to protect and safeguard the rights of the tribes, some tribal cultures became extinct either through the decrease in the population (caused by disease and poverty) or through their becoming caste or castelike groups. In the late 19th and 20th centuries, various anthropological surveys of the tribes of India were instituted and, as a result, we have a large body of anthropological data on the tribes of India. For example, Thurston's (1909) multi-volume *Castes and Tribes of Southern India*, and Iyer's (1928-35) *The Mysore Tribes and Castes* are excellent reference books on the tribes of southern India. A series of excellent comprehensive studies of the Tibeto-Burman-speaking tribes of northeastern India (in the Assamese-Burma border region) were undertaken in the early 20th century. For example, Hudson's (1911) *The Naga Tribes of Manipur*, Hutton's (1921) *The Angami Nagas*, Mills's (1922) *The Lhota Nagas*, Smith's (1925) *The Ao Naga Tribe*, and Mills's (1937) *The Rengma Nagas* are important ethnographic contributions. Books on the Austro-Asiatic-speaking tribes of India include Orans's (1965) *The Santal: A Tribe in Search of a Great Tradition* and Roy's (1970) *The Mundas and Their Country*.

Recent political developments in India facilitated the emergence of semiautonomous, separate states for the Tibeto-Burman tribes and for an Austro-Asiatic tribe in northeastern India, bordering Burma. These tribes have come under the influence of Christianity and Westernization more than under Hinduization. Thus, it is unlikely that they will transform into castes.

The tribes of central, eastern, and southern India who constitute minority populations in the various linguistic states are becoming more like castes due to their having to establish a kind of symbiotic relationship with the neighboring castes. However, the dichotomy between tribe and caste is likely to continue. As Mandelbaum (1970:577–78) points out:

> Jati and tribe are similar units in that each is considered by its members to be an endogamous entity composed of ritual equals. The crucial difference is that jati members, on the one hand, believe they must have nonkinship relations with others in their society and that these relations must be arranged in an order of dominance and deference. Tribesmen, on the other hand, tend to see their society as held together by kinship bonds and do not insist on hierarchical ordering. Further, jati people expect their village society to be culturally heterogeneous, each jati following a unique combination of customary practices; tribesmen expect their society to be homogeneous or, at least, not necessarily heterogeneous.

CHAPTER FOUR

ᔥ THE SEMIOTICS OF ALIEN ETHNIC IDENTITIES IN INDIA

i. Caste and Alien Ethnic Identities

In the last chapter I presented a brief discussion of how indigenous (i.e., Indian) religious sects and tribal groups acquired characteristics of caste groups, and I noted that the distinguishing feature of caste groupings is their functioning as components of a system of social relationships which links the caste (endogamous) groups in a hierarchy of religious purity and pollution. Historical scholarship of the past three decades suggests that formation of new castes and positional changes in the religious hierarchy occurred as adaptive devices of the caste system which responded or adapted to changes in the politico-economic fortunes of the caste groups. It is quite probable that during the past four millennia, hundreds of caste groups came into being with higher or lower religious and social identities in relation to their members moving up or down in the political and economic arenas of the different historical periods. Also, it is very likely that hundreds of indigenous sects and tribes had become castes or castelike groups through their adoption of social and ritual practices that enabled them to be located on particular social and religious status positions of the caste hierarchy.

An important fact of Indian history and society is that there is also a kind of group identity or group status validation that invokes the legitimacy of *non-Hindu ethnicity*, such as Christianity, Judaism, and Islam, and affirms the use of alien, that is, non-Indian ethnic identities, such as Persian, Turk,

Afghan, and Arab for practicing endogamy and status ranking. It may be noted that the term ethnicity refers to conceptions of peoplehood (such as beliefs about a group's origin and collective heritage), and that the binomial term ethnic group refers to endogamous social groupings which strive to maintain their biological or linguistic or religious distinctiveness. Caste groups also fit the descriptions of ethnicity and ethnic groups, but they have features that are unique to Hindu beliefs and practices that constitute the Hindu social order.

Due to the fact that greater politico-economic power of a group usually results in its having a higher social-religious status in the Hindu social order, various invading and trading groups from western and central Asia were included in the higher socioreligious categories, namely, the Kshatriya (warrior) and Vaishya (merchant). *But it was also possible for the invaders and foreign traders to maintain and use their alien heritage as symbols of superior social status without their being placed in the categories of Kshatriya or Vaishya.* There was great variation in how different invading and trading groups from western and central Asia adapted to the Hindu social order. There were regional differences, with the alien groups changing their status positions in relation to their political and/or economic strength.

In this chapter, I discuss the characteristics of certain foreign ethnic groups in India that dramatize clearly the semiotics of alien ethnic group identity in India. In many instances, the Muslims of India are hierarchically divided with reference to their alien or indigenous ethnic group identity. Indian Christians are hierarchically divided in some instances with reference to the dichotomy between alien or indigenous (Indian) ancestry, and in other instances with reference to the status of the corresponding indigenous Hindu castes. Indian Jews are divided by a combination of the above stated factors that operate among Muslims and Christians. Parsis, who do not incorporate indigenous (Indian) converts, are divided into priestly high-ranking caste and nonpriestly caste and have had high social status since the 18th century, reflecting their superior economic strength.

ii. Symbols of Islamic Ethnicity and Muslim Identities in India

It is necessary to make a distinction between *Islamic ethnicity* and *Muslim identities* because a significant number of Muslims in India use symbols of alien or foreign ethnic heritage as markers of their Muslim identity. Muslims in India are divided into castelike endogamous groups that are hierarchically ranked, with the upper-caste Muslims claiming alien or foreign (i.e., non-Indian) identity. Thus, although it is valid to identify all the followers of Islam as Muslims, it is important to note the fact that *there are several Muslim identities in India.* Whereas Islamic ethnicity refers to the religious symbols of groupness or peoplehood, the Muslim identities in India refer to conceptions of caste-like (endogamous) group boundaries that identify linguistic and bioethnic features as markers of distinctiveness. In other words, although Islam constitutes the foundation for Muslim peoplehood (ethnicity), Persian, Afghan, Arab, or other foreign origins provide the foundation for the ethnic group identities of Muslims with high social status.

India came under the influence of Islam in the first century of its beginnings (i.e., 7th century C.E.). Northwestern India became progressively linked with Islamic religious traditions of Arab, Persian, and Turkish invaders from the 9th century C.E. The coastal port settlements of western and eastern India began to accommodate Islamicized Arab settlements from that period. A brief discussion of Islam is presented here in order to identify some of the basic or central features of Islam as a system of ethnicity (peoplehood).

The word Islam means *submission* and *commitment,* and the word Muslim means *follower of Islam.* The five founding principles or *Pillars of Faith* of Islam are faith in god (Allah), praying five times a day facing Mecca, fasting in the month of Ramadan, giving alms, and undertaking pilgrimage to Mecca. Along with these pillars are six articles of faith, namely, "There is no god but Allah and Mohammed is his prophet," "Koran is the word of god," "Angels are the instrument of Allah," "The just will be rewarded in paradise and the unjust punished in hell," "Adam, Noah, Abraham, Moses, and Jesus were prophets who preceded Mohammed, the last prophet," and "Predestination of individual merit."

Due to the fact that these religious beliefs constitute guidelines for moral, social, and political action, there have been diverse interpretations, and these interpretations have frequently led to the emergence of theological schisms and religious movements that have become the religious traditions of different bioethnic groups or linguistic national traditions. Two main divisions of Islam arose early: The main division with the largest following is known as *Sunni* (from the word *sunna,* meaning *way*), and the other is known as *Shia* (*party of Ali*). Sunnis believe in elected successors of the prophet Mohammed (known as *caliphs*), and Shias believe in the hereditary successors of Mohammed. Shias believe that Mohammed's son-in-law (Ali) and Ali's son (Husain) were murdered, and Shia men commemorate this tragic event by engaging in self-flagellation and self-torture during the Muharram festival which is held every year to remember the martyrdom of Ali and Husain. Persia (Iran) became the center of the Shia Islamic tradition, and Arabic-speaking west Asians have continued to be predominantly Sunni Muslims.

Both Sunni and Shia traditions of Islam were introduced into India. The Turkish sultans and the Mughal emperors of India were, for the most part, Sunni Muslims. But they did not derive their legitimacy directly from the caliphs, and were, therefore, not opposed to the Persian Shia tradition of

Islam that was introduced in India by the Persian administrators and religious leaders.

iii. Persianization of Muslim Identity in India

For many years the Mughuls and their Central Asian followers continued to regard the Indian subcontinent as an alien environment, due partly to the strength of their cultural heritage they had brought with them from the lands beyond the Indus and partly to their instinctive rejection of the climate, living conditions, and patterns of behavior which they met with in India and which Babur denounced in his memoirs in no uncertain terms. *Above all, there was that antipathy between the Islamic and Hindu world view which has been a continuous factor in shaping the attitudes of Indian Muslims from the time of Sultan Mahmud of Ghazni [11th century C.E.] and al-Biruni down to the twentieth century.*

In dress, diet, and in many other respects the Mughuls only slowly and very partially adapted themselves to an Indian life-style. Persian remained the language of the imperial court, of higher administration, and of polite learning, while as late as the reign of Awrangzeb [late 17th century] the imperial princes and princesses were still taught Chaghatay Turkish. The Persian poetry written in India continued to mirror the tastes of Shiraz or Herat, and virtually everyone in the long list of poets attached to Akbar's court was a foreigner. Akbar's favorite authors were the classical masters of Iran—Firdawsi, Rumi, Sadi, and Hafiz.

—Farmer (1986:442–43)

For over eight hundred years, between the 11th and 20th centuries, Persian was used extensively by the literary, administrative, cultural, and political elites in northern and northwestern India (and also in certain parts of south-central and northeastern India that came under the political dominance of Muslims). If the British had not discontinued the use of Persian as an administrative language in the early part of the 19th century and if English had not been introduced to replace Persian, it is very likely that Persian would be the language of cultural and political elites today in many parts of India.

The legacy of the Persian language is evident in the emergence of *Urdu* as an ideologically distinctive language. Urdu acquired significance as the national language of the Muslims of India, and as a result Urdu was cultivated with Persian and Islamic orientations. Urdu was written in Persianized Arabic script, and Urdu literature was modeled on Persian literature with the incorporation of Persian themes as well as the inclusion of Persian and Arabic words. In the next chapter I analyze the origins of colorism in India—the aesthetic orientation of attributing higher social value for west Asian physical characteristics in women—to show that colorism was introduced in India by the Persianized Turks and the Mughals (Persianized Turko-Mongols who were ethnically Persian through several generations of marriages with Persian women).

Perhaps no other fact symbolizes more vividly and visibly the Persian influence in India than the Taj Mahal which was built in the 17th century by the Mughal emperor Shah Jehan in memory of his Persian wife, Mumtaz Mahal.

Although Indians and Persians were in close contact from the 7th century B.C.E. or earlier, Persianization of India did not begin until the 11th century C.E. The ancient connections or links between Persia and India, such as the common ethnic and linguistic heritage of Persians and Aryan-Indians, the role of Indian soldiers in the service of Persian emperors such as Darius and Cyrus, and the influence of the Persian empire in shaping the Mauryan-Indian empire in the 3rd century B.C.E. did not result in the process which I have identified as Persianization. Persianization in India began in the 11th century C.E. and it was initiated by the Turks—not by the Persians themselves. Once introduced, Persianization acquired momentum with the migration of large numbers of Muslim administrators, clerics, scholars, poets, and soldiers from Persia into India.

From about the 9th century C.E. Arab caliphs and sultans began to recruit non-Arab and non-Muslim soldiers and servants who were often purchased as slaves. The slaves of the caliphs and sultans became the trusted lieutenants. One ethnic group (composed of several tribal units) that was available for recruitment as slaves was the Turks. The Turks were moving out of central Asia from about the 7th century and were serving as mercenary soldiers in central and west Asia. As they were not Muslims, Islamic law permitted their enslavement. By the 9th century most of west Asia (including Persia) came under the influence of Islam, and as Islam prohibited enslavement of fellow Muslims, there was a great shortage of slaves in west Asia. Thus, Turks became the major source for slave recruitment from the 9th century. Turkish slaves known as *mamluks* were in great demand because of their reputation as brave warriors and loyal, trustworthy servants.

The Turkish word *mamluk* meant *slave*, but not in the manner that the word slave has been used in the post-16th century Western civilization where slavery became associated with a mythology of racial inferiority connoting inferior or subhuman moral and intellectual characteristics of slaves. The term mamluk identifies a person purchased as a slave for training to become a warrior, an administrator, a commander, or a chief assistant and to serve as a member of the ruling elite. Mamluks were often trilingual, speaking Turkish, Arabic, and Persian. They often rose to high military and administrative positions. Also, some mamluks became sultans (rulers) themselves, establishing empires and founding dynasties. One prominent mamluk or slave dynasty was founded in India and another in Egypt. As early as the 10th century it was common for Turkish mamluks to play a major role in the political landscape of west Asia. As Turks were being converted to Islam gradually, mamluks were often recruited from non-Turkish tribes of central Asia, Egypt, and Ethiopia. Ethiopian mamluks were known as *Habshis*. Turkish mamluks as well as free Turks, in most instances, adopted Persian language and customs, and in places where they had established political control, Persian administrative structures were introduced. In Afghanistan, a Turkish mamluk dynasty was established in the late 10th century by Sabuktigin. Sabuktigin's son, Mahmud of Ghazni, controlled not only Afghanistan but also eastern Persia and north-western India. This mamluk dynasty was replaced by the Persian Ghurid dynasty in the 12th century, but another Turkish mamluk dynasty emerged in northern India during the later part of the 12th century through a mamluk, who was in the service of Ghurids, and conquered Delhi. Qutbal-Din Aybak, the mamluk commander, became the sultan of Delhi and founded the mamluk dynasty of India. He was followed by other able mamluks such as Shams al-Din Iltutmish and Ghiyas al-Din Balban who served as sultans of the mamluk dynasty. The mamluk dynasty of India was followed by three other Turkish dynasties. The Khalji dynasty governed the Delhi sultanate from 1290 to 1320; the Tughluquid dynasty from 1320–1414; and the Sayyid dynasty from 1414–1451. An Afghan dynasty (known as Lodi dynasty) controlled most of northern India from 1451 to 1526, and in 1526 the Turko-Mongol conqueror Babur laid the foundation for the Mughal empire in India. It should be noted that Babur claimed descent from Timur (Tamerlane) who plundered Delhi in 1398 and massacred all the male adults of Delhi during his campaign. Timur claimed descent from the Mongol warrior of the 13th century, Ginghis Khan, and his army was composed of warriors from Turkish, Mongol, Afghan, and Turkic-speaking Mongol tribes; Babur is often identified as the first Mughal (Persianized Mongol) emperor of India although his ancestry was linked with both Turkish and Mongol tribes.

Between the 13th and 15th centuries, the Turks in India prevented the Mongols of central Asia from establishing a military or political base in India. During that period the Mongols established empires in eastern Europe, Persia, and China. The Mongol conqueror Chingiz Khan stopped short of crossing the river Indus into India in 1221, and there was no successful Mongol invasion of India. However, the Mongol influence in India began in the 13th century when large numbers of Persianized Mongols migrated into India.

Turkish political dominance in northern and northwestern India lasted about three hundred years, and in some ways shaped the making of modern India by introducing (1) Islam in northwestern, northern, northeastern, and central India, (2) the Persian language and Persian cultural supremacy in these regions, (3) an administrative system modeled after Persian bureaucracy, and above all, as I have noted earlier, (4) an ideology of colorism in India. The Turks very seldom permitted people other than mamluks, free Turks,

Arabs, Mongols, and Persians to hold any important position in the military or in the civil administrative services.

Thus, the Turks created the emergence of a non-Indian or foreign nobility who were Muslims. The Indian converts to Islam seldom held any high position during the Turkish period, unless they emulated the Persian customs, used Persian or Arabic, and acquired Persian wives. The Turkish sultans opened the doors for Persian, Arab, and Mongol immigrants to enter India in large numbers and these immigrants were often recruited to serve in important positions, a fact that resulted in making an automatic association between high status and foreign heritage, and in establishing a dichotomy between noble foreigners and indigenous commoners.

> Status within that nobility was conferred solely by service in the upper echelons of the sultan's government and, with few exceptions, promotion was through the ranks of the slave army. Skilled Iranian officials supervised the revenue administration and India-born Muslims and even some Hindus occupied subordinate posts, but the racial exclusiveness of the Turks and the intimate network of relationships that controlled the sultan's slave household made it virtually impossible for any who were not Turks and mamluks to acquire or retain real power.
>
> —*Farmer (1986:311)*

The Mughal Empire of India (from the 16th to 19th centuries) extended the Turkish patterns of military, government, and social class distinctions to a large extent, and intensified Persianization of India but departed from the Turkish pattern of granting exclusive economic and political privileges to free Turks and mamluks. The British who followed the Mughals continued many of the patterns established by the Turks and Mughals, but English replaced Persian as the official administrative language in the 19th century, and rational institutional structures were introduced in the military and administrative systems. Also, the British revived, although for different reasons, the Turkish pattern of assigning exclusive economic and political privileges for the members of the ruling class. In the Turkish sultanate, being a member of a Turkish ethnic group or a mamluk gave that person high status, with all the economic privileges and access to power, but the Turks did not have a theory of race to include or exclude a group or individuals as morally or intellectually inferior or superior. A seldom noted fact is that there were many powerful Egyptian and Ethiopian (Habshis) mamluks who in some instances even succeeded in establishing small sultanates (although short-lived) in India; the British, on the other hand, established a system of racial segregation after the 18th century when they became the political masters of India and promoted and affirmed their alien racial heritage as a symbol of political authority and legitimacy.

iv. Arabization of Muslim Identity in India

Islamized Arab traders must have introduced Islam in south India as early as the 7th century on the (western) Malabar and (eastern) Coromandel coasts because there were Arab settlements on these coasts before the advent of Islam in the 7th century. The upper-caste Muslims of the Malabar coast of south India (who are known as *Moplahs* or *Mappilas*) claim that their ancestors were Arab traders. The Muslims of the Coromandel coast of south India (Tamil Country) are known as *Labbays* and some upper-caste Muslims of the Tamil Country claim Arab descent. Moplahs speak Malayalam (the language of the Malabar coast) and Labbays speak Tamil (the language of the Coromandel coast), but they use several Arabic and occasionally Persian words in their speech that make their speech patterns into dialects of Malayalam and Tamil known as *Arabi-Malayalam* and *Arabi-Tamil.*

The Moplah Muslims of southwestern India have drawn the attention of scholars from many disciplines. Historians have investigated their links with west Asia and have shown that Arab traders who settled on the southwestern coast of India played an important role in the operation of the spice and textile trade that connected Europe, west Asia, southern India, southeast Asia, and China. It has been shown that Arab traders were indirectly involved in the development of different politico-geographic entitities in southwestern India, a process that began in the 10th century leading to the separation of the southwestern politico-geographic area of southern India from the Tamil politico-geographic area. Until the 16th century when the Portuguese weakened the Arab politico-economic power, and had finally succeeded in destroying the Arab dominance of the sea trade that connected Europe, west Asia, southern India, southeast Asia, and China, Arab influence in southern India was significant in the political, economic, and religious arenas. It should be noted that the Arab influence in southern India was not related to the Persianization and Islamization of northwestern and northern India. *Arabization of southern India was through trade, and this process led only to the development of Arab Muslim identity in southern India (rather than to any general trend toward southern Indians acquiring Arab customs or the Arab language). Persianization of northwestern and northern India, on the other hand, resulted in the adoption of Persian language and Persian customs by the upper-class Indians (as a whole), along with the use of the west Asian ethnic symbols of identity for defining or conceptualizing the identity of some Indian Muslims to signify their high rank or high social status.*

The Arabized Muslims of southwestern India (Moplahs), however, contributed to the emergence of certain distinctive linguistic, social, and cultural patterns of southwestern India, thus adding to the separation of southwestern linguistic, social, and cultural traditions from those of the southeastern linguistic, social, and cultural patterns. The Moplahs have continued to speak Arabi-Malayalam, a dialect of Malayalam language (spoken in southwestern India) which probably separated as a dialect of the Tamil language (spoken in southeastern India) after the 12th century. With the British politico-economic domination of southern India in the 18th century, the Moplah identity as an international trading community changed gradually, and a large number of Moplahs became involved in estuarine fishery and deep-sea fishing.

The use of Arabi-Malayalam as a mark of Muslim ethnic-Arab identity and the adherence to Islam, with the elaborate performance of Muslim rituals, have made Moplahs define themselves as culturally different from the Hindus and Christians of southwestern India.This type of claim for cultural distinctiveness was occasionally expressed in political terms, and violent conflicts between and among the Moplahs, Hindus, and Christians occurred in the 19th and early 20th centuries. Today, Moplahs are active in Kerala state (southwestern India) politics, and a significant number of educated Moplahs are gainfully employed as guest workers in the gulf states of west Asia.

I present below a brief discussion of the Tamil-speaking Labbay Muslims of the Coromandel coast of southeastern India (i.e., of the Tamil country) who claim Arab descent. Many who claim Arab descent have Arab physical features, and these Muslims seldom marry the Muslims who do not claim Arab descent; the Muslims who do not claim Arab ancestry generally have low social status. (See Chapters 12, 13, and 14 also for a discussion of the Arabized Labbay Muslims in southeastern India.)

There were several trading settlements of Arabs on the Coromandel coast (southeastern coast of India) before and after the advent of Islam, with the Arab Muslims having a major role in the sea trade until the 16th century when the Portuguese established maritime supremacy. Before the decline of Arab sea power, in many parts of the Coromandel coast small groups of Muslims had established village settlements with claims to non-Indian Arab ancestry, and these groups used the name *Labbay* as an emblem of their identity to signify Arabian descent. But the term Labbay was also used generically to identify Tamil-speaking Muslims of southeastern India as a whole, thus denoting that they were Tamil Muslims. The label Labbay therefore had a dual meaning of identification, one referring to Arabian and the other to Tamil origins; it was a label that was used by some Tamil-speaking Muslims to signify their Arabian origins, but it also delineated a category of all the Tamil-speaking Muslims. The distinctiveness of Tamil-speaking Muslims who claimed Arabian ancestry derived largely from their speaking Arabi-Tamil and their scrupulous adherence to Koranic injunctions, expressed in their food and dress habits and rites of passage.

From about the 16th century, southern India came under the influence of northern Indian Islamic kingdoms, and Muslim settlements with Urdu speakers had become established in the Tamil country and in other parts of southern India. These Muslims too had various labels of ethnic identity, but as their language was associated with the politico-economic dominance of Muslim emperors and kings, language also served as an emblem of identity, separating them from non-Urdu-speaking Muslims.

Thus, in any discussion concerning the Muslims of the Tamil country, it is necessary to point out that three variables of ethnicity operated. *Religion (Islam), language (Arabi-Tamil and Urdu), and alienism served as emblems of identity, with some Muslims using all three in association with politico-economic dominance and others using religion and alienness with no association with politico-economic dominance; the Tamil-speaking Muslims (Labbays) were ranked socially below the Urdu-speaking Muslims, but one segment of this population used the emblem of alien heritage to assert superior social status, associating the term Labbay with Arabic language.* The term Labbay was commonly used by government officials and census takers to identify indigenous origins (because the Labbay spoke Tamil), and in many parts of Tamil country Labbay was a stigmatized identity. For example, in the census reports of the British during the 19th and early 20th centuries, all Tamil-speaking Muslims were classified as Labbay, with low social status, as opposed to the Urdu-speaking Muslims who were classified under different categories with reference to their foreign ethnic origins and upper-class symbols. The generic use of the term Labbay to designate all Tamil-speaking Muslims and its lack of prestige as a symbol of reference and address in modern Tamil country were noted in a recent government report on ethnicity and caste in southern India. In this report, called *The Report of the Backward Classes Commission of Tamil Nadu* (1971:3), it was recorded that

> The exact connotation of the term "Labbai" puzzled us at first, as generally it is not considered to be a term of respectable address. Some witnesses who appeared before us, also testified to the fact that only some poorer sections of Muslims are described by this term. But reference to the Census Report of 1921 and of earlier decades confirmed the fact that this term was intended to cover all Tamil-speaking Muslims, as distinguished from Urudu-speaking Muslims. In fact, the Census of 1921 recorded Muslim population under four heads: Labbay, Shek, Syed and Pathan. Thurston who is generally referred to on caste matters, also confirms that "Labbai" covers Tamil-speaking Muslims.

In addition, the *Report* noted that the term Labbay was also used as a mark of sacredness and of Arab heritage:

> Labbai is the Tamil form of the Arabic word *Labbe*. Labbe means "Here I am, at your service." (Labbai is also derived from the root word *Labbae*.) The early converts to Islam were known as Labbai because of their ready response to the Divine call. ... In the Census Report of 1881 a very interesting description of the Labbai's is found: "found chiefly in Tanjore and Madura. They are Mappillas of the Coromandel coast, that is to say, converted Dravidians, or Hindus, with a slight admixture of Arab blood." (1971:235–36)

It is clear that despite the common characterization of Tamil-speaking Muslims as Labbay, the label of Labbay as an emblem of identity signifies different status identities in different sociopolitical contexts, and it is used to convey different meanings in different parts of the Tamil country. Among the Tamil-speaking Muslims in southeastern India, the term Labbay can denote Arab ancestry just as the term Moplah can have significance to denote Arab ancestry among the Kerala Muslims of southwestern India. But the Arab-Labbay connection or link is not as firmly established as the Arab-Moplah connection for legitimizing high social status.

v. Caste, Ethnicity, and Islamic Nationalism among the Muslims of India

A fact about the Muslims of India that has been noted by social scientists is that despite the egalitarian and nonracial ideologies of Islam, caste and ethnic divisions are common among the Muslims of India. A basic division is between the Muslims who claim foreign ancestry and higher social status (*Ashraf* or nobles of foreign descent) and the Muslims who are identified as converts from low-ranking Hindu caste groups (*Ajlat* or degraded). Mines (1973:68) points out correctly that "a characteristic feature of Muslim caste hierarchies in North India and the Deccan is the fact that the highest ranks are accorded to Muslims who claim an origin foreign to India." The Persianized, Urdu-speaking Muslims are divided into endogamous groups with group titles (such as *sharif* or *sayyid*) that signify their ancestral ethnic or class identity. Muslim caste and ethnic mobility (with low-ranking Muslim groups claiming high social rank and status) occurs through low-ranking groups adopting the titles that signify Afghan, Turkish, or Persian heritage. Also, class divisions among the Muslims have the potential to become castelike endogamous groups. Just as in the Hindu caste system new endogamous caste groups arise in relation to the politico-economic advancement of a section of a caste group which separates itself to form a new caste group, endogamous groups among the Muslims arise in relation to the political-economic fortunes of particular segments of the Muslim community. And, just as there is variation in the operation of the Hindu caste system in the different regions of India, there are variations in the castelike features of Muslims in the different regions of India. D'Souza (1959), in his study of the Malayalam-speaking Muslims of southwestern India (known as *Moplahs, Maplahs,* or *Mappilas,* discussed earlier), found that these Muslims are hierarchically divided into five castes, namely, *Thangals* (who claim sacred, lineal affiliation with Fatima), *Arabis* (who claim to be descendants of Arab traders of southwestern India), *Malbaris* (descendants of high-caste Hindus), *Pasalars,* and *Ossans* (who are considered to be converts from low-caste Hindus).

Summarizing several studies on Muslim groups that function in the Hindu social environment, Mandelbaum (1970:546–59) and Dumont (1970a: 205–12) have concluded that the social organization of Muslim groups is similar to that of Hindu groups. The institutional aspect which is characteristic of

Hindu civilization, namely, caste, is found to structure the relationship among Muslims and between Muslim and Hindu groups. Dumont (1970:211) further notes that Muslims as well as other non-Hindus, who function within the parameters of Hindu social order, have acquired the basic "psychological dispositions" of Hindus: Hindu worldview permeates and encompasses everyone who participates in Hindu civilization to the extent that the egalitarian ideology of Islam functions in only a modified form.

That this generalization tells us something about the use of the caste institution by non-Hindus cannot be disputed. However, it is not only misleading but also erroneous to infer that an understanding of the institution or principles of caste enables us to understand how Muslims in India organize themselves internally and externally. Muslims in India are not a homogeneous group. Historically and culturally they are diverse, having established distinctive adaptations to different politico-economic environments, and the kinds of relationships that exist between Hindus and Muslims vary greatly. See Aggarwal (1966), Ahmad (1973), Ansari (1959), Dale (1980), D'Souza (1959), Gopal (1964), Guha (1965), Khan (1968), Mines (1973), Mujeeb (1967), and H. Singh (1977).

Two features of caste, namely endogamy and hierarchical ranking, that are found among Muslims may result from the use of a number of different principles, not merely from the use of caste principles such as the Hindu hierarchical scheme and the ideology of purity-impurity. Internal endogamy and ranking among Muslims in India have their loci in alien or non-Indian ethnicity (Persian, Arabic, or Afghan) or in high-caste indigenous (Indian) origins, and in some instances politico-economic factors operate to signify the high or low status of particular sections of a Muslim group (as is the case with caste). The Hindu paradigm of *varna* (with the priesthood and the untouchable at opposite poles and the three other categories, namely, Kshatriya, Vaishiya, and Shudra, composed of various jati groups that strive for politico-economic power) does not serve as a model for the Muslim endogamous (jati) groups as it might for the Hindu endogamous groups. Muslims associate bodily cleanliness and ritual sanctity with their religious orientation that evolved in the tribal context of Middle-Eastern experience. They may believe scavengers and others who engage in similar occupations to be unclean, but such an association is not the same as that of the Hindu ideology of purity/impurity despite the fact that behaviorally both may produce the same results. Hindus and non-Hindus know how to function in the Hindu social environment, which is not to say that they share each other's worldview and ethos.

In a paper devoted to examining the contributions made by 20th-century scholars who have analyzed the societies in the geographical-political boundary of India, Ahmad (1972:172–77) makes some pertinent observations about the validity of generalizations made by sociologists and social anthropologists concerning the social structures and processes in India. He correctly points out that scholars have seldom investigated in detail the non-Hindu traditions of India and suggests that there is a "pronounced tendency among sociologists to equate Hindu society with India. ..." As noted earlier, the entry of Turks, Persians, Afghans, and Mongols into India after the 10th century and the introduction of Persian language and Turko-Persian administrative systems created profound changes in the Hindu civilization.

A civilizational complex that we identify as Hindu or Indian is composed of multiple linguistic/religious cultural traditions, and the similarities in the organization of groups occur as products of the universally applicable principles of boundary maintenance, or as Barth (1969) puts it, "the social organization of cultural differences," rather than from the application of a uniquely Hindu paradigm at macro and micro levels of Indian civilizations. People in any given sociocultural system can and do participate in its institutions with diverse motives and epistemological bases that result in similar behavior. The larger sociocultural systems—in terms of having large numbers of people and several types of groupings—maintain themselves through facilitating or institutionalizing cognitive and motivational nonsharing. Hindus and Muslims coexist in India with different worldviews (cognitive) and ethos (motivational).

Wallace's (1970) semiotic approach is ideally suited for the examination of group boundary maintenance and intergroup relationships in the Hindu or Indian society where hundreds of culturally distinctive groups coexist. Wallace explains that cognitive uniformity is dysfunctional to sociocultural systems. Knowing fully each other's motivations and cognitions is operationally counterproductive, and if cognitive uniformity is a prerequisite, it would severely handicap a system because the survival of a system would depend on the humanly impossible feat of everyone in the system knowing it in its entirety. Human beings function in a system with what Wallace refers to as "equivalence structure models" that permit them to participate in the system by predicting each other's behavior without having to replicate themselves cognitively or motivationally. *Hindus and Muslims in India function together (when there is no overt violence or conflict between them) with equivalent social models: Muslims have the caste structure of India, but the content or components of the Muslim caste structure differ significantly from those of the Hindu caste structure.*

Although Persianization, Arabization, and the use of Urdu language (along with universal Muslim acceptance of Arabic as the sacred language) have provided Indian Muslims with a measure of cultural-linguistic-religious integrity and distinctiveness, many Indian Muslim intellectuals have often exaggerated this distinctiveness to conceptualize the existence of a Muslim nation in India (see Ansari 1989). The 19th-century and early 20th-century elaboration of this concept of Muslim nation led to the creation of Pakistan in 1947, with an eastern wing in Bengal and a western wing in the region of Sind, Baluchistan, and Panjab; Urdu was adopted as the national language of both eastern and western Pakistan. This creation lasted only until 1971, when the eastern wing formed a separate nation-state called Bangladesh with Bengali as the national language. The western wing continues today as Pakistan. In recent times, Sindhis and Baluchis have emphasized their separate ethnic-linguistic identities in opposition to the Panjabi ethnic-linguistic identity, and it is possible that three or four separate nation-states could emerge in Pakistan in the future. Thus, Muslim identity, be it Indian Muslim identity or Pakistani Muslim identity, must be understood as a *relational* rather than as an absolute monolithic or uniform identity.

As Tinker (1989:20) notes,

> Pakistan, despite its relative religious homogeneity, has been unable to build a genuine Pakistani consciousness. Language and regional cultures have proved stronger than the unifying Islamic, Perso-Urdu culture of an elite. The alienation of the Bengalis and the bloody birth of Bangladesh signified the final breakdown of Jinnah's vision of a homeland for the Muslims of India.

vi. Symbols of Jewish Identity in India

It is very likely that Jews have been in India since the Roman period. The trading port centers of India were linked with the Greco-Roman world, and some Jewish traders must have settled on the Malabar Coast in ancient times. Jews of India illustrate two cultural aspects very clearly. They adopted certain Hindu beliefs about ritual purity and also adopted the ideology of colorism which began in India after the Turks established political dominance in northern India. As a result of adopting such cultural orientations, the Jewish community was divided on the basis of pure and impure Jews and on the basis of light-brown or dark-brown skin color. Light-skinned Jews were considered in some places to be pure and white, and they claimed a high or superior social status. There were Jews who had labels such as *Black Jews, Brown Jews,* and *White Jews.* There were altogether seven endogamous groups of Jews: (1) the Black Jews of Cochin whose ancestors had settled there either during the Roman period or a little later; (2) the White (Sephardic) Jews who emigrated from Spain and settled down in Cochin in the 16th century; (3) the Brown Jews of Cochin who were the converts to Judaism from the Hindu or Muslim servants of White Jews; (4) the Marathi-speaking *Gora* or fair-skinned Jews of the Konkan coast (south of Bombay in western India) who probably migrated into India during the early decades of the Christian era; (5) the Marathi-speaking *kala* or dark-brown-skinned Jews whose ancestors were probably the same as those of the Gora Jews; (6) the Baghdadi Jews, whose fortunes in India were linked with those of the British in India, with the Baghdadi Jews serving as important business or trade leaders in several cities of India during the 19th and early 20th centuries; and (7) the European Jews, mostly professionals like doctors, who left Europe in the 20th century to escape the Nazi terror.

Strizower (1959), in his study of the history and sociology of the Jews of India, noted the similarities and differences between and among the various

Jewish groups in India in terms of how they related with each other and in terms of their relationships with Hindu caste groups. I provide some of his observations and conclusions:

> Some 4,000 Jews from Baghdad, with small additions from Aden, Afghanistan, and Iran, are known as Baghdadi. The first of the Baghdadi arrived in India in the late eighteenth century. There are Baghdadi communities of some 2,000 each in Bombay and Calcutta; there is also a small group of Baghdadi in Poona. Baghdadi are on the whole fair-complexioned. They consistently use English. ...
>
> A few hundred European Jews, mainly from Germany and Austria, came to India in the nineteen-thirties. They live in Delhi, Calcutta, Madras, and especially in Bombay. Though the European Jews in Bombay often stress their differences from the Baghdadi, they join in Baghdadi social and religious activities. ...
>
> While the Baghdadi tend to imitate the Europeans, the social systems of the Bene Israel [the Marathi-speaking Jews] and Cochin Jewry show great resemblances to that of the Hindus.
>
> —*Strizower (1959:43)*

Mandelbaum (1970), in his discussion of the Jews of India, makes references to the Jewish ideology of color or colorism in India.

> The White Jews [of Cochin] were generally lighter in skin color than the Black Jews, though some of the White were as dark as any of the Blacks. ...
>
> The White Jews would not intermarry or interdine with the Black Jews and would not even count a Black Jew as one of the *minyan*, the minimum member of ten required for congregational worship. ...
>
> Like the Cochin Jews but independently of them, the Ben Israel [Marathi-speaking Jews] were separated into two jatis, the higher being called Gora, the fair ones, and the lower the kala, the dark ones. They too did not interdine or intermarry, though they did worship in the same synagogues. Those of the higher jati claimed purer Jewish ancestry; the lower, they alleged, was of mixed origins.
>
> —*Mandelbaum (1970:561-63)*

Most of the Jews emigrated to Israel during the decade following the establishment of the state of Israel, but there are still small pockets of Jewish communities on the west coast of India. Jewish identity was maintained through ritual dietary practices and the recognition of the Jewish sabbath (Saturday) as well as certain important festivals such as the Passover. Recently, the *Los Angeles Times* presented a lengthy article on the food and religious customs of the Indian Jews. Due to the fact that this article captures the indigenous Indian Jewish conceptions of themselves, I offer a lengthy quote from it.

On the tropical west coast of India, tucked away amid the vast Hindu population, there is a tiny but ancient community of Jews. You won't find chopped liver, potato pancakes or brisket of beef here, nor *matzo* ball soup. They serve *molagachi* (mahogany chicken with black pepper), *ellegal* (spice-rubbed fish in cool herb salsa), *masalachi* (mutton braised with garlic and coriander) and *appam* (coconut crepes with date sauce).

The oldest colony of Jews in India is known as the Bene Israel. Their origin is shrouded in mystery, but their traditions say they came in the second century B.C.E. and were shipwrecked at Konkan on the Malabar coast. The seven men and women who survived the disaster established the community, and today a memorial stands where, according to tradition, the bodies of those who were lost at sea are buried.

The second group—known as the Cochini Jews—say they arrived on the Malabar coast shortly after the Roman destruction of Jerusalem in C.E. 70. The Pardesi Synagogue in Cochin, which is of undetermined age—the present building dates from the 16th Century, but it preserves stone from a more ancient structure—has been designated a National Treasure of India. Iraqi and European Jews came later, in the last several centuries.

The Bene Israel and Cochini Jews remained relatively unknown to the Western world until recently, when they began to make an exodus from India to Israel and the United States, where they settled mainly in Los Angeles and New York City. Although temperamentally and linguistically similar to the Hindus, Indian Jews possess distinctly different customs and traditions, as well as a cuisine that is a wonderful amalgam of Indo-Jewish flavors.

"We are religious, of course," Sattoo Sabattai Koder explained to me in his centuries-old family house in Cochin, "but not orthodox." A stately looking gentleman dressed in a *mondoo* (the Malabari sarong), Rabbi Koder belongs to a family that traditionally provides wardens of the Pardesi Synagogue. He explained that Indian Jews strictly observe the Sabbath and its customs as well as Kashrut (Kosher laws), and the major Jewish festivals. But they have also adopted elements of India's secular spirit.

Hindu India, where everyone is born into one caste or another, not only allows but positively encourages ethnic groups to maintain their own traditions. As a result, Indian Jews socialize freely with other communities, celebrate each other's festivals and feast together without suffering from the ancient fear of unknowingly violating a dietary law.

"It is commonly understood that everyone will respect and abide by mutual dietary codes," said Koder.

—*Julie Sahn (1991:H-1)*

vii. Symbols of Syrian-Christian Identity in India

Syrian Christians constitute a distinctive religious group, quite different from the other Christians of India for several reasons. (1) Although Syrian Christians became very involved in the processes of Westernization in the 19th and 20th centuries, adopting Western customs, becoming competent in the use of English, and serving the British in various ways, they did not establish of Syrian-Christian churches in India as a result of the European conquest of India as in the case of the churches of Roman Catholic Christians and Protestant Christians in India. (2) Syrian Christians signify the existence of centuries-old contact between the peoples of the Malabar Coast and west Asia. (3) The prefix *Syrian* refers both to the claim that the ancestors of Syrian Christians came from west Asia and to the historical link between the churches of Syrian Christians of the Malabar Coast and the Syrian Orthodox patriarchs of west Asia. (4) Syrian Christians believe (a belief supported by some historical evidence) that Syrian-Christian churches on the Malabar Coast were established around 50 C.E. by St. Thomas, the disciple of Jesus Christ, who is believed to have converted the local Brahmins to Christianity, thus claiming the high status of a ritually pure caste. (5) They also believe that another Thomas (known as Thomas of Cana and as Thomas of Jerusalem) established Christian trade settlements in the 4th century C.E., securing military privileges from the local Rajas (kings), with claims to high political status of Kshatriya. (6) Until the end of the 18th century, that is, until such time as the British became the rulers of India, there was a close cultural affinity or bond between Syrian Christians and the Hindu warrior caste (Nayars), including intermarriages, the affirmation and celebration of each other's cult worship and festivals, and a close identification with the royalty (as defenders of the kingdom or state). (7) There was rapid decline in their ritual and social/political status which was brought about by the changes introduced by the British government and by Christian missionaries.

Syrian Christians, who are also known as St. Thomas Christians, have been linked with both the east and west Syrian patriarchates. Those linked with the east and those linked with the west differ in their beliefs about the nature of Jesus Christ, but they have not functioned as endogamous, hierarchical groups. The Syrian Christians who are committed to the theological orientation of west Syrian Patriarchate (Syrian Orthodox Church) believe that the divinity and humanity of Jesus Christ are an indivisible whole (monophysite), and they are identified as Jacobites. The others, who are identified as Romo-Syrians or Syrian-Catholics, believe that the divinity and humanity of Jesus Christ are not combined but are two separate states with different functions.

A new grouping of Syrian Christians, known as Mar-Thomites, came into being in the late 19th century. Missionary involvement in the internal affairs of the Syrian Christians had grave and tragic consequences. The Syrian-Christian community was fragmented and violent conflicts between them (i.e., between Jacobites, Mar-Thomites, and Romo-Syrians) and between Syrian Christians and the high-caste Hindus occurred as a result of the perception that Syrian Christians had lost their high ritual status through their association with missionaries and with low-caste non-Syrian Christians. Various separatist churches and messianic leaders emerged among the Syrian Christians. The missionary effort to convert them to protestant denominations did not meet with great success.

But in the 20th century, Syrian Christians were in the forefront of Westernization, becoming professional employees in the various British-established institutions in India and in other British colonies. Thus, although the Syrian Christians had lost their high ritual and political status in the 19th century, they reclaimed or regained it in the 20th century. As a result, the symbol of Syrian Christian has once again become a signification of high social status, and most Malayalam-speaking Christians use the label Syrian-Christian irrespective of whether they are members of the Syrian-Christian (Jacobite or Mar-Thomite or Syrian-Catholic) churches. It is not possible to distinguish Syrian Christians as a separate ethnic group with distinguishable physical features (different from the physical characteristics of other peoples of that region), but there are markers of distinction: personal names (such as Chacko, Cheriyan, Kurvilla, Mathai, Oommen, and Kurien) and house names (such as Tharkan), as well as a distinguishable style of life.

viii. Symbols of Parsi Identity in India

The Parsis, or the Zoroastrians of India, have for the most part been functioning as a trading caste. But they have not participated in the Hindu caste system, and in this regard they contrast with other non-Hindu groups of India that claim an alien heritage but have specific caste status, as for example the Jews or Syrian Christians of India. Numbering about 150,000, the Parsis have tried and succeeded in maintaining their ethnic homogeneity through a rigid application of endogamous marriage rules and through a highly stylized initiation-ritualism officiated by the Zoroastrian priesthood. Although Zoroastrian priesthood is hereditary, and despite the fact that the priesthood is considered to be endowed with superior spiritual qualities, attempts to divide the Parsi community into a priestly caste (like the Brahmins) and a non-priestly caste never succeeded. Divisions within the Parsi community occur largely in terms of the ethos of the traditionalists and modernists. Parsis perform most of the rituals in their homes with or without their family priests but maintain superior fire temples called *Atash Bahram,* and ordinary fire temples called *dar i Mihr.* A well-known Parsi ritual is the placing of corpses in the Tower of Silence for vultures to eat the flesh. The following two paragraphs summarize clearly the Parsi initiation-ritualism and funeral ritual that serve as markers of Parsi cultural boundary:

> For Zoroastrians, religious duties begin with initiation (*nanjote*) which occurs before puberty. Initiation, like most Zoroastrian religious duties, is the same for male and female. It comprises investiture with the sacred shirt (*sudre*) and cord (*kusti*). The sudre should be worn next to the skin at all times, while the kusti is retied five times a day accompanied by prayers which affirm allegiance to the Good Religion of God (*Ahara Mazda*) exemplified in pure thoughts, words and deeds and involving the rejection of evil. (Robinson 1989:361)
>
> Death is the work of evil in Zoroastrianism, hence all decaying and dead matter represent evil. As earth, fire and water are considered sacred, corpses are instead laid in a *daxma*, or "Tower of Silence" where they are exposed to vultures to avoid polluting the divine creation. (Robinson 1989:362)

Parsis entered India between the 7th and the 10th centuries C.E. to escape persecution in Persia when Arabs imposed Islam in most of Persia. They settled down in the region that we identify today as Gujarat in northwestern India and adopted Gujarati language and the international (trading) business culture of the Gujarati merchants. However, Parsis maintained their distinctive culture, and they were identified as an alien group with reference to their Iranian physical features and light-brown skin color. The involvement of Europeans in India's international trade (from the 16th century onwards) transformed the Parsi community from being one of several merchant communities to being a preeminent and extremely prosperous trading community with immense wealth that enabled them to become a leading community of industrialists, bankers, businessmen, politicians, intellectuals, and artists from the 19th century to the present day.

The city of Bombay became a Parsi stronghold from the 18th century, with Parsi economic collaboration with the British. Parsi loyalty was to international trade, and they became a leading vehicle for British-controlled international imports and exports from the 18th century. However, the Parsis resented the British procedures of taxing Indian goods, and the nontaxing of British-produced goods that were imported into India, and some influential Parsi businessmen and intellectuals became involved in the Indian nationalist movement (called the Indian National Congress) from the 19th century.

The "Grand Old Man" of Indian Nationalism was Parsi Dadabhai Naoroji (1825–1917), who established the first Indian business firm in

London and Liverpool in 1855. Author of Indian nationalism's major economic battle cry concerning the constant "drain" of resources and wealth from India by England, Dadabhai was also the first Indian to be elected to the British Parliament, and he was to be chosen three times to serve as president of Indian National Congress. Pherozeshah Mehta (1845–1915), the "Uncrowned King of Bombay," also a Parsi, established his title to fame and national power through his dexterity at the bar.

—Wolpert (1989:254)

While the services of the Parsi community to the strengthening of Indian economy lend themselves to the emergence of Indian nationalism, there are questions that should be asked about their role in Indian politics and in the perpetuation of colorism in India. Did the Parsi community contribute to the maintenance of a pan-Indian empire-state because they did not belong to any particular indigenous religious or linguistic national tradition and because it was economically advantageous to them to have the whole of India as a market? Did the Parsi community conceptualize their Persian (alien or foreign) heritage to locate their social position or rank high in the caste hierarchy with reference to their light-brown skin color?

ix. Symbols of Anglo-Indian Identity

For different reasons, the Anglo-Indians were, and still are, a category of people without a social rank. They did not and do not constitute a caste or ethnic group with conceptions of religious or cultural purity and principles of endogamy. Recruitment into the community resulted (and results) from European-Indian marriages and from some English-speaking Indian Christians from low-caste groups claiming Anglo-Indian identity. Depletion in the number of the Anglo-Indian community resulted from light- or fair-skinned Anglo-Indians identifying themselves as domiciled British subjects who aspired to return to the mother country (Great Britain) or to immigrate to New Zealand, Australia, or South Africa.

Thus, there was (and still is) no Anglo-Indian community with a particular locus in the politico-economic structure of any region. Anglo-Indians are found in all the major cities, and they have established associations to represent their goals, but they do not fit in any of the cultural idioms of status identity in India. They are united by their use of English as their native language or mother tongue and their emulation of what they believe to be the British religious, social, and cultural traditions. But, as the British disowned or disinherited the Anglo-Indians, attributing to them a negative, stigmatized identity from the beginning of the 19th century, English speech and mannerisms seldom accorded them a high rank in the Indian social hierarchy. The Anglo-Indians, in the Indian context, do not have a color-category identity, a race-category identity, or an ethnic- or caste-group identity: The Anglo-Indians are a people of noncolor, nonrace, nonethnicity, and noncaste.

To the reader who is not familiar with India, it would appear that the children of the late prime minister of India, Rajiv Gandhi, who was married to an Italian, are either classified as Anglo-Indians, or ought to be classified as Anglo-Indians. The fact is, the children are not considered to be Anglo-Indians. Partly as a result of the British use of the term Anglo-Indian from 1911 on to signify children of a European father and Indian mother and their patrilineal descendants, and partly as a result of the Indian custom of adopting and integrating new caste identities through the performance of certain Hindu rituals, Rajiv Gandhi's children are high-caste Hindus.

The following discussion of the origin and history of the Anglo-Indians should clarify the fact that light skin color does not automatically accord high status in the Indian caste system and that a community has to constitute itself into a regionally significant group with a particular politico-economic label or title (which roughly corresponds to the Hindu categories of social classification) in order to gain a social rank or identity. The Anglo-Indians have been a people outside the caste system and thus they are different from the Muslims, Jews, and the Syrian Christians who had either established their own internal caste hierarchy or formulated social ranks or identities corresponding to the Hindu caste hierarchy.

This lack of a social rank or identity within the caste system or corresponding to the caste system probably did not create a major problem because the Anglo-Indians were (and are) an urban community as a result of the British policy that prevented their establishing households or owning property in the villages. As caste identities have little significance in most cities, and as the Anglo-Indians were often located in specific quarters or towns adjacent to major railway terminals (because of their employment as railway engineers or conductors), they could function as urban dwellers with no particular affiliation with the Indian customs or civilization.

The history of Anglo-Indians begins with the Portuguese on the west coast of India although the term *Anglo-Indian* should technically be used to identify the descendants of British-Indian marital or nonmarital unions. The Portuguese admiral Vasco da Gama reached the port of Calicut in southwestern India in 1498, and Portuguese trade centers were established in 1500 in Cochin Harbor (south of Calicut) and in 1510 at Goa (north of Calicut). As the Portuguese had no racial antipathy toward the Indians, Portuguese traders and soldiers took Indian wives and/or concubines and gradually there evolved an Indian Christian community called the *Luso-Indians*. The other European traders and soldiers (i.e., the Dutch, the English, and the French) also took Indian wives or concubines, and this kind of European-

Indian contact continued until the beginning of the 19th century. As Gaikwad (1967:14) points out, "The merchants from different European communities used to mix freely with the natives. Up to the first half of the 19th century there was little or no racial feeling on either side. This feeling came only afterwards when the English became the rulers of India. Mixed marriages from which several well known families sprang and other irregular and temporary unions were more frequent than they were later."

The label Anglo-Indian was not used until the middle of the 19th century to identify those who are known today as Anglo-Indians. Initially, the term was used to denote the English who had either domiciled in India as employees of the East India Company, or as the employees of the native kings or princes. Terms such as Indo-British, Indo-European, Britasian, and Eurasian were used at different times to designate the Anglo-Indians. During the 17th and 18th centuries the English East India Trading Company and the Anglo-Indians prospered in a symbiotic relationship: Anglo-Indians served in the English military on par with English officers and fought in many Indian and European campaigns, and Anglo-Indians were also the valued employees in the civil services of the Company. However, by the end of the 18th century, the British had doubts about the loyalty of Anglo-Indians and began to worry about their increasing numbers in the employment of the company, and a series of policy decisions were made to keep them out of military and civil service. With the introduction of the railway and telegraphic systems in India, however, the Anglo-Indians found steady employment from the middle of the 19th century. With the steady guaranteed employment under the British, the leaders of the Anglo-Indian community strove to create a pan-Indian network of Anglo-Indians and sought from the British economic safeguards with job quotas for the Anglo-Indians, and the label Anglo-Indian was increasingly used as a cultural and racial marker.

> In 1911, the term Anglo-Indian was officially recognized by the government as descriptive of persons of mixed descent. By the Franchise rules of the India Act of 1935, the Anglo-Indian was defined as "A person whose father or any of whose other male progenitors in the male line is or was of European descent but who is a native of India. ..." In 1949, the Constitution of India accepted the same definition of "Anglo-Indian" as had been given in the Act of 1935. ... the term "Anglo-Indian" cannot be used for anyone whose father is an Indian and mother a European. Such a person born of Indian father and European or Anglo-Indian mother is known simply as an Indian.
>
> —*Gaikwad (1967:43–44)*

Abel (1988) in a study of Anglo-Indians has this to say:

The Anglo-Indian Community is today a living reminder to Indian people not only of the colonial presence which they might be glad to forget, but that there was something good which accrued from western culture and rule. This assumption is drawn from the place that Anglo-Indian education holds in India today and the fact that Anglo-Indian schools are packed to capacity by a vast majority of Indian students. This may be due to the excellent standard of scholarship that most of these schools maintain or it may be that the Anglo-Indian schools represent the common meeting ground of east and west. Anglo-Indians today preserve a distinctive character and at the same time enjoy equal opportunities with all other citizens of India.

—Abel (1988:185–86)

In contemporary India, it is estimated that there are between 150,000 and 250,000 Anglo-Indians (depending on who is included or excluded in the category). The use of the label Anglo-Indian has assets and liabilities just as the use of the label Harijan (Mahatma Gandhi's name for members of untouchable castes) has assets and liabilities. The Hindu caste system does not accommodate a loose category of people within a social status rank, and all labels such as Anglo-Indian or Harijan prevent members of these categories from acquiring region-specific politico-economic locus and from formulating symbolic associations with high social status ranks.

CHAPTER FIVE

✐ THE SEMIOTICS
OF COLORISM IN INDIA

i. Ethnic Symbols of Physical Beauty

Symbols of physical beauty may be delineated as group or culture-specific representations of physical traits such as skin color that are valued and idealized. As these representations become components in the conception of personal appearance or personhood, an individual may seek to present the idealized or valued physical traits of the group, often enhancing such traits through ornaments, clothing, hairstyles, facial makeup, and so on.

An infant acquires the representations of physical beauty through the enculturation of group symbols of beauty, and an infant will tend to have a natural affinity or attachment to certain physical characteristics of the group. Representations of ideal physical traits often signify the preference for certain types of physical characteristics such as black or white skin color, blonde or brunette hair, slim or round body, and small or large nose. Group representations of beauty develop historically, shaped by several factors such as borrowing from neighboring groups, dominant-subordinate relationships of groups, and social stratifications that stipulate the existence of certain ideal traits among only the upper classes.

An individual's natural affinity or attachment toward his or her group's representations of ideal skin color and other physical characteristics of beauty may change through processes such as (1) universalism, (2) alienation, and (3) dysjunction between membership group and reference group. (1) An individual may learn to transcend his or her group's ethnocentric cultural representations, accept the validity of other representations, and may even internalize another group's representations. (2) An individual may have psychological problems that make it difficult for him or her to function effectively as a member of a group, resulting in isolation and alienation. (3) An individual's membership group and reference group may differ to the extent that an individual may have to deal with two different sets of representations of beauty that could result in the individual conceptualizing the ideal physical traits not in terms of his own membership group but in terms of a different reference group. The individual could form negative attitudes toward the physical characteristics of his own group and could idealize the physical characteristics of another group.

In order to understand the ethnic symbols of beauty in India, we must note the fact that there is *no* membership group in India where all (or even most) of the members possess the idealized physical characteristics of beauty. The most significant membership group, namely caste, is internally varied or heterogeneous in terms of physical characteristics. Thus, although a caste group may have, and actively promote, certain representations of beauty such as light skin color, it does not necessarily mean that all or most of its members possess light skin color.

Another fact about India that we should note is that a different caste group (in which the members possess certain idealized physical features) cannot serve as a reference group for introducing such features into one's own caste (membership) group because rules of endogamy prohibit intercaste marriages. The membership group must also be the reference group for the physical characteristics unless an individual decides to break the caste boundaries (which happens occasionally), or unless the membership caste group is internally stratified with the upper stratum having different physical features from the lower stratum.

A third fact about skin color and status emulation in India is that although rules of endogamy essentially prohibit the use of a nonmembership group as a reference group for physical characteristics, a nonmembership group can be used as a reference group for the emulation or nonemulation of a style of life. Members of a low-ranking caste group may adopt a high-ranking caste group as a reference group for the purpose of emulating the customs of the high-ranking caste group. As the status of the caste group is relative in terms of its ritual purity that often corresponds to the economic and political strength of its members, different caste groups serve as positive or negative reference groups. When more members of a low-ranking caste group acquire greater wealth and political power, they would seek to secure for their caste group a high ritual status, comparable to that of a high-ranking reference caste group, and thereby move up in the social hierarchy with customs similar to those of the high-ranking reference group. Historically and in contemporary India, politically and economically powerful men and families have, in many instances, sought to secure brides who have West Asian physical characteristics and/or light-brown skin color.

ii. Symbols of Wheatish and Fair Skin Color in India

An interesting fact about India, which is puzzling to tourists and which has contributed to scholarly misinterpretation of prejudice and discrimination in India, is the phenomenon of matrimonial advertisements in newspapers. Thousands of matrimonial advertisements appear every day. Most of these advertisements, if they seek to secure a bride, stipulate that "wheatish skin color" or "fair complexion" is preferred and specify in some instances that fair-complexioned brides can cross caste boundaries (i.e., low-caste women could marry high-caste men) and can get married without dowry payments.

As Beteille (1968:173–74) points out:

> In many Indian languages the words fair and beautiful are often used synonymously. The folk literature places a high value on fair skin color. The ideal bride, whose beauty and virtue are often praised in the songs sung at marriages, almost always has a lighter complexion. A dark girl is often a liability to her family because of the difficulty of arranging a marriage for her. Marriages among educated Indians are sometimes arranged through advertisements in the newspapers; even a casual examination of the matrimonial columns of such popular dailies as *The Hindu, The Hindustan Times,* or the *Hindustan Standard* shows that virginity and a light skin color are among the most desirable qualities in a bride.

How did this type of cultural representation of beauty come into being in India? There can be no agreement on its origin and development for various reasons. There are, probably, multiple origins and diverse developmental processes, but I will identify six of the factors that prevent a dispassionate analysis of the phenomenon of colorism or the representation of high social value for wheatish or fair skin color.

(1) As historiography has little significance or relevance in the Hindu traditions, there have been constant rewritings in the past of particular caste groups, with various mythological histories of the origins of castes that justify, rationalize, or legitimize their present socioeconomic and politico-ritual statuses. *Therefore, one can never be certain about the origin of the physical characteristics of the members of any caste group.*

(2) Hindu scriptural materials have been altered constantly with various interpolations about who the true and pure Aryans are and about the true

meaning of the concept of *varna* (quality). *Therefore, only arguments can be presented rather than the verification of facts to settle issues.*

(3) An emotive cultural orientation of many upper-caste Hindus is their fabricated conception of themselves as lineally or biologically linked with Aryans although there is no scientific evidence of linking any particular upper-caste group with Aryans. *This fact of Aryanphilia distorts almost every aspect of scientific discourse.*

(4) As lower-caste men and women work in the sun from dawn until dusk—in agricultural fields, coastal fisheries, and urban streets—they are much more tanned than the upper-caste men and women who seldom are in the sun. *Many upper-caste members erroneously denote the deep tanning of low-caste men and workers who toil in the sun as indicative of separate origins of different castes.*

(5) As most lower-caste men and women cannot afford the ointments, powders, and clothing that upper-caste men and women use, most lower-caste men and women have a less refined appearance. *Upper-caste members frequently view the lack of decorative adornments such as expensive clothing and jewelry and the lack of literacy of the members of low castes as evidence of low-caste inferiority and biological separation of castes.*

(6) Although all the scientific studies prove conclusively that Brahmins (the highest caste or class) are physically heterogeneous and variable (they have different shades of skin color, are diverse in stature and in cephalic and nasal indices, reflecting the physical features of the populations of different regions in which they live), *there is a mythological affirmation of Brahmins as a homogeneous group which is lineally linked with Aryans because of an erroneous link between the Brahmanical priesthood and Aryans.*

Representations of beauty with high or higher social value for light-brown skin color (and for west and central Asian physical features in general) of women began after the 11th century in northwestern and northern India in the context of the invasions and settlements of Persianized Turkish Muslims. I noted in Chapter 1 that the migrations of various groups such as the Scythians, Persians, Greeks, and Huns between 7th century B.C.E. and 7th century C.E. resulted in these groups' being recruited into the upper ranks of the caste system. These groups were incorporated into the caste system, often in the ranks of Kshatriya or Brahmin castes, and it is possible that these groups strove to maintain caste endogamy with their political, socioeconomic, and religious status positions corresponding to Scythian, Persian, Greek, and Hunnish physical features. However, it was the emergence of the Persianized Turkish-Mongol Muslims in the 11th century C.E. that created the phenomenon of colorism, idealizing the light-brown skin color and the physical features of the Persians. The Persianized Turkish-Mongols cultivated an aesthetic cultural orientation that idealized everything that was Persian. They made Persian the court language although Turkish and Urdu-Hindi were also used and introduced Persian food and dress customs in India; Persian physical characteristics were considered to be ideal standards of female beauty. Gradually, a linkage arose between upper-class status and Persianlike physical features of women, and such a class-color orientation began to operate within caste groups with the upper-class members of high-ranking caste groups seeking Persian-looking brides.

iii. Pre-Islamic Symbols of Skin Color in India

The transformations in the representations and conceptions of beauty which began in the 11th century in northern and northwestern India had not reached southern India even in the 13th century. The Italian merchant traveler Marco Polo observed in his memoir (called *Travels*) that southern Indians considered black skin to be the ideal color of beauty.

> It is a fact that in this country when a child is born they anoint him once a week with oil of sesame, and this makes him grow much darker than when he was born. *For I assure you that the darkest man is here the most highly esteemed and considered better than the others who are not so dark.* Let me add that in very truth these people portray and depict their gods and their idols black and their devils white as snow. For they say that God and all the saints are black and the devils are all white. That is why they portray them as I have described. And similarly they make the images of their idols all black. [Emphasis mine]
>
> —*Marco Polo (1958:276)*

It is important to note the fact that, irrespective of whether southern Indians represented and conceptualized their gods as black and their devils as white, *Hindu religious color symbolism does not place a higher or lower value for either white or black color.* The god Siva can be black or blue or white although he is represented as black in most instances. God Krishna, who is represented as black and who is the idealized lover god, synthesizes black and white colors with reference to *black and white lights* complementing each other. In Krishna mythology, it is believed that in order to achieve sensuous pleasure Krishna manifested himself as black and white lights. The black light became the male principle or Krishna, and the white light became the female principle or Radha. Black Krishna impregnated white Radha (Radhita): "From Radhika, the white light, impregnated by Krishna, the black light, were born Universal Intellect (*Mahat-tattva*), Basic Nature (*Pradhana*), and the Embryo-of-Splendor (*Hiranya-garbha*), which is the principle and totality of all subtle bodies" (Danielou 1991:177). Danielou discusses in detail the color symbolism associated with gods, including even the serpent gods (*naga*s), and suggests that gods such as Krishna and Rama "are represented as dark in color" because they definitely were Hindu gods who were important in the cultural traditions that existed before Aryans entered India.

Danielou's interpretations are accurate historically and psychologically. Most aspects of what we identify as Hinduism today developed in the cultural traditions that existed before Aryans entered India; and psychologically, people create gods in their own image. (As the ancient Greek philosophers used to say, the red-haired Thracians created gods with red hair, the Ethiopians created black gods, and if horses created gods they would look like horses.) Southern Indians, as Marco Polo noted, created gods as black, resembling their own black-pigmented or tanned bodies, but they also created gods such as Siva, Krishna, and Rama who could be black, blue, or white.

The epics *Mahabharata*, in which the god Krishna has the prominent role, and *Ramayana*, in which the god Rama has the prominent role, were both first formulated in northern India in the Sanskrit language. In these epics, Krishna is represented as black or blue, and Rama is represented as black, blue, or white. It is reasonable to speculate that if these epics had been composed after the 11th century C.E., Krishna and Rama would have been represented as white.

iv. Post-13th-Century Symbols of Skin Color in India

As a result of the Muslim political dominance of northern and northwestern India, various Hindu reactionary movements came into being, and certain rigid Hindu practices were introduced along with certain reinventions of Hindu mythologies and codifications of Hindu beliefs. The taboo against cow slaughter became a political symbol of defiance against the Persianized Turks, and rules of caste endogamy were reinforced to prevent any Hindu from marrying outside his or her caste. Elaborate treatises were written on the dangers of caste mixing, and a new mythology of how different caste groups had come into being (with different ways of life) was invented.

The new mythology of caste origins found its full expression in *Manu-Dharma* (the Code of Manu) which was probably written in the 13th century. In the Code of Manu as well as in some other treatises, the origin of castes was attributed to the creation of castes by the creator god Brahma: The *Brahmin* caste evolved from the head (intellect) of Brahma; the *Kshatriya* caste evolved from the shoulder (arm to fight) of Brahma; the *Vasiya* caste evolved from the thigh (walk to trade) of Brahma; and the *Sudra* caste evolved from the feet (to work as serf) of Brahma. Added to this myth was the reference to *varna* (quality) as a physical trait (color). The Brahmin castes were represented as white (Brahmin varna); the Kshatriya castes as red (Kshatriya varna); the Vasiya castes as yellow (Vasiya varna); and the Shudra castes as black. Along with these representations of varna was added a theory of the mixing of colors (*varna sankara*): Miscegenation or varna sankara was believed to be responsible for the existence of people exhibiting diffused or different or diverse shades of the four primary colors (white, red, yellow, and black). Undoubtedly, this meaning of varna (and the related versions of color combinations) developed from the desire of Hindu scholars of the 13th century to emulate the Muslim representations and conceptions of beauty, and claim or accord high status to the Brahmins, Kshatriyas, and Vaisyas that was equal to that of the Turkish, Persian, Afgan, and Mongol invaders. Ironically, the Hindus made the Muslim invaders into a reference group for emulating the representations and conceptions of beauty even though there was widespread negative reaction to Islam and violent resistance to Islamic proselytization.

Originally, the word *varna* meant quality, and the categories of Brahmin, Kshatriya, Vaisiya, and Shudra were class categories of quality in which different *jatis* (endogamous groups or breeding populations) were located. Thus, although jatis were closed units, it was possible for jatis to move into different class categories in terms of their occupational and/or intellectual achievements. In the epic *Mahabharata* the god Krishna states: "*Chaturvarniyam maya srata guna karma vibaghasa*" ("The four aspects of humanity are manifested in terms of quality and action"). This implies that a Brahmin jati could lose its Brahmin quality and become a Shudra jati unless the quality of being a Brahmin is maintained, and a Shudra jati could acquire the Brahmin quality through the cultivation of Brahmin quality.

The Hindu theory of color mixing which developed in the 13th century acquired importance gradually in different parts of India. Brahmins (priestly class) and Kshatriyas (ruling class) were viewed as light-brown skinned, and whenever and wherever it was possible, jati groups of these categories sought to have brides of light-brown skin color, emulating the practices of the Muslim ruling classes of the Persianized Turkish-Mongol kingdoms of India. The Persianized Turkish-Mongol kings and nobles frequently sought their brides and concubines from Persia. The Mughal emperors followed the practice of taking brides from Persia and as a result their families were composed of members with very fair skin color.

> Babur, Humayun, and Akbar [16th century Mughal emperors] were of partly Turco-Mongol and partly Iranian descent. Jahangir, however, had a Rajput [Kshatriya] mother, and so had Shah Jahan. Shah Jahan, in turn, married an Iranian, in whose memory he built the Taj Mahal at Agra, and so Aurangozeb was Iranian on his mother's side. Two centuries later, European visitors at the court of the last Mughal padshahs [emperors] commented upon their pale complexions and central Asian features.
>
> —*Farmer et al. (1986:443)*

The colorism of Muslims and Hindus did not transform into a Western type of racism despite the efforts of the British and a few Indian scholars in the 19th and 20th centuries to equate colorism and racism. The main reason for the ideology of colorism not becoming racism is that in every caste or ethnic group (with the possible exceptions of the Parsis and some other groups in the Kashmir region) there occurs, among its members, a range of physical characteristics and skin color. It is not uncommon for members of the same family to exhibit West/Central Asian and indigenous/Indian physical characteristics, with some who are light brown and others who are dark brown or black.

The most visible operation of colorism today is in the preference for fair-skinned or wheatish-skinned brides, and in the movie industry where actors and actresses generally are those who look Western or central Asian. (An interesting fact is that some of the movie actresses are Jewish because of their west Asian physical features. The mother of Leela Chitnis, the most prominent actress of the 1940s, was Jewish; and an important actress of the 1950s, named Nadira, was Jewish.) This type of aesthetic preference, or the idealization of certain physical features, is entirely different from racism, a phenomenon of according power and authority to certain groups on the basis of their physical characteristics and of equating physical features with superior or inferior moral/intellectual characteristics.

v. Aryanism and Colorism in Modern India

The mythology of race, which the British introduced in India, had an unfortunate and unforeseen consequence for some Western-trained Hindu intellectuals. In their eagerness to be accepted by the British as equals, some Hindu intellectuals subscribed to the 19th century mythology of superior Aryan race and joined the British in promoting the view that Hindu civilization was created by the Aryan race and that the Hindu caste system developed out of a race war between the white-skinned Aryans and the black-skinned indigenous populations. The Aryan theory of Hindu civilization is not based on facts, but, as Slater (1976) observes, is rooted in the sentiment of Hindu intellectuals.

> Indian amour propre is gratified by the idea that Indians are Aryans, of the elder line. ... since very few Indians are aware of racial affinities and ancient cultural contacts, it appears to him that to be regarded as Dravidian rather than an Aryan is to deny his kinship with western Europeans and thus relegates him to an inferior category.
>
> —*Slater (1976:44)*

The historical invention of the existence of an ancient racial conflict in India, suggesting that such a conflict began with the entry of Aryans in 1700 B.C.E. and that the caste system developed as a result of this conflict, is based upon inferences made from the facts about the post-16th-century C.E. European politico-economic domination of non-Europeans that resulted in the emergence of a particular type of color-bound slavery. As the Europeans gradually succeeded in establishing politico-economic dominance over the indigenous populations of the New World, a hierarchical social arrangement with the Europeans at the top came into being. Along with this, the use of African slave labor after the 16th century was justified for over three hundred years with pseudotheories of race, racial superiority of the Europeans, and racial inferiority of the Africans. Africans in particular, and black-skinned people in general, were conceptualized as inferior morally and intellectually, and a hierarchy of races was constructed to defend the enslavement of Africans and the equation of black skin color and slavery. *A similar conceptualization did not exist in India; the caste system existed in India before the Aryans entered India, and the caste hierarchy was not based on color.*

The word *dasa* of the ancient Hindu texts is cited by some historians to suggest that black-skinned Dravidians were enslaved by white-skinned Aryans; in such a view, the words dasa and dasyu etymologically connoted slavery and blackness, denoting a correspondence between black skin color and slavery. But slavery in ancient India and elsewhere was colorblind, and the word dasa referred to a devotee or slave of the gods. When Aryans entered India, they encountered people who were devotees or slaves of gods such as Siva, Krishna, and Rama. And there were slave castes and master castes functioning within the framework of the caste system. The militarily victorious Aryans became members of the master castes.

There is, from a scientific perspective, no such thing as an Aryan race or a Dravidian race in India. Identities such as Aryan and Dravidian are cultural and linguistic categories. The notion that there is a dichotomy in India separating the Aryan north and the Dravidian south in terms of people in the north having Aryan physical features and people in the south having Dravidian physical features is inaccurate and unscientific. The term *Dravidian* did not exist before the 19th century when the philologist, the Right Reverend Robert Caldwell, introduced it to identify a group of non-Indo-European languages such as Tamil, Telugu, Kannada, and Malayalam. As Chatterji (1965:1) notes,

> The word *Dravidian* is an Anglo-Indian expression, a word created by British scholars in India, and is a hybrid consisting of the Indian or Sanskrit word *Dravida* and the English adjectival suffix -*ian*, which itself is from Latin. The original Sanskrit word has currently three forms,

Dramida, Dravida, and *Drawida,* and there are some subtle differences in the use of these forms. The form *Dramida* was definitely employed with regard to the Tamil-speaking section within the Dravidian family, just as the term Andhva is used with regard to Telugu-speakers and Karnataka with regard to Kannada-speakers and their country, and Kerala similarly stands for the Malayalam-speaking people of Malayali country.

Thus technically, *Dravidian* in its original usage referred only to the people of the country *Dramida* (the Tamils) and not even to a linguistic family (and definitely not to make a contrast between Aryan north and Dravidian south). As I noted in Chapter 1, the Aryan settlers of the northern region of India referred to that region as *Aryavarta,* or land of the Aryan speakers.

The notion that upper castes exhibit Aryan physical features is unfounded because there is no *uniquely* Aryan physical characteristic that can be identified as belonging to any caste. Studies show that it is not possible to make racial boundaries between the different regions of India. Light-brown or wheatish skin color occurs more in northern, northwestern, and southwestern India because of large numbers of people from west Asia and central Asia entering these three regions of India and *not* because of the entry of Aryans between 1700 and 1500 B.C.E. Aryans (central Asians) and Dravidians (Indians) had blended over the period of a thousand years (i.e., from 1500 to 600 B.C.E.). *The distinguishable west Asian and central Asian physical features that exist in northern and western India occurred mostly as a result of migrations after the 7th century B.C.E.* It should also be noted that variations in skin color occur significantly in almost all caste groups all over India. Members of the same caste in different regions manifest slightly different physical features and differences in skin color, reflecting historical connections with the ethnic groups of the different regions. Members of the *same* caste group living in southwestern India are generally lighter than those living in southeastern India. People of the southwest have mixed more with people of west Asia, and in climate southeast India is about 10 degrees hotter and much more humid than the southwest. Climatic differences resulting from the closeness to or distance from the equator, dry desert, or humid tropical zones, and the differences in altitude account for many of the phenotypic differences in India. The migrations from west Asia and central Asia which began after the 7th century B.C.E. account for some significant variations in skin color. In northwestern and southwestern India are caste groups whose physical features resemble closely those of the peoples of West Asia. In southwestern India it is common to find members of the same caste group, and indeed members of the same family, who are light-brown skinned (like West Asians) and dark-brown skinned. In physical features and skin color, peoples of eastern India, irrespective of whether they are from the north or south, exhibit similar physical characteristics and skin color; in this respect, the people of northeastern India (and the peoples of Bangladesh) and southeastern India look similar as compared with the peoples of the coastal settlements of southwestern India.

The Aryan speakers who entered around 1500 B.C.E. contributed very little to the existence of differences in physical features and skin color. As Possehl (1979:261) correctly notes,

> While Aryans imposed their language and established a new social order, they themselves must have been a small minority and rapidly lost their ethnic identity. So complete is the racial fusion, that the terms Aryan and Dravidian can now be used legitimately only in a linguistic context.

At the risk of being repetitious, it must be emphasized that caste hierarchy is not the same as racial hierarchy, and that although politico-economically powerful groups are accorded high-caste status, such a status is not legitimized or validated by racial or biological characteristics. Racism is rooted in assumptions about the inherent relationship between biological, intellectual, and moral qualities that make individuals or groups superior or inferior. The caste system is not rooted in assumptions of such an inherent relationship: The Brahmin who is black skinned (and there are many, depending on the region) is not ranked as ritually impure or low because of his or her skin color. The untouchable is not given a ritually pure or high status even when he or she has very light skin color (and there are many, depending on the region). The following two quotes illustrate the dynamics of colorism and descent groups (caste or jati) that reject physical features and color as criteria of membership in a caste or jati group.

> Among South Indian Brahmins, a dark girl has a low value in the marriage market. At the same time, a dark Brahmin girl will always (or almost always) be preferred to a non-Brahmin girl, however fair. ...
>
> In certain parts of North India, Muslim women are often very light skinned and have features that are positively valued. Nevertheless, a Muslim bride, however fair, would not normally be acceptable in a Hindu household. Likewise, a Kashmiri bride would not be acceptable in a Tamil Brahmin household in spite of her very light complexion.
>
> —Beteille (1968:175)

vi. The Pragmatics of Colorism in Modern India

I have suggested that colorism and racism are two different types of phenomena. Colorism in India operates as an aesthetic orientation, with a positive social value associated with light skin color and west Asian or central Asian physical features of women. I pointed out that colorism has little or no political value because no explicit association is made between moral/intellectual worth and light skin color, and it is an accepted fact that a man could have high socioeconomic-political-ritual status irrespective of whether he has light-brown or dark-brown skin color.

However, a puzzling political phenomenon began to unfold in 1991, which raised the possibility that the Nehru dynastic rule in India acquired *some* legitimacy or charisma from the light skin color and west/central Asian physical features of the Nehru family.

The political events in India in 1991 after the assassination of Rajiv Gandhi, the former prime pinister of India, brought Sonia Gandhi, his widow, to the attention of the world. Despite the fact that Sonia Gandhi is an Italian and a Roman Catholic Christian by birth, and despite the fact that she was never involved in political discourse or action on the Indian national political stage, the Congress (I) party nominated her to succeed her deceased husband as the leader of the party and to become the prime minister of India in the event of a political victory of the Congress (I) party in the national elections that were scheduled for 1991. She declined, and Dr. Narasimha Rao, a dark-brown-skinned diplomat from eastern India, became the prime minister. The fact that Dr. Rao became the political leader of India could be used as an example to suggest that there is no colorism or racism in India. However, Sonia Gandhi's political image in India does indicate the existence of the charisma of fair skin color in India.

It was a politically significant fact that there were many party members (and, if the news reports were accurate, "large masses of people") *who perceived the light-brown-skinned Sonia Gandhi as the rightful heir of the Nehru dynasty with the mandate to rule India.* It was reported that a group of party members had taken an oath to fast until death unless Sonia Gandhi was made her husband's rightful successor. There was hope that her daughter would become the prime minister after the mother. A leader of the Congress (I) party was reported as saying that "After all, historically, we have been ruled by dynasties" and that in order for the dynasty to continue lineally with Rajiv Gandhi's daughter Priyanka becoming the prime minister in the 21st century, it was necessary to have Sonia Gandhi serve as the "care-taker" prime minister.

In modern India the prime minister is often perceived by the masses as analogous to an emperor or king although the constitution identifies the prime minister as the head of the government and the president of India (a largely ceremonial office) as the head of the state. The Nehru dynastic rule began with Jawarhalal Nehru who was succeeded by his daughter Indira Gandhi (after a lapse of a few years when Nehru was succeeded by Lal Bahadur Sastri); after Indira Gandhi's assassination, her son Rajiv Gandhi became the prime minister. As the Nehru clan was originally from the region of Turkestan-Kashmir, most members of the Nehru family had the physical features and skin color of central Asians, and many of the members were Western-educated secularists (although belonging to the Brahmin class), a fact which enabled them to hold high administrative positions under the British. Jawaharlal Nehru was educated in England, and as he was independently wealthy due to his father's fortune, it was possible for him to devote the time and energy to secure freedom for India, and he became the first prime minister of India. Indira Gandhi was married briefly to Firoz Gandhi, a Parsi (Persian) from western India, with whom she had two sons. She groomed her younger son Sanjay Gandhi to succeed her but he died in a plane crash. After the death of Sanjay Gandhi, his widow Maneka Gandhi did not endear herself to her mother-in-law (Indira Gandhi) and was banished from the leadership of the Congress (I) party. Maneka, a Sikh by birth, joined a political party that opposed Indira Gandhi and thus furthered her estrangement from the Nehru dynasty. Then Rajiv Gandhi was recruited by his mother to take the Nehru dynastic mantle, and he became the prime minister after the assassination of Indira Gandhi. With the assassination of Rajiv Gandhi in 1991, the Nehru dynasty was faced with the possibility of an end to dynastic rule, and Rajiv Gandhi's window, Sonia Gandhi, was urged to become the prime minister.

A *significant fact about this political episode is that in political dynasties, it is common to recruit foreigners, and it is common that when a legitimate heir is not readily available, a temporary care-taking substitute will govern in the name of the child who is groomed to take over at a later date.* Sonia Gandhi refused to become the prime minister, and Priyanka Gandhi (Sonia's daughter) may or may not become involved in politics. Thus it is a moot point to argue whether or not a dynastic rule has been established. But it is legitimate to ask the following questions: Would the Congress (I) party members have considered Sonia Gandhi for the position of prime minister had she been a black-skinned sub-Saharan African rather than a light-skinned Italian? Did the Congress (I) members associate and equate her Italian heritage, as well as the heritage of her mother-in-law, who was a Brahmin, and the heritage of her father-in-law, who was a Parsi (Persian), with reference to some implicit meanings associated with the mythology of colorism and the Persian-Turkish-Mughal symbolic linkages of alienness or foreign heritage, west/central Asian physical features, upper-class status and nobility?

PART TWO

STATE SYSTEMS AND NATIONAL TRADITIONS OF INDIA

India under Emperor Asoka circa 240 B.C.E.

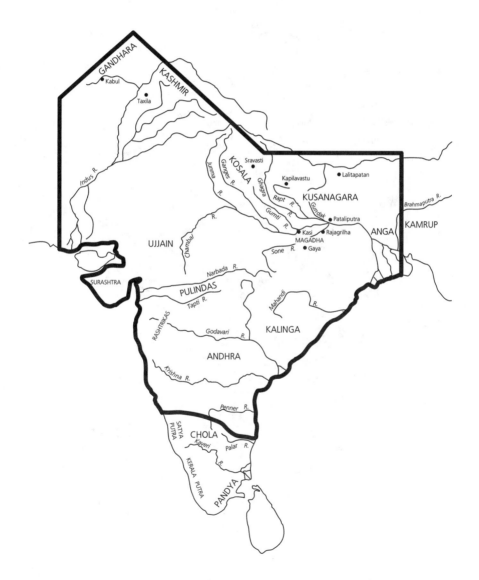

India in the 19th Century C.E. with British Territories and the Native Princely Kingdoms

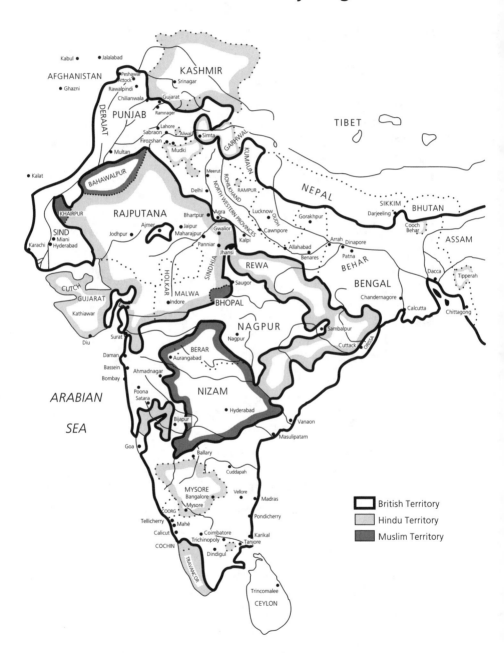

Contemporary Linguistic State Boundaries in India

Jammu and Kashmir

Himachal Pradesh Jan. 1971

Panjab November 1966

Haryana Nov. 1966

Delhi

Sikkim September 1974

Arunachal Pradesh March 1987

Rajasthan

Uttar Pradesh

Assam

Nagaland December 1963

Bihar

Meghalaya Jan. 1972

Manipur January 1972

Gujarat May 1960

West Bengal

Mizoram March 1987

Madhya Pradesh

Diu Daman

Maharashtra May 1960

Orissa

Tripura January 1972

Dadra and Nagar Haveli August 1961

Andhra Pradesh

Yanam to Pondicherry

Goa (Diu and Daman) December 1961

Karnataka

F Mahe to Pondicherry

Pondicherry May 1956

Karikal to Pondicherry

Kerala

Tamil Nadu

Gujarat
May 1990 — Date of formation of state on union territory

Union Territory

•••• Ceasefire line

F Former French territories under the government of Pondicherry union territory

119

✐ THE DEVELOPMENT OF EMPIRE-STATES AND THE FORMATION OF THE BRITISH-INDIAN EMPIRE IN INDIA

i. Empire-States and Nation-States

Webster's college edition dictionary defines *nation* and *empire* as follows:

nation, n. [M.E. and O.Fr. *nacion* L. *natio natus,* of *nascio,* to be born] 1. a stable, historically developed community of people with a territory, economic life, distinctive culture, and language in common. 2. the people of a territory united under a single government; country; stage; 3. a people or a tribe

empire, n. [M.E. *enpir;* O.Fr. *empire;* L. *imperium umperare*] 1. supreme rule; absolute power or authority; dominion. 2. government by an emperor or empress; 3. the period during which such government prevails. 4. a group of states or territories under one sovereign power; dominion of an emperor or empress. 5. a state unifying many territories and peoples under one rule

The term *state* is often used to signify existence of a political boundary in which laws are created and enforced. Usually, the term state is combined with terms that signify the source of political legitimacy or authority; for example, we refer to some states as *city-states, nation-states* or *empire-states.* In state systems that have multiple loci of political legitimacy or authority, certain internal segments will be identified as *states* as in state of California or state of Texas that are considered *sovereign states* but are subordinate to the republican state of the United States which binds all the sovereign states such as California and Texas under the constitutional charter of the *union of the states* with a natiunal government. Likewise, India has *linguistic, semiautonomous* states such as Karnataka and Kerala, and these states elect representatives for the government of the republican state of India which binds all the linguistic states with the constitution of India. The main difference between the republics of the United States and India is that the former does *not* make a distinction between the head of the republican state and the *national government*, and the latter has a separate head of state and head of the national government.

The use of the expression national government has a much wider significance than the characterization of the difference between the territorial state governments and the federal (union) governments. The national government represents the nation as a whole composed of several states or subnations. Thus, the government of the union of the United States is the American national government, and the government of the union of India is the Indian national government; the American government is the government of the people of *American nationality* and the Indian government is the government of the people of *Indian nationality*. Thus, both the American and Indian national governments function as *nation-states*, where the sovereignty or source of political legitimacy and authority is vested in the nation or people (or those who have the nationality as American or Indian). A major difference between American nationality and Indian nationality is in the manner by which these nationalities were created. *The British created the Indian nationality with peoples of different nations.* Through a historical process of British political amalgamation, some very different nations were put within the same state and some similar (or closely related) nations were maintained as separate states. For example, the Sinhalese of Sri Lanka and the Nepalese of Nepal have more in common with the majority of Indian nations although they have separate states, and the Tamils and Kannadigas have less in common with the majority of Indian nations although they are within the state of India.

Perhaps we should have a more precise discussion of the concepts of state and of the type of political entities that we identity as nation-states and empire-states. According to Watkins (1968:150), "The state is a geographically delimited segment of human society united by common obedience to a single sovereign. The term may refer either to the society as a whole or, more specifically, to the sovereign authority that controls it."

In a nation-state, the political legitimacy derives from a nation or people. When a state is constituted on the basis of the political rights of a single nationality or nation, the source of political legitimacy is the nation or people as a whole. Usually, a monarch or an elected group will represent the nation, and the monarch or the elected group will be vested with the authority by the people to rule or govern. On the other hand, in an empire-state there are many nations or peoples, and legal and religious formulations are invented to provide political legitimacy and authority to the rulers. The monarch or elected representatives of an empire-state may claim national political legitimacy, but due to the fact that an empire-state is constituted with more than one nationality or nation, political legitimacy is created through legal fictions. In order to understand how empire-states function, we should examine their origins and the political relationships of the different nations of the state. In general, an empire-state emerges through conquest and, therefore, political authority is vested in the conquering nationality. Historically, various political alliances between the various nationalities could develop, and the ethnic or national boundaries may become blurred through the use of an official language and the existence of common economic structures in the empire-state.

There are different kinds of empire-states. The kind of empire-state that is relevant for our discussion of India is the colonial empire-state. Colonial empire-states often control territories in different regions of the world. The expansion of Europeans, such as the Spanish, Portuguese, Dutch, and British, out of Europe resulted in the emergence of many empire-states which incorporated within their colonial territories various, diverse ethnic groups or nationalities. The dismantling of these colonial empire-states did not lead to the reconfiguration of the political boundaries. The political boundaries that were established by the colonial empire-states continued, and such a continuation often resulted in the emergence of violent conflicts among the diverse nationalities. Although these post-colonial empire-states were characterized as nation-states or even as democratic nation-states, political authority and the territorial integrity were most often maintained only through the use of military force. The governments of the post-colonial empire-states resembled the governments of the colonial empire-states, and the mentality of the political elite of the post-colonial empire-states resembled the mentality of the political elite of the colonial empire-states.

As the numerically dominant ethnic or national groups in the former colonial territories acquired the political authority to govern the former colonial territories, these dominant nationalities or nations identified the former colonies as nation-states, and often through military might prevented the division of the colonies along ethnic or national lines. In other words, the former colonial-territorial boundaries were claimed to be the national boundaries. Perhaps, as I noted earlier, the best phrase to characterize the former colonies is to identify them as post-colonial empire-states. In these post-colonial empire-states, the fiction of democracy is used to legitimize the governments as modern, universal, or progressive or nondictatorial. As the democratic elections would guarantee electoral victory for the dominant nationalities (because of their numerical dominance), the political and cultural elite were either members of the dominant nationalities or the clients of the dominant nationalities. Examples of post-colonial empire-states are India, Indonesia, Pakistan, and Nigeria.

Perhaps historians of the 21st century will provide a clear picture of why and how the post-colonial empire-states were created and maintained in the 20th century. There are several post-colonial empire-states in the world today, the largest of them being India. It is possible that the dismantling of the Soviet empire will serve as a model for the Indian empire to initiate the reconfiguration of the political boundaries along national lines, but it appears that such a possibility will arise only after a prolonged period of violent conflicts between and among the various nationalities of India.

The existence of violent conflicts between the various ethnic or national groups in India, Indonesia, Sri Lanka, Nigeria, Sudan, and Zimbabwe is primarily due to the conception of the former colonial territories or boundaries as *sacred* national boundaries. It is very important to note the fact that such a conception has its basis in the self-interests of the dominant groups of the colonial territories. Dominant groups have, in most instances, moved into or migrated to the regions or territories of minority groups. Since the official state or national language is, in most instances, the language of dominant groups (for example, Sinhalese in Sri Lanka and Hindi in India), members of the dominant group have greater access to the economic opportunities of the state and have more channels of political-economic control, thus giving them significant advantages. These realities have fostered violent conflicts in the post-colonial empire-states.

Scholars have been hesitant to discuss these facts, and when they discuss the ethnic or national group conflicts in the post-colonial empire-states, there is a general emphasis on the negative aspects of the conflicts without fully analyzing the foundations of these conflicts. It is possible that most scholars have accepted the post-colonial empire-states as true nation-states, and it is possible that most scholars perceive these states as agents of civilization, universalism, and pluralism. As a result, the legitimate political aspirations of minority nations have often been interpreted as irrational communalism or as expressions of backward, primitive, primordial loyalties. Consequently, many scholars have, directly or indirectly, become supporters of the dominant ethnic groups or nationalities of the former colonies such as India and Indonesia, and scholarly work is often used by members of dominant groups of the former colonies to promote what they claim is national integration or national unity. I suggest that scholars should examine the relevance of these claims in relation to how concepts such as civilization, universalism, and pluralism are used to serve the self-interests of the dominant ethnic or national groups of the former colonial territories.

ii. Pre-British Empire-States and Kingdoms

As historiography was not significant in the Hindu traditions, there was very little recorded evidence of the history of India prior to the Muslim invasions that began in the 10th century C.E. Hindus did not have a memory of their political dynastic past because history was seldom used to validate the political mythologies as it was used by the Christians and Muslims. Asoka, the supreme emperor of the 3rd century B.C.E. was completely forgotten until the 19th century C.E. when European scholars reconstructed Asoka's dynasty as well as that of the other dynasties of India with archaeological, ethnohistoric, Persian, Arab, Greek, and Buddhist sources.

Hindus developed an elaborate, rich religious mythological literature to validate political and social structures. The focuses of analysis and interpretation in Hindu tradition were the recurring patterns and processes rather than a lineal, progressive culmination of events. Thus, Hindu traditions often embodied a structural-functional orientation, with a commitment to synchronic analysis. As I noted in the introduction, a semiotic imagination, or a focus on exploring the relationships of symbols, their meanings, and their uses permeates every aspect of social and intellectual discourse in Hindu traditions. The two well-known mythological narratives that exemplify the semiotic imagination are *Mahabharata* and *Ramayana*. These epics deal with Hindu conceptions of the eternal truth of *dharma* (moral law or righteous order), the recurring conflict between good (represented as *devas* or celestial beings) and evil (represented as *asuras* or demons), the meaning of birth, rebirth and liberation (*karma-samsara-moksa*), and the pragmatics of Vishnu incarnations in society.

The two myths also represent and convey the meaning of territorial integrity and political autonomy. *Mahabharata,* which means *the story of the great king Bharata* or *the story of the great land of Bharat,* is the longest epic in the world. It contains several distinguishable segments that may be characterized as tours and detours into the cultural psyche of the Hindu civilizations. The term Bharat was used by the ancient Indians to designate northern India, but there was also a great sage named Bharata who is believed to have written the text on Indian classical dance called *Bharata Natyam* which is taught and practiced in southern India rather than in the north. The name Bharat is currently used by the government of India as an alternate name for India. *Ramayana* (story of Rama) identifies Ayodhya in northern India as the birthplace and nucleus of righteous kingdom (*dharmarajya*), narrating the story of Rama as an incarnation of god Vishnu who had taken human form to eliminate the demonic Ravana, but *Ramayana* is also a significant religious and political treatise on human relationships in different cultural domains, and Hindus in different regions of India have adapted the original script of *Ramayana* to convey diverse themes that have relevance in the different regions. Mahatma Ghandi used *Ramayana* to convey the legitimacy of a free India, which he called Ramarajya (kingdom of Rama).

It is likely that both *Mahabharata* and *Ramayana* were composed between the 4th century B.C.E. and the lst century C.E., and it is likely they reflect certain political upheavals of that or an earlier period. Historically, during that period northwestern and northern India were attacked by many invading armies from central Asia, Persia, and Greece, and there were many Hindu cults and sectarian conflicts. Ancient Hindu kings (rajas) were in many ways heads of powerful clans or tribal chiefs whose chief function was to lead in the battles. It is possible that some of these kings had acquired hegemony in certain regions and were given tributes by less powerful kings.

The Hindu Mauryan Empire emerged in the 4th century B.C.E. Its founder, Chandra Gupta Maurya, was, in all likelihood, influenced by both the neighboring Persians and by the Greek tradition which was introduced in India by Alexander the Great who invaded India in the 4th century B.C.E. However, the Indian empires had certain distinctively Hindu features. The symbiotic relationship between Hindu kingship and Brahmanical priesthood was evident in the fact that Chandra Gupta Maurya's chief counselor and aide was a Brahmin named Kautilya (also known as Chankya); Kautilya wrote an excellent manual on statecraft called *artha-sastra*, which has been acclaimed as one of the greatest treatises on politics and government.

Chandra Gupta Maurya's grandson, Asoka, ruled over the whole of India (except the Tamil kingdoms in the south) and parts of Persia and Afghanistan in the 3rd century B.C.E. Asoka converted to Buddhism and sent Buddhist missionaries to several neighboring countries. After the decline of the Maurya Empire in the lst century B.C.E., several small kingdoms flourished all over India, and in the early part of the 4th century C.E. an empire was founded by Chandra Gupta (different from the Maurya dynasty), and the Gupta dynasty lasted until the 6th century C.E.

One of the Tamil (Hindu) kingdoms of south India expanded territorially in the 9th century C.E. and established the Chola Empire which lasted until the 13th century. In northwestern and northern India, various Muslim sultanates and Muslim kingdoms came into being after the 10th century C.E., and some of them became empires. From the 12th to the 15th centuries the Turkish dynasties were politically powerful in most of northwestern, northern, and northeastern India, and there were regional sultanates (Muslim kingdoms) and Hindu kingdoms in different parts of India until the 17th century when the Mughal emperors consolidated their political dominance in India. The Telugu (Hindu) kingdom of Vijayanagar of southern India became a great territorial power in the early part of the 14th century and continued as an empire until the latter part of the 16th century. During the 17th and the early part of the 18th century, the Mughal empire was the most powerful political entity in India. The Maratha (Hindu) Empire of western India became an important regional power in central and southern India by the early part of the 18th century, and it might have established political dominance in northern India also had it not been defeated by the Afghans in the latter part of the 18th century and the British in the early 19th century. The Sikhs of Panjab in northern India established an empire in the early 19th century, but it was dismantled by the British, and by the middle of the 19th century, the British Empire in India included the whole of India, Pakistan, Sri Lanka, and Burma. The British became the paramount, supreme political and economic power in those territories for a century (until the middle of the 20th century), either controlling directly with territorial governors or ruling indirectly through subservient Hindu or Muslim kings.

iii. The Emergence of British Rule in India

The political scene in India of the 18th century was marked by incessant warfare and the existence of several independent Muslim and Hindu kings and governors who did not recognize the suzerainty of of the Mughal emperors. The Mughal Empire of the 18th century was essentially a regional power, with its primary locus in Delhi (in northern India). Various Hindu and Muslim kings had fought to expand their territories in India, and some sought to capture Delhi and displace the Mughal emperor. It was in this context that the British became the most important power brokers in southern and northeastern India, and this type of British activity eventually led the British to establish political hegemony in India.

The two European rivals of the British in India (the Dutch and the French) had for different reasons been unsuccessful in their dealings with Muslim and Hindu kings and governors. As the Dutch had a monopoly in the spice trade in southeast Asia, and as there was no political rival to the Dutch in Indonesia (the Dutch colony), they did not become involved in the political intrigues of different ethnic groups. Also, with their superior navy, the Dutch had become more involved in the African slave trade and were active in securing laborers from India and elsewhere to work in their Indonesian plantations. During the 18th century, the trade contacts of the Dutch in India became limited to a few commercial relationships with Indian merchants who engaged in international trade. (See Chapter 13 for a discussion of a Dutch center known as Pulicat in eastern India.) As the French and the British had frequent conflicts in Europe, they developed antagonistic relationships in India, but due to the fact that the British had acquired a superior understanding of the political culture of India, the French failed in their efforts to use the Muslim or Hindu kings or governors against the British. Also, the British had the advantage over the French in having some exceptionally able (but corrupt) soldier/administrators who successfully sought glory and wealth in India.

The two outstanding or eminent soldier/administrators who were instrumental in establishing the British Empire in India during the 18th century were Robert Clive and Warren Hastings. The impeachment of these two men in the British Parliament for corruption reveals a good deal about British culture and how the British succeeded in becoming the world's superpower for two hundred years from the middle of the 18th century to the middle of the 20th century.

It is necessary to discuss briefly the European expansion into Asia before presenting an interpretation of how the British succeeded in establishing the empire in India. The Portuguese were the first European nation to make significant scientific advancements in navigation in the 15th century. The Portuguese monarch, Prince Henry the Navigator, wanted the Portuguese to engage in trade for ivory and gold without interference from any Muslim middlemen and the Arab navigators who controlled international trade. The Portuguese established bases on the coastline of West Africa, and with the help of Arab sea captains learned about the monsoon winds that would take them to the west coast of India from the east coast of Africa. The Portuguese admiral Vasco de Gama arrived in the port city of Calicut in southwestern India in 1498 and established a settlement in Goa (a port city located north of Calicut and south of Bombay) in 1510. The Portuguese gradually succeeded in eliminating Arab hegemony of the spice trade in the 16th century, and became the preeminent sea power with bases in Ormuz on the Persian Gulf coast, Malacca on the coast of Malaysia, Macao in China, and in various other places. The Dutch became involved in the spice trade, beginning in 1595, and the English followed the Dutch in 1600. During the 17th century, the Dutch replaced the Portuguese as the dominant European sea power and succeeded in establishing political dominance in southeast Asia and Sri Lanka (Ceylon), and they were successful in preventing the English from becoming involved in the spice trade of southeast Asia. The English established several trade settlements in India during the 17th century when the Mughal Empire of India was at its zenith. A trade center was built in 1612 at Swat in northwestern India, and a trading factory was built in 1640 at the port city of Madras (south of Pulicat where the Dutch had a port) in southeastern India; also, during the latter part of the 17th century, the English procured and cultivated the harbor city of Bombay (located north of the Portuguese colony of Goa) and succeeded in establishing a base in Calcutta near the mouth of the Hughli river on the Bay of Bengal (northeastern India).

The French and the Danes were the two other northwestern European powers that established bases in India. In 1720, the French secured a trading port at Pondicherry (south of English-held Madras and north of Dutch-held Nagapattinam), but the Danes, who had built a fort at Tranquebar (north of Nagapattinam), were primarily concerned with missionary work and eventually founded the leading Christian missionary college at Serampore near Calcutta (northeastern India). There were a few other new English, Dutch, and French settlements in India by the middle of the 18th century, but from the middle of the 18th century the European power of significance in India was Britain (the union of England and Scotland).

Despite the existence of all these European ports, trade centers, and factories, the European cultural impact on India was minimal until the middle of the 18th century. With the exception of Goa, where the Portuguese actively promoted marriages between the Portuguese and the indigenous people and converted large numbers to Roman Catholic Christianity, there was no clash or synthesis of European and Indian cultures between 1600 and 1750 because none of the northwestern Europeans (the Dutch, English, or French) had the military strength to challenge or defeat an Indian king or a Mughal governor (*nawab*), and none of these Europeans could impose their values on the Indians. The Indian kings and the Mughals could have eliminated the European bases at any time during that period, but their existence was tolerated by the Mughal emperors and their governors (as well as other kings or warlords) because of the commercial advantages in securing European and southeast Asian and Chinese commodities. Also, because the Europeans had established dominance as sea powers, Indian merchants progressively became dependent on them for international trade.

Due to the commercial nature of the European involvement in India, many Indian merchants and traders were drawn into the world of the Europeans, and the loyalty of these merchants and traders was to the Europeans rather than to the local kings or governors. When the British and French were in the process of establishing port (trade) settlements in the territory of the Tamils in southeastern India, Tamil merchants studied English and French and had personal loyal relationships with the Europeans. For example, a Hindu merchant named Ananda Ranga Pillai (1709-1761) was a close friend of the French governor of the French port settlement called Pondicherry, and Pillai became the chief agent of the settlement as the trusted assistant to the governor, Francois Dupleix. Pillai maintained a diary in which he recorded day-to-day activities of the government and the traders and provided interpretations of the personal characteristics of the leaders.

Despite the thoroughness and the openness of Pillai's descriptions in the diary, there is no evidence of his having any loyalty to an Indian king or governor, but there is evidence that he favored the French over the Indian Hindu or Muslim kings or dynasties. In an introduction to a segment of Pillai's diary, De Bary notes:

> One striking feature of *The Private Diary of Ananda Ranga Pillai* is the total absence in its author of national consciousness or sense of political loyalty to fellow Indians, as opposed to Europeans. Trade was his family's hereditary occupation and he therefore entered naturally into a symbiotic relation with the merchants from across the sea. He ardently supported the empire-building ambitions of his sponsor, Francois Dupleix, and identified the latter's fortunes with his own, regarding Dupleix not as a foreigner but simply as an individual with whom he enjoyed a mutually profitable connection. At the same time Ananda Ranga remained a staunch and orthodox Hindu, never violating in the slightest the rules of his religion. In this respect he is representative of many generations of Indians from his day down to our own whose interest in things Western remained at the level of externals, and for whom European culture and thought seemed of little importance in comparison with the time-tested value of their traditional beliefs.
>
> —*De Bary (1958:3)*

iv. Company Raj and the British Empire-State of India

The Englishman who had the capacity to acquire loyal partners from among the Indian traders and soldiers was Robert Clive (1725–1774), who became the rival of Francois Dupleix in the Tamil territory, and who through successful military campaigns in the Tamil territory and Bengal (northeastern India) laid the foundations for the emergence of the *Company Raj* of the British Empire in India. Robert Clive was a son of a well-to-do English family who never did well in school, and who, like other never-do-well Englishmen, went to Madras in southeastern India as a clerk in the East India Company operations. Some historians have compared Clive to Napoleon and he has been called "the father of the British empire in India" (as in the *Encyclopaedia Britannica*). It is possible that he could have become a *nawab* (a semi-independent ruler or governor under the Mughal emperor) and founded a dynasty in northeastern India had he not continued to be an employee of the Company and returned to Britain to become a member of Parliament, face impeachment, and kill himself. Clive was successful in his political and military shenanigans in the Tamil territory of southeastern India, and in 1751, at the age of 26, he was no longer a clerk but a military and political strategist of the Company. Thus, he was called upon to save the Company's interests in northeastern India (Bengal) in the middle of the 18th century. In a military campaign of 1757, Clive asserted a clear military and political victory for the Company, and thus steered the emergence of the Company Raj. It should be noted that Clive was known later as Baron Clive of Plassey in recognition of his military victory in a place called Plassey in northeastern India, comparable to how, in recent times, Admiral Mountbatten was given the title Lord Mountbatten of Burma in recognition of Mountbatten's victory over the Japanese in Burma in 1944.

It is possible to characterize the hundred years from 1757 (when Clive won the war in Plassey) to 1857 (when the Indian soldiers revolted against the British commanders) as the era of Company Raj (Company Kingdom). The original charter given to the East India Company in 1600 (which essentially gave commercial monopoly to the Company in return for a fixed tax revenue to the English crown and later the British government) was changed several times during the 18th and 19th centuries to reflect three factors: (1) The Company was being transformed to become a powerful military, political, economic, and legal organization with a role to represent the economic and political interests of the British government; (2) the British home government began to assert a supervisory role over some of the major decision-making activities of the Company; (3) the commercial monopoly of the Company was gradually replaced with an ultimate reversal of the original trading charter, and the Company became the administrative arm of the British government until 1858 when the administration was brought under the direct rule of the British Crown.

The significant transformation of the Company's original role in India occurred when the Company acquired the right to collect revenues in northeastern India. Clive's victories enabled him to negotiate a settlement with the Mughal emperor to provide the Company with *diwani* (administrative and revenue-collecting rights) status in Bengal, Orissa, and Beihar (regions in northeastern India). Through such an agreement, the Company became a vassal of the Mughal Empire, with the emperor receiving a small tribute from the Company. In practice, the Company became a sultanate or kingdom and the Company governor became a nawab, although technically and legally the Company functioned with a British charter and the Company governor was appointed by the British board of directors of the Company.

The *Encyclopaedia Britannica* lauds Clive's success in India in the following way:

From the emperor [Clive] secured the most important document in the whole of British history in India up to that time, which appears in the records as "firmaund from the King Sah Aalum, granting the dewany [the right of collecting taxes and revenues] of Bengal, Behar, and Orissa to the company, 1765." The date was August 15; the place, Benares; the throne, an English dining table covered with embroidered cloth and surmounted by a chair in Clive's tent. It is all pictured by a Mohammedan contemporary, who indignantly exclaims that so great a "transaction was done and finished in less time than would have been taken up in the sale of a jackass." *By this deed the company became the real sovereign rulers of 30,000,000 people, yielding a revenue of £4,000,000 sterling.* [emphasis mine]

—*Vol. 5:835*

v. The Constitution of Rational Political and Legal Institutions in India

Eighteenth-century Britain and 18th-century India were worlds apart. In Europe (including Britain), the community of philosophers examined every aspect of nature without fear of persecution, and a commitment to free and critical inquiry of culture and all human institutions became the hallmark of 18th-century Europe, a century which is rightly called Enlightenment. Most scholars believed that human misery and suffering could be removed with the creation of rational institutions, and most scholars believed that through acquisition of knowledge it was possible to progress and attain the blessings of a civilized society where human beings would be free from the shackles and bondage of superstition, tyranny of the state, and ignorance. As most philosophers had implicitly accepted the validity of empiricist and rationalist epistemologies in human affairs, there was a belief that all human beings could progress. Despite the emergence of racism in the 16th and 17th centuries in conjunction with the linking of physical features and slavery, transforming the colorblind institution of slavery into a racial institution, the Enlightenment philosophers believed in the common psychic unity of humankind and in universalistic ideals.

From the British ethnocentric perspective and assumptions about reason, universalism, progress, and civilization, India of the 18th century appeared to be the opposite of what the Enlightenment thinkers would have favored. The caste and religious practices appeared to be superstitious and irrational, and from the British perspective there were no progressive institutions such as law courts and civic administration; civil disputes and high crimes were resolved or settled by kings or chieftains who made the decisions either whimsically or on the basis of what they regarded as the custom (which varied from group to group and from region to region); the life of the rural people was at the mercy of village councils and caste councils that functioned with no clearly delineated codes of conduct; and above all, the right to own property and the private ownership of property that had become the central, most fundamental aspect of the British capitalist society, were not defined or affirmed clearly.

The Company, with its transformation from a commercial enterprise to a political entity, began to devise ways to collect revenues in a systematic manner. And the Company introduced certain institutions to maintain order and legal standards of conduct in order to function as a political authority. British models of economics and law were gradually applied, adapting them to suit the local conditions. Thus there came into being different kinds of administrative orientations, some modeled after the Mughal system and some modeled after the British system. Clive left India before these administrative systems fell into place, but his protegé Warren Hastings (1773–1784) proceeded swiftly and initiated what he believed to be necessary reforms. Warren Hastings has been hailed as the second most important person in establishing the British Empire in India, but he, too, like his mentor Clive, was impeached in the British Parliament. The impeachment proceedings and the debates on the affairs of India were ritual affirmations of British civilized society. The intellectuals and most members of Parliament developed a schizophrenic attitude toward India, simultaneously having a positive and negative image, which has continued up to this day; the impeachments and debates validated the British democratic, rational institutions of order and dramatized the autocratic and corrupt practices of particular individuals who had been corrupted by the Indian society. Despite his impeachment, Warren Hastings was admired. The *Encyclopaedia Britannica* extols his services with the following laudatory comments:

> He [Warren Hastings] was the first to attempt to open a trade route with Tibet and to organize a survey of Bengal and of the eastern seas. He persuaded the pundits of Bengal to disclose the treasures of Sanskrit to European scholars. He founded the Madrasa or Mohammedan education at Calcutta, primarily out of his own funds; and he projected the foundation of an Indian institute in England. The Bengal Asiatic society was established under his auspices, though he yielded the post of President to Sir William Jones. No Englishman ever understood the Indian character so well as Hastings; none ever devoted himself more heartily to the promotion of every scheme, great and small, that could advance the prosperity of India. Indians and Anglo-Indians alike venerated his name, the former as their first beneficent administrator, the latter as the most able and most enlightened of their own class. *If Clive's sword conquered the Indian empire, it was the brain of Hastings that planned the sys-*

tem *of civil administration and his genius that saved the empire in a dark hour.* [emphasis mine]

—Vol. 11:247

The Company's role as a commercial or trading enterprise was abolished in 1833, and it became a military, political, and administrative organization controlled by bureaucrats whose actions could be questioned only by their superiors in India or in Britain. It is beyond the scope of this book to illustrate how commercial and governmental or imperial concerns merged or complemented each other. The Company, whether or not it was a trading concern, was the financial backbone of the British Empire and served to provide the resources for British global dominance. The Company in India was the base for the British to embark upon rapid industrialization and colonization of Africa and Oceania. The British essentially used a pattern of relationship between commerce and imperialism that developed in Europe after the 15th century. The national monarchies of Europe that led in the expansion of Europe had established a pattern of an alliance among the merchants, soldiers, and the monarch; the monarch provided the charter for trade which gave legitimacy for the merchant as representing an imperial power; the merchant, in turn, shared the profit with the monarch; and the monarch gave military support to the merchant through the recruitment of military and administrative officers. In the case of the Company in India, the same structure operated: The Company had a monopoly on trade, with its charter or sanction of the monarch; the monarch through the government trained civil and military officers in various public schools and academies to serve as officials of the Company (in its role as the British government in India); in return, the Company enriched the monarch's imperial government by establishing global economic dominance. India became the foundation of the British Empire, providing the empire with wealth, raw materials, soldiers, indentured servants, and low-level civil servants. Thus, India was the goose that laid the golden egg for the British. To resolve their trade deficit with China (due to the British import of Chinese tea in large amounts), the Company's government took over the manufacture of opium (as its monopoly in 1779), and private merchants bought opium from the Company for sale in China. This enabled the Company to get back the silver bullion paid to the Chinese for tea. Although many Indian merchants and civil servants who worked with the Company prospered because of the Company's success in trade, the prosperity of the few Indians did not help the Indian economy.

Because commercial colonialism meant rule by a foreign company for the profit of an alien people thousands of miles away, it eventually provided a disaster for Bengal and ultimately for all of India. Most of India's previous intruders had settled permanently in India and, as a ruling elite, had sought to retain its capital resources within the subcontinent. Now India was ruled by remote control with the result that valuable wealth was drained from the country to enrich another country. It is estimated that between 1757 and 1780, 38 million pounds sterling was drained out of Bengal alone, either in the form of bullion or in articles of export in exchange for which Bengal received little, if anything. It was wealth such as this, derived from overseas colonies, that provided Britain with the capital to launch the world's first industrial revolution.

—*Farmer (1986:557)*

The British established complete political control over India only by the middle of the 19th century. Although certain regions of India came under the direct control of the British by the middle of the 18th century, most of India was under Muslim and Hindu kings until the middle of the 19th century. The British had to declare war against the Nizam of Hyderabad and Tippu Sultan of southern India in the late 18th century to acquire their political submission, and the Marathas and the Sikhs were not defeated until the early part of the 19th century. An interesting and important fact, which had great significance in the political history of the two-hundred-year period, roughly from 1747–1947, was that the British fought their battles with large numbers of Indian soldiers (called *sepoys*). Because of regional differences in India (such as the Maratha nationals in western India, Bengali nationals in northeastern India, and Tamil nationals in southern India) and the existence of antagonistic religious communities (such as Hindus, Muslims, and Sikhs), the British could use these groups to fight each other. The British fought and won their wars with Indians fighting Indians, and it was this political reality of India that helped the British survive the great revolt of the soldiers (*sepoy mutiny*) in 1857. It was with a large contingent of Muslim soldiers that the British were able to defeat the Sikhs in the early part of the 19th century. During the sepoy mutiny, the Sikhs and Rajputs fought with the British to suppress the revolt of the Muslim and Maratha soldiers. The British favored the Sikhs and Rajputs after the revolt, and they constituted the majority of Indian soldiers in the British army during the latter part of the 19th and early part of the 20th centuries. The British also devised ways to disperse the low-level commands in the various ethnic regiments such as the Maratha regiment, Sikh regiment, and Bengali regiment that preempted any major revolts in the military after 1857; until the 20th century, no Indian could become a commissioned officer in the military, and all command positions were held by the British officers. The British Indian army was deployed in several military engagements outside of India in places such as China, southeast Asia, Africa, west Asia, and Europe. During the two world wars, Indian military regiments were important units of the British army. There were over two million Indian soldiers who fought with the British in the Second World War.

vi. The Introduction of the Politics of Racial Hierarchy in India

For analytic purposes we can identify three periods of British colonialism in India: the period of 1640–1740, when the British found the political elite of India to be superior to them, and the British strove to emulate the Indian elite; the period of 1740–1840, during which the British perceived the Indian elite to be equals in some aspects, and inferiors in others; the period of 1840–1940, when the British asserted themselves as morally, intellectually, and racially superior to the Indian elite. The seven years (1940–1947) before the British left India were marked by British personal and cultural anguish over the impending loss of India, which often transformed into hatred toward the Indian elite. The demarcation of the three periods is, to some extent, arbitrary and should not be taken as major dividing points; there were some elements common to all three periods, but a delineation of time periods is useful to understand the political and cultural factors in India and Britain (and the West in general) that determined the shifts or changes in the British orientation toward India and Indians.

In the 16th and 17th and in much of the 18th centuries, the Europeans were not in a politically powerful position in relation to the rajas, nawabs, and sultans of India. Economically, the European merchant's power did not exceed that of the Arab and Indian merchants (who were involved in international trade). The Portuguese married the local women of Goa and were involved in making Goa a Portuguese outpost culturally. The English, during the 17th and 18th centuries, emulated the lifestyles of the wealthy Indian merchants or soldiers. The acquisition of *diwani* rights, or the authority to collect revenues, in a large area of northeastern India (following Clive's victory in the battlefield of Plassey in 1757 and a later success in 1765) changed the status of the British from that of supplicators and political manipulators to that of rulers. The British, as a group, saw themselves as semiautonomous governors (nawabs) after 1765, and maintained an effective army to protect their political and economic interests. As Wolf correctly notes,

> Before the victory at Plassey, the characteristic Englishman in India was a merchant who, through life in his "factory" and trade dealings in the hinterland, acquired a sense of equality with the members of the Indian elite with whom he dealt. The merchant, or the Company merchant act-

ing as official, often lived like the Indian notables, with an Indian mistress, or zenana, and surrounded by Parsi or Muslim servants, Portuguese or Goanese cooks, and Malabari or Malagassy slave butlers.

—Wolf (1982:245)

In the later part of the 18th century, the Company governors ruled the Company territories comparably to how the Muslim and Hindu kings ruled their kingdoms rather than how the British society operated. The Company officials were seen as superior nobles by the Indians just as a king's relatives and officers were seen as noble superiors. By the end of the 18th century the British separated themselves from the Indians and the Indian institutions, and the Company ceased to function within the cultural and political framework of Indian society. The Company began to introduce political and legal structures that were enforced by the military that was under the command of the governor general of the Company. Despite the changes, the British politico-military administration in India was quite similar to that of Turkish sultans (12th to 15th centuries) and the Mughal emperors (16th to 18th centuries): At the top of all administrative units were British officers (similar to Turco-Mongol and Persian officers), and lower-level civil servants and soldiers were recruited from the Indian communities.

The Company opened schools, or encouraged the opening of schools, to teach English to recruit English-speaking clerks and gradually began to replace Persian with English as the commercial and government language. In 1813, the Company lost its trade monopoly, and private merchants began to flood India along with Christian missionaries who had finally secured permission from the British government to enter India to proselytize and to become involved in the reform of Indian society. By 1833, the Company ceased to be a trading enterprise altogether; it had become strictly an organization of military officers and civil servants, mainly fighting battles to subjugate Indian kings, annexing large territories to the British-Indian territory, and governing the British-Indian territory with the rules and laws that were approved by the British home government. In the same year (1833), English was proclaimed the official language.

By the end of the second phase or second century of British presence in India, a major change occurred in how the British perceived Indians and in how they perceived themselves in relation to the Indians. Indians were no longer considered as equals to the British, and the Indians themselves were ranked hierarchically in terms of attributing positive or negative qualities to the different Indian communities. Some Indian communities were favored to serve in the military and others in the lower levels of civil service. The British saw themselves as endowed with superior moral, intellectual, and physical characteristics. The British cultural assumption was that the British race had a mission to reform, educate, civilize, and govern Indians. Initially, the British used the Hindu structure of ritual hierarchy and the Mughal structure of class hierarchy to legitimize or assert their dominance. But gradually the conception of racial hierarchy acquired significance as the British legitimizing authority. A dichotomy between the British and Indians was made on racial terms and an insurmountable division between the British race and the Indian race was created.

The third phase or third century of British presence in India (1840–1940) was characterized by activities in several realms (political, economic, literary, scientific, religious, military, social, etc.) that affirmed the separation of the British white race and the Indian black race. The distinction between the British white race and the Indian black race was conceptualized in cultural terms because in a few instances the Britishers had darker skin color than the Indians. A clear cultural-racial boundary was drawn between the British and Indians, and a legal barrier was erected to prevent the Indians from moving into the higher ranks of British military and civil hierarchy. As noted in Chapter 4, there was a buffer between the British and Indian races with the existence of a mixed race of Anglo-Indians whose members were granted some job preferences in government employment.

The racial ideology of biological, moral, and intellectual superiority combined with the myth of Aryan race. Initially proposed by Sanskrit scholars of Germany, European scholars of the 19th century began to link race, language, and culture, and there came into existence an interpretation that the Aryan race was responsible for the creation of great languages and great civilizations. Hinduism and Hindu civilization were viewed as creations of the Aryan race, and hundreds of pseudoscientific, philological and Indo-European theories were formulated to show the superiority of the Aryan race and Aryan civilizations.

Despite the fact that the initiator of the Aryan myth, Max Muller, rejected theories that connected race, language, and culture, it became fashionable to write racial histories of humankind and civilizations in the 19th and early 20th centuries, with the Aryan race given importance as the originators of great civilizations. Historians and anthropologists applied a pseudoscientific comparative methodology to prove that contemporary Hindu civilization was comparable to the ancient Greco-Roman civilization. The implication of this interpretation was that the Aryan invaders of India established a great civilization in India but that its progress was stopped by the mixing with indigenous races and that it remained at the same level of the ancient Greco-Roman civilization whereas the pure Aryans of the West progressed and produced still greater, more rational civilizations. Needless to say, this interpretation was not only nonsense but was a total fabrication. When the Aryans entered India, they were tribal peoples with few or simple systems of philosophy, economy, or politics, but the indigenous populations lived in urban centers of great sophistication that existed for well over a thousand years before the Aryan entry into India. The facts about Indus Valley indigenous civilization were not known in the 19th century, but even after it was conclusively shown that the basic, essential features of Hindu civilization were a continuation of the features of Indus Valley Civilization, many scholars were reluctant to give up their Aryan model of Hindu civilization. Vincent Smith, the influential Indologist historian, promoted an Aryan theory of Hindu civilization in his books, particularly in his widely used book, *Early History of India, from 600 B.C.E. to the Muhammedan Conquest, Including the Invasion of Alexander the Great* (1924). Inden, who analyzed the British writings about India in the 19th and 20th centuries, has this to say about Smith's interpretation of Indian history:

> Like so many other Indologists, Smith held that the world-ordering rationality which he assumed was needed to bring about this unity [i.e., of empires and civilizations] was the property of Aryans and not of India's indigenes, the so-called Dravidians. But he differed from most in his belief that India's moments of imperial unity were precipitated by the Eastern, Iranian Aryans, bearers of the world-bearing force we know as oriental despotism, and not by the European Aryans, bearers of the reason and will that gave forth Europe's superior political and economic institutions (1924:158–59, 289–90). *The effect of this theory of Persian influence, of course, was to justify the transcendent despotism of the British Raj by showing that the polity that the British had erected in India was not only true to India's history, but even an improvement on it.* There is no question, in Smith's India, of returning to a glorious Aryan past that was Indian. That past, which in his scheme meant empire, was necessarily the product of an active male and Aryan rationality that was foreign. It arrived by conquest and imposed itself on a non-Aryan populace that was inherently divisive and not contingently divided. Indians, thus, needed outside rule in the remote past, as they did now, if they were to remain in a single unitary state. Smith's history of ancient India was, thus, really a history of the present. As it had been in antiquity so it is in our own day. [emphasis mine]
>
> —Inden (1992:185)

CHAPTER SEVEN

✸ HINDI RAJ AND THE CREATION OF THE INDIAN EMPIRE-STATE

i. Crown Raj of the British-Indian Empire

The Crown Raj of the British-Indian Empire came into being in 1858, the year following the sepoy mutiny in 1857. Queen Victoria assumed responsibility as the ruler of India and the governor general of the former Company Raj assumed the title of viceroy in addition to the former title as the governor general of India. In her proclamation, assuming the role of the ruler of India, Queen Victoria included the following statement:

> We declare it to be our royal will and pleasure that none be in anywise favoured, none molested or disquieted, by reason of their religious faith or observances, but that all shall alike enjoy the equal and impartial protection of the law; and we do strictly charge and enjoin all those who may be in authority under us that they abstain from all interference with the religious belief or worship of any of our subjects. ... And it is our further will that, so far as may be, our subjects, or whatever race or creed, be freely and impartially admitted to offices in our service, the duties of which they may be qualified, by their education, ability, and integrity, duly to discharge.
>
> —*cited in Wolpert (1991:58)*

It was evident to the educated, wealthy class of Indians that there was a discrepancy between what the British administration in India practiced and what the Crown preached. While the masses (Indian soldiers, low-caste Christian converts, and peasants) as well as the Hindu and Muslim princes worshipped Queen Victoria and her surrogates in India, the Indian nonprincely upper class composed of Western-educated lawyers, civil servants, and intellectuals felt deprived or cheated. Members of this Indian upper class were descendants of the Indians who made fortunes in the late 18th and early 19th century through the use of, or the expropriation of, the changes that were introduced in Indian society by the Company Raj. Many of them were from northeastern India because it was in this region that the British laws of private landownership helped to destroy the Mughal patronage system and created in its place a class of wealthy landlords, bankers, money lenders, civil servants, and intellectuals (who were independently wealthy because of the British laws that enabled their ancestors to locate themselves in cities but own large estates or cash-crop plantations in the countryside or hills). Bengali names such as *Roy, Sen,* and *Tagore* became synonyms for immense wealth. In western and northern India also there were Indian families who had made immense fortunes because of the British presence in India. Many of these families, such as the Tatas, Birlas, and Sarabhais, were willing to work as partners of the British in international trade, commerce, and industrialization, but they resented the British racist attitudes toward the Indian elite and, as a result, gave support to the nationalist movements of the Indian intellectuals. Queen Victoria conveyed the impression that the British were divinely ordained to own India as a sacred trust, that this sacred trust should not be broken, and that it was the moral and religious duty of the British to save and protect India. The Crown Raj promoted a patron-client relationship in India, with the British as the patrons, and projected an attitude of paternalism and White Man's Burden toward the native children of India. Spear (1968) notes,

> Queen Victoria took her relationship to her new subjects very seriously and contrived, by some esoteric magic of her own, to convey her concern to them. At any rate the new regime was more personal, something which Indians liked. In the next thirty years, helped by the Queen's initial proclamation, there grew an extraordinary attachment and even reverence for the queen's person which littered Indian cities with her statues and certainly strengthened Anglo-Indian ties. Without apparent effort Victoria had captured the mystique of Akbar.
>
> *—Spear (1968:148)*

ii. The Emergence of the Dominions of India and Pakistan

In the last decade of the 19th century and in the first two decades of the 20th century, there were sporadic revolts and terrorist activities that resulted in the assassination of about two dozen British officers, but it was widely recognized by both the British and the Indian intellectuals that self-rule and dominion status would be granted to India by the end of the second decade of the 20th century. Particularly, there was a tacit understanding that India's support to the British during the First World War would be rewarded with an announcement of the date of the transfer of power from the British to the Indians. These expectations proved to be false, and there was widespread protest and unrest all over India in 1919 against the British. The British reacted by imposing martial law types of regulations and suspended civil liberties. The reason for these contradictory signals, misunderstandings, and misinterpretations of British intentions was that although there was ample goodwill toward India and genuine desire to transfer the government to Indians at the highest levels of the British government and Parliament, there was great bureaucratic and military resistance and intolerance to the transfer of power to Indians; the Crown Raj, at its top, lived up to the promise given by Queen Victoria in her proclamation of equality, but it could not implement its will because of pervasive British racism and mistrust between the British administrators and Indian elite. A tragic enactment of British racism and mistrust occurred in a park called Jallianwala Bagh in the city of Amritsar in northern India. A British general named Reginald Dyer (who has been called a "lunatic," "savior," "misguided," and so on, depending on who is writing about him and with what sympathies) ordered his Muslim and Nepali troops to fire, at close range, at unarmed Hindus and Sikhs, resulting in the death of about 500 and the wounding of about 2000 people.

Despite the British bureaucratic and military resistance to change and the opposition of Winston Churchill and a few other diehard racist politicians, there was widespread support for India's dominion status. However, major problems arose at various levels of negotiations for the dominion status because of the conflict between the leaders of the Muslim League (who for the most part wanted to create a new Islamic state or nation) and the leaders of the Indian National Congress (who, for the most part, wanted to keep a united India after the departure of the British). It was very clear after 1940 that independence or dominion status for India was imminent, but the declaration of independence was postponed to take place after the Second World War, and the British contributed to major unrest in northern and northeastern India by shooting and bombing civilian protesters in 1942. Thousands of Indians were killed, tens of thousands wounded, a hundred thousand or more arrested in the undeclared war that was waged by the Crown Raj against what was no longer the brightest jewel in His Majesty's Crown. Due to a peculiar combination of universalism, secularism, ethnocentrism, religious fundamentalism, and political naiveté, most of the leaders of the Muslim League and the Indian National Congress were unable to compromise over federalist composition of a free and united India, and from 1946 violent conflicts among Hindu, Muslim, and Sikh masses became common. In 1947, the dominion of India and the dominion of Pakistan were created over the dead bodies of millions of Muslims, Hindus, and Sikhs.

iii. Hindi Raj and the Indian Empire-State

The two chief architects of Hindi Raj and the Indian empire-state were Mahatma Gandhi and Jawaharlal Nehru. They came from different backgrounds, and had different assumptions about the world of politics, but they shared a common bond of affection and respect that helped them to promote and achieve each other's political goals. At crucial moments of leadership contests, Mahatma Gandhi came to the rescue of Jawarharlal Nehru, as when there was a contest between Nehru and the radical leader Subhas C. Bose for the leadership of the Indian National Congress Party, or when there was a contest between Nehru and the authoritarian leader Sardar V. Patel for the leadership of the Indian government. And, Nehru deflected criticisms of Gandhi's discussions of his personal sexual and spiritual struggles as well as Gandhi's religious humanism and helped to focus on the real significance of Gandhi's role in India's politics. In his book *The Discovery of India*, Nehru made a brilliant and insightful assessment of Gandhi's contribution to India:

> Much that he said we only partially accepted or sometimes did not accept at all. But all this was secondary. The essence of his teaching was fearlessness and truth and action allied to these. ... So, suddenly as it were the black pall of fear was from the people's shoulders, not wholly, of course, but to an amazing degree. ... It was psychological change, almost as if an expert in psychoanalytic method had probed deep into the patient's past, found out the origins of his complexes, exposed them to his view, and thus rid him of that burden.
>
> —*Nehru (1946:361–62)*

Neither Gandhi nor Nehru would have used terms like *Hindi Raj* (Hindi kingdom) or *Indian empire-state* to characterize the political identity of post-British India. But, knowingly or unknowingly, they transcended specific caste identities and particular national traditions of India and became the most important political pan-Indian symbols of modern India, representing the political unity of India and they helped to keep the geographical and political boundaries of the British-Indian empire and to make Hindi into the medium of all-India or pan-India national politics. I will discuss in Chapter 8 the implications of the use of Hindi with reference to Indian nationalism and particular regional-national identities. In this section I will discuss briefly how Gandhi and Nehru served as leaders (and as symbols) to maintain the political unity of India and promoted pan-Indianism as a territorial-political-state entity. It is likely that if leaders like Gandhi and Nehru were not on the political scene of the early 20th century, the British might have left India with a different political map. Some of the princely states or kingdoms would have become separate countries, such as Jaipur, Kashmir, Hyderabad, Mysore, and Travancore, and there would have emerged separate, linguistically uniform nation-states such as Maharashtra (speaking Marathi), Panjab (Panjabi), Hindistan (Hindi), Baluchistan (Baluchi), Sindh (Sindhi), Bengal (Bengali), and Tamil Nadu (Tamil).

Gandhi and Nehru offered two different but complementary perspectives. Gandhi's perspective was to keep the traditional roots of Hindu India (which he called Ramarajya, or the kingdom of god Rama), while getting rid of inhumane practices such as untouchability and creating self-sustaining agricultural village republics. Nehru's perspective was to create a secular India, with industrialization and democratic socialism. Both were universalists and idealists, but Gandhi was a religious humanist and Nehru a scientific humanist. Both had acquired Western education, lived in England, and were admitted to the bar, but Gandhi experienced great angst in England and rejected Western lifestyle after briefly experimenting with it, while Nehru was enrolled in an English public school (Harrow) and Cambridge, and acquired an English lifestyle. Both were prolific writers, but they focused on different experiences to communicate their ideas about humanness and being Indian. Gandhi confronted human imponderables of fear, death, aggression, and love with a total commitment to truth and honesty in his *Autobiography* and in other writings. Nehru reflected on the history of humankind and civilizations in his two well-known books *Discovery of India* and *Glimpses of World History*. Both were unselfish, altruistic, and generous individuals, but Gandhi had an estranged relationship with his family and never acquired monetary and material rewards for his family or relatives, while Nehru had a very close relationship with his family and enhanced the family wealth he inherited; his relatives served as highly placed officials of the British government. Both were influenced by the writings of British Jacobians, utilitarians, and liberals, and had socialist commitments, but Gandhi sought to establish egalitarian castes while Nehru sought the help of the wealthy Indian industrialists and bankers to transform Indian society into a just and casteless society. Both were intimately involved in shaping most of the political developments of the first half of the 20th century, but Gandhi never held a political office and therefore could firmly adhere to his ideals and be uncompromising, while Nehru held politically important positions in the Indian National Congress organization and became India's first Prime Minister—which undoubtedly made him pragmatic and opportunistic.

Gandhi promoted the use of Hindustani or Hindi as an alternative to English, labeling English as a colonial language and Hindi as the nationalist language. He believed that the continued use of English would maintain a native slavish mentality, and he was correct in making such an assessment. But his belief in Hindi as the nationalist language was not only unfounded but had tragic consequences for hundreds of millions of non-Hindi-speaking Indians. Gandhi's position on Hindi as the nationalist language contributed to the emergence of the Hindi Raj as a replacement for the Crown Raj, and Gandhi's desire to create the righteous kingdom of the god Rama in India helped to continue the British empire-state after the British left India. If Hindi had not been promoted as the nationalist language to be used as a substitute for English, the colonial language, and if Gandhi and Nehru had not promoted the maintenance of a united India that was created by the British, there would be no Hindi Raj and no empire-state in India today; in their place would be several politically autonomous nation-states with their own national languages. (It is conceivable that Gandhi made an unconscious, symbolic link between Hindi and Hinduism because his hero, god Rama, ruled from Ayodhya which is located in a Hindi-speaking region of northern India.)

Nehru's contribution to the creation of the Hindi Raj and the empire-state was as important as Gandhi's. Nehru believed that the national aspirations of the linguistic groups, such as the Bengalis, Marathis, and Tamils were expressions of irrational communalism. Nehru, whose intellectual heritage was more in tune with that of the 18th-century European Enlightenment, did not recognize the fact that the national aspirations of the various linguistic groups were logical and rational within their cultural framework and did not take into account the fact that nationalists or communists were labeled terrorists or freedom-fighters depending on the perspective of who labeled them. In many ways, Nehru was committed to continuation of the empire-state because he was a product of the British upper-class culture which extolled the values of civilization, progress, and universalism. The British upper class generally transcended the nationalism and national boundaries of Europe, and although Europe was divided into nation-states based on linguistic divisions, the British colonial policy makers (who were mostly members of the upper class) disregarded and dismissed the ethnic-linguistic boundaries of the colonized peoples as irrational and created political-territorial boundaries that included many nationalities whose members were occasionally dispersed in different antagonistic, colonial empire-states. Gandhi was totally honest in discussing the reasons why he promoted a united India: He believed in the Hindu unity of India and he believed that a united India would serve humankind very well; Gandhi's pan-Indian empire-state was a Hindu conception. Nehru believed that Indians would prosper and achieve greater things if they learned to transcend the communal and parochial sentiments and acquired the orientations of conceptualizing India as "the nation"; the Indian nation, in his view, would have immense natural resources and manpower to become a great national superpower and could influence and shape the future of the world. Thus, Nehru was eager to inherit the Crown Raj and the empire and to maintain them under the control of Indians, and he helped create the Hindi Raj and the empire-state of India.

The following quotes summarize Nehru's legacy:

Nehru [did not] question the continuing relevance of the pillars of the Raj, which the British had set up—the bureaucracy, the police and the army—when he fashioned his new India. In his indictment of British rule, Nehru especially let himself go on the subject of the Old Indian Civil Service. ... Of all those in the I.C.S. Nehru most disliked its Indian members, *plus royaliste que le roi* (rather overlooking the ample representation of the Nehru clan in that service). Yet when independence came, Nehru yielded to the persuasion of Patel and others and agreed to the rights and privileges of the "Twice Born" being entrenched in the constitution.

[In southern India] [t]he security forces were soon engaged in a full-scale operation of represssion on the orders of Nehru and Patel. In Telengana and what was soon to be Kerala, a peasant revolt against the landlords achieved widespread success. The army sent in 50,000 or 60,000 troops, supported by armed police and the village soviets were liquidated at the cost of 4,000 killed and 10,000 arrested. There was no room for militant peasant power in new India.

The acceptance of these pillars of the British Raj as the main pillars of the Congress Raj contributed much to continuity, to institution-building, to the strengthening of the national superstructure.

—*Tinker (1989:12–13)*

iv. The Constitution of the Linguistic States in India

Hindi speakers in India seldom comprehend the reasons why the peoples of some linguistic states are concerned about the official language problem. Beyond the obvious ethnocentric and self-serving protestations about the need to have a national language of India and the belief that Hindi is the most suitable for such a pan-Indian national language status, there are political-structural reasons that cause difficulty for the Hindi speakers to comprehend the official or national language problem of India. As there are six linguistic states in which Hindi is the national-official language, Hindi speakers often assume that the language-national differences of India are little more than the dialectical variations that exist among these linguistic states and wonder why the south Indians make a big fuss over the language issue; seldom do the Hindi speakers realize that the difference between Hindi and Tamil (a southern Indian language) is greater than between Hindi and Farsi (Persian).

The framers of the constitution of post-British India contemplated a fair and just delineation of internal political boundaries. Linguistic-national identity was considered the most fair marker of internal political boundaries, but there was opposition to this because of a fear that it would lead to the disintegration of India. As a result, until the Telugu speakers forced the government of India in 1953 (following the protest death of the Telugu leader Potti Sriramalu in 1952) to create a linguistic state for the Telugus called Andhra Pradesh, the integral internal political boundaries of India were essentially those that were created by the British who had delineated provincial territories or presidencies that cut across national or cultural-linguistic boundaries. A reorganization of the internal political boundaries was undertaken in 1956 which resulted in the creation of several new linguistic states, and in 1960 and 1966 additional linguistic states were created. Major reorganizations of the internal political boundaries occurred recently in northeastern India (in the region bordering Burma and Bangladesh) where Tibeto-Burman- and Austro-Asiatic-speaking linguistic states were created.

Today, there are six linguistic states for the speakers of Hindi in central-north India that are identified as Rajasthan, Haryana, Himachal Pradesh, Uttar Pradesh, Bihar, and Madhya Pradesh. As the linguistic states are politically semiautonomous, most Hindi speakers assume that the difference between the Hindi-speaking and non-Hindi-speaking states is similar to the difference among Hindi-speaking states and that since there are several Hindi-speaking states as opposed to single non-Hindi-speaking states (with each having only one national or regional language), Hindi is not just a regional national language but is the intercultural or pan-Indian language of India.

I have already discussed in Chapter 6 the history of the use of Hindi as the nationalist language. The introduction of Hindi in non-Hindi regions of India was justified as a political necessity, and the process of *Hindi-ization* began in the early part of the 20th century as a vehicle to achieve an indigenous political integration of India, replacing English which had served the purpose of fostering the political integration of India with the political, economic, and cultural elites using English in all the regions of India.

As a result, Hindi-ization has (since the 1930s) been identified by many pan-Indian nationalist leaders to be the same as *Indianization,* or opposition to Westernization and the use of English. Had the nationalist leaders devised ways to switch from English to the use of all the national languages (not just Hindi), it is possible that all the national languages would have acquired, by this time, the vocabulary and orientations necessary to have textbooks in the sciences and arts. And the nationalist leaders could have created national republics, with a federation of the republics that might have been called the Union of the Linguistic Republics of India. But it did not happen, and the language problem in politics and in higher education has continued to plague the peoples of India. Professor Clarence Maloney, whose research in different parts of India over the past three decades has contributed much to our understanding of linguistic nationalism in India and elsewhere, recently made the following perceptive observations about the future of India:

Languages with many speakers are also likely to be stronger because they may have more specialized modes of speech for particular professions, trades, and experiences. If a language does not have enough speakers using the concise modes of speech in technical subjects, the language may give way in those subjects to a stronger one.

But civilizational creativity is related more to how indigenous ideas come up, adapt, and flourish in a language. Korea, Israel, and Netherlands, though not very large, are creative societies because the people from bottom to top in society contribute to the process. A historical lesson for India is that civilizational creativity cannot be maintained by a minority elite speaking among themselves in a foreign language—there is hardly an example of such to be found in history. South Asian societies will be creative in the modernization process when foreign and elite influence are better balanced by grassroots influences, which can only be through the people's languages.

In the long perspective of India's future history, what will remain, after all the civilizational ups and downs, is the ethnic realities—the 77 million Marathis, the 65 million Telugus, or the 56 million Tamils, not to mention the 360 million Hindus. This is what ultimately will make history—not political boundaries, nation-states, national ideologies, or government policies about language. And these peoples' creativity can be released mainly in their own languages.

The electoral process in India has moved society in this direction somewhat, but the real language problem remains.

—*Maloney (1991:8)*

Language is likely to become even a bigger issue in India.

Some regions of India might well fall away from the union of states—maybe the southern or eastern hill linguistic states. This may not lead to nirvana, but neither will they be much worse off than they are as part of India. Some language groups also may drop off that other great linguistic conglomerate in the world, the Soviet Union, despite its fervid effort to hold them with Russian.

The linguistic regions of India may look at the prosperity of Korea, Thailand, or Italy, and think that, since they are the same size, they could achieve the same level of prosperity. That could have been true decades earlier, but now, with the vast and growing populations, their besetting poverty, and the constriction of resources, it may be too late.

—*Maloney (1991:9-10)*

Currently there are six politically semiautonomous states where Hindi is the national and official language. Technically, if we establish a correspondence between language divisions and political divisions, there should be only one Hindi state (which incorporates the territories of all the six states) and it could be called *Hindistan* or *Hindi Pradesh* (the land of Hindi speakers). In most instances, regional-national languages serve as official languages, but Sanskrit (which is recognized as a national language) does not have a separate linguistic state, and Tibeto-Burman linguistic states have, for the most part, kept English as the official language although Tibeto-Burman is used on ceremonial occasions.

v. India and Western Democracy

With some justification, India is frequently referred to as the world's largest democracy, and it is not uncommon that the democratic institutions of India are viewed as more stable than their counterparts in most other non-Western countries. While a nationalist Indian can take pride in the expression of such sentiments, we should note the fact that the democratic institutions of India were introduced in India by the British primarily to safeguard the political/economic interests of the Crown Raj. It is legitimate to ask whether the British-sponsored democratic institutions safeguard the political/economic interests of the Hindi Raj in contemporary India, or whether those institutions protect the rights of all the Indians.

As the democratic institutions did not evolve or develop in India, there is a dysjunction between these institutions and the traditional status-oriented Hindu and Islamic customary legal/political institutions. India acquired the rule of law, and the democratic and bureaucratic (rational) institutions as a consequence of the empire-building efforts of the British who strove to create uniformity and impose standardized rules for governing a huge empire-state, as opposed to how the European nation-states acquired the rule of law (and the democratic and bureaucratic institutions) through a prolonged process of asserting individual rights and the elimination of the feudal order. As a result, the Western rule of law and the democratic institutions that exist in India coexist with the customary laws of the Hindus and Muslims along with the feudal systems of the rural areas. The caste system has survived because of the coexistence of the Western-imposed models and the traditional models of political/legal action. Despite the efforts of many all-India and regional leaders to enforce the Indian constitution to protect the civil rights of the low-caste Hindus, untouchables, and tribal peoples, there have been innumerable instances of abuse and violation of the rights. In most regions, the high-caste Hindus have continued to assert what they believe to be the privileges and prerogatives of high-caste status, and government-sponsored aid to low-caste Hindus, untouchables, and tribal peoples has been opposed violently with tragic consequences.

Western democracies of the modern historical period (i.e., post-15th century C.E.) developed gradually with the emergence of national monarchies and a merchant class, rise of experimental science and capitalism, and the expansion of Europe outside of Europe with large numbers of Europeans emigrating to non-European regions and the European accumulation of immense wealth from non-European regions. Among the European states, Great Britain became the leading world power by the 18th century and introduced the British models in many of its non-Western territories. *When Great Britain introduced the Western type of legal and political models in India, they altered irrevocably the Indian concepts of land ownership, banking, and trade, but left intact many other customary (caste and religious) laws. The Indians who learned to use the British laws prospered, and this led to the emergence of an upper class of Indians, particularly in the region of Bengal, which supported the British rule of law and the Western models of social contract. These Indians viewed the customary laws of the Hindus and Muslims (as well as the status obligations of village community), and the authoritarian orientations of maharajas (kings) and nobles as irrational and capricious anachronisms. Thus, the Western-educated Indians became the carriers or custodians of the British democratic tradition in India, and when India became independent, the Western-educated elite drafted the constitution of India based on the European models of democracy.*

The constitution of India provides a framework for the existence of semiautonomous states with elected assemblies and state governments headed by chief ministers, but the constitution gives greater, a near-absolute power to the federal or union (central) government which is headed by the prime minister. The prime minister is elected by his or her political party members (the majority) in the Parliament and is directly or indirectly responsible for all the internal and external affairs of India. However, the constitution identifies the head of the Indian empire-state as the president who is elected by the Parliament but is not involved in the governing of the country so long as the prime minister has the support of Parliament. Although the Indian presidency is a largely ceremonial office (like the constitutional monarchy of Britain), the president is the commander-in-chief of the military and has the authority to dissolve the Parliament and impose President's Rule in India if the prime minister loses the confidence of the Parliament. Each semiautonomous state has a governor who is appointed by the president (upon the recommendation of the prime minister), in addition to the elected chief minister who heads the government. The governor has the authority to dismiss the chief minister if he or she loses the confidence of the elected assembly of the state, dissolve the assembly, and to impose the President's Rule in the state.

The following quote clearly describes the political dynamics of the Indian empire-state.

While the structure of the republic is federal, considerable power is concentrated at the center. Flexibility is assured by the provision that the Central Government and the states have concurrent powers over economic and social planning, commerce, social security, health, and education. All the residual powers not specified in the constitution rest with the Central Government, which controls foreign policy, defense, internal security, and revenue—the subjects which the British had listed as reserved topics under the dyarchy.

The Central Government has emergency powers to act in situations "whereby the security of India or any part of the territory thereof is threatened, whether by war or external aggression or internal disturbance (actual or potential)." In such a case the President may issue a proclamation of emergency which remains in force for two months or longer if approved by both houses of Parliament. During that period, the guarantees to individuals under the Bill of Rights may be suspended, the President may issue administrative orders for any state, and the Union Parliament may legislate on subjects normally restricted to states' actions. This provision of the constitution, which has been invoked on several occasions, during which periods a presidentially appointed government has functioned in the states affected, gives the Central Government a weapon against recalcitrant states or states which might try to subvert existing institutions—for example if the Communists in Kerala should try to introduce totalitarian methods.

—Dean (1969:84–85)

In her important book *Modern India: The Origins of an Asian Democracy,* Judith Brown draws our attention to the fact of how the Hindi Raj has inherited the legacy of the Crown Raj.

A further element of continuity in the ideas behind governmental practice before and after independence needs stressing if one is to understand a dimension of India's democratic experience which was most powerfully demonstrated in Mrs. Gandhi's "Emergency Rule" thirty years after independence. Although Congress in opposition had bitterly opposed government's ability to rule with emergency powers, yet as the party of government intent on welding a new state it incorporated into the constitution very significant provisions for just such rule after 1947. It permitted the President to suspend the right to freedom and to constitutional remedies in situations of national emergency, and also provided for preventive detention of those thought likely to injure society. The family likeness to the raj's coercive powers was even greater when in the early 1960s a Defence of India Act provided for the detention of anyone thought likely to prejudice the defence of India. *The old emergency powers of Viceroy and provincial governors reappeared in those given to the states' governors and the President: both, like their British predecessors, have power to promulgate ordinances.* Furthermore, the President can in certain circumstances suspend a state government and bring the state under Union control—so-called "President's Rule." Here is potential for coercion and authoritarian rule as stern as anything the British had produced.

—Brown (1985:345)

Brown (1985:363) also states that "the 'Emergency' has proved conclusively that democratic politics and government can be demolished almost overnight at Union and state level if the government of the day chooses to use its potential and has a pliant President and Parliament."

CHAPTER EIGHT

✦ THE ETHNOLINGUISTIC STATES AND NATIONAL TRADITIONS OF INDIA

i. The Linguistic States of Hindistan, or the Land of the Hindi Speakers

The Hindi language developed in the 12th century in northwestern India in the political context of the Turkish rule in India and therefore acquired Persian vocabulary and some Persian phonological characteristics. In Chapter 1, I pointed out that the Indian dialect known as *Khari Boli* had come under the influence of Persian and had become Hindi. Today, Hindi is spoken by the people of the central-north territory of India, and roughly about 40 percent of Indians use Hindi as their mother tongue. When the British established political dominance in central-north India, some areas were ruled directly by the British governors and other areas were ruled by Hindu or Muslim kings who had accepted the suzerainty and authority of the British. The political configuration and the political boundaries of central-northern India were, to a large extent, shaped by the British. After the departure of the British, the princely states or kingdoms were eliminated, and gradually the following Hindi-speaking, semiautonomous political entities or linguistic states came into being.

(1) *Rajasthan state* of Hindistan was composed of kingdoms that were recognized by the British as princely states; the princely states had internal autonomy but were subservient to British authority and needs. Rajasthan continues to have royal houses or Rajput lineages who claim to be descendants of

ancient and medieval kings, and the land is studded with beautiful palaces, the most famous of which are in Jaipur (known as Rose Red City) and Udaipur.

(2) *Uttar Pradesh state* of Hindistan was known under the British variously, at different times, as Northwestern Provinces, United Provinces of Agra and Oudh, and United Provinces. The sacred rivers Ganges and Jamuna meet in this state at Allahabad, the birthplace of India's first Prime Minister, Jawaharlal Nehru; Hindus believe that an invisible river named Saraswati meets Jamuna and Ganges from underneath. Also in this state are the Taj Mahal, the mausoleum for the Persian wife of the Mughal emperor Shah Jahan, the Hindu sacred cities of Benares and Mathura, and the Buddhist sacred center of Sarnath.

(3) *Bihar state* of Hindistan was governed by the British from the 18th century when the Mughal emperor bestowed *diwani* (revenue-collection) rights to the British. The state has Dravidian- and Austro-Asiatic-speaking minority populations and a significant number of Muslims. The city of Bodhigaya, where Buddha attained enlightenment under a *bodhi* (banyan) tree, and the city of Patna which used to be known as Pataliputra, when it was the capital of ancient and medieval Hindu kingdoms, are in this state.

(4) *Madhya Pradesh state* of Hindistan was once the region of several princely states. During the British period and until 1956, this state had a different political state boundary than what is identified as its political state boundary today. There are several Dravidian- and Austro-Asiatic-speaking minority groups in the state. The famous city of Ujjain, which is located on the banks of Kshipra river, is near the ruins of a prosperous Hindu city which was destroyed by the Muslims in the 13th century.

(5) *Haryana state* of Hindistan was formed in 1960 for the predominantly Hindi-speaking Hindus in the Panjab territory of northern India; as a result, the Panjab linguistic state of India (discussed in the next section) is inhabited mostly by Panjabi-speaking Sikhs. Haryana was the site of a major Hindu revivalistic movement in the 19th century. Known as *Arya Samaj*, it was founded by a Gujarati Brahmin to purify Hinduism of what he believed to be degenerate forms of idol worship and caste practices; the ancient Vedas (Hindu sacred scriptures) are viewed by the devotees of Arya Samaj as containing all the spiritual and scientific truths about the world.

(6) *Himachal Pradesh state* of Hindistan has the luxuriant Siwalik hills and the rivers Jamuna and Satlaj, making it into a most sought after summer resort and a place of immense natural resources. It has magnificent Mughal gardens and British hill stations; the recent increase in population density has altered the nature of Himachal Pradesh, and it is an important agricultural state today.

An important fact about distinctiveness of the linguistic states of Hindistan, distinguishing them from the rest of India, is the identification of the

Brahmins as *Panc Gauda Brahmins,* whereas the other Brahmins (with the exception of Orissa Brahmins) are identified as Panc Dravida Brahmins.

> Brahmans are also classified by region and dietary prohibitions. The southern or Panc Dravida Brahmans are pure vegetarians while the northern or Panc Gauda Brahmans may eat fish. As the names imply, each division traditionally contains five sections. Included in the Panc Dravida division are: Dravida Brahmans of Tamilnad and Kerala; Andhra Brahmans of Andhra Pradesh; Karnataka Brahmans of Mysore; Maharashtra Brahmans of Maharashtra; and Gurjara Brahmans of Gujarat. The Panc Gauda division includes: Saraswat Brahmans of the Panjab; Gaur Brahmans near Delhi; Kanakubja or Kanaujia Brahmans from the Ganges in eastern Uttar Pradesh; Maithil Brahmans of Bihar; and Utkal Brahmans of Orissa.
>
> *—Tyler (1973:200)*

ii. The Linguistic States of Panjab and Kashmir: The Land of Panjabi and Kashmiri Speakers

A large majority of Panjabi speakers and a significant number of Kashmiri speakers are citizens of Pakistan. When the state boundary of Pakistan was established, western Panjab was made part of Pakistan because the majority of the people in that region were Muslims. When the Hindu king of Kashmir declined to take quick action on whether to annex the kingdom with Pakistan, Pakistan tried to annex it by military action and secured about one-third of the territory, and thus Kashmiri speakers are in both Pakistan and India.

Although the Panjabi language and Hindi are closely related, and although both Panjabi and Hindi were Persianized, a distinguishable Panjabi literary tradition has existed since the 12th century. Many linguists divide Panjabi into Western Panjabi (spoken mostly in Pakistan) and eastern Panjabi (spoken mostly in India), and Western Panjabi is grouped with the Sindhi language as belonging to a distinctive language subfamily in contrast to eastern Panjabi which is grouped with Hindi, Urdu, Gujarati and Pahari. Panjabi is written in Perso-Arabic script, Devanagari script, and Gurmukhi script, corresponding to the religious affiliations of the speakers. Muslims have favored the use of Perso-Arabic script, Hindus use Devanagari, and the Sikhs use Gurmukhi (script of the gurus). Sikhism, which came into being in the 16th century, has about 15 million followers, most of whom live in the Panjab linguistic state of India. The Golden Temple of the Sikhs is in the city of Amristar, which has been the scene of many interethnic and interreligious conflicts since the Mughal period. Although a significant number of Sikhs are Khatris and Jats (Hindu castes), Sikkhism eschews the Hindu ideology of untouchability and caste ranking and strives to promote an egalitarian unity of the community of Sikhs. Such a community consciousness, coupled with a history of a Sikh military order seeking to protect the Sikh political interests, has created a desire and goal among many Sikhs to form a separate state or country for Sikhs. Sikhs have pointed out correctly that a Sikh kingdom or nation-state would have existed today but for the British military campaigns against the Sikhs in the early 19th century which led to the annexation of Panjab territory (both western and eastern) to the British Empire.

I present a detailed discussion of the history of Sikh religious and national traditions in Chapter 10. In this section I offer certain facts and interpretations that will enhance the reader's understanding of the factors that have contributed to the emergence of religious and linguistic conflicts. Sikhism is the religion of over 15 million people in India. Beginning as a devotional, pacifist, inner-directed, redemptive religious movement, it evolved into a community of militant brotherhood, with a military type of sociopolitical order known as the *Khalsa* (pure) which is dedicated to the preservation of the religious ideals that were propagated by its founder Guru Nanak (1469–1539) and his nine successors. The development of Sikhism into its present form was shaped by the Mughal policies of the period (early 16th to early 18th centuries), and it is reasonable to state that the policies of the government of India will shape the future religious orientation of Sikhism as well as determine the identity of Sikhs as Indians. Sikh identity is not linked with or modeled after Hindu or Muslim identities despite the fact the Guru Nanak borrowed extensively from the Hindu devotional (*Bakhti*) and philosophical (Upanishadic) traditions and was also influenced by the Shiah and Sufi traditions of Islam. Thus Sikhism cannot be labeled as an offshoot of Hinduism (as many Hindus might believe) like Buddhism or Jainism, and it cannot be identified as an Islamic sect like Ahmadiyyas or Ismailis. There are certain religious beliefs and practices of Sikhism that separate it completely from both the Hindu and Islamic folds. I noted in Chapter 4 that Jews of India had adopted some Hindu social practices and had become castelike groups and that Syrian Christians had essentially become a Kshatriya caste with beliefs and practices that accommodated them in the Hindu society. Historically, the various religious movements that arose against Brahmanical priesthood ended up becoming caste groups within the Hindu social order. (Jainism and Lingayats are two well-known examples of this phenomenon.) However, the Sikh tradition has prevented the Sikhs from becoming Hindus or castes.

Why did the Sikhs not become a Kshatriya caste group, corresponding to the warrior-model of their culture? The reasons are several. Guru Nanak traveled extensively inside and outside of India and concluded that the rituals and social practices of both Hinduism and Islam stood in the way of knowing god's truth. He composed several hymns which he dedicated to one god, whom he conceptualized as True Name (*sat nam*); he believed that these hymns would serve as aids to discover god's truth in one's own self. The following morning prayer" or hymnal (known as guru Nanak's *japji*) is recited every day by devout Sikhs.

There is one god.

He is the supreme truth.

He, the creator, is without fear or without hate.

He, the omnipresent, pervades the universe.

He is not born, nor does he die to be born again.

By his grace shalt thou worship him. Before time itself there was truth.

When time began to run its course he was the truth.

Even now, he is the truth, and evermore shall truth prevail.

Guru (teacher) Nanak's teachings attracted followers or disciples (the word *sikh* means disciple) from all the castes because he disavowed the Hindu belief in untouchability, and he formed a community of brotherhood or commune where members from different castes ate together and shared their wealth. The teachings of Guru Nanak were recorded and were identified as the "original book" (*adi granth*), and the tenth guru Gobind Singh (1666–1708), who created the Khalsa (warrior-religious brotherhood) as a defense against Muslim persecution, abolished the succession of gurus and consecrated the book (*granth*) as the guru. Thus, the sacred scriptures acquired the status of religious teacher or guru for the disciples. These scriptures are known as *Guru Granth Sahib* and are kept in the Sikh temples known as *gurdwara* (teacher's abode). The most important and famous gurdwara is the Golden Temple of Amritsar which was built with the support of the Mughal emperor Akbar who promoted religious tolerance during his rule. It is the intolerance toward non-Islamic religions and the persecution of Sikhs which the Mughal emperor Aurangzeb practiced that resulted in Guru Gobind Singh making the disciples into warriors. As a sign of this change, he instituted the custom of men taking the title of *singh* (lion) and women taking the title of *kaur* (princess). Guru Gobind Singh also declared that all the warriors should carry the emblems of uncut long hair (*kaesh*), comb (*kangha*), underwear (*kacha*), steel bangle (*kara*), and knife (*kirpan*), which initially had functional consequences but now have become mostly markers of Sikh identity. There is no Sikh priesthood, but there are committees constituted to maintain the affairs of the gurdwara, and *granthis* to read the *granth sahib.*

Sikhism may be compared in its initial inspiration to many other movements of reform which arose within northern Hinduism under the impact of the religious challenge of Islam in the medieval period, but it is distinguished from them by the success with which it has resisted the general tendency towards reabsorption within mainline Hindu orthodoxy. It is therefore rightly to be regarded as the youngest of independent religious traditions of India where the Sikhs (1.8 percent of the population) significantly outnumber the combined totals of all Indian Buddhists and Jains, and significantly outweigh the Indian Christians in political and economic importance.

—Robinson (1989:343)

Thus, given the cultural developments in the Sikh tradition, it is logical for Sikhs to aspire for a separate nation-state (*Khalistan*) in India. It is very likely that the powerful Sikh kingdom which was established by the Sikh king Maharaja Ranjit Singh early in the 19th century would have continued in the 20th century had not the British become involved in the governing of India.

The linguistic state of Jammu and Kashmir has had a distinctive political and religious history. In ancient times, it was a special area of the Hindu mystics (yogis) and ashrams (monasteries) and it was a Buddhist stronghold which linked India and central Asia (through Turkestan). After the 12th century, it became the favored place of Muslim sultans and emperors, and the population was converted to Islam. In the early part of the 19th century, the British installed a Hindu king and annexed Jammu and Kashmir as a princely state of the British-Indian Empire. When the British left India, the king of Jammu and Kashmir waffled over whether to annex the kingdom with the state of Pakistan, as he was expected to do because of the preponderance of Muslims in the kingdom, or try to establish an independent kingdom. Pakistani leaders, fearful of the king's indecision, permitted nonregular, paramilitary units to infiltrate the kingdom to depose the king. The king sought the help of Indian leaders, and the Indian army marched into the kingdom ostensibly to protect the sovereignty of the king but used the military presence there to encourage the king to merge the kingdom with India. However, about one-third of the kingdom came under the Pakistani paramilitary forces, and that area is called Azad (free) Kashmir. Later, China claimed the northeastern region (Ladakh) of Kashmir as its territory, and in 1962 waged a successful military campaign to take over Ladakh.

The Kashmiri language is a member of the Dardic subfamily of the Iranian language family. Thus Kashmiri is closer to Persian than to the Indo-Aryan languages such as Hindi and Panjabi. However, ethnolinguistically,

Kashmiri has closer connections with Panjabi and Hindi; Urdu is used as one of the official national languages of the Kashmiri state (in addition to Kashmiri language). As the majority of Kashmiri speakers are Muslims, there have been recurrent political campaigns to either establish a separate country (nation-state) or merge the state with Pakistan.

iii. The Linguistic States of Gujarat and Maharashtra: The Land of Gujarati and Marathi Speakers

The linguistic states of Gujarat and Maharashtra are located on the central-western region of India. As noted earlier, Gujarati is usually grouped with Hindi, eastern Panjabi, and Pahari, and Marathi is grouped with western Panjabi, Sindhi, Oriya, Bengali, and Assamese languages. However, ethnolinguistically, Marathi is closer to Gujarati. Although they belong to the Indo-Aryan language family, they have been influenced heavily by the Dravidian languages, and both have correspondences with Dravidian grammar. Also, both Gujarati and Marathi were influenced phonologically by Persian and underwent Sanskritization through the adoption of Sanskritic idiom and vocabulary in religious discourse. Both Gujarati and Marathi acquired distinctive dialectical features about the same time that Hindi dialects became distinctive in northern India about the 12th century. Whereas Hindi acquired importance as a language of mass communication under the Turkish and Mughal emperors between the 12th and 19th centuries and came under the influence of Persian (and to a minor extent, Turkish and Arabic), Gujarati and Marathi developed as separate languages. Gujarati was spoken primarily by Gurjar caste communities who are believed to be descendants of central Asian Huns who settled down in Rajasthan and other areas of western India and was cultivated as a literary form by the Jains, a religious-caste community of very successful business and industrial entrepreneurs. The Jains follow the philosophical-religious orientation of the Hindu prophet Mahavira who lived in the 6th century B.C.E. There is scholarly consensus that Jainism was the continuation of the Hindu orientation that prevailed in northwestern India prior to the entry of the Aryans between 1700 and 1500 B.C.E., and that this fact of cultural continuity accounts for the existence of the Dravidian cultural and social structures in the Gujarati tradition.

The Gujarati linguistic state was established in 1960, with the division of the British-created political region called Bombay Presidency into Gujarat and Maharashtra. Under the British, the Gujarati region contained several princely states such as Baroda, Saurastra, and Bhavnagar. Gujarat has a large Muslim population and a large merchant class of traders, bankers, and landowners belonging to the caste communities of Jains, Muslims, and Hindus. (Mahatma Gandhi was a Gujarati speaker from a Bania caste; the word *Gandhi* means *grocer* and signifies merchant caste identity.) The coastline of

Gujarat has served from ancient times (possibly 3000 B.C.E. or even earlier) as an important area for international trade, connecting India, west Asia, and southeast Asia. Gujarat became a stronghold of Muslim traders by the 13th century, and Gujarati Muslims introduced Islam in southeast Asia during the 13th century.

The Marathi linguistic state (Maharashtra state) has peoples who are ethnically very diverse due to the fact that there have been continuous migrations of people from west Asia into that area. Bombay, the cosmopolitan capital of Maharashtra, is India's version of New York City. (A section of Bombay, like Manhattan in New York City, is an island.) Maharashtra has highly Westernized Brahmin communities, such as Citpavan and Konkani Brahmins, as well as large numbers of Parsis (who settled there about the 9th century C.E.), Turkish traders, and Bagdadi and Bene Israel Jews.

Nationalism in Maharashtra state has certain distinctive features. By the 17th century, Marathi speakers were aware that they constituted a politically united community against Islam; the symbol of this nationalism was and has been a Maratha chief named Shivaji who crowned himself the king of Marathas in the late 17th century in defiance of the Mughal emperor Aurangzeb who had called a *jihad* (holy war) against the Marathas in defense of his Islamic empire in India.

Maharashtra witnessed the rise of two important anti-Brahmanical movements in its recent history. A social-religious reformer, Jyoti Rao Phule, founded a society called *Satya Shodak Samaj* in 1873 to promote self-respect among low-caste and untouchable Hindus and to negate the importance of the Brahmanical priesthood in Hindu rituals. In 1956, just before his death, the untouchable leader B.R. Ambedkar (who is known as the father of the Indian constitution) led the Mahar untouchable caste of Maharashtra in a mass conversion to Buddhism as a protest against the Hindu ideology of untouchability which he blamed on the existence of a Brahmanical priesthood.

iv. The Linguistic States of Bengal, Orissa, and Assam: The Land of Bengali, Oriya, and Assamese Speakers

The Bengali linguistic state of India is small in territory, but the Bengali language is the second largest language community in south Asia with about two hundred million speakers. (The largest language community in south Asia is Hindi.) The majority of Bengali speakers are in the state of Bangladesh which was known as East Pakistan until 1971. When the British left India, East Pakistan was created with the division of Bengal into Hindu and Muslim areas. The Hindu-Bengali area became the linguistic state of West Bengal in India, and the Muslim-Bengali area became East Pakistan (which was renamed

Bangladesh after it separated from West Pakistan—now known as Pakistan—and acquired its status as an autonomous country or nation-state).

Bengal came under the domination of the British in the latter part of the 18th century. British domination resulted in the impoverishment of the Muslim nawabs (semi-independent governors linked with the Mughal empire) and the Muslim nobles who held political hegemony over Bengal before the British, and, in turn, helped the Hindus of Bengal. Muslims held onto their past glory and Persian learning, and as a result very few Bengali Muslims learned English or acquired an understanding of the British norms and laws that were introduced in the late 18th and 19th centuries. The greater participation of Bengali Hindus in the British government and British commercial enterprises created an exceptionally wealthy class of Hindus from different castes, and the emergence of some Hindu families like the Tagores, Sens, and Roys, whose immense fortunes enabled them to cultivate the arts and sciences. The wealthy Hindus were concentrated in the western area of Bengal, and western Bengal progressed economically in contrast to eastern Bengal which had become economically impoverished with a large Muslim population.

The wealthy Hindus of west Bengal helped to produce what has been termed a Bengali renaissance of the 19th century. Every field of intellectual activity developed. For example, Raja Ram Mohan Roy (1774–1833) founded *Brahmo Samaj* (divine society) to reform Hinduism and cultivate the philosophical foundations of the Vedas (Hindu sacred scriptures); Ramakrishna Paramahamsa (1834–1886) revived the Krishna devotional cult of the 16th-century Hindu mystic Chaitanya (1486–1530); Keshab Chandra Sen (1834–1884) synthesized Hindu and Christian ideals and promoted a spiritual orientation that might be characterized as pantheistic monotheism; Bengali literature flourished with writers such as Michael Madhusudan Datta (1824–1873), Bakim Chandra Chatterjee (1838–1894), Sarachandra Chattopadhyay (1876–1938), and Rabindranath Tagore (1861–1941). In Calcutta, the capital city of Bengal, a new upper-class elite called *bhadralok* (the people of quality) emerged, with members recruited from Brahmin, Baidya, and Kayastha castes. Members of this class dominated the political, governmental, and banking arenas in the 19th and early 20th centuries. Historically, in Bengal, the British contributed to the destruction of the Muslim aristocracy and the creation of a Hindu aristocracy which was not linked with royal privileges of pre-British India.

The Oriyan state or the linguistic state of Orissa was in the shadow of Bengal from the 18th to the 20th centuries. However, its early history and religious orientations make the state quite different from Bengal. In ancient times, Orissa was the center of a powerful state known as the Kalinga Empire which was destroyed by emperor Asoka in the 3rd century B.C.E. Asoka's conversion to Buddhism is attributed to his existential transformation which apparently occurred when he saw hundreds of thousands of dead bodies in the battlefields of Orissa. Until the 16th century, there were several Hindu kingdoms; the Mughals established political hegemony in Orissa in the middle of the 16th century, and the British took over its administration in 1803. Although Oriya, the Indo-Aryan language, is the national and official language of Orissa, there are many Munda (Austro-Asiatic) and Telugu (Dravidian) speakers in the state.

Orissa is famous, or well known, for its thousands of temples and shrines, many of which have very elaborate erotic carvings. The capital city of Bhubaneswar has remnants of very ancient temples; the city of Konarak has 13th century temple structures with sculptures that depict all humanly possible sexual unions; it is very likely that these and other temple erotic carvings were related to *Tantric* Hinduism, which focused on sexuality for conceptualizing spirituality and cosmic energy. Orissa has the famous city of Puri where the Krishna cult of Juggernaut (Jagannath) was established. In an annual ritual, the deities of the cult are mounted on the decorated temple chariot which is drawn by hundreds of Krishna devotees (with no caste distinctions); occasionally, devotees perform the act of self-immolation by lying in front of the wheels of the chariot.

Although there were Hindu kingdoms in Assam and despite the fact that the Assamese language developed as a branch of Bengali, Assam was never an integral part of any Indian empire until the early part of the 19th century when the British defeated the Burmese (who had established political authority in Assam) and added Assam to the British-Indian Empire. (Burma was also made a British colony, and in the latter part of the 19th century, the British Empire in India was labeled "the empire of India, Burma, and Ceylon.") As the mighty Brahmaputra River and the smaller Surma River flow through Assam, there are very fertile valleys for agriculture, and as Assam is at a high altitude with mountain plateaus, the British-introduced tea plantations have continued to be an important source of the state's wealth. Also, the state has important mineral and oil deposits.

v. Austro-Asiatic and Tibeto-Burman Linguistic States of India

Over the past thirty years, partly in fear of Chinese invasions (which actually occurred in 1962) and partly to prevent internal unrest in Assam, limited political autonomy was granted to the Austro-Asiatic-speaking and Tibeto-Burman-speaking groups in Assam, and several new linguistic states were created by the Union government of India. These are Nagaland, created in 1963; Meghalaya, Tirupura, and Manipur, created in 1972; and Mizoram and Arunachal Pradesh, created in 1987. As a result, Assam today is a territorially small state. Assam has continued to have internal conflicts, largely due to the

Assamese grievances against the Bengali landlords who had taken control of much of the arable lands during the British rule.

vi. The Linguistic States of Karnataka and Andhra Pradesh: The Land of Kannada and Telugu Speakers

Kannada, a Dravidian language, which is the national official language of the state of Karnataka, acquired literary distinctiveness in the sixth century C.E. Politically, the boundary of Karnataka shifted several times. There were several small Hindu kingdoms until the 17th century when Muslim nawabs and generals captured large tracts of Karnataka land, and in the 18th century the Muslim warlords Hyder Ali and his son Tippu Sultan posed a major threat to the British rule in India. After Tippu Sultan was defeated, the British installed a Hindu king in southern Karnataka and the princely state of Mysore was formed. South of Mysore was another small Hindu princely state known as Coorg, which became part of the British Empire in the 19th century. In the 18th century the Marathas held political hegemony in northern Karnataka, but after they were defeated in the early 19th century, northern Karnataka was made a part of the territory of the Bombay presidency of British India. In 1956, the Karnataka linguistic state was created, with the territory which included the states of Mysore, Coorg, and northern Karnataka.

Karnataka has had a distinctive Hindu religious and caste history which distinguishes the state's cultural configuration and social structure. In this state, conflict between Brahmins and non-Brahmins has a long history, and a socioreligious movement called the *Lingayat* movement emerged in opposition to Brahmanical priesthood and caste. Founded by a Brahmin official (in a Hindu kingdom in the 12th century C.E.) known as Basarappa in recognition of his belief that he was an incarnation of god Shiva's bull *Basawa* (*nandi*), the Lingayat movement revived Jainist and Shaivite religious orientations in opposition to Brahmanical priesthood and caste. The main focus of Lingayat ritual was the attainment of union with Shiva, and Lingayat rituals were officiated by Lingayat priests known as *jangama* (non-Brahmins). Now, Lingayats are divided into four subcastes, and all of them wear a copper or brass replica of *Shiva-lingam* (divine phallus) around the neck.

The Telugu linguistic state, known as Andhra Pradesh, was once the center of powerful Hindu kingdoms that controlled most of central and southern India between the 2nd century B.C.E. and 3rd century C.E. and between the 14th and 16th centuries C.E. (The ancient Telugu-Hindu empire was established by the Andhra dynasty, a name which has been used by the Telugus to identify their territory today.) From the late 16th to early 18th century, most of Andhra Pradesh came under the political authority of Turkish sultans and the Mughals. In 1724, one of the Muslim governors proclaimed himself an independent monarch with the title *Nizam of Hyderabad.* By the late 18th century, the British succeeded in establishing political control over the Nizam, but the Nizam was permitted to maintain his kingdom (known as Hyderabad) as a princely state or British protectorate. The territory east of Hyderabad was annexed to the British territory called the Madras Presidency. The Nizams of Hyderabad cultivated the learning of Persian and Urdu and promoted Islam. As a result, some of the cities of Hyderabad were populated by large numbers of Persian and Urdu-speaking Muslims. When the British left India, the Nizam tried to establish an independent kingdom or nation-state. As the majority of the population of Hyderabad were Telugu-, Maratha-, or Kannada-speaking Hindus, the government of India wanted Hyderabad to be merged with India, and the Indian army was sent to subdue the Nizam's army for its merger with India.

There is evidence of Telugu literary orientation, beginning in the 11th century C.E. However, Telugu literary style was heavily influenced by Sanskritic literature and scriptures; it is likely that the Telugu literati were mostly Sanskritized Brahmins;Telugu translations of the epics *Mahabharatha* and *Ramayana* as well as the Telugu devotional literature show the influence of Sanskritic forms. The Telugu Empire of the period from the 14th to the 16th centuries initiated a Telugu renaissance with both Brahmin and non-Brahmin writers but was stifled by later Muslim invasions. However, the classical, southern Indian musical forms known as Carnatic music derived impetus from the writings and performances of Telugu artists, and this musical tradition was often linked with the classical southern Indian dance forms known as *Bharata Natyam* which were cultivated in the Tamil country adjoining the Telugu territory.

vii. The Linguistic States of Tamil Nadu and Kerala: The Land of Tamil and Malayali Speakers

The southern tip or the deep south of India has been the land of Tamil-speakers for at least three thousand years. Although the myths and legends of the Tamils suggest that they are the autochthonous peoples of the south and that in prehistoric times they lived in a much bigger land area in southern India (which they believe to have submerged under the sea), it is very likely that the memory of the submergence of land refers to the floodings and sea erosions on the coastline of what is identified as Gujarat and Sindh (in Pakistan) during the last decades of the Indus Valley Civilization (1700–1600 B.C.E.). Volcanic eruptions on or near the Thira island (known as Santori island at an earlier time) in the Aegean Sea around 1700 B.C.E. caused major climatic changes as far as China, and it is reasonable to speculate that the decline of the Indus Valley Civilization was associated with such climatic changes. Some Dravidian-speaking people might have moved southeast of the Indus Valley into the interior of India and other Dravidian-speaking people might have used the coastline of western India and settled down in the area identified as Konkan Coast of Maharashtra state. Still other Dravidian speakers probably went farther south on the western coast and settled in the territory identified as the Malabar Coast of Kerala state and gradually moved to the eastern seaboard of south India and the northeastern coast of Ceylon (Sri Lanka). This last group of Dravidian speakers were probably the ancestors of the Tamils. From literary and religious records, we can state with certainty that by the 5th century B.C.E. there were Tamil kingdoms on the western and eastern regions of the southern tip of India. In the next chapter I describe and discuss the characteristics of these Tamil kingdoms.

The emergence of Malayalam as a distinctive language, separating from Tamil, began in the 15th century C.E., that is, after almost two thousand years of a common Tamil literary foundation or heritage which was not directly linked with the Sanskritic literary and religious heritage of northern India. Beginning in the 15th century, the literary compositions of the western region of southern India began to incorporate Sanskritic vocabulary and styles, and eventually by the 17th century a Malayalam literary tradition emerged in southwestern India which was quite different from the Tamil literary tradition of southeastern India. Although the literary separation of Malayalam from Tamil began only in the 15th century, the sociopolitical separation of southwestern India (Kerala) and southeastern India (Tamil Nadu) probably began in the 10th century.

There were several factors that contributed to the emergence of Malayalam as a separate language. The primary reason was that the Brahmin castes of southwestern India known as Nambutri (sometimes spelled Namboodri) Brahmins became a landowning community with a distinctive type of symbiotic relationship with the warrior (Kshatriya or sata-Shudra) castes of southwestern India. The warrior castes, known collectively as Nayars (or Nairs), focused on training all the males in martial arts and had an elaborate matrilineal and quasi-matriarchal system that provided sexual freedom for the women to take paramours from the Nambutri caste members. Nambutri males were frequently bachelors because of the Nambutri patrilineal custom of only the oldest male establishing a family household and inheriting all the property, a practice that facilitated the maintenance of large landholding by a few Nambutri households.

It is not certain when this custom became established in southwestern India, but it probably began after the 7th century C.E. After the 7th century, literary compositions in southwestern India were primarily the works of Brahmins. As opposed to the literary and religious compositions of the southeastern regions which were undertaken by both Brahmin and non-Brahmin castes, non-Brahmin participation in the literary output in the southwest was limited. The reason was that Nayars involved themselves mostly in martial arts and there were no other high-ranking non-Brahmin castes in the southwest.

As Brahmins in general, and the Brahmanical priesthood in particular, cultivated Sanskritic learning and rituals, the influence of the Sanskritic tradition became very pronounced in the southwest. The Tamil of the southwestern region was so infused with Sanskrit that the Tamil script was modified to express Sanskritic phonemes, and the spoken Tamil in the southwest became nasal and acquired a large percentage of Sanskrit vocabulary.

The secondary factors that contributed to the emergence of southwestern Tamil and southeastern Tamil were those related to the immigration and settlement of various west Asian peoples in southwestern India and the emergence of small Hindu chiefdoms. The coastline of southwestern India, known as the Malabar Coast, had trade connections with ancient Greeks and Romans and had continuous trade links with Arabs and Persians; Christianity was introduced in the southwest before the 7th century C.E. and a large Syrian Christian community with religious affiliation with the Syriac Episcopiates thrived in the southwest, functioning as a warrior caste comparable to that of the Nayars. After the 7th century C.E., Muslim Arabs settled down in the southwest, and their descendants, known as Moplahs or Mappilas, acquired a caste status comparable to that of Hindu and Christian merchants who were involved in international trade. (I discussed in Chapter 4 the role of Moplahs and Syrian Christians in the development of west Asian ethnic identities in southwestern India.)

Due to the extensive use of the Malabar Coast for international trade, various wealthy warrior caste (Nayar) families emerged, and some of these families began to provide protection for the traders. The most successful of these Nayar families took titles of royalty such as Perumal, Varma, and Raja, and there were many royal households with territorial and ceremonial rights. There were cultural and dialectical variations that affirmed the distinctiveness and the boundaries of the different royal houses. At the time when the West (Portuguese, followed by the Dutch and English) began to challenge the Arab hegemony of the Arabian Sea and to establish bases on the Malabar Coast in the 16th century, there were three major royal houses: The northern part of the Malabar Coast had a household whose head was known as the Zamorin or king of the sea (derived from the Tamil word *samudram* for sea) and he was based in the port city of Calicut (Kozhikode); south of Calicut were the Cochin and Quilon (Kollam) ports that were under Nayar Rajas. There were a few other minor ports under the control of Nayar royal houses as well. In the 17th century a powerful Nayar kingdom called Travancore emerged south of Cochin. Although for brief periods the Portuguese and Dutch controlled some of the Malabar ports, eventually, by the end of the 18th century, the British established political authority over the entire area. Cochin and Travancore became princely states under the British, and the territory of the Zamorin was annexed to the Madras Presidency and ruled directly by the British.

The two major Tamil dynastic kingdoms of the southeast were known as Pandyas and Cholas. The Pandyas were the primary patrons of Tamil learning and scholarship although the Cholas (and the Cheras of the southwest) were also promoters of the Tamil literary tradition. There were Brahmin and non-Brahmin scholars, as well as Jain, Buddhist, Muslim, and Christian scholars, who contributed to the enrichment of the Tamil literary tradition. Early Tamil literature of the period 5th century B.C.E. to 9th century C.E. produced secular and religious treatises, epics, and poetry, and the influence of Sanskrit on the literature of this period was minimal. After the 9th century C.E. the influence of Sanskrit was greater, and the participation of Brahmins in Tamil learning became important. Nevertheless, the contributions of the non-Brahmin saints of the Shaivite and Vaishnavite sectarian traditions of the post-9th-century period produced one of the most sophisticated renditions of devotional worship in the framework of "love for and grace of divine being."

As I present a detailed discussion of the Tamil political and literary traditions in the next chapter, it is unnecessary to discuss the characteristics of the Tamil linguistic state here. Suffice it to say here that the British established political authority in most of the Tamil territory by the end of the 18th century, and it, along with other areas (some with Malayalam, Kannada, and Telugu speakers), became the British-administered Madras Presidency.

The boundary reorganization of the states of India in 1956 resulted in the creation of the linguistic states of Kerala and Tamil Nadu. The Western Ghats, or the southern mountain range which divides peninsular India into the western rainforest and eastern semidesert (because most of the monsoon rainfall is on the west), form the general boundary that separates Kerala and Tamil Nadu. Kerala has many mountain estates and plantations where a variety of food and cash crops grow. Tamil Nadu is predominantly a rice-growing region with river and deep-well irrigation. Despite the common cultural, linguistic, and literary origins of Kerala and Tamil traditions, they have become very different from each other in contemporary cultural orientations. Thus, it is inconceivable that they would be united or merged to form a single nation-state. But because, economically, it is very advantageous for Kerala and Tamil Nadu to have a common irrigation board, a common transport system, and a common trade system, there is a possibility that they could function as a federal unit called United States of Kerala and Tamil Nadu if and when the division of India occurs with the formation of separate nation-states or republics.

In this chapter I have offered interpretations of different linguistic states and national traditions of India, focusing on certain distinctive aspects of these territories in order to reveal the linguistic-religious-cultural patterns that make them different and distinctive. Although they share a common Hindu and social heritage (caste), their histories and contemporary orientations have given them separate national traditions. There is every indication that these traditions are in the process of cultivating their languages into viable mediums of discourse in all domains of arts and sciences. However, the imposition of Hindi as the official language and the patronizing attitudes of Hindi speakers toward the non-Hindi speakers have had negative consequences for both the Hindi and non-Hindi speakers. India's potential can be realized only when each of the nationalities has an equal role in channeling its intellectual and emotional energies.

In the next chapter I present a discussion of a southern Indian national tradition and state in detail. And in Chapter 10, I present an in-depth discussion of a northern Indian national tradition state. The southern Indian tradition is rooted in *linguistic nationalism* and the northern Indian tradition is founded upon *religious nationalism*. These two chapters will show why we should have an in-depth understanding of the histories of the linguistic states in order to reveal the symbols and aspirations of the people. An in-depth understanding of the states and the national traditions will also reveal the structure of the dialectics of ethnicity and history that create and maintain the cultural/national boundaries.

LINGUISTIC NATIONALISM AND THE QUEST FOR DRAVIDASTAN (THE LAND OF DRAVIDIAN SPEAKERS): THE TAMILS

i. National Autonomy and the Quest for Statehood

In contemporary India many linguistic states seek national political autonomy, and if a referendum were to be taken on this question, it is likely that all the linguistic states, with the possible exception of the six Hindi states (Hindistan), would opt to establish separate or independent, autonomous nation-states. The six Hindi states would probably assert that the territorial unity of India is sacred because it is to their advantage to keep the non-Hindi states within the political framework of the Indian empire-state: Keeping the non-Hindi-speaking states in India provides enormous economic and political advantages for the six Hindi states.

In Chapter 7, I pointed out that the departure of the British resulted in the substitution of Hindi Raj for British Crown Raj, and that the political status of India as a colonial empire-state did not change because the political aspirations of the non-Hindi speakers, as well as those of Christians, Sikhs, and Muslims, were never given an opportunity in the ballot box to determine their future. Political discourse on national-political autonomy of the linguistic states was banned as an act of treason. Parallel political developments occurred in various regions of the world where European nation-states established colonial empire-states. When the European powers established their colonies in Asia and Africa, political boundaries were created without any regard or concern for the diverse ethnic groups who were either included or not included within the colonial boundaries. Colonial empire-states such as India, Indonesia, Nigeria, and Kenya were created, and when the Europeans left, the colonies they created were transferred to the numerically or economically dominant ethnic groups. This resulted in violent conflicts within the colonial empire-states, and the boundaries that were created by the European powers became immutable and sacred for the numerically or economically dominant groups because it was economically advantageous for the dominant groups to keep the other ethnic groups as subservient partners. Military force has been the primary mechanism or vehicle in the maintenance of these post-colonial empire-states. In India, the Kashmiri Muslims, the Tibeto-Burman Christians of northeastern India, the Panjabi-speaking Sikhs, the Tamils, and the Telugus have sought national autonomy in different ways, and the use of Indian military force has muted their claims with tragic consequences in human lives.

Ethnic aspirations for nation-statehood or national political autonomy have been frequently explained or interpreted as *separatism* or *irrational communalism* by the empire-states as well as by many scholars. But it is important to recognize that the words separatism and irrational communalism have meaning only within the perspective of what is defined as a whole or rational. Thus when a country's boundaries denote the wholeness of the country, any claim of a group or segment of the country to establish a new country would be called separatism, and one group's political rationality would often be identified as irrational by another group unless both groups share common political commitments or goals. When we attempt to understand the various linguistic nations or states in India, we should examine how they relate to or not relate to their being a part or segment of the Indian whole. Different linguistic states or nations may have different reasons for being linked with the Indian whole. The linking of Kashmir with India was not expected, but once the link was established it became the sacred duty of India not to permit the Kashmiri nation to become a separate nation-state. The Telugu nation had voiced concern over Hindi, Maratha, and Bengali dominance and wished to have its own national state boundary, but it never materialized. Panjabi-speaking Sikhs have sought to establish a separate nation-state (for Sikhs) on the basis of their religious faith and have had ongoing violent conflicts with the non-Hindus and the military. The Tibeto-Burman- and Austro-Asiatic-speaking nations in northeastern India have very little in common with the rest of India culturally or religiously, and they would be delighted to have their own countries, but the Indian military has overwhelming power to prevent the secession of the Tibeto-Burman- or Austro-Asiatic-speaking states. One of the states, Nagaland, came close to achieving autonomy but was crushed into submission by the Indian military.

Of all the linguistic states of India, the state of Tamil Nadu in southeastern India has shown the continuity and persistence of nationalist aspirations for political autonomy. The Tamils have used the Tamil language for well over two thousand years to seek and maintain political-territorial integrity although they came under the political domination of various non-Tamil kings and governors during that period. I present in the following pages an interpretation of the two-thousand-year-old quest for Tamil national political autonomy and offer an analysis of Tamil symbols that have been used by the Tamil to foster and maintain the Tamil ethnic identity.

ii. Dravidian Speakers of India and the Linguistic-Cultural Distinctiveness of the Tamils of India

There is scholarly consensus that the language spoken in the Indus Valley Civilization (of the period 3000 B.C.E.–1500 B.C.E.) was Dravidian. There is controversy, however, about the relationship between Dravidian and other language families. The widely accepted view is that Dravidian was a branch of proto-Elamo-Dravidian that had a large distribution in west Asia, with later branches of Elamite (spoken in eastern Iran) and Dravidian (spoken in the Indus Valley); some scholars have found evidence to place Dravidian in the Altaic linguistic family. There are small and large groups of Dravidian speakers all over India (including central and northern India) and Baluchistan (now part of Pakistan but once part of Persian empires at different periods until Mughal political dominance). But only in peninsular (southern) India did Dravidian languages establish political and linguistic dominance. It is reasonable to infer that the ancestors of the Dravidian speakers who established the Dravidian kingdoms in southern India came from the Indus Valley Civilization. However, it is very important to note that "full-fledged mesolithic-type" cultures existed in southern India at about 4000 B.C.E., and that there is no evidence to suggest that these early inhabitants of southern India were not Dravidian speakers (see Fairservis, Jr. 1975:87). In all likelihood, Dravidian speakers and Austro-Asiatic speakers coexisted in central, northeastern, and southern India, and the movement of Dravidian speakers from the Indus Valley into southern India after 1500 B.C.E. provided the impetus for cultural elaborations, the rise of urban centers, and the emergence of literary traditions.

Maloney's (1986) interpretation of the cultural origins of the Dravidian speakers in southern India, that they migrated into southern India from the Indus Valley, appears to be accurate, but further research is needed to settle the relationship between the populations that existed in southern India and the populations that migrated into southern India after 1500 B.C.E. following the decline of the Indus Valley Civilization. There is no evidence to preclude the possibility that the populations in southern India had trade contacts with the populations of Indus Valley Civilization by sea, and it is highly probable that this contact facilitated and enabled the movement of the Dravidian-speaking populations from the Indus Valley into southern India where they merged with the preexisting Dravidian-speaking and Austro-Asiatic-speaking populations of southern India.

Maloney notes:

Dravidian-speakers spread into South India and Sri Lanka from western India. It may be deduced almost certainly that Dravidian speech was current in Pakistan at the time of the Indus Civilization (2300–1700 BC), and it highly influenced the evolution of Sanskrit and other Indo-Aryan languages, causing divergence of that language group from the other Indo-European languages. Dravidian-speaking peoples moved from Gujarat southwestward through Maharashtra in the wake of the expansion of Indo-Aryan speaking states of the North Indian plains from about 1000 BC. Then they overran all South India in the Iron Age, with their horses, iron weapons, state systems, and settled village life. They left megalithic monuments to the dead all over the peninsula.

The main Dravidian languages could have diffused over such wide areas as each now occupies only with the establishment of state systems, which were in place before the 4th Century BC. Tamil, Malayalam, and Kannada are more closely related to each other than to Telugu, which must have spread over its huge area in a separate wave. It is not known who the pre-Dravidian people of South India were, as there is no relic language, and they have been absorbed in the Dravidian peasant society or as tribals who have picked up Dravidian speech. But in Sri Lanka, the Veddas persisted into this century as a relic of pre-Dravidian hunting society.

Tamil literature of the Sangam period, 1st through 3rd Centuries AD, comprises a small shelf-full of books. It has very little Sanskrit infusion and the style is not Indo-Aryan. For example, the rhyme in poetry is on the first syllables of the line, not the last syllables. With stronger Brahmanical influence in medieval times, many Sanskrit words were borrowed by Tamil, so that in a Tamil dictionary today about half of the words are from Sanskrit, but the percentage of Sanskrit-based words commonly used is far lower. Malayalam borrowed so heavily from Sanskrit in medieval centuries that it became recognized as a language separate from Tamil. Telugu and Kannada also have more infusions of Sanskrit, while other Dravidian languages have heavy infusions from Hindi and Marathi.

There were three Tamil kingdoms at the time of the Sangam literature: the Pandiyas ruling from Madurai in southern Tamil Nadu, the Colas ruling from Tanjavur, and the Ceras ruling in Kerala. These persisted throughout most of history, though in medieval centuries there were other dynasties such as the Pallavas on the Madras side and the Kongus around Coimbatore. The three classical kingdoms were established by the Mauyan period and are referred to in King Asoka's inscriptions. The Pandiyas, at least, existed even earlier, from the 4th and possibly the 5th Century BC.

The Sangam was a literary academy enlisting about 490 authors of the period. There are persistent legends that the Samgam whose literature we have today was the 3rd Sangam, and that the two earlier such academies were in two earlier Pandiyan capitals on the coast opposite Sri Lanka. The literature refers often to cities with high buildings, merchants, and sea trade, including some with the Roman Empire. The body of Sangam literature is essentially secular, extremely concise in style, and distinguishes themes of the "inner" life, such as love, from themes of the "outer" life, such as war.

—Maloney (1986:2-3)

The fact that the Tamils had a literate civilization in the first millennium B.C.E. is a cultural premise of great importance. From a Western scholarly perspective, some of the claims to literary antiquity might appear fanciful, but as the Western scholar Schiffman (1973:127) observes: "The study of language issue in Tamil Nad should begin in approximately 1,000 B.C. or even earlier, for one of the cornerstones of this problem is the argument of the antiquity of Tamil culture."

For further discussion on the linguistic, cultural origin of the Tamils, see Arokiaswami (1956), Arunachalam (1974), Beck (1972), Chatterji (1965), Egnor (1978), Hart (1973, 1975a, 1975b, 1976), Kanakasabhai (1966), Krishnamurthi (1966), Meile (1965), Nadarajah (1966), Nayagam (1973), Pandarathar (1967), Paramasivanandam (1960), Pillay (1969), Sastri (1967), Schiffman (1973), Shulman (1980), Singaravelu (1966), Stein (1977), and Subramaniam (1966).

iii. Ancient Tamil Kingdoms and Tamil Polity

During the Tamil classical period (5th century B.C.E. to 3rd century C.E.) the Tamil country had three major kingdoms: Pandya Nadu (the country of the Pandyan dynasty) in the southern tip of India, Chola Nadu (the country of the Chola dynasty) in the southeast, and Chera Nadu (the country of the Chera dynasty) in the southwest. Each of these kingdoms had several vassal kings (*kurunilamannargal*) and chieftains (*nattukon*). After the 3rd century C.E. the kingdoms declined and large areas of the Tamil country, with the exception of a small region of the Pandya kingdom, came under the political domination of non-Tamil kings, but from about the 9th to the 13th century the Chola kingdom became a powerful empire in southern and eastern India with a superior navy that had bases in several ports of southeastern Asia and Ceylon. The Pandya kingdom reasserted its hegemony briefly at different periods from the 13th to the 18th centuries. After the 15th century Tamil political autonomy in large areas of the Tamil country was lost to the Telugu, Muslim, and Maratha rulers of the central and eastern regions of India, and finally to the British, who by the end of the 18th century had established direct political control over most of the Tamil territory with the exception of the southern tip of the Tamil territory, which became a part of the princely kingdom of Travancore. (This region of the Tamil territory is known today as Kanyakumari district, or *Nanchil Nadu.*)

In ancient times, the Tamil concept of *nadu* (country) was used to identify different regions of the Tamil speakers. Village settlements (called *oor* or *gramam*) were grouped within regions that were controlled by chieftains from hereditary aristocratic families (identified often as petty kings or *kurunila mannargal*). The political significance of nadu varied from time to time during the past 2000 years, largely due to the introduction of non-Tamil principles of governance. For example, the Telugu kings who established supremacy over the Tamil country by the 15th century governed through retainers and local military chieftains called *palayakaras* (see Paramasivanandam 1960:125). Also, as Stein (1977:16) notes, the settlements of Brahmin literati which were established in the nadus "profoundly altered certain aspects" in the conceptualization of nadu.

A brief discussion of the British land system is necessary to show how the Tamil country is conceptualized and governed today. The British did not unify the Tamil regions into a single political entity. Several Tamil regions were included in a large territorial unit called the Madras Presidency composed of Malayalam, Kannada, and Telugu-speaking regions of the modern-day Kerala, Karanataka, and Andhra states. As indicated earlier, the concept of nadu underwent major changes after the 15th century, particularly after the 18th century when the British developed a uniform method of collecting revenue. The British retained the institution of *mirasidars* (landlords), which had been introduced earlier by the Muslim kings, but they appointed Englishmen to collect revenue from the mirasidars. The collector was also empowered to deal directly with the cultivators, and this method of direct taxation was called the *ryotwari* system. The method of taxing the landlord instead of the cultivator was called the *zamindari* system (see *The Imperial Gazetteer of India*, Vol. IV, 1907, particularly p. 207). The British also recognized the institution of *inam* or gifted property that the Muslim kings introduced during their rule. Thus there were three kinds of villages under the British. The zamindari village was leased by the government to a *zamindar* or landlord; the land was heritable but not transferable. In the ryotwari village, land was owned and was transferable by individual *ryots* or cultivators. The inam village was a trust that was exempt from taxation; it could not be sold or transferred.

The British territory was divided into districts, headed by the revenue collector who had judicial and executive powers. The district was divided into *taluks*, headed by native officials known as *tahsildars*. Villages were grouped into revenue villages on the basis of population and revenue. The head of the revenue village was the *munisiff* whose powers were similar to those of the collector of the district but were confined to the village level. The post of munisiff was hereditary, as it came into being during the Muslim rule. The village munisiff was generally a wealthy man who was already recognized as headman of the village. A clerk assisted him in collecting revenue, and two or three runners (*talayari* and *vettian*) helped him police the area. The power of the revenue collector was greatly reduced when separate judicial and executive authorities were established. After the departure of the British in 1947, the zamindari system was abolished, but in almost all other aspects the British pattern exists today.

In 1956, the government of India reorganized the territories on the basis of language, and the linguistic state of Tamil Nadu, initially called *Madras State*, came into being.

iv. Ancient Tamil Social Organization and Religion

Ancient Tamils referred to the Tamil regions or territories collectively as *Tamilakam* (the home of the Tamils). The social organization, religion, and values of Tamilakam (as conceived by the ancient Tamils) are known to us mainly through several classical anthologies of poems and lyrics and an ancient treatise on Tamil grammar called *Tholkappiam*, and through *Thirukkural*, a book of aphorisms and morals, all of which were probably written between the 3rd century B.C.E. and the 3rd century C.E. We also learn about the ancient Tamils through the well-known Tamil epics, *Silapathikaram* and *Manimaekalai*, which were probably written between the 3rd and 5th centuries C.E. (The dates are disputed. Some scholars assign *Thirukkural* to the 4th century and the epics to the 7th century, whereas others assign all the classical literature to the period between the 3rd century B.C.E. and the 3rd century C.E.)

The ancient Tamils believed that Tamilakam had five ecocultural zones (*Ain-thinai*) in which there were five distinctive cultural adaptations. The Tamil term *thinai* represented both land area and morality; from this it may be inferred that the ancient Tamils probably had a theory that cultural variations were associated with specific ecological adaptations. The people living in the mountain ecological zone (*kurinchi*) were identified as hunters (*kuravar*); the people of the forest (*mullai*) as herdsmen (*ayar*); and those of the fertile plains (*marutam*) as cultivators (*vellalan*). The people on the coast (*neithal*) are described as seafarers and divers (*paravar* and *mukkuvar*), and in the desert (*palai*) as warriors (*maravar*). In large urban settlements, such as administrative and commercial centers, there were classes of people known as nobles (*arasa parambarai*), literati (*anthanar* or *chantor*), merchants (*vanikar*), and messengers (*paravar*). Also, as Tyler (1973:106) points out, the ancient Tamil literature recognizes the existence of aristocrats and untouchables. Thus, it is certain that notions of purity and pollution were prevalent from ancient times and that the caste system existed in ancient times.

People in each of the several ecological zones worshipped a special deity: In the coastal zone, the god of the sea (*Vannan*); in the fertile plains, the god of the sun (*Vaenthan*); in the desert, the goddess of war (*Kottavai*); in the mountains, the god of hills (*Chaeyon*), and in the forests, the god of cattle (*Mayon*). Worship of mother goddesses and of the god Muruga was popular among the Tamil at all periods. Pillay (1969:494) observes that "Muruga has been doubtless the pre-eminent God of the Tamils through the ages." Mother goddess (*amman*) worship constituted the single most important form of religious expression of the Tamil masses from ancient times, and such worship is most popular among the Tamils today, particularly among the villagers. Saivism, or worship of the god Siva, has had princely patronage from ancient times, and Tamil saints and poets elaborated a doctrine of Siva worship called *Saiva Sidhanth* (Siva and true end, or knowledge of Siva). Worship of the god Vishnu was also popular in Tamil society, and a Brahmin saint, Ramanuja, who lived in the 11th century, elaborated upon the foundations of Vishnu worship. *Bhakthi*, or devotional worship of particular deities, became very important in the Tamil country from about the 9th century C.E. There have been numerous, highly valued lyrics written by *Alvar* and *Nayanmars*, saints who were dedicated to the propagation of Vishnu or Shiva worship.

Between the 3rd century and the 9th century C.E., a period often referred to by Tamil historians as the "dark age" of the Tamils, very little Tamil literature of the earlier naturalistic kind was produced, but many ethical and religious poems that show Jain and Buddhist influence were written. Much of Tamil territory was under non-Tamil kings (*Pallavas*) during that period. From the 9th century onwards, Tamil writings consisted of lengthy attacks or apologia of Jainism, Buddhism, Saivism, and Vaishnavism. The authors seldom referred to social conditions, although some decried the existence of jati (caste) and religious conflicts. Disputes over caste groups' privileges and prerogatives were common, and upward social mobility of members of a caste group or of an entire caste group was also prevalent. Ramauja, the social reformer of the 11th century who founded a Vaishnavite religious sect, is thought to have helped many members of non-Brahmin caste groups become part of a Brahmin caste group. Referring to this aspect of Tamil society, Stein (1968:78) states that "Medieval Indian history appears to present widespread persistent examples of social mobility. It is known that members of lower rank ethnic units assumed roles and statuses which are usually reserved for higher units and with the consent of such higher groups."

v. Brahmanical Priesthood and State Temples in the Tamil Territory

The most common social anthropological fallacy in the study of the religious systems of India is to make a spurious distinction between Brahmanical and non-Brahmanical Hinduism, and to suggest by implication that the former has an all-India distribution with Brahmanical deities, and that the latter belongs to non-literate regional traditions with regional or village deities who are propitiated by non-Brahmins. I think that a more valid distinction would be to identify the temples sponsored by kings, merchants, and the wealthy, in general, with large land endowments as *state* temples as opposed to the smaller temples in the village communities that are *communal* temples. The Brahmanical priesthood had the patronage of the Hindu kings who ruled the Tamil territory, and several Hindu temples with Sanskrit-educated Brahmins as officiating priests sprang up in the Tamil territory. The kings often commissioned Sanskrit-educated Brahmin priests to officiate over the rituals in these temples, and several of these religious practitioners were given entire villages as gifts.

Large Hindu temples were usually built by rich merchants or kings who endowed the temples with property, and the maintenance of the temples was entrusted to those families claiming descent from the founders. Maintenance involved collecting funds from the endowed property and providing for the temples' upkeep and the salaries of religious practitioners and other servants of the temple. The custodians of the temples, called *Dharmakarthas* (upholders of the moral order), are known today as trustees. The temple custodians often used the collected funds for their own personal needs rather than for temple upkeep. This caused a number of disputes, with claims and counterclaims over custodianship. Custodians often claimed to be the owners of land which had been attached to temple. In the 19th century the British (who by this time had established political hegemony throughout India, including the Tamil territory) instituted a semiautonomous body called the Hindu Religious Endowment Board that looked into matters of fraud and into the finances of temples with endowed property. The board took many rich temples under its jurisdiction, replacing the hereditary trustees. The powers and jurisdiction of this board grew over the past 100 years, and today there is a cabinet minister whose special duties are supervision of this board (see Derrett 1966; Presler 1978; Mudaliar 1965, 1974). In recent times, legislative acts have been enacted to substitute Tamil for Sanskrit invocations (*archanai*) in the temples and to appoint non-Brahmin priests.

Historically, communal temples have been associated with the worship of amman (mother goddess) and the god Muruga. As mentioned earlier, the Tamils have viewed amman and Muruga worship as distinctive aspects of Tamil civilization. I discuss the various aspects of amman worship as it occurs in a Tamil village in Chapter 15.

vi. The Symbol of Chenthamil, or Pure Tamil

As noted earlier, the whole or parts of Tamil territory came under the political and religious domination of non-Tamils at different times for long periods during the past 2000 years, but the Tamil literary tradition served and continues to serve as the custodian of Tamil ethnicity through the conception of the Tamil language as the core symbol of Tamil ethnic identity. From ancient times to the present, the Tamils have made a fundamental distinction between standard, chaste, or pure Tamil language (*Chenthamil, Suthathamil*) and the colloquial, impure Tamil (*Kodunthamil*). To those who believe in such a distinction, pure Tamil has remained unchanged from its original ancient form in classical literature and is considered to be a bounded, closed system in terms of its archaic idiom, structure, and vocabulary. Colloquial Tamil, in contrast, is viewed as open and responsive to changing existential conditions, functioning as the primary medium of verbal communication among the masses. To the Tamils, pure Tamil language symbolizes Tamil ethnic identity.

In linguistics, the coexistence of two varieties of the same language, with one having a continuous link with the past and the other responsive to change, is called diglossia. According to Lehmann (1972:242), "When an elevated form of language exists side by side with the spoken language and is reserved for special uses, the situation is referred to as diglossia." The examples of diglossia most often cited are Latin and Sanskrit. Tamil, however, differs from these languages in one important respect. Whereas Latin and Sanskrit have become specialized to be used for only particular religious/ritual goals, pure Tamil has not been confined to a particular religious/ritual use. The distinction between pure and impure Tamil is made by nearly all Tamil speakers. The Tamils regard literary Tamil as pure Tamil and believe that through education they can participate in its use. Schiffman (1973:129) states that the native hypothesis of immutability in Tamil culture reflects the "phenomenon of diglossia in Tamil." The literary language, he says, is morphologically and phonologically rooted in the past, and the spoken language in the present. He notes that no other language in India has such a dichotomy and goes on to observe, "We have then, an attitude about language that is manifested in reverence for the ancient stages of the language and attempts to keep that stage pure from non Tamil and non ancient sources" (1973:132).

Spoken Tamil is itself dichotomized, with one version following the pure, standard tradition and the other being highly varied with regional and group dialects. In such a context, we can use the term diglossia to distinguish between two kinds of spoken Tamil, namely, pure standard Tamil and impure colloquial Tamil rather than between literary and spoken Tamil. One version of written and spoken Tamil is common to all educated Tamils and is used in certain contexts such as in writing and speeches, and the other is the medium of everyday verbal communication and is differentiated into dialects peculiar to different regions and groups. *In the conceptual framework of the Tamils, being educated in pure Tamil links a person to the past, to the primordial ooze of Tamil beginnings.* Standard pure Tamil (Chenthamil or Suthathamil) has continued to serve as a vehicle for the codification of what is proper in both language and culture, and in this sense serves as a sacred symbol of authority for the conception of justice, ethics, and boundedness at different levels of cultural experience. The symbol of pure Tamil represents what is believed to be the unchanging morality of the Tamils and links the past and the present, relating the purity/spirituality/immutability of the Tamil language with the purity/spirituality/immutability of Tamil womanhood.

vii. Tamil Poets and Tamil Literary Academies

The emergence of pure Tamil as a symbol of Tamil cultural boundary may be traced to classical Tamil literature, particularly to the contributions of the Tamil poets (*pulavan*), many of whom were women. From ancient times, the Tamil poet has been viewed by the Tamils as a kind of culture hero, a mythical, exemplary model who embodies the essence of Tamil values. Hundreds of poets have been canonized, including a number of Western scholars who became Tamil poets or commentators. Any discussion of Tamil civilization in general and of Tamil ethnic identity in particular must take into account how the ancient literary tradition is conceptualized by the Tamils. The antiquity of this tradition, according to the Tamils, goes back to a thousand or more years before the Christian era. The difficulty of assigning dates to the classical works is due to disagreements as to when Sanskritic literary and religious ideas began to influence the Tamil literary tradition; it is equally difficult to assess the extent of such influence. It is important to the Tamils that their classical literature be accepted as autochthonous, free from any alien influence, but at the same time they recognize the fact that many of the early poets were influenced by Sanskritic idioms and by Jain and Buddhist ideas. It is likely that some of the ancient Tamil poets (between the 3rd century B.C.E. and the 3rd century C.E.) were either Buddhist or Jain converts. Historians have recorded the prevalence of conflicts between Hindus and Buddhist/Jain monks between the 3rd and 9th centuries C.E. With the political ascendancy of the Chola empire in the 9th century, Hinduism was rejuvenated, and Buddhist/Jain ideas were discussed. The classical literature is seen by many Tamil scholars as only the most recent addition of a thousand-year-long literary output in the Tamil country. According to them, Tamil literary tradition began long before the emergence of Jainism and Buddhism and before Sanskritic orientations were introduced in Tamil civilization. Although the dates will have to be settled by future scholarship, there is evidence that the Tamil ethnocentric perspective on the antiquity of Tamil classical literary tradition is not totally unfounded.

The rejuvenation of Hinduism in the Tamil regions from the 9th century C.E. generated new ideas about the antiquity of Hinduism and the Tamil literary tradition. It was held that there were three academies (*sangham*) of Hindu poets under the patronage of the Pandya kings and Hindu deities: These academies were identified as the first academy (*muthal-sangham*), the middle academy (*idai-sangham*), and the final sangham (*kadai-sangham*). In this interpretation, the first academy lasted 4440 years and had 549 residential poet panelists or judges and 4449 peripatetic poets; the middle academy lasted for 3700 years and had 59 judges and 3700 other poets; and the final academy lasted 1830 years and had 49 residential poet judges and 499 poets.

A myth of the ancient homeland of the Tamil developed probably after the 9th century C.E. According to this myth, a large area of land south of Cape Comorin (which is the present southern tip of India and the Tamil country) was occupied by the Tamils; the first two Tamil academies were believed to exist there. The last or third academy was thought to be stationed in the city of Madurai, which became the capital of the Tamil Pandya kingdom after the catastrophic submerging of the land mass that was the original homeland of the Tamils. Historical evidence suggests that the capital of the Pandya kingdom had to be moved from the coastal area because of flooding by tidal waves to the interior where the city of Madurai is located (Sinnatamby 1973; Maloney 1975:13). The legend of the three academies was probably based on this fact and upon the Buddhist concept of sangham, meaning congregation of worshippers. As the Tamils have always had a community and culture of poets associated with religiosity, individual poets made reference to the sangham as a symbol of their antiquity. Many Tamil poets were elevated to the status of saints. The literature began to function as Tamil hagiology for all practical purposes. The Tamil poet (*pulavan*) became a prototype for authority in the discussion of Tamil values.

viii. Naturalism and Supernaturalism in the Tamil Literary Tradition

Scholars agree that early Tamil literature did not use Sanskrit as a model and that a separate literary tradition came into being by the 4th century B.C. E. in the Tamil country. Hart (1976:320) believes that neither Tamil nor Sanskrit borrowed from each other directly, but both "derived their shared conventions, meters and techniques from a common source."

The existence of ancient Tamil literature became widely known in the 18th century. Until then, the early manuscripts (which were written on palm leaves and had to be copied every hundred years or so because of leaf decay) were in private, mostly religious, libraries. The existence of these manuscripts was known to Tamil literati, and in the 17th century Christian missionaries had access to some of the manuscripts. One of the manuscripts, *Thirukkural,* was printed in the 18th century. Many of the manuscripts had several versions as well as commentaries that were written by poet saints other than the original authors. A systematic study of the authenticity and the classification of the literature began in the 19th century. The dating of the manuscripts has long been a matter of controversy. It is believed that only a small portion of the classical literature survived, and that much of it was revised by commentators who promoted or attacked particular religious perspectives. However, with the existing epigraphic and internal linguistic evidence it can be said that the pre-18th-century literature belonged to two different periods of cultural experience in the Tamil country.

The literature of the first period (identified as the classical or sangham literature) is to a large extent world-affirming and naturalistic. Descriptions of music and dance, ethics and morality, grammatical rules and standards of pure Tamil, heroism and polity, domestic life and aspects of love, beauty of nature and ecology constitute the bulk of this literature. The ancient poets used the dyadic categories of *akam* (interior, love, etc.)/*puram* (exterior, war, etc.), and the triadic categories of *aram* (vireo)/*porul* (wealth)/*inbam* (happiness) and *iyal* (rhetoric)/*isai* (music)/*nadagam* (drama). Scholars have classified the ancient literature with these categories, but the modern classifications and interpretations should be accepted as tentative. The second period of Tamil literature can be identified as lasting for about fifteen hundred years, from the 3rd to the 18th century. The literature of this period includes treatises on Buddhism, Jainism, and philosophical Hinduism, as well as the prolific writings of the *Nayanmars* (devotees of god Siva and related symbols) and *Alvars* (devotees of god Vishnu and related symbols) who initiated the Bhakti tradition, and the Tamil renditions of the northern epics such as *Ramayana* and *Mahabharatha*.

ix. The Symbol of Karppu: The Tamil Theme of Female Chastity-Spirituality

From ancient times to the present, purity or chastity of women has been associated with sacredness or spirituality which in turn is linked with Tamil language and Tamil culture. Just as Tamil language must retain its purity or chastity to retain its sacredness or spirituality, Tamil women must retain their purity or chastity to retain their sacredness or spirituality.

Tamil literature stresses that a distinctive aspect of Tamil civilization is the worship of divinity as female. In ancient times a number of poets were women, and many women attained sainthood in the Bhakti (devotional worship) tradition of the Tamil country. Several recently published textbooks deal primarily with the chastity and other virtues of Tamil women of ancient times. Some of these publications are *Ilakia Matharkal* (Women of the Classic Epics), *Peria Purana Penmanikal* (Women of the Puranic Medieval Period),

Nadanda Nagayar (Women Political Chiefs), *Thavachelvi Manimaekalai* (the heroine of the epic, *Manimaekalai*), *Pengal Olukkam* (Morality of Women), *Thamil Valartha Makalir* (The Women who Fostered the Tamil Language), *Kannagi* (The Chastity Goddess, heroine of the Tamil epic, *Silapathikaram*), *Madavi* (a central woman character in two epics), and *Aram Valartha Mangaiyar* (Women who Fostered Virtue). Tyler (1973:100) states: "Associated with fertility and disease, the cult of the mother goddess represents one of the most ancient and persistent expressions of Indian religion. Since mother goddesses are practically nonexistent in the earlier Aryan religious works, it is certainly a cult of non-Aryan origin."

Egnor (1978) shows the existence in Tamil culture of the theme of inner self as female. Egnor (1978:174–75) found through interviews with a Tamil informant, Themozhiar, that there was a basic difference between Sanskritic and Tamil cultures in terms of their conceptualization of ultimate reality: "Sanskrit culture is male-dominated: the male is the locus of purity and the center of ritual. Tamil culture (as embodied in T.) is female-dominated: *the female is the locus of purity and the center of ritual.* In Sanskrit the self *purusa* is male and the body *prakrit* is female. In Tamil the self *uyir* is female and the body *al* is male. In Sanskrit power is hard (so semen is called a 'hard' substance and the teacher is *guru*, 'heavy'); in Tamil power is soft." [emphasis mine]

The Tamil word *karppu* means female chastity, fidelity, and faithfulness, but it evokes a number of associations that include supernatural power, sacrifice, suffering, penance, virtue, morality, justice, ethics, austerity, and asceticism. From the earliest times, karppu has been an important sacred symbol that has been used to conceptualize female spirituality and a variety of cultural experiences. (A distinction is often made between *ara-karppu*, meaning moral chastity, and *mara-karppu*, meaning brave and righteous chastity; the goddess Kannagi, discussed later, is associated with the latter.) There are a number of female images, the most important being that of Kannagi, the goddess of chastity, that represent the deified, divinized, or idealized karppu in association with important Tamil values.

Hart (1973:230–50) points out that the now widespread chastity/spirituality complex in India probably had its origin in Tamil civilization. From a comparative study of ancient Tamil and Vedic literature, Hart concludes that chastity was not a religious category for the early Aryans. He notes that the later Hindu scriptures refer to chastity due to their borrowing the concept from the south. In a later contribution, Hart (1976:321) documents the references to chastity and supernatural power in the ancient literature: *Ananku* (the Tamil concept of impersonal supernatural power) "was strongly present in a chaste wife; if she should fail to keep her chastity, then ananku would go out of control, bringing destruction to her husband and perhaps to others." From the Tamil perspective, karppu, in its ideal state, incorporates supernatural power and thus can protect everything that is considered by the Tamils to be important. Karppu can safeguard the Tamil family, Tamil country, Tamil culture, and Tamil language. As discussed later, the symbol of Tamilakam (home of the Tamils) serves as a vehicle for the conception of Tamil country. Karppu is evocative of the Tamil home with one's chaste mother, chaste wife, and chaste sister, all of whom protect the sanctity of the house. In the last section it was shown that Chenthamil represents chastity/purity/spirituality of the Tamil language; karppu, symbolized in imageries such as Kannagi, represents chastity/spirituality/home. Thus, the units of the symbols of Tamil home, pure Tamil, and chastity can combine to convey a similar meaning, or can individually convey each other's meaning in different contexts.

In this conceptualization, the purity/chastity of Tamil women protects the Tamil country and the Tamil language. The loss of purity/chastity of the language is analogous to the loss of purity/chastity of Tamil womanhood, and such a loss would result in the loss of sacredness or spirituality of the household, and ultimately the Tamil country. Karppu has been, in this sense, an important sacred symbol of boundary maintenance.

x. Kannagi: The Representation and Interpretation of Chastity in the Tamil Epic *Silapathikaram*

An early literary formulation of chastity through the image of a particular woman was presented in the Tamil epic of the classical period, *Silapathikaram*, believed to have been authored by Ilango Adigal, a Jain monk who was the brother of a Chera king. Adigal's narration of the various episodes in the life of the heroine, Kannagi, is presented as the documentation of actual events that happened in the three ancient kingdoms of the Tamil country. Tamil culture is described in great detail; every episode of Kannagi's life is positioned in the context of the author's elucidation of the Tamil notions of fate, love, omens, deities, monarchy, morality, and art forms.

The following is a brief outline of the story of Kannagi's apotheosis. Kannagi and her husband Kovalan were members of the merchant (*vanikar*) community who lived in the city of Puhar in the Chola kingdom. They were temporarily separated due to Kovalan's infatuation with a courtesan named Madavi. Kovalan severed his relationship with Madavi, suspecting her of infidelity, but by that time had lost all his wealth. After Kannagi's reunion with Kovalan, she offered her diamond-embedded golden ankle bracelets to be sold for business investments, and both husband and wife decided to proceed to the city of Madurai in the Pandya kingdom to begin a new life.

At the start of their journey they met a Jain lady ascetic named Kavunthi Adigal who accompanied them to Madurai. At the end of their journey they rested at the outskirts of Madurai, and on the recommendation of Kavunthi Adigal, Kannagi resided in the house of a woman named Mathari who was a member of the herder community. Taking one of Kannagi's ankle bracelets to the Bazaar, Kovalan encountered the chief goldsmith of the Pandya king. The goldsmith had recently stolen an ankle bracelet of the queen that resembled Kannagi's, and when Kovalan asked him to evaluate Kannagi's bracelet he decided to place blame for the theft on Kovalan. Asking Kovalan to wait in the goldsmith's house, the goldsmith went to the king and accused Kovalan. The king accepted his word and bade his soldier to recover the ankle bracelet and execute Kovalan. On hearing the news of Kovalan's execution, Kannagi, overcome with grief, ran to the palace of the king and sought an audience with him. The king defended his act by stating that he had rendered justice by killing a thief, but Kannagi proclaimed her husband's innocence by producing her ankle bracelet which contained diamonds. As the queen's ankle bracelet contained pearls, the king asked his soldier to compare bracelets. Kannagi dashed her bracelet to the floor and a diamond fell on the king's face. The king, unable to bear the idea that he had committed an injustice, dropped dead to the floor, and on seeing her husband die the queen also died. Outside the palace, Kannagi tore her breast, cursed the city where her husband had been wrongfully executed, and invoked the gods to burn it. Fire broke out in Madurai. From Madurai, Kannagi proceeded to the Chera kingdom. People of the hill region in the Chera kingdom saw her being transported to the skies in a chariot. The Chera king, told of this supernatural event, decided to dedicate a temple with Kannagi as the presiding deity. She was honored as the goddess of chastity in Vanchi, his capital city. The epic narrates how the Chera king had to fight and defeat the enemies of the Tamils when he marched with a large army to the Himalayas to procure a large stone to make the idol for Kannagi.

The author of the epic conceptualized the spirituality of chaste women and the ideals of Tamil justice with reference to the life and acts of Kannagi. The objective of the author was to characterize the distinctive customs and the unity of the Tamils. According to the epic, although the Tamils lived in three different kingdoms and were divided into several occupational categories (along with the existence of Jain, Buddhist, and Hindu religions), all the Tamils shared a common cultural heritage. Kannagi represented all the ideals of Tamil womanhood but also manifested the ability to render justice in a domain outside the household. In the experiential domain of political and legal authority, Kannagi drew upon her spirituality, the source of which was chastity, declared the innocence of her husband, and caused the burning of a city. Being married to Kovalan she could not escape his fate but at the same time manifested fully the essence of Tamil womanhood/motherhood. Her existence was a demonstration of the operational relationship between chastity, a principle of female spirituality, and political authority.

The epic showed that chastity, in combination with justice, became an operative principle in different domains of the cultural experience of the Tamils. The justice Kannagi sought was a political ideal of the Tamils. Her challenge to the erring king as to whether it was proper on his part to be a king when he made the grievous mistake of ordering an innocent man's death was a repudiation of political authority that had lost its moral and legal base. The king himself realized this fact and was destroyed. Although everything that occurred to Kannagi was preordained, she was rooted existentially in the cultural experience of the Tamils, and her quest for justice was a Tamil quest.

xi. The Symbol of Tamilakam: The Home of Tamils

Stein (1977:11, 25), writing on "the historical geography of Tamil country," notes that the Tamils used the symbol of *Tamilakam* from at least the 1st century B.C.E. He says that this illustrates that the Tamils had "a unique culture." It is not known how widespread this use was in ancient times, but numerous references to Tamilakam are found in the literature of the Tamil classical period between the 3rd century B.C.E. and the 3rd century C.E. Tamilakam is a combination of two words, *Tamil* and *akam* (home or interior), which together mean the home of the Tamil language, culture, and/or people. The symbol of Tamilakam evokes the imagery of the internal psychic/emotional unity of the members of a household, and by doing so conveys the meaning of the internal psychic/emotional unity of all Tamils. The symbol serves as a vehicle to comprehend and conceptualize the territorial and cultural boundary of the Tamil by contrasting the "internal Tamil" with the "external other."

In the conceptual framework of the Tamils, the imageries of the Tamil language and culture evoke the sentiments associated with one's own home. One's mother is the focus of cultural/emotional integrity in the Tamil household and one's father is the focus of territorial integrity. The mother is expected to be an embodiment of virtue, and her virtue is believed to uphold the sanctity of the home and bring divine blessings. The father is expected to protect the home and to bring wealth and fame for the home, and all men are rendered the protectors or patrons of the home of Tamil culture and language. Tamilakam is thus rendered into a political symbol. This symbolic association makes it possible for a Tamil to comprehend the social, political, and religious divisions of his society without the integrity of Tamil culture being undermined. The Tamils are internally divided into a number of endogamous status groups (known in Tamil as *kudi, kulam,* or *caste*); they have been dispersed, often living in different political entities; they follow diverse Hindu sectarian traditions as well as Jainism, Buddhism, Christianity, and Islam. But despite this diversity, the Tamils are united, with a common commitment to safeguard the Tamil language and culture.

A linkage exists between maleness and territoriality. Just as a Tamil male is expected to protect the sacredness of Tamil womanhood, he is expected to protect the Tamil language and culture and thus the territory of the Tamil language and culture. The symbol of Tamilakam can be regarded as a master symbol that synthesizes the role of male and female by using the imagery of the interior (female) and exterior (male) aspects of home for protecting Tamil language, culture, and territory.

xii. The Politics of Linguistic Nationalism

It is likely that the importance of Tamilakam as a symbol of boundary maintenance arose in ancient times because historically there was no politically bounded single territorial entity for all the Tamils until the 1950s. The ancient Tamil kings (of the period between the 3rd century B.C.E. and the 3rd century C.E.) possessed different regions within the Tamil country and were continuously at war. The decline of the ancient kingdoms was followed by political and religious strife, during which a non-Tamil kingdom was established in the northeast of the Tamil country. Two of the ancient Tamil kingdoms became powerful after the 9th century and one kingdom (the Cholas) acquired the status of empire but they did not develop a culturally homogeneous territorial political identity for the Tamils. By about the 15th century, the Tamil kingdoms ceased to be a significant political force in southern India; a number of local Tamil chieftains claimed kingly heritage but thus were subservient to the Telugu, Muslim, or Maratha kings and to the British after the 18th century. The Tamil kings and chieftains, however, promoted the idea of Tamilakam as the symbol of the home of the Tamils. The main exponents of the idea of Tamilakam were the hundreds of poets, both male and female, who from the earliest times had the patronage of Tamil kings and chieftains. Stein notes that the idea of Tamilakam was sustained and conveyed primarily by the "peripatetic poets and hymnists" and that "a sense of Tamilakam suffuses" the poetry of the Tamil classical period. Hundreds of poets, despite their serving under particular Tamil kings and chieftains scattered throughout the Tamil country, transcended their parochial loyalties and served as the custodians of the Tamil language and culture as a whole.

In the 19th century, after the expansion of channels of communication and the spread of Western education, industrialization, and urbanization, many changes occurred in the relationships among the various caste groups. In occupation, religion, education, and politics, variability became more pronounced within caste groups than it had previously been; thus, variability among caste groups, with regard to these characteristics, became less noticeable. Several members of the Brahmin caste groups acquired Western education and established themselves in the academia and in the judicial and executive branches of the British government of India. A few members of occupationally specialized and unspecialized non-Brahmin caste groups sought employment in industry, and some founded commercial enterprises in the cities. Conversion to Christianity provided protection and employment for a large number of persons from non-Brahmin caste groups.

As pointed out earlier, several ancient Tamil texts (which were buried in private libraries during earlier centuries) began to appear in print during the 19th century. Thus ancient Tamil epics and other forms of religious literature became accessible to a large number of educated and wealthy members of non-Brahmin caste groups. Many Tamil scholars who did extensive research on this ancient literature concluded that *Saiva Sidhantha* was the essence of Tamil religion or Hinduism before the establishment of the Brahmanical priesthood and Sanskritic authority in Tamil society. Saiva Sidhantha was referred to as the Dravidian religion, and the leaders of the Dravidian movement in the 20th century sought to strengthen it. Two Tamil scholars who were both Brahmins, Suryanarayan Sastri and U.V. Swaminatha Aiyar, wrote extensive commentaries on ancient Tamil literature in the late 19th century. Aiyar was instrumental in publishing a large number of ancient poems and epics that had long remained in palm-leaf manuscripts (Spratt 1970:11). Sastri was a leader in the efforts that began in the 19th century to strengthen the Tamil language and culture through the elimination of what many Tamil scholars believed to be Sanskritic or Aryan words and customs. This was the beginning of what may be called the Tamil Purity Movement. Sastri changed his Sanskritic name to a Tamil name and was known as Paritimal Kalaingar. Another leader in the Tamil purity movement was Swami Vedachalam Pillai who took the name of Maraimalai Adigal. Adigal wrote and published extensively on the Tamil cultural heritage. Christian missionaries from the West also played a significant role in the revival of Tamil scholarship. In the late 18th century, Father Beschi became a renowned Tamil poet under the Tamil name Veerama Munivar. The Right Reverend Robert Caldwell undertook a comprehensive study of Tamil grammar and customs as well as a comparative study of Dravidian languages in the 19th century.

Western scholarship of India in the 19th century produced dubious categories and classifications as well. The idea of race was introduced, and scientifically fallacious associations were made between race, culture, and language. The identification of the existence of Dravidian and Aryan groups of languages gave rise to a spurious assumption of the existence of Dravidian and Aryan races. Western scholars derived the word Dravidian from the Sanskrit word *Dramida* or *Dravida* which was used by non-Tamils to identify Tamil speakers (see Chatterji 1965:1). In the dramatization of Tamil ethnic identity, from the late 19th century these scientifically fallacious Western epistemological orientations began to be deployed by the Tamils themselves. Many Tamil leaders explicitly or implicitly made racial and cultural distinctions between Dravidians and Aryans.

The Tamil purity movement and Western scholarship provided non-Brahmin politicians with a rhetoric that on the one hand helped to revitalize the Tamil language and culture, and on the other to promote their political aspirations. Brahmins were identified as Aryans and the custodians of Sanskritic civilization, and non-Brahmins were identified as Dravidians and the custodians of Tamil civilization. Along with this development, the sanctity of ancient Tamil literature was affirmed, and the sacred symbols of ancient Tamil literature acquired cultural, social, and political significance in the modern context.

xiii. The Quest for Dravidastan

A political party known as the *South Indian Libertarian Federation* was founded in 1916, principally to oppose the economic and political power of the Brahmin caste groups. The party was later named the Justice party, and its stated goal was to render social justice to non-Brahmin caste groups. In order to gain the support of the masses, non-Brahmin politicians began propagating an ideology of equality among all non-Brahmin caste groups. The Brahmanical priesthood and Sanskritic scriptural authority were blamed for the existence of inequalities among non-Brahmin caste groups. It was argued that a classless Dravidian-Tamil society existed before the incorporation of Brahmins into Tamil society. The Brahmanical priesthood and Sanskritic scriptural tradition were considered responsible for the decay of Dravidian-Tamil culture.

In their effort to curtail the economic and political interests of Brahmins, non-Brahmin politicians had the tacit support of the British. The British had become disenchanted with Brahmins, who through their involvement in the all-India nationalist movement for independence posed a serious threat to the British. Non-Brahmin politician supported the British, arguing that the departure of the British from India would result only in complete domination by Brahmins. Non-Brahmin politicians claimed and secured communal representation or protected employment opportunities for non-Brahmins in the British government. They justified their preference for British political hegemony by saying that once non-Brahmin caste groups acquired enough economic power and educational skill, they could liberate themselves from the foreign yoke, both British and Brahmin. Politically and economically powerful non-Brahmins deserted all-India national politics in favor of the quest to establish a separate political entity in peninsular India composed of all Dravidian linguistic groups. In the latter stages of its history, the Justice party preached the secession of peninsular India to form a separate nation-state called *Dravida Nadu* (Dravidian country) or *Dravidastan* (Dravidian nation-state).

In 1926, a charismatic leader named Periyar (a Tamil title that means the great) E.V. Ramaswamy Naicker launched an open revolt against the Brahmanical priesthood and Sanskritic scriptural authority. In contrast with the Justice party, which had the support of only the very wealthy and well-educated members of non-Brahmin caste groups, Periyar attracted thousands of non-Brahmin youth who were mostly semiliterate and poor. Periyar's association was called *Suya Mariyathai Iykkam* (Self-Respect Union), and its main goal was to give pride and dignity to non-Brahmin youth. Periyar was a rationalist and a social reformer. His main thesis was that Brahmins had debased Dravidian culture, which in turn had demoralized non-Brahmin youth, and that in order to salvage Dravidian culture from its impure state, the Brahmanical priesthood and Sanskritic scriptural tradition must be destroyed and Brahmin religious practitioners expelled from Dravidian-Tamil society. Young people were exhorted to stop performing religious ceremonies that had the sanction of Sanskritic scriptural authority in the temples and at home. They were encouraged not to employ the services of Brahmin priests to officiate over crisis rites, and marriages were often solemnized by the leaders of the movement in the absence of a Brahmin priest. It was pointed out that in the primordial Dravidian culture, only the elders of the community officiated over crisis rites. These marriages were called self-respect marriages or reform marriages (*suya marivathai kalyaanam* or *seerthirutha kalyaanam*).

The writings of Ingersoll and other rationalists were serialized in the association's journal. The ideology of hierarchy (status differences between castes), commensal separation (segregation of castes), and ritualized vocation (caste vocations) were characterized as alien to Dravidian culture, and non-Brahmin youth were asked to disregard notions of pollution and rank in social intercourse. Books on Tamil culture and ancient Tamil literature were made available, and young men were given training in Tamil rhetoric. A popular slogan of the Self-Respect Union was, "If you see a snake and a Brahmin, beat the Brahmin" (*Pambaium parpanaium partha parpanai adi*). The Justice party weakened in the absence of mass support, and Periyar took over the leadership of the party. Under his tutelage the party prospered, but almost all of the party's conservative members, most of whom were rich and educated, withdrew from active participation. In 1944, Periyar renamed the party *Dravida Kalagam* (Dravidian Association). The Dravidian Association became immensely popular with the urban masses and students, and many villages were influenced by its propaganda. Hindi and ceremonies that had become associated with Brahmanical priesthood were identified as alien symbols that should be eliminated from Tamil culture. Brahmins, who were regarded as the guardians of such symbols, came under verbal attack.

In 1949, Periyar's chief lieutenant, Aringar (a Tamil title which means "the wise") C.N. Annadurai established a separate association called *Dravida Munnetra Kalagam* (Dravidian Advancement Association), generally referred to as the DMK. The DMK made the efforts of Periyar and his Self-Respect Union relevant to the villagers and the urban students, particularly to male students. Many non-Brahmin leaders and students changed their Aryan names to Tamil names, usually translating the original name into Tamil. The DMK advocated the thesis that the Tamil language was immensely richer than Sanskrit and Hindi in content and thus was a key that opened the door to all subjects to be learned. The DMK appealed to the school-going and educated youth both in the city and in the village. An important medium of the DMK was the Tamil cinema. By the 1940s, Tamil cinema had become the chief source of entertainment in Tamil society, and most of the leaders of the DMK were directly or indirectly involved in stage and cinema productions. These presentations depicted the Tamil woman as the embodiment of purity and chastity, and many films dealt with the following themes: the cult of Kannagi (queen or goddess of chastity), the glory of Tamil kings and queens, Tamil nationalism (the sanctity of the Tamil language and culture), egalitarianism, eradication of caste inequality, and opposition to Brahmanical priesthood and rituals.

The leaders of the DMK were great orators in Tamil, and many had done original research on Tamil culture. Most of these leaders had been trained to do public speaking in Periyar's Self-Respect Union. Their public speaking was more than a forum for attacking the Brahmanical priesthood; the leaders developed a distinctive skill in expressing the ideas of the movement, and the audience participated. Platform speech (*maedai paechu*) acquired the characteristics of dramatic art and became a form of transcendental expressiveness. The talks combined both modern and ancient forms of Tamil speech and were highly alliterative and rhythmic. They attracted large audiences not only in the urban areas but also in villages. In their speeches, the leaders of the association stressed the values and morality of the ancient Tamils as mentioned in the ancient Tamil literature and extolled these forms as essential for a satisfying life. The leaders were also very popular writers in Tamil. They wrote in chaste or pure Tamil, avoiding the use of Sanskrit derivatives. Thousands of books, booklets, and journals were published, elaborating on the theme of the greatness of Tamil culture and Tamil language. The Tamil language was equated with the Tamil woman and was referred to as Tamil mother (*Tamil Thai* or *Tamil Annai*). Every Tamil was asked to protect his mother. Abstract ideas related to virtue and the unity of humankind were also expounded. Slogans such as *Kadamai-Kanniyam-Kattupaadu* (Duty-Dignity-Discipline), *Ontrae Kulam, Orae Theivam* (One Community, One God), *Ellorum Innattu Mannarkal* (All are Rulers of this Country), and *Yathum Urae Yavarum Kaeleer* (Let the World Hear that I Belong to Every Country) became popular in Tamil society.

The leaders of the DMK presented themselves as the custodians of the Tamil cultural heritage and identified Brahmins as the custodians of Sanskritic heritage and authority. Although non-Brahmin leaders in many instances proclaimed themselves to be rationalists and atheists, they attempted only to discredit the beliefs in what they perceived to be Brahmanical gods and goddesses and not the beliefs in what they perceived to be Tamil gods and goddesses, including the mother goddess. The divinity of Tamil womanhood/motherhood was made more significant, and the goddess of chastity as well as the symbol of the mother goddess acquired a greater significance. The leaders of the movement affirmed that through Kannagi's life and acts the mystical power of chastity (the spirituality of Tamil womanhood/mother-hood) had acquired symbolic significance in the realm of politics and ethnic-ity. To have a chaste language and culture was to share in the spirituality of chastity. Just as Kannagi sought justice and claimed ultimate victory, the Tamils as a whole could seek justice and be victorious in their conflict with Brahmins and Hindi speakers. Victory was the realization of political autono-my for the Tamils and Tamil literary greatness.

Any references to chastity had at once several meanings: Chastity linked the integrity of the Tamil family, the spirituality of Tamil womanhood/moth-erhood, political victory, and ethnicity. Tamil culture and language were equated to Tamil womanhood/motherhood (*Tamil Thai*) and any threat to Tamil culture and language was considered a threat to Tamil woman-hood/motherhood. Frequently, the association between the spirituality of chaste women and the glory of a chaste language and culture was made, and as indicated earlier, a significant number of Tamil publications in the 20th century extolled the chastity and justice of ancient Tamil princesses, poet-esses, and other prominent women, in particular the chastity and justice of Kannagi. Thus, in 1965 when Hindi was introduced in Tamil society as a lan-guage to be taught in schools and used in governmental work, self-immola-tions occurred.

With its opposition to Hindi, the DMK became a powerful political power. In 1957, it polled 14.6 percent of the votes in the state (Tamil Nadu) general elections, and 27 percent in 1962 (Hardgrave, Jr. 1965). In 1967, the DMK polled 41.2 percent of the votes and became the ruling party in the state of Tamil Nadu (Spratt 1970:49), and in the 1971 elections it gained a larger percentage of votes. Many traditional leaders of Tamil villages began to sup-port the DMK. This was partly a result of the villager's desire to be identified with the winning political party, and partly as a result of major changes in the relationship between dominant and subordinate jati groups in the village. The DMK began to consolidate its village support by various adaptations which included less open verbal attacks on the jati hierarchy and eliciting the support of the rich and the elders of dominant jati groups. In spite of these adaptations, mainly undertaken to strengthen the financial position of the party, the DMK's followers were members of subordinate jati groups and its support came especially from young men who gave voluntary services during the elections. The DMK leadership split on important political issues and a new party called *Anna DMK* was formed in 1977. Anna DMK gained a majori-ty in the Tamil Nadu legislature and formed the government, and since then Anna DMK has continued to be the most powerful political party in the state of Tamil Nadu.

Although the nation-state of Dravidastan has not materialized, the polit-ical landscape of Tamil Nadu has been dominated by leaders and followers who have either overtly espoused the idea of creating Dravidastan or have covertly given support for such an idea in opposition to Hindi and Hindistan.

✣ RELIGIOUS NATIONALISM AND THE QUEST FOR KHALISTAN (THE LAND OF THE PURE): THE SIKHS

i. Religious Nationalism and the Quest for Statehood

In the last chapter I discussed the cultural factors that fostered the emergence of linguistic nationalism among the Tamils of India. The Tamils have conceptualized their national identity, focusing on what is believed to be pure Tamil language (*chenthamil*) and have sought to establish the nation-state of Dravidian speakers (*Dravidastan*) to protect the purity of Tamil.

In this chapter I examine the cultural factors that have fostered the emergence of religious nationalism among the Sikhs of India. The Sikhs have conceptualized their national identity, focusing on what they believe to be the pure Sikh community known as the pure ones (*Khalsa*), and have sought to establish the nation-state of the land of the pure (*Khalistan*) to protect the purity of the chosen disciples known as the *Khalsa Sikhs*.

Sikhs, which literally mean disciples, number about 15 million today. Their religious tradition, known as Sikhism or Sikh Panth (the path of the disciples), was originally known as Nanak Panth, or the path of Guru Nanak, its founder. Guru Nanak was born in the Panjab in 1469 and from the age of thirty until his death in 1539 he traveled extensively in northwestern India and preached devotion to God. Most Sikhs live in the Panjab state of India, where they constitute a numerical majority and are the politico-economically dominant community. Sikhs are found in other parts of India also although they are almost always ethnically Panjabi speakers belonging to the endogamous caste communities of the Panjab such as the Jats, Khatris, Auroras, Mazhabhis, and Ramdasis. There are also many domiciled Sikhs in England, the western United States and Canada, and a large community of Sikhs exists in Toronto. North American converts to Sikhism, known as *gora* or white Sikhs, are found mostly in the western United States and Canada.

The emergence of Sikh nationalism was largely a consequence of violent conflicts between Sikhs and other communities from the 17th century. From the middle of the 17th century to the middle of the 19th century, for about two hundred years, Muslims and Sikhs had major conflicts and battled each other. Sikhs and the British fought in the middle of the 19th century. From the late 19th century to the present, Sikhs and Hindus have had violent conflicts and tense or stressful relationships. All these violent encounters had individually and collectively produced a Sikh sense of a persecuted community, and Sikh aspirations for a homeland to protect the Sikh religion and the Sikh community developed out of the real and imagined persecution. Had there been no conflict between the Sikhs and the other communities, it is very likely that the Sikhs would be viewed and accepted as a Hindu sect today like the Jains or the Lingayats rather than being identified as a separate religious community of India like the Christians or Buddhists or Muslims. Although Sikhism is commonly viewed as a synthesis of Hindu and Islamic mystical traditions, it is more accurate to interpret Sikhism as an aspect of the Hindu religious complex that combines Yoga-Sant-Guru orientations that deal with the mastery of psychic and spiritual powers and the teaching of such techniques by holymen or saints. In a later section I discuss this religious complex in greater detail.

Sikhs attained a kind of national autonomy and politico-economic dominance in the early 19th century when Sikh kingdoms emerged in the Panjab and Kashmir. Sikh political power might have waxed had it not been for the British military presence in India in the 19th century. The British defeated the Sikh armies of the Panjab in the middle of the 19th century, and, after that, for a century the Sikhs became the staunch supports of the British Empire with thousands of Sikh soldiers serving in British military campaigns both inside and outside of India. Christian missionary activity in the Panjab began in the middle of the 19th century, but it did not have a major impact on the Sikhs although a few westernized Sikhs and a prominent Sikh king had become Christians.

A major impetus to foster Sikh religious national identity emerged in the middle of the 19th century as a consequence of the British policy of permitting the Sikhs in the British military to wear the emblems of Sikh Khalsa identity (symbols of communal purity) such as the turban and the beard. Sikh-Muslim animosity was strengthened by the British policy of using Muslims to fight the Sikhs and vice versa. In 1857 when many Muslim and Hindu princes and soldiers revolted against British authority, Sikh princes and soldiers supported the British and the victorious British rewarded the Sikhs through various means.

In the late 19th century, Hindu-Sikh animosity acquired great significance. With the emergence of Arya Samaj, a conservative Hindu revivalist sect in the late 19th century, Sikhs felt threatened. Arya Samaj propagated the holiness of the Vedas (ancient Sanskritic scriptures) whereas Sikhism promoted the divinity of the Adi Granth (the Sikh holy book containing the sayings of the Sikh gurus or teachers). The opposition between the devout followers of Arya Samaj and Sikhism became so intense in the late 19th and early 20th centuries that attempts were made by the Sikhs to purge all Hindu influence on Sikhism and to purify Sikhism from what the devout Sikhs believed to be the corruption of Sikhism by Sikhs who often had Hindu and Sikh dual identities.

In the early 20th century the *Akali Dal* movement (political party of the immortal Sikhs, known also as the eternal party) was in the forefront of protests against Hindu and non-Khalsa (non-pure) Sikh managers of Sikh temples and endowments. The efforts of Akali Dal between 1920 and 1925 resulted in the creation of a Khalsa-Sikh supervisory committee called *Shromani Gurdwara Parbhandak Committee* (central temple management committee) to oversee Sikh temple practices and endowments. Since 1925, members of this committee have been democratically elected from the Khalsa-Sikh community, and since then the committee has acquired enormous political significance, functioning as the political wing or unit of Sikhism, claiming to represent the entire Sikh community and the Sikh way (*Sikh Panth*). Leaders of Akali Dal hoped that the British would safeguard Sikh political interests if and when India became independent of British rule. There was some expectation that a Sikh nation-state would be created. Such an aspiration for Sikh statehood never materialized, and Sikh claims for political autonomy were never seriously considered by the British. Many Sikhs felt betrayed by the British when India was divided to create Pakistan for Muslims without fully developing a mechanism to protect the lives of the Sikhs in the western section of the Panjab which became the core unit of Pakistan.

The departure of the British in 1947 brought misery not only to the Sikhs but to the Muslims and Hindus as well. The uprooting and exodus of Sikhs, Hindus, and Muslims in the wake of the partition claimed an estimated two million lives. The Sikhs in the Panjab region of Pakistan were reduced to a small minority, but in the Panjab region of India they constituted a majority in the northern and central areas although Hindus outnumbered them in the total population of the Indian Panjab. An uneasy political alliance between the Sikhs and Hindus lasted for about two decades, and in 1966 the Panjab of India was divided into Panjab state (*Panjabi Saba*) and Harayana state, ostensibly as linguistic states with the Panjabi language as the national official language of Panjab state and Hindi language the national official language of Harayana.

The real reason for the division of the Panjab region of India into the Harayana and Panjab states in 1966 was to appease the Sikh religious claims for national autonomy. In the newly created Panjab state of India, Sikhs were not only a numerical majority but they also became economically and politically much more powerful than the Hindus of the state. The politics of the Panjab state during the past twenty-five years have been marked by conflicts between moderate or pro-India Sikh leaders and extremist or pro-Khalistan Sikh leaders. Also, there have been several instances of negotiations between Sikh leaders and the Indian government that produced unresolved concerns. All these factors have fostered violent terrorist activities that are blamed mostly on Sikhs but at least some of which must be attributed to Hindus and the police. The moderate pro-India segment of the Sikh population has been usually identified as loyal to the all-India Congress political party, and the extremist segment is usually linked with the *Akalis* (immortals or timeless ones, or eternal ones) and the *Akali Dal* (party of the immortals or the army of the immortals). The creation of the Panjab state in 1966 was a concession to Sikh demands for political autonomy, but according to the Akalis, the formation of Panjab did not meet all the demands of the Sikhs. Also, despite the fact that Sikhs constitute the numerical majority in the Panjab state, there is still a large minority population of Hindus in the state, and if the Sikhs are divided among themselves politically, Hindus would play a major political role in the state.

In the 1970s, factional politics among the Sikhs became very intense, and the Akalis themselves were divided on defining the goals of the Panjab state. In this politically volatile contest, the all-India Congress party supported a factional leader named Sant Jarnail Singh Bhindranwale who was associated with the Sikh sectarian group of *Nirankaris*. Bhindranwale defied his Congress party members and became a secessionist leader: His ultimate goal was to create Khalistan (land of the pure) and he advocated armed rebellion to achieve this goal.

In 1984 Bhindranwale and several of his followers were killed in a gun battle between them and the Indian army which invaded the temple complex where he and his followers had barricaded themselves. The prime minister of India, Mrs. Indira Gandhi, who had authorized the army attack on the temple complex, was assassinated by two of her Sikh bodyguards in the same year, a fact that illustrated Mrs. Gandhi's flawed understanding of Sikh history, the sant-Sikh tradition, and Khalsa-Sikh sensibilities.

As McLeod (1989), the leading authority on Sikh history and Sikhism, notes, there are several interpretations of the events that occurred between 1946 and 1986, and it is likely that one can never reconcile the journalistic/academic versions of the history of those forty years with the interpretations of the Sikh faithful. For the Khalsa-Sikhs, the period of forty years was characterized by betrayals by Hindus and the Indian government, and such a view of the Hindus and the Indian government fostered the rejuvenation and strengthening of the Khalsa and Sant traditions of Sikhism.

> Bhindranwale has predictably been the object of respect and adulation, denigration and fear. A considerable hagiography has gathered around him, matched by a corresponding demonology. Although he was killed during the Indian army assault on the Gold Temple complex in 1984 his reputation lives on, both for those who revered him and also for those who feared or despised him. An unbiased impression is, needless to say, very difficult to acquire at such close quarters and we shall have to wait until the dust settles before accurate assessments can be made. This much, however, can be affirmed. Jarnail Singh Bhindranwale has carved for himself a martyr's niche in the Panth's [Sikh way] tradition, and no amount of journalistic or academic reassessment will dislodge him from that place in the popular affections.
>
> —*McLeod (1989:116)*

ii. The Socioreligious and Political Contexts of 15th-Century Northern India

The rise of Guru Nanak Panth (way of the divine teacher Nanak), the Hindu sectarian orientation that later acquired the name Sikh (way of the disciples) or Sikhism (which means learning from divine teachers), and the development of the theology of this religious orientation cannot be understood fully without a discussion of the social, religious, and political environments of northern India in the 15th century.

The beginning of the 15th century marked the decline of the Delhi sultanates of the Turkish Muslims that had been in existence for about three hundred years. As early as the 11th century, Turkish Muslims invaded northern India, and from the 12th to 15th centuries, very powerful Turkish sultanates controlled northern and northwestern India. However, in 1398, the Turko-Mongol conqueror known as Timur the Lame or Tamerlane invaded and sacked Delhi, killing almost all the adult male population, and in 1451 the Delhi sultanate of the Turks came under the Afghans known as Lodis.

> The triumph of the Lodi Afghans indicated new forces at work in fifteenth century India. … Fierce fighters, they encountered little difficulty in taking over the sultanates of Delhi and Malway, while those with ambitions still unsatisfied passed down the Gangetic plain to establish strongholds of Afghan power in Bihar and Bengal. Another element

that contributed to the prevailing instability was the Habshis, or Ethiopians, brought into India as *mamluks* after the supply of Turkish *mamluks* had dried up with the Mongol conquests of Central Asia and the conversion of the Turks of the steppe zone to Islam. Habshis were to be found mainly in the sultanates of Gujarat, the Deccan, and Bengal, all of which had access to the sea. The Khalji [a Turkish dynasty of Delhi sultanate from 1290–1320] commander Malik Kafur was a Habshi, as was the founder of Sharqi dynasty [1394–1479] of Jaunpur, and so were several short-lived sultans of Bengal.

—Farmer (1986:314)

Babur, the Turko-Mongol Muslim ruler of Kabul in Afghanistan, defeated the Lodi sultan of Delhi in 1526 and established the Mughal Empire which included large areas of northwestern and northern India as well as the Kabul region of Afghanistan. The Mughal Empire lasted for over three hundred years, but from the middle of the 18th century the Mughal power waned and the British began to exercise politico-economic dominance in India.

As a result of the long period of Islamic influence, conversions to Islam, and the existence of Muslim sultanates, several Hindu revivalist, reformist, and syncretic religious movements arose in northwestern and northern India. Also, both Hindu and Muslim (Islamic) mystical traditions acquired importance among the peasants and the poor due to the fact that these orientations cut across caste and religious boundaries.

Three orders of Sufi saints [Muslim mystics] had appeared in India by the thirteenth century: the Chishti, Suhrawardi, and Firdawsi, all of which appealed to the same mystical yearnings for union with God, experienced by so many Hindus as well as Muslims and other "God-intoxicated" seekers the world over. The fervent love of god, which played so important a role in the passionate yearnings for "the mother goddess" ... characterized Bengali religious consciousness from time immemorial. ... The wandering *pirs* (Sufi preachers), who went into Bengal's remote villages to bring their message of divine love to impoverished peasants, sounded much the same as Hindu *bhakti* ("devotional") saints offering salvation through worship of the mother goddess, or Mahayanist Buddhists bearing the promise of divine salvation by grace of a Boddhisattva's blessing.

—Wolpert (1989:117–18)

The mystical and devotional orientation of Islam and Hinduism produced several sants (saints with the reputation of having direct experience or communion with god) who transcended the parochial ritualism of Islam and

Hinduism. The Muslim sant Kabir (1440–1518), who was a member of a low caste of weavers, "inspired millions of followers to abandon their sectarian perceptions of Islam and Hinduism in favor of his syncretic path of simple love of God" (Wolpert 1989:12). Guru Nanak (1469–1539), a high-caste Hindu, began to propagate love and devotion to god, rejecting Hindu ritualism and caste ranking. It is a significant fact that Kabir's mystical poems are included in the Sikh sacred book (*Adi Granth*) as are the poems of another Muslim sant named Sheik Farid. The Adi Granth contains also the devotional hymns of earlier sants named Namdev and Ravidas. In the next section I will discuss briefly the foundtion of the sant tradition and its relationship to Sikhism.

iii. The Sant Tradition of Hinduism and Sikhism

Guru Nanak's significant role as the founder of Sikhism was his synthesis of various religious currents of Hinduism into a new way (panth or path) to comprehend the name (nam) and message of the timeless (eternal) and formless being. Nanak belonged to the sant tradition of Hinduism, and his elaboration of this tradition developed into a new way which was identified by his followers as Nanak panth.

The sant tradition of Hinduism probably developed in the 12th century in northern India. It denounced Hindu ritualism and caste hierarchy (based on the belief in ritual pollution) and promoted universal community of human beings. Sants were either monotheists or pantheists who emphasized the need to meditate for interior or inner illumination. Sants were often mystical poets who sang or recited hymns in ecstasy. Their religious foundation was rooted in communion with (or experiencing) God. The sant tradition was influenced by the Hatha-Yoga emphasis on the attainment of spiritual and psychic powers and was influenced also by the devotional (*Bhakti*) orientation of Hinduism. However, most of the sants, including Guru Nanak, considered their approach to spiritual self-realization to be different from the Bhakti and Hatha-Yoga orientations. Guru Nanak condemned Hatha-Yoga's excessive asceticism. Sants were often viewed as gurus, or divine teachers, and Sikhs believed that divine teachers were important to communicate god's truth. However, the sants themselves were not disciples of gurus because sants received true knowledge from god who was their divine teacher, the *Adi-guru* or *Sant-guru* (first preceptor or true preceptor).

In his important book, *The Guru in Sikhism*, Cole (1982:98–99) notes:

> The doctrine of Guru, in common with many other aspects of the Sikh faith, owes much to its Hindu parent. To witness the ways in which disciples manifest respect for their spiritual guides and to observe the rela-

tionship of Sikhs to the Guru Granth Sahib ... is to note many similarities. However, Sikhism has been remarkably successful in resisting the temptation to deify its leaders or to perpetuate the line of human gurus. ... The principal single reason for this success must be the care which the Gurus themselves took to point beyond themselves to God who, manifesting himself as Guru, revealed himself to mankind through words entrusted to Guru Nanak and his successors.

The succession of guruships came to an end with the tenth guru, Guru Gobind Singh, whose children had been executed. He declared the Adi Granth (Sikh holy book), containing the sayings of the gurus and others, to be the divine guru and thus the role of the divine teacher was conferred on Adi Granth.

iv. Guru Nanak Panth and the Sikh Panth of Nanak's Successors

As noted earlier, guru Nanak was an exponent of the sant tradition which formulated new teachings on how to receive God's name and word. His teaching was called the Nanak panth (the way or path of Nanak, which was also known as Nanak community), and Nanak panth was more like a school of spirituality instead of a new religious order. Nanak appointed his successor from among his disciples rather than annointing his son as his successor. This created some schism among Nanak's followers and a subsect called *Udasi* panth, which focused more on yogic types of asceticism, came into being. Guruships were accorded to disciples who were selected for their spiritual qualities until the installation of the sixth guru, Guru Har Gobind, who was the son of the fifth guru, Guru Arjan.

An important feature of the Sikh panth was that the disciples of the gurus were both Hindus and Muslims, and the gurus for the most part encouraged the disciples to continue with their respective religious affiliations. The first six gurus had many Muslim disciples. The fifth guru (Guru Arjan) who built the holy temple of the Sikhs, Har Mandir or Temple of God (known as the Golden Temple) in the city of Amritsar, honored a Muslim holy man named Mian Mir by having him lay the temple's foundation (Engle 1980:84). Engle (1980:102) also notes that due to the fact that many of the sixth guru's (Guru Har Gobind) "followers were Muslims, he had a mosque built for them—letting it be known that he had not sided against any sect of people but against the oppression and religious intolerance which had become prevalent. Men were to remain within their own social bodies and all modes of worship were to be respected."

The transformation of the Sikh panth from an inner-directed, redemptive, pacifist, spiritual training school occurred gradually, and by the time of the fifth guru, Guru Arjan (guru from 1563 to 1606), the martial tradition of the Sikhs began. Guru Arjan instructed his son, Har Gobind, to "wear weapons at his side and command an army" (Engle 1980:92). Guru Har Gobind had two swords symbolizing spiritual and temporal authority and started the tradition of receiving arms and horses as offerings to him, and he built a community hall for engaging in both spiritual and political discussions. This hall was built opposite the Golden Temple and was called *Akal Takht* (Throne of Timeless). Engle (1980:96) notes that Guru Har Gobind put into action what his father (Guru Arjan) had contemplated doing and had trained his son to do. Har Gobind became a spiritual and temporal ruler, trained in religious and military functions. He combined the military and spiritual traditions with the following rationale:

> The ideal man is a saint within and outwardly a prince: spiritual and temporal powers combined. Arms are for the protection of the weak and the poor and to overthrow tyranny and cruelty. Moreover, Baba Nanak did not renounce the world but simply renounced Maya.
>
> —*Engle (1980:102)*

v. Guru Gobind Singh and the Khalsa Panth

Perhaps the second most important guru of Sikhism is Guru Gobind Singh (1666–1708). It was Guru Gobind Singh, the tenth and last living guru, who created the religious-military order of Sikh brotherhood known as *Khalsa Sikhs*. The word Khalsa can be translated as the chosen, but it has acquired the meaning of "pure ones" or "pure community."

The Khalsa Sikh brotherhood was founded in 1699. Guru Gobind Singh assembled his followers on Baisakhi festival day and demanded a disciple's head. A volunteer was taken into a tent by the guru; after a brief period the guru returned with a blood-soaked sword and again demanded a volunteer. The guru repeated his actions until he had five volunteers, and then proclaimed that the five volunteers were "the chosen ones" or "the pure ones" and that they had not been killed because the guru had slaughtered goats instead. The guru prepared *amrit* (nectar) of sugar water, stirring the cup with his sword, and made the chosen ones drink. After the guru had also sipped the nectar, he called for other volunteers to join the chosen ones, and with such an initiation ceremony the community order of the pure ones (Khalsa) was created. The first five volunteers were called the Five Beloveds because of their love for the guru and willingness to sacrifice their lives. The guru wanted all the Sikh men to adopt the surname of *Singh* (lion) and all the Sikh women to take the surname of *Kaur* (princess), and ordained that Khalsa Sikh men should not cut their hair, should carry a comb and a dagger, and wear a steel bangle and a particular type of undershorts (known as the *five K's* with reference to the Panjabi words *kes, kangha, kirpan, kara,* and *kachh*). The Khalsa was originally conceived of as a community of saint soldiers to fight the Muslim persecutors, but it gradually acquired other functions, including the work of keeping the Sikh community from being corrupted by Hindu beliefs and rituals. The primary objective of Guru Gobind Singh was to make the Sikh community into a martial community which fought for god's victory. As McLeod (1976:13) notes:

> God, for Guru Gobind Singh, was personified by steel and worshipped in the form of the sword. For him the characteristic name of God was *sarab-loh,* the "All-Steel," and it is no accident that in the preparation for Sikh baptism, the baptismal water is stirred with a two-edged sword.

vi. The Quest for Khalistan

It is important that we should be aware of the fact that not all Sikhs are Khalsa Sikhs and that there are subsects such as Nirankaris and Namdharis that divide the Khalsa Sikhs. There are also Sikhs who identify themselves as Nanak Panthis or Sahajdharis to signify the fact that they are anti-militaristic. It is also important to note the fact that the Sikh tradition acquired militaristic characteristics only in response to (or in reaction to) persecutions and political oppression. The fifth guru (Guru Arjan) was persecuted and tortured by the Mughal court, and as a result it became necessary to use the soldier disciples for defending the Sikh community. The tenth guru (Guru Gobind Singh) lost all his children to Mughal executions and many of his disciples lost their lives in battles with Muslims or Hindus in his attempts to defend or protect the Sikh community against the Mughals or Hindus. There was a gradual development of a Sikh political community in the 18th century, and they became a politically dominant group, largely through the efforts of the Khalsa Sikhs and their core of volunteer fighters known as *Akalis* (immortals). In the late 18th century, Sikh kingdoms developed, culminating in the rise of a Sikh Empire under Maharaja Ranjit Singh (1780–1839) who was known as the "one-eyed lion of Panjab." The British defeated the Sikhs in the middle of the 19th century, annexed most of the Sikh territories to the British Empire, and established an overall political dominance over the princely Sikh states such as Patiala and Nabha. For about a century, a large contingent of Sikh soldiers fought defending the British Empire, but during that period there were also a few British actions that caused unrest among the Sikhs, and Sikh opposition to the British became evident in the early 20th century. Attempts were made by Khalsa Sikhs to strengthen their Sikh identity and distinctiveness as a non-Hindu religious tradition. The *Akalis* (immortals) became active, and in the early 20th century the party of immortals (Akali Dal) acquired political importance in the Panjab. Master Tara Singh (1885–1967), who was the undisputed Khalsa leader in the early 20th century, demanded the creation of a Sikh nation in 1942.

> In March 1946 the Shiromani Akali Dal resolved formally to demand a separate Sikh state of "Sikhistan" or "Khalistan". … in the wake of Partition with its mass migration and slaughter of Sikhs, Master Tara Singh trenchently remarked, "The Muslims got their Pakistan and the Hindus got their Hindustan, but what did the Sikhs get?" It was a question that was to ring louder in the minds of millions of Sikhs after more than a quarter century of Indian independence brought no peace but the sword of growing conflict to Punjab.
>
> *Wolpert (1991:114)*

During the past forty years, the quest for Khalistan has taken many turns, some political compromises, and some violent conflicts. It has been said that the Sikh identity as a separate religious-ethnic group would not have continued beyond the middle of the 19th century had it not been for the British who fostered this identity for political reasons, mainly to keep Sikh soldiers separated from the Hindus and Muslims so that the Sikhs could be used to fight the Muslims and Hindus. According to this interpretation, the Sikhs were on their way to becoming a Hindu sect, having come under the influences of Hindu practices and rituals, and it was the British divide and rule policy that helped reinvent and recreate the Sikh identity. It can also be said that the policies of Jawaharlal Nehru and Indira Gandhi in the 20th century helped to reinvent and re-create the Sikh identity. The fact is, however, that Sikh leaders have responded and reacted to real or imagined persecution and threats in such ways that a militant lifestyle has been integrated with a pacifist philosophy as a mechanism for the survival of the Sikh community and the maintenance of the Sikh national tradition. Irrespective of whether the Sikhs achieve their goal of establishing Khalistan or the Land of the Pure in this or the next century, the Sikh community will not be absorbed into the Hindu caste fold, and the Sikh national tradition will not be merged with any other national tradition of India.

PART THREE

VILLAGE TRADITIONS OF INDIA

Tamil Nadu, India

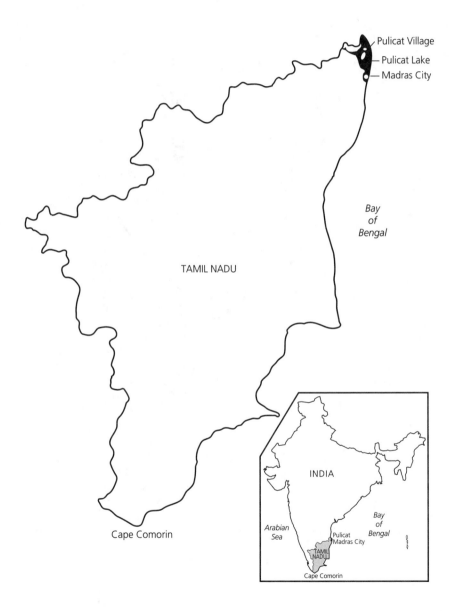

Pulicat Village
Pulicat Lake
Madras City

Bay
of
Bengal

TAMIL NADU

Cape Comorin

INDIA

Arabian
Sea

Bay
of
Bengal

Pulicat
Madras City

TAMIL
NADU

Cape Comorin

Pulicat Village and Its Vicinity

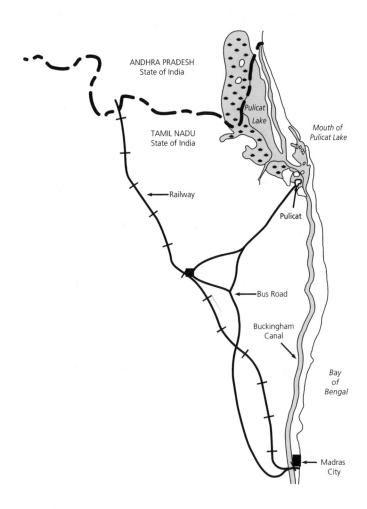

ANDHRA PRADESH
State of India

Pulicat Lake

Mouth of
Pulicat Lake

TAMIL NADU
State of India

←Railway

Pulicat

←Bus Road

Buckingham
Canal

Bay
of
Bengal

Madras
City

Pulicat Lake Showing Territory of Pulicat Revenue Village

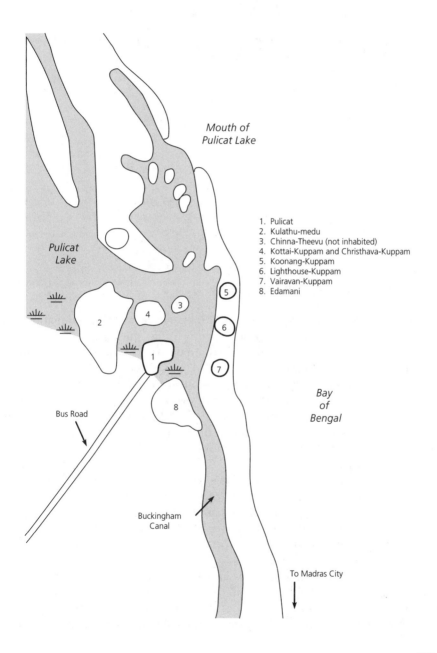

Mouth of
Pulicat Lake

Pulicat
Lake

1. Pulicat
2. Kulathu-medu
3. Chinna-Theevu (not inhabited)
4. Kottai-Kuppam and Christhava-Kuppam
5. Koonang-Kuppam
6. Lighthouse-Kuppam
7. Vairavan-Kuppam
8. Edamani

Bay
of
Bengal

Bus Road

Buckingham
Canal

To Madras City

CHAPTER ELEVEN

ꙮ THE STUDY
OF VILLAGE TRADITIONS

i. The Village Communities of India

Ever since the British acquired Diwani Rights (securing the legal mandate to collect land taxes) in Bengal (northeastern India) during the 18th century, legal and political discourse on the foundations and nature of the Indian community has been undertaken by both Europeans and Indians in an effort to establish a just and rational system to collect land taxes from the different types of village tenure. The 19th century writings of Sir Henry Maine (who served in India as a legal administrator) evoked great interest among evolutionary anthropologists and promoted the development of legal anthropology (anthropology of law). Maine's books such as *Early History of Institutions and Village Communities* became classics in the study of the origins and parallel developments of customs and social institutions. Drawing upon ethnographic facts from India, Maine argued that humankind passed through a cultural stage of development when kinship-based status defined the privileges and prerogatives and that this stage was replaced by a more advanced system of contractual arrangements between peoples which specified the legal rights and obligations of such agreements.

An important area of concern in Maine's discourse on legal institutions and village communities was to show that ancient Indians held or owned land communally, and that the communal ownership of land created village communities that were inhabited by kin-based groups. Maine attempted to demonstrate the existence of universal principles of village tenure as well as to show that there were differences in the conceptions of group ownership and group use. Also, Maine discussed the possibilities of variations in relation to Aryan and pre-Aryan institutions of India. Maine strove to discover whether the principles of village tenure regulated the rights of the villages with heads of the related families making the necessary decisions, or whether there were village headmen who enforced the principles of village tenure.

Baden-Powell (1896) offered a brilliant critique of Maine's thesis in his important study *The Village Community*. Baden-Powell noted that Maine had erred in not taking into account the existence of the *ryotwari* village community which had no "appearance of joint or common ownership": In the ryotwari village community, land holdings were held "separate and independent" by individual families, and land holdings did not constitute a "proprietary unit." Baden-Powell pointed out that even in communally owned joint-villages, there were different principles of village-tenure, with some villages having aristocratic lineages of the kin-based groups owning the land, and some villages operating in a democratic mode through the adoption of the principle of equal sharing. Baden-Powell also noted that historically different or similar principles of village tenure came into being for various, diverse reasons and that it was wrong to conclude that there was a causal regularity in the emergence of a particular type of village tenure throughout India. He noted that village communities could be established by a kin-based clan by conquest, by an individual receiving land from the king as a gift, or by a group of colonists who associated voluntarily. It was fallacious to argue that ryotwari village communities "resulted from a natural evolution" of common ownership because there was no evidence that the characteristics of ryotwari village community developed from the communal village community of earlier times and because of the fact that it could be shown that characteristics of communally owned village communities could arise from the type of ryotwari village community.

Baden-Powell provided extensive documentation on the existence of regional variation in India. He showed that there were differences between northern, northwestern, northeastern, central, southeastern, and southwestern regions of India because of the historical patterns of migrations, tribal orientations, and the variations in the uses of land for cultivation or pastoralism. Baden-Powell concluded his discourse on the Indian village community as follows:

> In south India, there is a universal village formation, but there is no claim, either joint or individual, to ownership of the whole village; there the village is a group formed of several families who settled, or are now resident, together, but whose contiguous holdings within the village boundary are independent, and always have been so, as far as any evidence goes. In north India, the village as an area of land is also the essential feature, not a causal result of the fission of a class and where

such a village is jointly owned, it is really that the village is the limit of the original acquisition by a single person, and continues as the sphere of ownership, succeeded by joint inheritance of the founder.

I described in Chapter 9 the systems of village tenure that became established in Tamil Nadu. During the 18th century, the British developed a uniform method of collecting revenue. The institution of *mirasidars* (landlords), which was introduced by the Muslim kings, became important, and the method of collecting land taxes through the landlord was called the *zamindari* system. The method of collecting taxes directly from the land-owning peasants of the village was called the *ryotwari* system. As the British also affirmed the existence of *inam* or *gifted* villages, there were three types of villages, namely, the zamindari village, the ryotwari village, and inam village. The zamindari village was leased by the government to a zamindar or landlord; the land was heritable but not transferable. In the ryotwari village, land was owned and was transferable by individual *ryots* or cultivators. The inam village was a trust that was exempt from taxation; it could not be sold or transferred.

ii. Anthropological Studies of Indian Village Communities

Anthropological studies of Indian village communities began in a systematic manner during the middle of the 20th century. Largely influenced by the writings of Radcliffe-Brown who promoted the social anthropological tradition of using the concept of "social structure" for identifying the positional and functional relationships of human groups and equally shaped by the teachings of Robert Redfield who applied the concepts of "community" and "little traditions" for the study of peasant cultures, several monographs and books on the Indian villages appeared after 1950. Two important collections of essays on the Indian villages appeared in 1955: The book *Village India, Studies in the Little Community* was edited by McKim Marriott (1955), and the book *India's Villages* was edited by M.N. Srinivas (1955). These two sociocultural anthropologists set the standards for the anthropological study of villages in the subsequent two decades. Some other important anthropological books on Indian villages that appeared before 1970 were *Indian Village* by S.C. Dube (1967), *Gopalpur: A South Indian Village* by A.R. Beals (1962), and *Shivapur: A South Indian Village* by K. Ishwaran (1968). In some ways, the publication of *Information and Behavior in a Sikh Village* by M.J. Leaf (1972) marked the beginning of the application of eclectic approaches and models in the study of Indian villages. It is also important to note the fact that during the past two decades graduate students and scholars from the University of Chicago have focused on the study of symbolic forms and systems in both the village and urban settings of India. There have also been innumerable other studies by European, American, and Indian scholars that have shed much light on the actual operation of the village caste system, jajmani economic system, panchayat political system, and the Hindu religious system.

The study of village traditions often focused on the examination of the caste status, village deities, and rituals and the relationships among caste, religion, and economics (jajmani system). Anthropological studies of the caste system have shown the existence of multiple labels of caste identity and multiple levels of caste ranking and suggest that the explanation or interpretation of the caste system as a static system operating within the Hindu scriptural model of fourfold varna (Brahmin, Kshatriya, Vaisya, and Shudra) categories is erroneous. I will discuss briefly a few studies of Tamil villages of India to show how the caste status system operates in the villages and how the labels of jati identity are used in different ways in diverse contexts.

Gough (1960:60n) in her study of a Tamil village in the 1950s found that a jati group with the name *Idaiyan* (herdsmen) had the jati title *Konan* (king). The use of the title was, according to her, indicative of the group's desire to enhance its status. She notes: "The Konans were formerly called Idaiyans (fem. *Idaicchi*). The title 'Konan' ('king') has been adopted in an effort to raise the rank of the caste."

Sivertsen (1963:31) studied a Tamil village in the same region where Gough undertook her study, and according to him the jati group called Idaiyan had been attempting to discard the jati title Konan. Sivertsen, who delineates jati titles as "surnames," has this to say about Idaiyans: "Herdsmen, especially wealthier herdsmen and herdsmen in salaried jobs, no longer style themselves Konar, but use Pillai as their surname, thus simulating the name used by a non-Brahmin high caste, the Vellalas. By Brahmins and other castes, however, they are still referred to, and addressed as, Konars." Whereas Gough's Idaiyans considered the title Konan (which means king in Tamil and corresponds with the Kshatriya varna) prestigious and used it for claims to a higher status, Sivertsen's Idaiyans regarded the title Konan as inferior to the title of an agriculturalist jati group.

Beteille (1965:97–98) also studied a Tamil village in the same vicinity where Gough and Sivertsen had conducted their research. He does not make a clear distinction between jati names and jati titles; for example, he refers to *Padayachi* (warrior) and *Ahamudaiyan* (owner of homestead) as jati names, when in fact they are jati titles. His main thesis is that, despite the ambiguities and lack of any uniform standard in the criteria used for ranking jati groups, both jati titles and varna symbols are aspects of the same principle of hierarchy; in other words, names and titles are both local expressions of the all-India idiom of varna hierarchy. He notes the difficulty of trying to fit data into the Hindu ideological scheme:

> One major obstacle to a brief and clear discussion of non-Brahmin castes lies in the confusion of terminology. Caste names among non-Brahmins have been undergoing transformation by a process which

seems to be fairly widespread. Members of a certain caste A begin to adopt a particular title or surname B and soon they return B as their caste name. As a consequence, members of the same caste may return different caste names, and sometimes members of different castes adopt the same title or caste name.

—*Beteille (1965:80)*

Beck (1972:2–17; 301), who studied the social organization of the western region in the Tamil country, refers to endogamous social groupings as subcastes, which she represents by the term jati in noncapitalized form. The social groupings composed of several such subcastes are referred to as castes, which she represents by the term jati in capitalized form. A subcaste, or noncapitalized jati, is defined as a "specific grouping of alleged kinsmen identified within a larger caste category on the basis of their ritual, territorial, and/or occupational identity." A caste, or capitalized jati, is defined as a "socially recognized grouping of persons that is formed on the basis of general economic, occupational, and ritual criteria."

Beck's definitional criteria do not point out the fact that although the symbols of group identity converge, they also provide for the perception and conception of distinctiveness at the level of kinship, politics, and ritual. She states that symbols of group identity such as Kavundar, Chettiar, Pillai, and Nayakkar are caste (jati) names, but fails to note that these labels are also used as titles (that signify politico-economic authority) by a number of jati groups who would not be classed as subcastes (jatis) of Kavundar, Chettiar, Pillai, and Nayakkar castes.

The use of the varna category Kshatriya in the conception of the jati title Vannia-Kula-Kshatriya (warriors of the fire race) by a number of cultivating jati groups is common in the northeastern and northwestern regions of the Tamil country. Most of these jati groups use a number of different jati titles also, but the titles generally convey the meaning of land ownership or politico-economic authority. In the Tamil Nadu government document on jati groups (1971, Vol. II: 89) it is recorded that 79 jati titles are used by the northern cultivating jati groups of Tamil society. The most commonly used title in the northeast is *Padayachi* (warrior); the popular titles in the northwest are *Padayachi, Nayakkar, Rediiar, Mupanar,* and *Gounder.*

From Thurston's (1909:7 vols.) description of the use of jati titles in south India, I cite below a selected number of references that pertain to the Tamil country, all of which convey a sense of the diversity and confusion in the use of labels of jati identity:

The ordinary title of the Agamundaiyans is Servaikkaran, but many of them call themselves, like the Vallalas, Pillai. Other titles, returned at times of census, are Adhigari and Mudaliars. (Vol. I:8)

It is noted in the Census Report, 1891, that "the name Chetti is used both to denote a distinct caste, and also a title, and people bearing this title describe themselves loosely as belonging to the Chetti caste, in the same way as a Vellala will say that he is a Mudali. This use of Chetti had caused some confusion in the returns, for the subdivisions show that many other castes have been included as well as Chetti proper." Again, in the Census Report, 1901, it is recorded that "Chetti means trader, and is one of those titular or occupational terms, which are often loosely employed as caste names. The weavers, oil pressers, and others use it as a title, and many more tack it on to their names, to denote that trade is their occupation." (Vol. II:91–92)

It is noted, in the Salem Manual, that "some of the agricultural classes habitually append the title Goundan as a sort of case nomenclature after their names, but the word applies, par excellence, to the head of the village, or Ur Goundan as he is called." As examples of castes which take Goundan as their title, the Pallis, Okkiliyans, and Vellalas may be cited. (Vol. II:300)

Other titles, indicating authority, bravery, and superiority, assembled by Pallis are Nayakar, Varma, Padaiyachi (head of an army), Kandar, Chera, Chola, Pandya, Nayanar, Udaiyar, Samburayar, etc. Still further titles are Pillai, Reddi, Goundan, and Kavandan. (Vol. VI:14)

Some Pattanavans give themselves high-sounding caste titles, e.g., Ariyar, Ayyayiraththalaivar (the five thousand chiefs), Ariya Nattu Chetti (Chettis of the Ariyar country), Accu Vellala, Karaiturai (sea-coast) Vellala, Varunakula Vellala or Varunakula Mudali. ... Some Pattanavans have adopted the title Pillai. (Vol. VI:178)

I suggest that honorific titles are labels that convey the meaning of politico-economic authority and are conceptually different from the varna categories. For example, the term *Muppan*, which is used by many Tamils as a title, means elder or leader, and elders and leaders of different groups use it as a title in a region where its meaning is understood as such, but a segment of any group which acquires a leadership position in a locality may use the term *muppan* or *Muppanar* as a group title as well.

Data on jati titles show that although jati titles and varna categories may in some cases share the same characteristics or attributes, their usage and meaning differ greatly. A jati group may have several titles at the same time, and some of these may correspond with Kshatriya, Vaishya, or Shudra varnas. Jati groups with titles that are linked with Vaishya varna may function as land-owning, politically dominant jati groups (Kshatriya) rather than as traders.

Jati names may be defined as labels of group identity that refer to or represent and connote endogamy and ritual purity/pollution. Members of a jati group, with a distinctive name, conceive of themselves as having a common historical/biological heritage, thus reflecting a kin-based identity. The function of jati titles, on the other hand, is largely political in the sense that they are expressions of authority within a jati group and among jati groups. Jati groups that use the same title do not have a common ceremonial complex, and although in some cases a title can be considered a larger category within which several endogamous units are incorporated, the titles do not generally indicate the ritual boundaries of endogamy.

Jati names can be labels of defilement or purity, but jati titles seldom have such meaning. If and when titles become and are regarded as names, they acquire the meaning of defilement or purity. Groups that engage in ritually degrading occupations are usually subservient to groups which perform ritually pure occupations, and their names generally refer to defilement. But such groups may have titles that are the same as those of ritually superior groups.

Subservience is a political matter; defilement is relevant only in the context of interaction among members of different jati groups. Thus the use of jati titles is both an indicator of power relationships among jati groups and a procedure for testing the flow of power. The use of titles in the context of interaction within a jati group denotes the authority of a leader or leaders of that group, and the use of titles in the context of interjati group relationships denotes the authority of a group or of several groups. If a title is used frequently as a term of reference and address, then it acquires the meaning and function of a jati name by becoming a label of endogamy, and new titles emerge along with it.

The political authority of an individual or group in the village is expressed in the use of jati titles or political symbols that are the locally accepted vehicles of leadership and decision making.

Beyond jati names and jati titles, there are varna classificatory categories that the villagers occasionally use to validate their ritual and social rank. Varna categories such as Brahmin (class of priesthood), Kshatriya (warrior class), Vaishya (trader class), and Shudra (class of serfhood) refer to a hierarchy of social and sacred value. As indicated earlier, most of the theorizing, model building, and debate in the sociological and anthropological literature on India concerns the problem of the relationship between the conceptual paradigm of varna and the behavioral jati group statuses. The general assumption is that there is a correspondence between the varna categories and the manner in which members of jati groups conceptualize their status in the social hierarchy. In this view, jati is the behavioralized unit of varna: Varna is the archetypical symbol-complex or the prototypical model for all social relationships, and jati is the behavioral replication or duplication of varna. Scholars generally use the term caste (or subcaste) to characterize jati groups and use the term as a concept to identify the organizing principles, such as ritual pollution and hierarchy, which govern interjati group relationships. The labels of group identity such as jati names and jati titles are subsumed under the categories of caste or subcaste, and the caste system is explained as homologous and analogous to the varna hierarchical system. For example, Dumont (1970a:34) has argued that the conceptual reality of the caste system is in the hierarchical opposition between "pure" and "impure" and that this factor "accounts for the structural character of … caste and sub-caste being the same thing seen from different points of view." Tyler (1973:151) emphasizes "that the underlying logic of the jati system is identical to that of the varna system." But it is very important to note the fact that varna hierarchy, as I have indicated, relates to jati names: Both varna categories and jati names refer to ritual purity/pollution. The locus of this ritual purity/pollution is the occupation, and the principles of endogamy and hierarchy affirm the ritual status of the jati group and the group's rank in relation to other groups.

The importance of studying the history of the labels of group identity and their contextual significance in the village community cannot be emphasized enough. Without such analysis, the multiplicity of labels and their constantly changing roles will, understandably, result in massive confusion. Both jati names and jati titles may refer to occupational or territorial identities. In some instances a jati group's name may reflect its occupational prerogative but its title does not. In other instances the title may be indicative of occupational identity whereas the name signifies neither occupation nor place of origin. A name which in one group refers to occupational identity may be used as the title of another group which does not engage in that occupation. In some instances the name and title are inseparably linked, and in some cases the title is used as the preferred name by all or some of the members of a jati group. Titles and names are interchangeable labels of group identity, but the meaning and function of the labels differ depending on whether they are used as names or as titles.

The anthropological study of human groups is predicated on the assumption that it is possible to reveal the emic or native categories of thought and that anthropological descriptions approximate accurately the cultural reality, or the organization of cultural experience in a given setting. Modern anthropologists, however, seldom assert that their studies are totally objective or accurate: There is a recognition of the fact that the anthropological description is a particular version of the cultural reality of the people studied and that the people themselves have different versions of their cultural reality. Anthropologists attempt to be true to their commitment to reproduce a cultural reality as accurately as possible and try to avoid bias and distortions as much as possible.

The reader must also note the fact that the cultural realities of villagers may differ significantly. And, it is also necessary to keep in mind that although the study of a village community can be presented as a microcosm of the macro-Indian cultural reality, with a theoretical assumption that villagers everywhere enact similar cultural patterns of the Hindu civilization, studies of village communities should be viewed as partial data in our effort to understand India. Regional variations and historical factors often produce distinctive features in village cultural reality, and the diverse ethnolinguistic traditions shape the village cultural reality in multiple ways so that there are significant cultural differences between and among India's villages.

CHAPTER TWELVE

✣ *PULICAT: AN ESTUARINE VILLAGE OF EASTERN INDIA*

i. A Note on the Physical Structure of Pulicat Village

In this chapter I describe the physical features of Pulicat village as it existed (or more accurately, as I observed it) in 1970 to 1971 when I studied Pulicat as well as a number of other villages in southeastern India (politically demarcated as the state of Tamil Nadu). Pulicat is not a typical Indian village, if there is such a thing as a model Indian village that can be used to illustrate the typical village social structure (caste system), economic structure (jajmani system) and the Brahmanic/non-Brahmanic structure (religious system). The nature of Indian villages varies greatly in relation to whether they are agricultural villages (with land-owning and service castes), or whether they are single-caste coastal fishing villages. Some villages have very effective village councils and caste councils (panchayats) with rigid hierarchical arrangements of castes ranked in the social continuum of the most pure castes that are included in the Brahmin category, pure castes that are included in the Kshatriya and Vaisya categories, the impure castes included in the Shudra category and the most impure castes included in the Untouchable category. But, there are villages with two or three castes that exist in a relatively egalitarian relationship, and there are single-caste villages as well in some parts of India. Some villages are closely linked with urban centers and others are relatively autonomous; some villages are part-societies that are economically and politically related to neighboring towns; and some are isolated, functioning as relatively autonomous economic/political entities.

The study of the physical structure of a village often provides clues to the understanding of the ecological adaptations and the social structure of the village. The village center is generally occupied by pure castes and the households of impure castes usually radiate toward the periphery of the village with the most impure castes living in the peripheral areas of the village, reflecting the conceptions about occupational purity and impurity. It is not uncommon to have different sections of the village reserved for use by only certain castes and different water wells may be reserved for different castes. Religious centers (temples) frequently are built to serve different castes, and some temples may be out of bounds for impure and most impure castes. Social interaction in the village often dramatizes the existence of exclusive and inclusive privileges of the castes in the use of village physical space.

Pulicat village structure is typical in some senses and is atypical in other ways. Due to its historic association with sea trade in textiles and spices and its current association with fisheries and lake/sea fishing, Muslim and Hindu traders and fishing-caste communities constitute the important economic-sociopolitical components, but Pulicat village also manifests many social, economic, and religious characteristics that can be found in typical Indian villages. It is also an arguable question of whether Pulicat is a village or a town. *Pulicat was once identified as a town and it was once the center of the Dutch colonial settlements in eastern India, but at the time of my study, Pulicat was identified legally as a "revenue village" and politically as a "village" rather than as a "town."*

The castes (jati groups, to be more precise) who lived in Pulicat at the time of my study were:

Gurukkal Purohitar	Caste (jati) groups generally accorded *most pure* status. (Jati groups that claim to be included in Brahmin category.)

Beri Chettiar Idayar Kammalar Kanakar Kusavar Labbay Muslim Mudaliar Nadar Naidu Saliar Vanniar	Caste (jati) groups generally accorded *pure* status (alphabetized). (Jati groups that claim to be included in the Kshatriya and Vaisya categories.)

Ambattar	
Bebedel and Rengen Muslims	
Karaiyar	Caste (jati) groups generally accorded *impure* status.
Nattar	(Jati groups included in the Shudra category, although
Pandaram	some members may claim to be included in kshatriya or
Pattanava	Vaisya categories.)
Villiar	

Harijan (Parayan)	Caste (jati) group generally accorded *most impure* status.
	(Jati group included in the Untouchable category.)

I chose to study Pulicat village because it was an ideal setting for several reasons. The study of Pulicat's estuarine ecology provided insights into the cultural configurations of agricultural and coastal (fishing) settlements; the study of Pulicat history provided insights into the ancient trading settlements of India and indicated how European colonial domination occurred; the study of Pulicat ethnicity and caste provided insights into the emergence of Arabic traditions in India and showed how Telugu and Tamil caste groups coexisted; the study of Pulicat religious traditions provided insights into the historical development and functional similarities and differences between and among Hindus, Muslims, and Christians.

In this chapter, I describe the physical features of Pulicat in an effort to present the reader with an understanding of the settlement patterns of Pulicat. In the next chapter I present a discussion of the historical facts about Pulicat that indicate how the modern settlement patterns of Pulicat came into being. At the time of my study, Pulicat was identified as an estuarine fishing village that served as a market center, linking several villages surrounding Pulicat estuarine lake (see map page 205). Very few people imagined that Pulicat was once a major port settlement of eastern India and that for over two thousand years Pulicat Harbor was visited regularly by ships from southeast Asia and west Asia. The only reminders of the ancient and colonial heritage of Pulicat are the hundreds of dilapidated mansions that were once used by the wealthy traders and the decayed ancient Hindu temples tombstones of the Dutch, the remains of the Dutch fort (named Geldria) and the remnants of masonry work of the Dutch chapels.

ii. Pulicat and Its Hamlets

Pulicat lies at 80°19' longitude and 13°25' latitude, and covers an area of 4.57 square miles. The present territory of Pulicat was part of a much larger area administered by the Dutch between the 17th and 19th centuries. Hundreds of ruined mansions are found in Pulicat and the neighboring Karimanal village, which lies about two miles northeast of Pulicat. Pulicat revenue unit is composed of Pulicat village, four fishing hamlets (subvillages) across the Pulicat lake on the east, four fishing hamlets on the north, one semifishing hamlet on the south, and another semifishing hamlet on the northwest. The four hamlets on the east can be reached from Pulicat only by boat across the lake. There is a regular ferry service. The southern hamlet can be reached by wading through knee-deep water, but during the monsoon the water column exceeds three feet. The northwestern hamlet is separated from Pulicat by low-lying marshy ground which is inundated in the rainy season. The four northern hamlets are connected to Pulicat by a road along elevated embankments. (See map page 204.)

Pulicat Lake is India's second largest brackish water lake, and the southern portion covers an area of approximately 180 square miles, most of which lies in the territory of the state of Andhra Pradesh, north of the state of Tamil Nadu. From north to south, the lake is about 40 miles long; its breadth varies from 1 to 12 miles. About fifty islands, small and large, dot the lake. Most of the small islands lacked human settlements at the time of my study, but human skeletons and potsherds in lower layers of the earth indicate the presence of former settlements. Large settlements were found in two islands, both of which were in the territory of Andhra Pradesh. Thick layers of subfossil shells were found in all the islands and in the lake. The shells are excavated for commercial use and bring a large revenue. Between the sea and the lake is a strip of sand on which several fishing villages are situated. Four of these villages are included in the revenue unit of Pulicat. The sandy tract is thought to be caused by the recession of the sea, as subfossil shells and other fauna abound in deeper layers, but some think that the lake was formed during a storm when the sea "topped the low lying ridge of the coast line" (Crole 1879:76).

About two miles northeast of Pulicat village the lake opens into the Bay of Bengal. This opening, about two miles wide, is occasionally clogged by silt, during which time the low-lying areas surrounding Pulicat village are inundated by the waters of the lake. Because the lake is connected with the sea, it is subject to tidal influence, and commercial fishing in the lake is profitable mainly because of this influence which keeps the fish and shrimp moving in and out of the sea. The depth of the lake varies from 2 to 40 feet. The water column near Pulicat is relatively deep, which enabled the Arab and Western traders to enter the lake through its opening and dock the boats on the islands near Pulicat.

Pulicat village serves as a commercial center for several neighboring villages. Apart from the fish trade which brings the people of the surrounding hamlets to Pulicat, a variety of commodities from food and clothing to toilet articles are sold in Pulicat; Pulicat also has a number of tea shops and restaurants. Pulicat is the bus terminal for a number of neighboring villages: Ten private and government-owned buses ply from 4:45 a.m. to 7:45 p.m., and fish, shrimp, and crabs that are not transported by vans are transported by bus. Until a road was constructed in 1955, the main mode of transport was by boat on the canal; firewood and subfossil shells are still transported by boat.

Pulicat had twenty-eight streets at the time of my study, and I group them into four areas or zones. The four zones are (1) the northeastern zone where the Labbay, Rengen, and Bebedel Muslims lived; (2) the central zone inhabited mostly by Beri-Chettiars; (3) the southwestern zone where most of the non-Chettiar Hindus lived; and (4) the south peripheral zone in which members of the Villiar tribe lived.

The sacred places of the Hindu jatis were in the central and southwestern zones except for an amman temple known as Asalathamman Kovil where regular worship was performed, and a ruined temple that was once maintained by the Kaikolar jati. It is probable that the eastern section was once inhabited by Hindu jatis: An eastern street was named after the Karaiyar jati, although there was no Karaiyar living there. Bebedel Muslims lived in this area. A ruined temple in the south peripheral zone and a temple that was maintained by the Potters indicated that the zone delineated as southwestern was once the southern and western extremities of the village and that the Villiar who lived in the south peripheral zone were newcomers to the village.

The northern extremity of the village was once the Dutch residential area, and the street there, once called Gentlemen's Street, became known as Kottai Theru (Fort Street). On the southern side of this street were Labbay Muslim houses and shops, and a newly constructed fish market existed there. On the northern side of Fort Street toward the eastern extremity was the hospital maintained by the Panchayat Union (union of village councils); the hospital building was once the residence of the Dutch secretary of Pulicat. West of the hospital was the ruined Dutch fort Geldria, encircled by a moat used by the fisheries department of the Tamil Nadu government. North of the hospital was a building called Ari Bungalow, once the house of an Englishman, that eventually came to be used by the fisheries department. To the west of the Dutch fort was the road that connected Pulicat with the four northern hamlets, and further west was one of the two Dutch cemeteries found in the territory of Pulicat. North of the cemetery was a building where French Polish was sold as an alcoholic drink, and beside it a dilapidated movie theatre. A large margosa tree shadowed the Dutch cemetery, and nearby a thatched hut was used by a political party (Dravidian Advancement Association). Across the street to the west were the ruins of a Dutch church.

On the south side of Fort Street were several ruined buildings. Fort Street was cut by a diagonal road called Peria Theru (Big Street), on which Labbay Muslims lived. The mansions on this street were dilapidated, and several were in ruins. On the northeastern end of this road was a two-story building newly constructed by a Harijan (Untouchable) leader who had rented it to a government-controlled bank. A Christian doctor lived across the street in one of the dilapidated houses of a Labbay that he purchased and renovated. On the southern end of the Peri Theri was a mosque called Peria Palli (Big Mosque).

Chinna Theru (Small Street) was parallel to and south of Fort Street and was inhabited by Labbay Muslims. Labbay and Rengen Muslims lived on Kammala Chinnapayan Street, which was diagonal to Small Street and parallel to Big Street, and turned eventually toward the west. Rengen Muslims also lived in the area northwest of Kammala Chinnapayan Street called Bumikottai. The area south of Small Street, and between Kammala Chinnapayan Street and Big Street, was the burial ground of Rengen and Bebedel Muslims. Before it was converted into a burial ground for Rengen and Bebedel Muslims, who were newcomers to Pulicat, the area was lived in by the Labbay, whose residences were in ruins. The Labbay buried their dead within the premises of the mosque and not in the burial ground.

South of the burial ground was a mosque called Chinna Palli (Small Mosque). In the northwestern section where Labbay, Rengen, and Bebedel Muslims lived were four sacred places of the Muslims: a mosque named Haji Palli; a place called Zikiri Palli which once served as the Muslim school (the Zavia); a scripture-reading hall called Pungavanam Kaerimi; and a devotional hall of Rengen Muslims, called Ujira. On Big Street were a Muslim scripture-reading hall called Mauletu Hana and a Muslim youth center called Rauna-Hul Majalis Mohamadia Sangam (now in ruins); on the southern end of the street was Big Mosque.

Parallel to Big Street, on the east, was Asalathamman Kovil Street; Karaiyar Theru ran diagonally toward the east. Karaiyar jati members used to live there before Bebedel Muslims moved in. The ruins of houses and Hindu temples indicated that the area south of Karaiyar Theru was once a Hindu area, but Bebedel Muslims moved in, and there were two Muslim sacred places, a mausoleum called Nayainama Meday and the Ujira of Bebedel Muslims.

Adjoining the Ujira on the south was an ancient and very large Saivaite temple called Ishwaran Kovil, which was probably built by Telugu-speaking Chettiar traders about three hundred years ago. South of this temple were ruins of houses and two Brahmin households. Bebedel Muslims lived to the south and west of this area. Also in this area were an ice factory and the quarters of the factory staff. Some of these buildings housed the police station and police personnel before the station was shifted to another village in 1941.

The Telugu-speaking Chettiar traders lived in the central zone area when Pulicat prospered as a port village. Now there was only one house inhabited by a Telugu-speaking Chettiar, and the central zone was predominantly a residential area of Tamil-speaking Beri Chettiar. A temple called Adinarayana Kovil, which was dedicated to the patron deity of the Telugu Chettiar, remained in ruined condition. A huge Vaishnavaite temple called Perumal Kovil and two Saivaite temples named Pillaiar Kovil and Nattupillaiyar Kovil were in ruins. Regular worship took place in two Amman temples; one of the temples was distinguished as Dharmaraja Kovil by the Beri Chettiar who maintained it. Dharmaraja Kovil was built by the Beri Chettiar who were violent partisans in the disputes between left-hand and right-hand divisions of the caste groups of Pulicat. There were three Hindu devotional halls called Bajanakovil, Ranga Ramanuja Baktha Saba, and Shanmuganantha Saba. The Central Inland Fisheries office and the post office were located in the central zone.

The Padma and Pattu Saliar (weavers), Vanniar, Mudaliar, Naidu, Idayar, Kusavar, Ambattar, Kanakkar, Kammalar, and Pandaram lived in the southwestern zone. The ruined state of houses and temples in this zone indicated the migration of artisan groups to other places after the decline of Pulicat as a port town. Bavanarishi Kovil, the temple of the patron deity of Saliar (weavers), was in a ruined condition and there was no worship there. Kaliamman Kovil, maintained by the Kammalar (smiths), was in dilapidated condition. Kanakkar (accountants) worshipped their patron deity, Munieswaran, under a pepul tree. An amman temple known as Mukkunthamman Kovil, was the popular temple of the village. On the west was a Saivaite temple called Subramania Kovil which was built by the Beri Chettiar in recent times. A secondary school and a grade school, a Weaver's Society, the Panchayat (village council) Office, a pre- and post-natal center, a library, and a recreational center were in the southwestern zone.

In the south peripheral zone lived the Villiar (classified as a tribe) who were ranked above the Harijan (Untouchable castes). (Scavengers lived outside the village on the bus road, north of the village.) The nineteen Villiar houses were thatched huts. To the east of the Villiar residential area, at the southeastern extremity of the village, was an estuarine biological lab which was run by the Madras Christian College. Within the premises of the lab were the ruins of a temple once known as Anumantharayan Kovil. On the day of Naga Chatturthi (snake workshop), Hindus worshipped an anthill on these premises. The village latrine for women lay between the lab and the Villiar quarters; the surrounding area was used as a dump for rags and other items. West of the Villiar residential area was a pond called Kusavan (potter) Kulam from which clay for pottery making was taken. West of the pond were a temple called Vinayagar Kovil, maintained by the potters, and a mausoleum of a Hindu saint named Ama Sami, now in ruins.

The zones were not inhabited exclusively by any particular caste group. A few non-Chettiars lived in the central zone; and Christian and Hinu professionals were found in all the zones except the south peripheral zone. But in former times the physical structure reflected the social structure: The Labbay (Moors, as they were known then) lived in close proximity to the Dutch gentlemen on the north side of the village. Telugu-speaking Chettiar lived in the center of the village. Weavers, other artisan castes, and agricultural serfs lived in the south part of the village. The zone delineated as south peripheral was settled by the Villiar after the Dutch left the area.

iii. The Kuppams (Hamlets or Subvillages)

Until 1970 the revenue unit was also a political unit: Pulicat panchayat (village council) was composed of Pulicat and ten hamlets. In 1970 eight hamlets seceded and formed a separate panchayat. Since I have defined the boundary of Pulicat as the revenue boundary, both panchayats were included in the study. Also, the eight hamlets were closely linked with the economy of Pulicat proper.

The word *kuppam* usually meant a fishing hamlet, but there were kuppams in the interior of Tamil Nadu where the people did not engage in fishing. Sometimes the word kuppam indicated the existence of a single caste group in a bounded territory. The residential area of the Harijan (Untouchable) was generally called *cheri* in the state of Tamil Nadu, but a cheri was also referred to as a colony. The word colony indicated the status position of the Harijan—the Harijan did not participate fully in the society and functioned as the economically and politically powerless colonized peoples.

The Bay of Bengal lay to the east of this hamlet known as Koonang-Kuppam. Pulicat Lake was on the west and opened into the bay to the north of the hamlet. The two hamlets of Lighthouse-Kuppam and Nadu-Kuppam lay to the south. There were 111 houses, most of which were thatched huts. On the northern extremity of the hamlet was a Hindu devotional hall called Narayana Bajanakovil. Southwest of this temple was a grade school, and further west were two amman temples called Tulukkanapamman Kovil and Samalapeviamman Kovil. West of these temples was a banyan tree in which Mariamman was supposed to reside, and further west was an improvised shed for the worship of another amman called Kudaluriviamman. Close to the coast about half a mile south of the hamlet were the clay idols of Kanni (virgins) and Annanmar (elder brothers).

The hamlet called Nadu-Kuppam was bordered by the sea coast on the east, by a hamlet called Lighthouse-Kuppam on the west, on the north by the hamlet of Koonang-Kuppam, and on the south by another hamlet called Vairavan-Kuppam. In Nadu-Kuppam were nineteen houses, of which four had plastered walls and tiled roofs. At the southwest end of the village was an amman temple called Tulukkanathamman Kovil, and further west was a palm tree in which a spirit called Adiyarthu Muni was supposed to reside. On the northeast side of the hamlet, the goddess Sakthi was worshipped in an improvised shed, and north of this shed beside the sea coast were idols of Kanni and Annanmar. In the center of the hamlet was a palm tree said to be possessed by a spirit called Val Muni. Bajana Kovil (Hindu devotional hall) was located within the hamlet.

A lighthouse on the sea coast identified the hamlet of Harijans, called Lighthouse-Kuppam. Pulicat lake was on the west and Nadu-Kuppam to the east of Lighthouse-Kuppam. To the north was Koonang-Kuppam. There were fifty-eight houses, of which seven were tiled. Southwest of this hamlet was a large banyan tree where a spirit (nameless but of the Muni species) was supposed to reside. Close to this tree on the east was a devotional hall called Narayana Bajana-kovil and an amman temple called Dadiamman Kovil, both encircled by an outer wall. A bit to the north of the temple was a banyan tree with a platform built around its base; the tree was supposed to be possessed by an amman called Mannadiamman. A grade school was located at the southwestern end of the hamlet. On the western side was a palm tree supposed to be inhabited by a spirit of the Muni species. On the northern side an amman called Gengamman was worshipped in a hut.

Vairavan-Kuppam was the only hamlet in which three caste groups lived: Karaiyar, Pattanava, and Harijan fishermen inhabited three exclusive zones. The hamlet was bounded to the east by the Bay of Bengal, and on the west by Pulicat Lake. Lighthouse-Kuppam was on the north, and on the south, about two miles away, was a hamlet called Sathan-Kuppam, which was not part of Pulicat revenue unit. This hamlet had temples common to all the caste groups, but the Karaiyar and Pattanava castes used certain temples exclusively, and some temples were used only by the Harijan. Amman temples called Araniamman Kovil (also called Periapalathamman Kovil) and Samalathevi-amman Kovil and a banyan tree supposed to be possessed by an amman called Mariamman were maintained by the Pattanava and Karaiyar who lived on the northern side of the hamlet. The Harijan, who lived on the southern side, had an amman temple called Periapalathamman Kovil. Ellamuthuam-man Kovil, Yelumalayam Kovil, and Samalatheviamman Kovil (an improvised shed), Kodalaypallan Kovil, and a palm tree, supposedly possessed by Sadayamman, were used in common by all three caste groups. Idols of Kani and Annanmar were kept on the northern extremity of the hamlet. Of the 37 houses in Vairavankuppam, 16 belonged to the Karaiyar, 12 were inhabited by Pattanava, and 9 belonged to the Harijan; all were thatched huts.

Members of many caste groups lived in Edamani hamlet at the time of my study. The Nattar lived in twelve houses, most of which were tiled, in the northern section. The Harijan lived in twenty-eight houses, most of which were thatched huts, in the southwestern section. The Harijan section was called Edamani Colony. In the northern section were three amman temples. Two of these, Ponniamman Kovil and Lakshmiamman Kovil, were in small sheds, and the other, Ellamuthuamman Kovil, was in a small building. In the southwestern section was an amman temple called Ellamuthuamman Kovil; near the temple was a devotional hall (Bajana-Kovil). Both the temple and the hall were thatched sheds.

Kulathu-medu hamlet, which lay northwest of Pulicat village, was used by the Hindu caste groups of Pulicat for various purposes, from cattle herding to cremation of the dead. About three centuries ago, two large tanks were dug. One was probably dug by the Dutch government and the other by a Telugu-speaking trader, Tongu-Muthu Chetti. One tank was called Tongu-Muthu Chetti Kulam. The temples and pilgrimage centers that were maintained by the Chettiar were in ruins at the time of my study. Tongu-Muthu Chetti Kulam was used by a number of people from the northern hamlets, as well as by the Tamil-speaking Beri Chettiars of Pulicat who claimed to own it. Part of the territory was the cremation ground for the Pattanava and Harijan fishermen who lived in the north and for a number of other Hindu caste groups living in Pulicat; the Beri Chettiar had a building there to perform mortuary rites. The tank dug by the government was not used because the water was too saline.

Kulathu-medu had two settlements: On the west lived the Villiar in seventeen thatched huts; on the east lived Hindu and Muslim jati groups (two Vanniar households, one Mudaliar household, one Brahmin household, and three Muslim households) in tiled houses. In the eastern section were two amman temples called Asalathamman Kovil and Dhraupathiamman Kovil. In the western section a small amman temple called Sensurveramman Kovil existed. Near this temple was a banyan tree believed to be possessed by a spirit called Maduriveran. In the northern section of the hamlet, paddy cultivation is undertaken on a limited scale.

The northern hamlets were Kottai-Kuppam, Kottai-Kuppam Colony, Christhava-Kuppam, and Andi-Kuppam on a piece of land that was once an island but which the Dutch connected to Pulicat by road. On the east of Kottai-Kuppam, Christhava-Kuppam, and Andi-Kuppam was Pulicat Lake. Kottai-Kuppam was further north than the other three hamlets. A Dutch cemetery lay to the west of these hamlets, and at their southern border lay Andi-Kuppam. In the cemetery, the earliest burial of a Dutch soldier, as indicated by dates on the tombstones, took place in 1647. Kottai-Kuppam Colony was south of Christhava-Kuppam. It is likely that during the Dutch period this island had a small population of only Christian fishermen. Pattanava fishermen settled at the northern end of the island early in the 19th century. The Christians, who were of the Pattanava caste group, distinguished themselves from the Hindus by delineating the area where they lived as Christhava-Kuppam (Christian community). The Harijan settlement, known as Kottai-Kuppam Colony, was established in the 19th century. The Harijan were employed in boat transport along the Buckingham Canal which had been commissioned as a commercial route in the 19th century connecting eastern coastal villages to Madras city. The Harijan of this settlement lost their work with the construction of the road connecting Pulicat with other villages, and since 1955 were employed as laborers for fishermen and as agricultural serfs and construction workers. In the Harijan settlement were two Valluvar (potter caste) households, indicating that lime burning was done extensively until recent times. There were lime-burning kilns between Kulathumedu and the

Dutch cemetery. Andi-Kuppam came into being in the 20th century when a few Pattanava fishermen settled down on the southern extremity of the island.

There were 134 houses in Christhava-Kuppam, most of which were tiled. A Roman Catholic church, a Catholic devotional hall, a Catholic-maintained school, and a parish bungalow existed in the hamlet. Kottai-Kuppam had 67 houses. Kottai-Kuppam Colony had 36 houses, of which two belonged to the Valluva caste. Andi-Kuppam had 50 houses. Most of the houses were thatched huts. Kottai-Kuppam had its own separate amman temple and Hindu devotional hall.

CHAPTER THIRTEEN

✣ A BRIEF HISTORY OF PULICAT VILLAGE

i. Political History of Pulicat

Pulicat was an important seaport of eastern India in ancient times, and it was a major center for the manufacture and distribution of cotton textiles. Its name was derived from the Tamil word *Pazhavaerkadu* (forest of fruit trees), and it was called *Paliakata* by the Dutch in documents dating back to the 17th century. When Tamil kingdoms flourished in southern India from the 5th century B.C.E. to the 3rd century C.E., Pulicat was a northern outpost of Tamil territory (Moses 1923:75). With the decline of Tamil kingdoms in the 3rd century C.E., a major part of Tamil territory, including the northern region, came under Pallava kings of the north. In the 9th century one of the Tamil kingdoms in the south expanded to include the northern territory. This northern territory was called *Thondaimandalam* (identified by the Europeans as the Coromandel Coast). The shores of Thomdaimandalam were studded with ports containing Arab settlements, among which was Pulicat.

In the oral tradition of Pulicat, there are different interpretations of the origin of the name Pulicat and different histories of the founding of Pulicat as a seaport. I give below a few of these interpretations and oral histories. Many villagers believe that the name *Pazhavaerkadu* is derived from the Tamil words *pazhia* (old) and *vaerdadu* (babul-forest), but in the vil-lage folklore the name Pazhaverkadu is also traced to four other sources: (1) Pazhavaerdaku owes its name to the fact that the region was under the jurisdiction of *pazhia* (old) *arkadu* (the region of Arcot) *navabu* (Muslim-prince); (2) Pazhaverkadu was named after a princess called *Pavazha-kodi* (pearl-tendril); (3) Pazhaverkadu was once a forest (*kadu*) full of fruits (*pazham*); (4) the coast of Pazhaverkadu was well known for the abudance of *pavazham* (pearls).

Muslim traders (known as Labbay) believe that Pulicat was once a dense forest that was cleared by Arab settlers. In this tradition it was the Arab settlers who developed Pulicat into a harbor, and it was they who secured land from the Muslim prince of Arcot for the Dutch to found a factory there and undertake trade in spices, precious stones, and textiles; these Muslims also believe that they were once so very wealthy they they turned down a grant of land from the Muslim prince of Arcot to maintain their mosques.

High-caste Hindus believe that the village of Pulicat was settled by wealthy Telugu-speaking Chettiars who developed the port there to expand their sea trade between eastern India and southeast Asia. The Dutch had, it is believed, settled in Pulicat with the approval of a Hindu prince, and Pulicat was, for several centuries before the arrival of Arabs and Dutch, an important trading and pilgrimage center. This tradition links Pulicat to fifteen surrounding hamlets (and to dozens of ancient Hindu dynasties), and there exists a rich folklore of Hindu temples and deities of Pulicat.

The Roman Catholic Christians believe that Christianity was introduced in 1515, as the *Catholic Directory of India* denotes that year as the founding of the Catholic church in Pulicat. Many Christians and some Hindus believe in an oral tradition that refers to a miracle that led to the building of a Christian church in Pulicat. The legend is that a Hindu fisherman came across an idol of Virgin Mary, and that he was paralyzed when he struck it with his axe, mistaking it for firewood. On hearing this, Portuguese settlers who lived about 30 miles south of Pulicat (in San Thome which became a French port temporarily and is now a suburb of Madras city) came and built a church, placing the idol in it.

In the 14th century, Tamil kingdoms in the south were invaded by Muslim kings and generals from the north, but for the next two hundred years Telugu kings held hegemony over a large part of Tamil territory, including Pulicat. In the twilight of Telugu martial power, and when the Muslim kingdoms of the north were expanding, the trading companies of Portugal, The Netherlands, Denmark, France, and England sought to establish trading posts in a number of coastal villages of eastern and western India.

When the Dutch arrived on the coast of Tamil territory in the early 17th century, they tried to eliminate the Portuguese trade centers in India (that had been established in the 16th century) as well as the Arab traders, who functioned as middlemen in the trade between the peoples of southern India and the Straits settlements (southeast Asia). In 1609 the Dutch secured permission from a Telugu king to build a trading post in Pulicat. They fortified the village as a defense against the Telugu, Tamil, and Muslim kings as well as against the Portuguese and within four years established control over sea trade in eastern India. Pulicat served as the seat of Dutch government in India, and under pressure from the Dutch, an English trading post established in Pulicat in 1619 was disbanded in 1622.

The frequent changes in the fortunes of Telugu, Tamil, and Muslim kings and generals did not destroy trade or the handloom industry of Pulicat. The Dutch presence in Pulicat was beneficial to the weavers and the Hindu and Muslim traders. During their rule, the population of the village must have been over 10,000, and it is likely that over 1000 handlooms operated in Pulicat alone. The sole occupation of several jati groups in Pulicat and in the hinterland of Tamil, Telugu, and Kannada territories was the manufacture of cloth for export. Muslim and Hindu traders controlled internal commerce, and external sea trade was controlled by the Dutch (after the Dutch settlement was established in Pulicat).

Pulicat figured prominently in history because Telugu, Tamil and Muslim kings vied with one another for the control of the port. Port revenue provided a major source of income for those who controlled Pulicat. Barbosa, traveling through Tamil territory in the early 16th century, described Pulicat as a "grand port which was frequented by an infinite number of Moorish vessels from all quarters" (Moses 1923:78). Famine, resulting from the looting of Hindu and Muslim armies, wiped out a large number of people in port villages. In Pulicat and in a southern port village called San Thome that was controlled by the French, an estimated 30,000 died of starvation in 1647 (Sewell 1932:279). A few years later, San Thome became a suburb of Madras city (located about 30 miles south of Pulicat), which was established by the English as the main port settlement of southeastern India with a foritification called Fort St. George.

In the 1630s a chaplain stationed at Pulicat with the Dutch trading post wrote that "among Shudras there are many and diverse groups whereof each pretendeth to surpass the others; and therefore it doth oftimes hap that great strife ariseth in the land, insomuch as one caste or another, be it in marriage or in burial of the dead goeth beyond what is the custom" (quoted in Mandelbaum 1970:217–18). The same writer mentions a specific instance of inter-jati dispute which occurred at Pulicat in 1640: A particular method of burial that was the privilege of one jati was adopted by another jati, and this gave rise to physical violence (see Singer and Cohn 1968:6).

As the following quote suggests, the Dutch and Pulicat were, in some ways, part of the European discovery of India and contributed to the development of oriental scholarship:

> The Dutchman Abraham Roger was sent out to the Dutch settlement at Pulicat on the Coromandel Coast of southeast India in 1632 and stayed there for 10 years, followed by five in Batavia (now Jakarta). He knew Tamil and he made friends with Brahmins who could introduce him to

Hindu customs and Sanskrit classics. In a book put together after his death there is a full account of the caste system and of various Hindu sects, of the social and religious duties of Brahmins, the temples and religious ceremonies, the devotion of Siva and Vishnu, the Hindu conception of the soul. He showed ... a "willingness to study Hinduism as a living religion which must be understood in its own terms," and his book was still useful in the age of the Oriental scholar Max Muller, two centuries later.

—Holmes (1993:16)

Pulicat and its vicinity came under a Telugu king temporarily in 1626, and in 1644 a Muslim general from the north defeated the Dutch. But these incursions did not hamper the Dutch monopoly of trade, and Pulicat continued to exist as the principal trading post of the Dutch in southern India. The Dutch participated vigorously in many of the battles of Telugu princes and Muslim generals, supporting the side whose success would most benefit the Dutch presence in Pulicat. In 1689 the seat of Dutch government in India was moved to another port village in eastern India which the Dutch had captured from the Portuguese, thus reducing Pulicat to the rank of a principality. (See Burgess 1913:67–114; Sewell 1932:273–83; Krishnaswamy 1964:322–60; and Sridharan 1965:61–63.)

The Dutch rule in Pulicat lasted, with a few interruptions, for 214 years. In the 17th century, the area surrounding Pulicat was ruled by a Muslim prince, and this area was ceded to the British in 1760 as a *jagir* (estate) by the Muslim prince. The British fought and defeated the Dutch in 1781, and again in 1785 and 1795. (On the main road in Pulicat there is a marker with the inscription, "Site of the first Dutch Settlement in India, Fort called Geldria. The spot was finally captured by the English in 1795.") Dutch control of Pulicat lasted until 1825, when the village was annexed to the British territory (which had been given to the British by the Muslim prince in 1760).

Under British rule, villagers were allowed to participate in political activities that transcended the village. Natives were elected to quasi-autonomous political units called District Boards which advised the British revenue collector on matters relating to education, public health, and general development. Pulicat was identified as a "town" and administration of Pulicat was entrusted to the "elected town council members." The members of the town council were often nominees of the jati elders, and the chairman was either a member of the economically powerful Beri Chettiar jati group, or the Muslim Labbay (trader) jati group. The town council became defunct in 1938, as the income from the taxes in Pulicat was insufficient to maintain the amenities offered by the town.

After the demise of the town council, Pulicat territory became a "revenue village" with a state-appointed revenue-legal official called the *munisiff.*

The munisiff was aided by the village accountant (*karnam*) and the village watchmen (*thalayari*). The munisiff was empowered to conduct trials and jail miscreants but was eventually supposed to hand such persons over to the police. Most of the interhamlet disputes were settled by the munisiff, who usually received gratuitous gifts for not reporting them to the police, or by the village and jati panchayats. Police involvement in the village disputes was rare. If someone reported acts of violence to the police without consulting the panchayat or the munisiff, he was censured by the panchayat. The main function of the munisiff was to record births and deaths and collect revenue. The karnam maintained the revenue records and exerted considerable power, as he wrote legal documents for the villagers.

ii. Recent Economic and Social History of Pulicat

With the departure of the Dutch in 1825, Pulicat changed from a center of trade and textile production to a health resort and fishing village. Retired British officials acquired land and mansions in the area, and Pulicat was probably a popular summer rendezvous. Casuarina (*Casuarina muricata*) was cultivated and sold as firewood, primarily by British settlers. But the official concern of the British was to consolidate their interests in the town of Madras, which was about 30 miles south of Pulicat; and when the blue hills (*Nilagiri*) of southern India became accessible for establishing summer residences or bungalows (to escape the extremely hot and humid climate of eastern India), even the little importance that Pulicat had as a health resort vanished. (In 1895 the lighthouse at Pulicat was rebuilt, and its function was to warn ships away from the dangerous shoals of Pulicat.)

The decline of Pulicat as a trading and textile center started even before the Dutch left Pulicat. In the 19th century the British-controlled port at Madras expanded, and eastern trade of southern India was channeled mostly through this port. By the latter part of the 18th century the Dutch were no longer the major sea power. The fact that the customs house at Pulicat was closed and Pulicat ceased to be a port of call in the 19th century did not by itself destroy the traders and weavers of Pulicat, because the Muslim and Hindu traders of Pulicat had access to the port at Madras via a canal which the British had built in the early 19th century (Buckingham Canal connected Pulicat Lake and Madras city). What caused the decline was the British policy of systematic annihilation of the indigenous textile industry and trade of eastern India. Whereas the Dutch had been satisfied to eliminate middlemen and amass the profits of trade for themselves, the British took over the entire trade operation and imported British goods, particularly cloth and yarn, for local consumption. Heavy taxation of indigenous goods, particularly cloth, and the banning of direct imports and exports by the natives, and the presence of tax-exempt British commodities in the market, eventually led to the destruction of the local economy.

A few Muslim and Chettiar traders of Pulicat continued their profession collaborating with British businessmen based in Madras. The main commodity of trade was the colored cotton cloth called *lungi*, which was in great demand in countries known today as Malaysia, Indonesia, and Thailand. A few Muslim traders who had relatives living permanently or temporarily in those countries had trade connections there. The British tolerated native trade in lungi because it brought them revenue. The cloth became so popular during the Dutch rule of Pulicat that the Dutch trade mark *paliakat-lungi* (cloth made in Pulicat) was used for all colored cotton cloth exported from eastern India. (Pulicat lungi is famous even today in southeast Asia, particularly in Malaysia.)

By the early 20th century all the Dutch mansions had decayed, and building contractors from Madras came to strip them of their wooden doors and windows for use elsewhere. Some of these mansions were occupied by the Muslim traders (Labbay) of Pulicat, but others were owned and used by wealthy Europeans and natives of Madras only as holiday homes. All the mansions were neglected and remained in a dilapidated condition. An anthropologist who studied the Muslim traders (Labbay) in 1923 wrote:

> The houses built at a time when Pulicat was a flourishing emporium are very pretentious but unfortunately many of them are in ruin owing to the neglect to repair the blighting effects of biting winds loaded with salt spray. Many of the inhabitants are poor and eke out a precarious living selling stones, timber, pillars etc. from the ruins of the palatial residences built by their rich forbears.
>
> —*Moses (1923:82)*

Historically, the Labbay came to acquire an identity comparable to that of the Brahmin jati, and a status comparable to that of the Hindu warrior jati. The Labbay prohibited intermarriage between themselves and other Muslims and maintained separate cemeteries. The Tamil spoken by the Labbay contained Arabic words because they sent their children to learn and read Tamil in Arabic script and to memorize the Koran. The Labbay were ranked high in social status because of their history of great wealth and claims to Arabic heritage. Their poverty in the 20th century did not deprive them of high status as they continued to officiate over religious ceremonies.

The jatis of Pulicat were grouped into left-hand and right-hand jatis as it was the custom in the Tamil territory. The right-hand jatis in Pulicat were Mudaliar (Vellalan), Kanakkar, Vannan, Ambattar, Balija Naidu, Labbay (Muslim), Benedel Muslims, Pattanava fishermen, Pattu and Padma Saliar,

Idayar, Udayar and Parayan (Harijan). The left-hand jatis were Beri Chettiar, Kammalar, Vanniar, Nattar, Kaikolars, Chempadava fishermen, Rengen Muslims, and Christian Pattanava. Three jatis, the Thotti (scavenger), Panachavan (the temple assistant), and Pandaram (non-Brahmin priest) were not included in either segment. Each division had its own temples in Pulicat, and a few temples were built as a result of disputes over custodianship. A few jati groups which were involved in the violent conflict between the two divisions migrated to other villages in the 20th century, and after this dispersion disputes seldom occurred.

At the time of my study, the Hindu jatis no longer identified themselves with left-hand or right-hand segments for political or social reasons. However, Muslims continued to be divided into Labbay and Rengen and Bebedel Muslims, and violent disputes between Rengen and Bebedel Muslims were common.

iii. Recent Religious History of Pulicat

As noted above, there were Hindu, Muslim and Christian traditions in Pulicat when the British possessed the village. Hinduism was the only powerful and important religious tradition during the period when Tamil and Telugu kings ruled Pulicat. There existed many large Hindu temples dedicated to the gods Siva, Vishnu, and Subramaniya, and there were several Hindu temples dedicated to the *amman* (mother goddess) and Hindu shrines dedicated to the *kula theyvam* (deities who were also worshipped as family deities). The amman was worshipped as the *grama theyvathai* (village goddess). Hinduism continued to prosper in Pulicat during the Dutch and British periods, but Islam and Christianity also acquired importance in Pulicat during these periods.

The practice of Islam in Pulicat probably dates back to the time when Islam was first introduced to the coastal settlements of India in the 8th century C.E. There were Arab settlements on the Coramandel coast of eastern India (including Pulicat) prior to the advent of Islam, and Islam was introduced in Pulicat by the Islamicized Arab traders. After the fortification of Pulicat by the Dutch, mosques were built by the Arab traders in Pulicat proper, and the mosques that were built before the Dutch rule were used primarily by non-Arab Muslim converts. Two large mosques, named *Periapalli* (big mosque) and *Chinnapalli* (small mosque), and smaller places of worship and scripture reading were built in recent times. The Muslim traders, who claimed to be racially different from the other Muslims, were associated with the proper maintenance of the large mosques. The other Muslims, who were divided into sociopolitical groupings known as the Rengen party and the Bebedel party, built sacred halls known as *ujiras* for conducing special ceremonies and festivals associated with each group.

All the Muslims in Pulicat belonged to the same sectarian tradition (*Sunni-Shaf'i*) and spoke Tamil, but the Muslim traders (Labbay) kept themselves isolated as an endogamous group within the Muslim community of the village. The Labbay were the only Muslims who could read and write Arabic, and as a result religious and political authority came to be vested in them. The Labbay functioned as the *peshimams* (priests), *kazis* (registrars), and *mauluvis* (commentators of the Koran). In Pulicat, as a result, the term Labbay became synonymous with priest; every male Labbay, by virtue of his education, could perform priestly duties that required recitation of scriptures.

In contrast to the stigmatized meaning which the label Labbay had in different parts of Tamil country and to its use as a classificatory category of Tamil-speaking Muslims in general, the Muslim traders of Pulicat used the label to signify their Arabic heritage as well as their social and cultural superiority over the other Muslims in Pulicat and to denote their exclusive style of life and religiosity. The mythology of the Arabic heritage was written down in Tamil, using Arabic script, about fifty years ago. The following is a translation of this document:

This is a chronicle which tells about our ancestors and about how they came to establish their settlement in Pulicat.

In ancient Medina there lived a group of Muslim devotees known as Khadims, or servants of the prophet, whose main occupation was to conduct prayers and to tend to the up-keep of the tomb of the prophet Mohammed; the Khadims possessed supernatural powers and they could perform miracles for those who asked them to intercede with the prophet; they lived in isolation, away from the people of Medina. Medina was governed by Bathushas who were the successors of the Imams Hanifi, Banbali, Shafi and Malik who had founded separate sects. At the time of the rule of Bathusha Yusuf the Khadims were persecuted: the Kathusha demanded the Khadims to give tributes to him. …

As the Khadims declined to meet the demands of the Kathusha the latter tried to deprive them of the supernatural powers before he could punish them. He asked them to bring him eggs as gifts and put the eggs in the same basket. Then he asked them to identify the eggs that belonged to each of the Khadims and decreed that they should consume the eggs. The duplicity of the Bathusha was unknown to the Khadims, and they committed the sin of consuming food that belonged to another, and, as a result, they lost their supernatural powers. When the Bathusha asked them to perform miracles they could not, and convinced that punishing the Khadims would not affect him any more, the Bathusha decided to deport them. This occurred in the year of Hijiri 668. The Khadims and their families were placed in four ships.

The four ships drifted in four different directions; one reached Malay; two reached the south-eastern coast of India; and another reached the south-western coast of India. *The Khadims who reached the south-eastern coast identified themselves as Labbays and were distinguished from the natives as marakabu, or the people of the ship* [emphasis mine]. Those who reached the south-western coast of India identified themselves as Navitha, or the new people, and those who arrived in Malaya identified themselves as Hana-Hajee.

One of the Labbay settlements was in the Chozha kingdom of Tamil Nadu. The settlers flourished in the port town of Kahir-Pattinam, but the king started persecuting them. As a result the Labbays migrated towards the north of Pulicat. By this time, the Labbays adopted the Tamil language and were engaged in trade, but, as they found the place unsuitable, moved south to the Thoni-Revu (harbour of boats) section of Pulicat.

Long after the Labbays had established themselves in the Thoni-Revu section of Pulicat, a Dutch ship arrived there and the captain wanted water. Mustafa Maricayer, who was the head of a prosperous Labbay lineage, received the captain and offered to trade with the Dutch. The Dutch ship called on Thoni-Revu again, and Mustafa Maricayer promised the captain that he could procure land for the Dutch to build a factory and fort. With his trade connections with the Dutch Mustafa Maricayer became a very wealthy man, and he went to the king of Arcot with gifts for procuring land for the Dutch. Mustafa Maricayer was successful in getting land, and Pulicat forest was cleared for the building of the Dutch fort in Hiriji 772. The Labbays moved their settlement from the Thoni-Revu section of Pulicat to Pulicat proper.

The Dutch provided capital for the Labbays and the latter prospered. Mosques were built in Pulicat proper and in the Thoni-Revu section of Pulicat. In Hijiri 1091, the mosque in Thoni-Revu section was renovated. In Hijiri 1121, a smaller mosque called Chinnpalli was built and this was renovated in Hiriji 1261. The Labbays belong to the Shaf'i sect. The fort in Pulicat was under the Dutch for 143 years. In Hijiri 1218 the English captured the fort but the Dutch returned in Hijiri 1233 and ruled for five more years before the English dislodged them permanently.

Not long ago when the king of Arcot offered a gift of land for the maintenance of the mosques in Pulicat, the Labbays turned the offer down as they were very wealthy. The prince gave the gift to a Muslim in a near-by village, but this gift was stolen from him by a kazi.

Christianity in Pulicat has had a long tradition (the Roman Catholic church was probably built in the 16th century) but was confined to one hamlet of Pulicat. The people of this hamlet belonged to the Pattanava Hindu jati before their conversion to Roman Catholicism. The Dutch had two churches, one outside and one inside the Pulicat fort known as Geldria. According to

Dutch records, a Dutch chaplain was stationed at Pulicat, and from the existence of a large number of tombstones of the Dutch within the boundaries of the fort, it can be inferred that Pulicat was inhabited by large numbers of Dutch. There is no evidence that the Dutch converted the natives to Christianity. Conversion to Christianity in Pulicat occurred through the proselytization of Hindus by Roman Catholic (primarily Portuguese) missionaries from Goa and other Roman Catholic strongholds in the coastal areas of southern India. The Roman Catholic Christians of Pulicat were served by priests from the Madras bishopric who were stationed in a bungalow near the Pattanava Christian hamlet. The Pattanava Christians prospered in the 20th century, becoming a significant political bloc in Pulicat.

CHAPTER FOURTEEN

ECONOMIC AND SOCIOPOLITICAL TRADITIONS OF PULICAT VILLAGE

i. Patrons and Clients in the Economic Structure of Pulicat

At the time of my study, the Beri Chettiar monopolized the sale of rice, groceries, and textiles and gave financial credit to the fishermen jatis (Pattanava Hindu, Karaiyar, Nattar, Pattanava Christian, and Harijan). The Labbay and the weavers (particularly the Pattu and Padma Saliars) also borrowed from the Beri Chettiar in time of need. Artisan jatis (Kammalr or blacksmiths and goldsmiths, and Kusavar or potters), Ambattar (barber), Pandaram (non-Brahmin priest), and Brahmin (temple priest and officator over crisis rites) rendered services and received payment in cash. Idayars (herdsmen) sold milk; several members belonging to Balija Naidus (a Telugu-speaking jati), Nadar, Vanniar and Mudaliar (cultivating jatis) and Bebedel and Rengen Muslims (who were mainly engaged in the fish trade) operated tea or cigarette shops, and some were professional tailors. Villiars (generally classified as a tribe) engaged in fishing but also served as household servants and laborers.

The financial credit provided by the Beri Chettiar was pivotal to the functioning of the village social system. In the lean seasons of fishing, the fishing jatis borrowed money to ward off starvation. Other jatis also borrowed from the Beri Chettiar. Thus the Beri Chettiar were the patrons and all the other jatis were the clients in the credit structure which enabled the survival of all the jatis. The fishing jatis controlled the lake and sea and were the source of wealth for the whole village, but were dependent on the creditors, the Beri Chettiar.

A combination of tenure, credit, and mortgage permeated every economic transaction in the village. Lease agreements and readily available credit kept the village economy viable. Persons selling fruit, vegetables, meat, and fish, as well as breakfasts and lunches, and the widows and elderly women called *angadikarichi* who were permitted to sell food in the hamlets, were ancillary to the Beri Chettiar creditors and fish contractors, upon whom the complex credit and mortgage structures depended. All wealth derived ultimately from the fishermen.

Intensive fishing was done in named zones and areas of Pulicat Lake. Those engaged in lake fishing acquired rights of ownership over specific areas in the lake. These rights to specific areas alternated between individuals, and between groups. The rights could also be mortgaged. Fish contractors paid sums ranging from $1000 to $2000 to secure exclusive rights to purchase the fish caught by all the fishermen in a hamlet. This money was called lease money (*kuthakay panam*). The jati council, which represented the hamlet, agreed that no one in the hamlet would sell fish in the open market. The lease money was considered a gift rather than a loan. The contractor usually paid less than the market price and thus was able to make a profit. Female contractors paid lease money to fishermen who caught crabs in the lake. Occasionally, hamlets surrendered or mortgaged their rights to allotted areas in the lake in exchange for lease money. The contractors employed either the fishermen of the same hamlet or of other hamlets to fish in the allotted area. If the fishing enterprise proved successful, the contractor was obliged to share part of his profit with the fishermen who gave him the mortgage. A hamlet might also decide to secure lease money without surrendering rights over fishing or selling. In this case, the lessee (the person who made the gift to the hamlet) was entitled to tax or impose a levy on every fishing expedition undertaken in the hamlet. This form of lease applied more often in the hamlets engaged in sea fishing than in those engaged in lake fishing.

Lake tenure was an essential part of the village economy. The money secured from the lessee was used to return the loans accrued by the hamlet at an earlier time. Any surplus was either spent on amman temple ceremonies, or distributed equally among the male adults. In the hamlet, every adult male was an economic unit (*thalaykattu*, literally "head tie") required to share in the fortunes and misfortunes of the hamlet. Every male adult had a share (*pangu*) in the money received from a lessee or borrowed from a creditor, and he was obliged to honor the agreement with the lessee and the creditor. Only those who had a share acquired fishing rights in the lake.

Jati groups who engaged in lake fishing, such as Pattanava Hindus, Pattanava Christians, and Harijans, had an elaborate economic regulatory system called *padu muray* (area system). Padu muray determined the time, place, and personnel of the fishing operations and bestowed equal rights to every adult male (*thalaykattu*). Persons within this system were shareholders in the corporate enterprise by which fish were caught. Padu muray may also be seen as a limited concern or licensing authority that functioned as an economic leveler.

On attaining the age of 18, a boy became an economic unit (thalay-takku). He was required to pay a nominal fee to the village council for such recognition. Until this time, he was not given a share, and he was not held responsible in any of the hamlet's credits and liabilities. In some hamlets, a distinction was made between those who had shares, and those with shares who also had areas in the lake registered in their name. In order to have a registered area, it was necessary to have a share, but this was not sufficient. In the hamlets where a distinction between shareholder (*pangukaran*) and area owner (*padukaran* or *padu urimaykaran*) was made, area owners were recruited from among the shareholders when areas in the lake were being reallocated. Usually only married men and those who possessed fishing nets were allotted *padu* (a registered area), which encouraged shareholders either to get married or to buy nets. The eldest son inherited the padu of his father, and the other sons were required to file applications for padu with the village council. The successful candidates were obliged to make nominal payments to the village council and were then given the title *padu urimaykaran* (owner of area rights). Owners of area rights who neglected to make use of their areas were removed from membership, and if they applied for admission again they had to pay a heavy fine to the village council.

Shrimp fishing was the lucrative form of fishing in the lake. The lake was divided into a number of named zones, and each zone into a number of named areas. Each area was registered in the name of a person, but each person had to circulate, moving from one registered area to another according to a fixed schedule. Fishing with drag nets (*badi valay*) required the labor of 50 to 60 persons. Usually most labor was recruited from among the shareholders of the same hamlet, but individuals from other villages were also employed. The owner of the net paid half of the wages in advance and shared with the laborers 50 percent of the earnings above and beyond their wages. Only a certain number of nets could be used in the lake at a time; therefore, a net used on a particular day could be used again only after all the other nets in the hamlet had been used in turn. Nets were put out in particular areas where their owners had area rights. The wealth of a fisherman was measured by the number of nets and boats he possessed. By lending the nets and boats, he could secure one or more shares in the earnings. The number of shares given in return for the use of the nets varied, and the most profitable property was the drag net which provided the owner with 50 percent of the earnings.

In some hamlets, adult males (economic units or thalaykattukaran) were divided into groups called *jamay* or *jamat*. Each jamat had particular areas and days allotted to it. A jamat was usually composed of 15 to 26 persons and had a leader. Earnings of the jamat were evenly distributed among members of the jamat, and if one of the members was sick and could not partici-pate in the fishing operations, he was still entitled to a share.

Not only were different hamlets allotted areas, but hamlets exploiting the same zones in the lake shared the fishing rights among themselves on an egalitarian basis. Each hamlet was allotted specific days. Usually two hamlets operated in a given zone, although they had different areas, and the type of net that could be used was also specified. The following table illustrates the circulation of individuals and hamlets in the lake. Four hamlets labeled A, B, C, and D, and three groups in each hamlet numbered 1, 2, and 3, would cir-culate as in Model I. If two hamlets agreed to exploit a zone on the same day, the circulation would be as in Model II.

Not all fishing in the lake came under the area system. One section of the lake had no demarcated areas and was fished by area owners on days when they had no area allotment and by the elderly who seldom used the areas. There was no registered area for angling, which was commonly done. Villiars and Nattars who also fished in the lake along with the Pattanava Hin-dus, Pattanava Christians, and Harijans had no elaborate area system. Catch-ing crabs was undertaken regularly by fishermen of three hamlets and was very remunerative. The three hamlets took turns using the lake for this activi-ty. The area in the lake where crabs were abundant was called *nandu padu* (crab area), and Harijans had no rights in the area. Crab catching and fishing occurred simultaneously in the lake; men caught crabs when it was not their turn to fish.

As fishing operations in Pulicat Lake increased, Bebedel and Rengen Muslims, who had been household servants of Muslim traders (Labbay) when they were prosperous, became fish contractors. The increase in the fish trade

Model I

	Mon.	Tues.	Wed.	Thurs.	Fri.	Sat.	Sun.
Week 1	A-1	B-1	C-1	D-1	A-2	B-2	C-2
Week 2	D-2	A-3	B-3	C-3	D-3	A-1	B-1

Model II

	Mon.	Tues.	Wed.	Thurs.	Fri.	Sat.	Sun.
Week 1							
Zone I							
area (i)	A-1	A-2	A-3	C-1	C-2	C-3	B-1
area (ii)	B-1	B-2	B-3	D-1	D-2	D-3	A-1
Week 2							
Zone I							
area (i)	B-2	B-3	D-1	D-2	D-3	A-1	A-2
area (ii)	A-2	A-3	C-1	C-2	C-3	B-1	B-2

led to rivalry among the fishermen of different hamlets, and conflict among them was common. In one of the conflicts, a few Pattanava Hindus were murdered by Pattanava Christians. Eventually the fishing hamlets agreed to use the fishing areas in Pulicat Lake on alternate days.

As fish contractors began to export fish and the fishing enterprise expanded, groups previously engaged in other occupations became indirectly or directly involved with fishing. A number of Mudaliars, Vanniars, Idayars, Bebedel Muslims, Rengen Muslims, and Naidus opened coffee shops and cigarette shops to cater to the fishermen. Two other economic enterprises were palm-leaf basketry and weaving by handlooms. Almost every adult female in the households of Muslim traders (Labbay) took up basketry, which often enabled the traders to subsist. Kammalar (smiths), Kusavar (potters), and Ambattar (barbers) continued their traditional occupations.

ii. Sociopolitical Structure of Pulicat Village

In social status, the Beri Chettiar and the Muslim traders who identified themselves as the Labbay ranked high, and Harijans were ranked at the bottom. The Villiar, although similar in food habits and rituals to the Harijan, were regarded as clean, and many served as household servants. All three Muslim groups had the same food habits, but only the Labbay were considered clean. After the migration of the Telugu-speaking Chettiar and the impoverishment of the Labbay, the Beri Chettiar ranked above every other group. However, Mudaliars and Saliars did not acknowledge the high rank of the Beri Chettiars. The ranks of jati groups (given below) are only approximate, because different groups ranked themselves and others in different ways at different times. Further, the rankings are meaningless if it is not known how the people using them interpret them in different contexts.

Jati groups in Pulicat had multiple status labels that could be identified as representing jati names, jati titles, and *varna* or scriptural ascriptions and attributes. These labels were often used interchangeably so that an observer would find it difficult to identify the basic endogamous groups and relate them to larger categories of social classification. Only through the study of the history of the labels of group identity and their contextual significance—what the group names and titles mean to the users and how such usages acquired significance at different intra- and intergroup levels of interaction—can jati labels be understood. Without such an analysis, the multiplicity of labels and their constantly changing roles can result in massive confusion and erroneous interpretation.

I found that the three most popular jati titles in Pulicat were *Mudaliar* (capitalist), *Chettiar* (trader), and *Nayakkar* (chieftain). The title Mudaliar, which was used as a prestigious title by a number of jati groups throughout the Tamil country, was adopted by a jati group of fishermen named Karaiyar as well as by a cultivating jati group whose name had reference to a particular locality called Ponneri. The title Nayakkar was used by a cultivating jati group

(Vanniar) and by the herdsmen jati group called Idaiya. There were five jati groups with the title Chettiar: the fishermen jati group called Pattanava, two trading jati groups called Beri-Chettiar and Vaduvu-Chettiar, and two jati groups of weavers, named Padma-Saliar and Pattu-Saliar, but the two trading jati groups, Beri-Chettiar and Vaduvu-Chettiar, used the title as their jati name. Whether a label was a name or a title depended on its meaning to the person who used the label. Jati *names* were associated with ritual purity and with occupational purity/pollution and endogamy. Jati titles were associated with village authority and politico-economic power, and hence with the panchayat.

It is possible to present a model of status structure of Pulicat village with reference to the economic, political, and religious power attributes of the jati groups. In many instances, the social status of a jati group (and, in turn, the status of a member of the jati group) was the sum of the economic, political, and religious attributes. In other words, there was a correspondence or congruence between those attributes, and jatis with greater economic and political strength tended to have higher religious and social statuses. However, there were exceptions, and there were frequent reinterpretations and reevaluation of status positions in relation to the different social contexts in which members of different jatis interacted.

The following model of the ranking of the jati groups in Pulicat was based on the analysis of self-conceptions and external attributes and identifications. The ranking identifies 1 as the highest and 5 as the lowest.

JATI STATUS

	Economic	Political	Religious	Social
Beri Chettiar	1	2	2	1
Brahmin	3	5	1	2
Labbay Muslim	3	3	1	1
Mudaliar	3	2	2	2
Balija Naidu	3	4	2	2
Saliar (Pattu and Padma)	3	3	2	2
Idayar	3	4	2	3
Kanakar	3	3	2	2
Kammalar	3	3	2	2
Vanniar	3	1	3	3
Kusavar	4	4	3	3
Nadar	2	5	3	2
Ambattar	3	4	3	3
Pattanava Hindu	3	3	3	4
Pattanava Christian	3	3	3	3
Karaiyar Mudaliar	3	4	3	4
Pandaram	4	4	3	3
Nattar	4	4	3	4
Bebedel and Rengen Muslim	4	2	4	4
Villiar	5	4	4	4
Harijan (Parayan)	5	3	5	5

iii. Corporate Authority in Pulicat Village

The traditional village and/or jati panchayat (council of elders) was the primary institution of corporate authority in the village. From the 1950s, the government-sponsored village panchayats, which were linked to the regional and state agencies of community development, began to coexist with the traditional village and/or jati panchayats. The members and the president of the government-sponsored panchayats were elected public officials, entrusted with functions such as the upkeep of roads, lighting, sanitation, children's schooling, and village developmental projects. These officials were often affiliated with particular political parties and ideologies, and many were young social activists. However, the traditional village and/or jati panchayat was the custodian of village and jati custom. The villager subordinated himself to the adjudication of the traditional panchayat and accepted the authority of the traditional panchayat as the adjudicator and arbitrator of all matters that related to the corporate life in the village. The traditional panchayat was perceived by the villager to be the village or jati itself; when the villager conceptualized what it meant to subordinate himself to the village or jati (*urukku adangi nadappathu*), he used the imagery of the traditional panchayat as the agency of social/moral control. The traditional panchayat was required to protect the cultural and territorial interests of the jati or village. In some ways, the council was like a king's council, protecting the territorial and cultural integrity of the kingdom, and conflicts among jatis and among villages were not common.

Hamlets with more than one jati group had a panchayat for each group (called *jati panchayat*) as well as a hamlet panchayat (known as *ur panchayat*). The terms jati panchayat and ur panchayat were used interchangeably in hamlets in which only one jati group existed. The number of members in the panchayats varied from hamlet to hamlet; the average number was six including the headmen. Jati titles were used when referring to or addressing the headmen, but other members were often referred to as councillors (*panchayathars* or *kariastar*). In a few hamlets, members performed specific duties, for example, as convenor of the council (*tandakaran*, or *tandagar*) or temple trustee (*dharmakartha*, or *dharmagar*). Such offices were hereditary.

Harijans did not use jati titles but referred to their chief headman as *peria kiramathar* and the assistant headman as *chinna kiramathar*. In one hamlet, in which three jati groups lived, the ur panchayat was composed of the headmen of the three jati panchayats. Each headman held the position of leader (*thalaivar*) in turn. In one Pattanava jati hamlet, households were differentiated into seven families (*kudumbam*). Each kudumbam had a headman who was a member in the jati panchayat. One of the seven families was identified as the head family (*thalay kudumbam*), whose headman was also the leader of the jati group of the hamlet.

The main function of the panchayat was adjudication (*mathiyastham*). If someone deviated from tradition or custom, the panchayat was convened, which meant that the entire village was assembled. At such assemblies, the headmen and other members of the panchayat usually sat in an elevated position. Offenders who were not members of the panchayat had to stand before the panchayat; in a few hamlets, the offenders were required to prostrate themselves on the ground before the members of the panchayat at the beginning of the hearing. The plaintiff (*yathi*) was given the chance to state his case first. The defendant (*prathi*) was, on certain occasions, required to "swear by the village" (*ur maela chathiam*).

The headman pronounced the verdict after consultations with members of the panchayat, and after hearing the views of the people of the village. In some cases, the offender was required to acknowledge the authority of the panchayat by placing a leaf or a stone before them; this act was known as *macholika*, or symbolic statement of agreement. In one hamlet, macholika was performed soon after the offender was judged guilty by the panchayat. The common practice was for the offender to make a pledge (*chathia vakku*), and enter into an agreement (*udanpadikkai*) with the panchayat never to deviate from the tradition and custom of the village.

The punishment for most offenses was payment of fines, which were either given to the aggrieved party or spent on the temple. Men were punished by having to circle the village with a broken pot containing cow dung and urine (*mankuda malar*), and women had to collect village refuse. Such punishments were forms of censure, in contrast with the most serious sanctions (*kattupadu*) of ostracism and exile. The terms *jati kattupadu* or village kattupadu indicated that an offender was living on conditional agreement with the village; if the conditions were not met, the offender was exiled from the village. Conditional stay entailed ostracism until the offender had met all the stipulations of the panchayat judgment. A kinsman was usually required to provide bail (*jamin*). If the stipulations were not met within a stated period, the villagers were required not to speak to or aid the offender. Cooperation was necessary for the village to survive. If the offender did not honor the judgment of the panchayat, he was forced to leave the village.

The panchayat, particularly the headman, was in charge of collecting and dispersing money in the village. The ritual function of the headman, and of the panchayat in general, varied from hamlet to hamlet. The headman and panchayat played relatively minor roles in the Christian hamlet, but in the Harijan hamlets they were consulted and honored in every crisis and cyclical rite; the headman officiated over the marriage negotiations and ceremonies and received the bride on behalf of the village.

Traditional relationships and authority (as exemplified in the jati and village panchayats) coexisted with the newly established democratically elected councils in the village. After an initial attempt to dominate the elected council, the traditional elders confined themselves mostly to their traditional functions in the village. The youth and others who had no hereditary authority involved themselves in the elected councils and party politics that linked the village to the outside; the members and president of the elected council had links with political leaders of the region and the state. These nontraditional leaders could take pride in their achievements in the village, in securing government aid for constructing a reading room, schools, latrines, water tanks, and other amenities. But in matters of morality, ritual, and corporate prerogatives and obligations that had the sanction of custom, the traditional panchayat continued to serve as an important institution of political authority and as a symbol of boundary maintenance.

CHAPTER FIFTEEN

℘ RELIGIOUS TRADITIONS OF PULICAT VILLAGE AND THE PAROCHIAL MODELS OF VILLAGE HINDUISM

i. Brahmanic Rituals and Jati Identity

In Pulicat, members of each jati group perpetuated the belief that religious and moral standards of jati groups were distinctive, and that these standards were special privileges that had to be dramatized on religious, that is, ceremonial occasions to reaffirm jati identity. The only jati group that did not have such a specific attitude about its ritual privileges and prerogatives was the Harijan. Only the Harijan had no overt claims to high status. Bebedel and Rengen Muslims, who acknowledged the ritual supremacy of the Labbay Muslims, believed in distinctive privileges and prerogatives. The crisis ceremonies of the Rengen and Bebedel Muslims resembled Hindu ceremonies more than Labbay ceremonies. Christian Pattanava performed all the crisis ceremonies of the Hindus but had the idol or picture of the Virgin Mary instead of the Hindu deities.

The separateness of jati groups in matters of crisis ceremonies and commensality helped sustain the belief in the existence of distinctive moral and religious standards. All Hindu jati groups except the Harijan, Villiar, and Kammalar employed the services of Brahmins in specific rites during marriage and mortuary ceremonies, but every jati group had a particular method of conducting the ceremonies. Commensality (*panthi pojanam*) was usually restricted to those within the jati group, but jati groups such as Mudaliar, Balija Naidu, Idayar, Kusavar, Nattar, Ambattar, and Vanniar occasionally participated in commensality.

The performance of distinctive types of crisis rituals (rites of passage) and jati-specific cyclical rituals helped maintain the religious/social boundaries of individual families and jatis. The affluent performed a special ceremony for a pregnant woman, called *valaykappu*, usually in the seventh month. On this occasion, the women wore several glass bangles to amuse the fetus with the sound of jingling. A rite of waving a pot which contained a red-colored watery mixture of lime and turmeric (*alam*) was performed, and the liquid was placed on the forehead of the pregnant woman by relatives and well-wishers. In the seventh or ninth month of pregnancy, a special ceremony called *chimantham* was performed. The woman was seated on a dais in the central place of the house, and alam was waved in front of her. On that day the woman was usually returned to her mother's house, where the child was to be delivered.

A midwife or an elderly relative attended the childbirth. For the first three days, the child was usually given only sugar water, but if the child was found to be very weak a lactating kinswoman or the mother suckled the child. The mother was given a concoction of various herbs called *kava masala* every day, and she was given a ritual bath on the fifth day. She consumed regular food from that day on and was regularly given a mixture of asofoetida (*perunkayam*) and palm candy (*panankarkankandu*). For the first three months, she was permitted to have only the food that was considered hot, and ideally she was required to abstain from sexual intercourse during this period.

A naming ceremony was performed in the first month, when the father lifted the child and uttered its name before handing it back to the mother. There was no restriction on the frequency of breast-feeding; the child was fed when it was restless. At the end of one year, the mother applied a paste of yellow gram, cayenne, or margosa leaves to her nipples, or tied the nipples with a string to discourage the child from breast-feeding. If there was no later child, weaning occurred at the age of two. Toilet training was done by coaxing and teasing. By the time a child was three, he was expected to be toilet trained. Before the child reached the age of seven, an ear-piercing ceremony was conducted by all the non-Brahmin jati groups. Elaborate arrangements were made by the child's *ammangan* (maternal uncle). A seance with the family deity was usually held to secure the deity's approval. All the mother's consanguineal relatives (who were the father's affinal relatives, or *sampanthi*) were required to offer gifts (*moi*). Hair was shaved from the baby's head by a special barber, and ear piercing was done by a ritual goldsmith. Brahmin priests were not required to perform this ceremony. An elaborate female initiation ceremony was performed by all the non-Brahmin jati groups. The girl was usually isolated for seven, nine, or eleven days. The *ammangan* (mother's brother) bore all the expenses connected with the purificatory rites for her acceptance into the household. A seance with the family deity was held, and a special *alam* rite for the girl was performed. A Brahmin priest was not required in this ceremony. However, the services of a Brahmin priest were secured occasionally by every jati group except Kammalar, Villiar, and Harijan. Brahmin jati groups performed a male initiation rite called *upanayanam,* at which time a thread was worn by the boy as a mark of his becoming a twice-born and was permitted to acquire secret formulas of the Sanskritic scriptural authority.

Among non-Brahmins, preferential mates were cross cousins, and the marriage was generally performed at the bridegroom's residence. Marriage was preceded by a ceremony called *nichayartham,* at which time the terms of exchange of gifts for the bride and groom were decided. Three, five, or seven days before the marriage ceremony, a long pole (*panthal kal*) was planted, and special rites were performed. On the day preceding marriage, special rites called *nalangu* were performed which involved ritual bathing, particularly of the bridegroom. The ammangan (maternal uncle) and *athay* (paternal aunt) had special privileges in this rite. Beri Chettiar and Saliar grooms donned a thread as a mark of jati privilege before the marriage rite. As the final rite of the marriage ceremony, the bridegroom tied a turmeric-stained string around the bride's neck. With the exception of Kammalar, Villiar, and Harijan, all jati groups employed a Brahmin priest for the marriage ceremony.

Both burial and cremation occurred. Adults were usually cremated. Mortuary rites called *punniathanam* or *kariam* were usually performed on the first, seventh, eleventh, and sixteenth day after death. A Brahmin priest was employed to perform purificatory ceremonies by all the jati groups except Kammalar, Villiar, and Harijan to purify the house. Christians differed from the non-Brahmin jati groups only by employing the Christian priest to officiate over the ceremonies, and by having a naming ceremony in which a godmother had special responsibility for the child. The Christian dead were always buried. Rengen and Bebedel Muslims had adapted most of the Hindu rites but performed the Muslim ceremonies also and employed the Labbay priests. The most characteristic adaptation of a Hindu rite by the Rengen and Bebedel Muslims was the performance of the female initiation rite, to which the Labbay did not give much importance.

The Labbay Muslims gave great importance to reading scripture and to having special prayers. They also gave special significance to the process of eating together from a common pot (*sahan*). The Labbay placed great value on their women having black teeth, which they acquired by rubbing on them a black powder called *thasana. Maruthani,* a red substance taken from leaves, was applied to beautify the nails and palms, a practice performed by Hindus and Christians as well. The Labbay had an elaborate naming ceremony. Soon after the child was washed, a priest or elder touched the ears and forehead of the child and recited scriptures before pronouncing the names of the saints selected by the family. The child's name of reference and address was, however, given on the seventh day. The ear-piercing ceremony was restricted to females. An elaborate initiation rite called *kathana,* or *sunnathu* (cutting) *kalyanam* (marriage) was performed for boys, during which the foreskin of the penis was removed. Marriage was a contract which the *kazi* (Muslim registrar) confirmed, and divorce was permitted with the approval of the kazi. A man was required to pay a dowry (*mahar*), and the marriage rite (*nikka*) was held in the bride's house. The father of the bride represented her in the marriage rite, and either the mother or the sister of the groom represented the bridegroom. The Labbay buried their dead within the compound surrounding the mosque. The dead of the Rengen and Bebedel Muslims were buried in a Muslim cemetery.

The following chart identifies the major festivals performed in the village of Pulicat and refers to the jati groups that performed them. (These ceremonies were associated with Brahmanical Hinduism.)

Major Festivals in Village of Pulicat

Time	Festival	Participation of Jati Groups
January	Pongal; harvest festival	All jati groups participated. Bogi rite is performed by a few of every group. Only the Brahmins performed the rite of *Aditya puja* (sun worship). Cow rite was done by all with cattle. *Kanum* rite was performed more vigorously by fishermen, particularly by the Harijan who sang and danced.
February	Sivaratri	A few of every group stayed awake, but Beri Chettiars gave more importance to the festival.
March	Karaday Nonbu	No non-Brahmin jati group performed it.
March	Sri Rama Navami	No non-Brahmin jati group performed it.
April	Tharpanam	No non-Brahmin jati group performed it.
July	Avani Avittam	No non-Brahmin jati group performed it.
July, August	Kur Utum Vila	An amman festival performed with great elaboration in Mukkuntha amman temple on five Sundays. All the non-Brahmin jati groups participated.
August	Krishna Jayanti	A few of every jati group performed it. Hindu Pattanava of one hamlet performed the ceremony elaborately.
August	Agni Utsavam	An amman festival; only in Draupathi amman temples of Pulicat proper. Sanskritic myth was combined as the amman was identified as Draupathi, heroine of *Mahabharatha*. Fire-walking rite was the main feature. Jati groups of Pulicat participated on a left-hand, right-hand basis.
August	Vinayakar Caturti	A few Saliar performed it.
September	Mahayala Amavasy	Ancestor worship. A few of every jati group except Harijans and Villiars performed it. Beri Chettiars, Mudaliars, Saliars, and Vanniars gave more importance to its performance.

Major Festivals in Village of Pulicat (*cont'd*)

Time	Festival	Participation of Jati Groups
September	Navarathri	Nine-day festival of dolls. A few Beri Chettiar women performed it at home. Ammans were decorated and special lullaby rites were conducted for nine nights. Each night's expenses were borne by the person who performed the *upayam* (special invocation). All jati groups participated. On the ninth day a rite called *ayuta puja* (weapon rite) was performed by most Beri Chettiars, Saliars, and Kammalars. A few fishermen also conducted it.
September	Saraswati puja	Nine-day learning festival. Most Beri Chettiars and a few Saliars performed it.
September, October	Puratasi sanikilamay	Special *bajana* rites (singing and religious hymns) were conducted on five Saturdays. Expenses were borne by a person or group performing *upayam* (special invocation).
October	Vaikunt ekatesi	A few of all jati groups stayed awake.
October	Dipavali	All the jati groups participated by bathing ritually and eating well.
October, November	Skandapuranam	Six-day festival of Muruga in the temple maintained by Beri Chettiars. All the jati groups participated.
November	Naga Chthurti	Snake worship. A few Beri Chettiar, Mudaliar, and Saliar women performed it.
December	Kartikay thipam	Muruga worship. All jati groups performed it.
December, January	Margali Bajanay	Special rites were performed in all the amman temples. Singing religious hymns was done in the hamlets. In Pulicat proper, a few from every group performed it.

ii. Non-Brahmanical Shamanism and Group/Individual Rituals in Pulicat Village

Shamanism coexisted with other kinds of religious orientations in Pulicat. Shamanism involved communion with supernatural beings and/or powers in contrast to the scriptural orientations which required a religious practitioner to learn and use particular religious knowledge to communicate to supernatural beings and powers. Although it was possible to distinguish the existence of two types of religious practitioners, namely, shamans and priests on the basis of *communion with* and *communication to* supernatural beings or powers, it is important to state that these two types overlapped considerably.

Spirit mediums in Pulicat could be identified as shamans. Mediums (shamans) of mother goddesses (amman), godlings, and spirits usually did not receive payments for their services. There was no Tamil word for shaman in Pulicat: The villager referred to the shaman as *avarukku chami varum* (deity comes to him), or as *avarukku muni irangum* (spirit will descend on him). There were male and female shamans, and public and private shamans. On all ceremonial occasions, the ammans descended on the public shamans of amman temples. The ammans could also be invoked on other occasions. Public shamans were attached to specific ammans. Pulicat amman temples had shamans from the Mudaliar and Vanniar jati groups, and each was attached to a particular amman temple in the village. Shamans of the amman temples in the hamlets were members of the jati groups of the hamlets.

When a person showed signs that an amman or a spirit was using him as a medium or vehicle, the community confirmed him as a shaman by either piercing his tongue *(nakku alaku)* or by pouring hot oil on his palm (*pu alaku*) in special initiation ceremonies. Shamans divined causes of sickness and other difficulties of persons or the village, exorcised demons, and or spirits. When possessed, they had no identity distinctive from that of the deity or spirit, and their prescriptions were the prescriptions of the deity or spirit.

There were also private mediums or shamans of the family deity (*kula theyvam*). The family deity could be ammans, spirits of dead magicians (*muni*), and spirits of persons who met with untimely death. A member of the household usually functioned as the medium of the family deity. The deity could use several mediums, although it would possess only one at a time. When spirits of dead relatives were solicited to function as family deities or guardians of the household, special ceremonies were held with the aid of shamans to invoke the ammans and other recognized spirits. If the solicited spirit consented to accept one of the living relatives as the medium, the medium swallowed burning camphor or poured hot oil on his palm to confirm that the spirit had become an ally of the medium. All familial ceremonies were conducted only with the permission of the family deity, as conveyed through the shaman. Spirits of the muni class, amman deities, and wandering spirits of those who committed suicide or had been murdered (*pey*) were reputed to have the power to possess and cause harm. On such occasions, the public or private shamans divined the identity of the possessor and the reason for the possession. Special propitiatory ceremonies, as prescribed by the shaman when in a state of possession, were held to propitiate the possessor. When these ceremonies proved ineffective, professional exorcists called *manthrakaran* were consulted. Cholera and smallpox epidemics were attributed to particular ammans, and temples were built frequently in their honor to propitiate them. When a death was attributed to an amman or a muni, a temple was built to appease the amman, or special rituals were performed under the peepul, palm, or margosa tree that was considered to be the abode of the muni. At times, a magician's aid was sought to control a muni, and iron-nailed wooden sandals were kept under the trees to prevent the muni from alighting from the trees. On ritual occasions when the shaman became the medium of the muni, he wore the iron-nailed wooden sandals, and the muni moved about and was appeased through the shaman.

A number of diseases were attributed to possession. Amulets called *billay* were tied around the neck, waist, or arm to ward off possession and attacks by the ammans and spirits. In many Hindu, Christian, and Muslim households, brass plates with Koranic inscriptions were hung on the wall or nailed on the doors to protect the homes from spirits. No one from within the village or the hamlets was ever accused of sorcery, but villagers feared sorcery by outsiders. Blood sacrifices for certain spirits were occasionally done through the aid of a magician from outside the village, but supernatural assistance was secured mainly through known shamans of particular ammans or spirits in the village. Diseases believed to have been caused by the ammans were seldom treated by medicine. Smallpox was known as *ammay vilayadukiral* (mother goddess is playing), or as *ammay uthirukkal* (mother goddess has poured). Margosa leaves, considered sacred in amman worship, were placed on and around the sick person. Those attending the sick were required to take a ritual bath, wear clean clothes, and abstain from sex. Mumps were called *ammay kattirukkiral* (mother goddess has settled), and a paste of margosa leaves was applied. No other treatment was given. Very elaborate annual festivals took place in the hamlets in honor of the ammans. No time was fixed for these festivals. When a hamlet could afford to spend about $1000, the ceremony was performed, and it was not uncommon for a year or two to be skipped. Apart from the annual amman festival, Hindu Pattanava, Nattar, and Karayar fishermen conducted a special annual ceremony called *kanni jodi* (virgin pairs). The propitiatory offering of fire was an important rite in this ceremony. The fire was carried by a shaman and dumped into the sea. Idols of the virgins and their brothers (*annanmar*) were kept on the seashore. Each hamlet had a specific place for keeping the idols, and new idols were added every year. Some mother goddesses were referred to by certain diseases as their prefix, and others were not directly linked to any particular disease and had as their prefix the name of a local woman or place. The temples of some of the goddesses were marked only by the existence of a sacred pot (*kalasam*) believed to be possessed by the goddess, or a shrub marked by garlands and neem leaves. Some were thatched huts, whereas others were well-constructed brick-walled buildings with an inner room where the idol of the goddess was kept and an outer verandah which served as a meeting place for the devotees on ceremonial occasions and as a resting place for men in general. A few temples were located on spacious grounds surrounded by walls. The idols of the goddesses in the walled temples were usually made of stone, but some were of wood.

There were five mother goddess temples in Pulicat: Asalath-amman temple; Left Draupathi-amman temple; Right Draupathi-amman temple; Mukkunth-amman temple; and Kali-amman temple. With the exception of the Kali-amman temple, all were brick-walled buildings, and three had compound walls encircling the temples. Asalath-amman was the *grama-devatai* (village goddess) who belonged to every jati group in the village and was worshipped daily in her temple. A man of Pandaram jati officiated as her priest, but she had no confirmed shamans, and recent efforts to secure a shaman were unsuccessful. Two Draupathi-amman temples existed because of disputes between the jati groups of the left-hand category and right-hand category. The dominant jati group of the village (Beri-Chettiar) which belonged to the left-hand category undertook the construction of the Left Draupathi-amman temple, and its maintenance was largely controlled by this jati. The priest of this temple belonged to the Mudaliar jati, and the priest of the Right Draupathi-amman temple was of the Pandaram jati; daily propitiations occurred in both temples, and both goddesses had shamans. The Mukkunth-amman temple belonged to every jati, had a confirmed shaman, and the goddess was propitiated every day by her priest of the Saliar jati.

Asalth-amman was identified as the oldest and was fond of cow's meat and human flesh. Mukkunth-amman, the youngest, was less ferocious, and Draupathi-amman was the fire woman. Among other features distinguishing the ammans were the different idols that were kept in the inner sanctum of the Mukkunth-amman and Draupathi-amman temples. In the Mukkunth-amman temple were the idols of Mukkunth-amman (largest of all the idols in size), Renuku-amman (conceived of as another form of Mukkunth-amman), Parasuraman (the son of Mukkunth-amman and Jamathagri Maharishi), Pillaiyar and Subramaniya (the sons of Siva and Parvathi), and the three deities Siva, Vishnu, and Brahman who were conceived of as the supreme divinities. In the Draupathi-amman temples were kept the idols of the five Pandava brothers (the mythical heroes of *Mahabharatha*) and Pothi-raja who was conceived of as the bodyguard of the goddess.

Elaborate annual ceremonies occurred in the two Draupathi-amman temples and in the Mukkunth-amman temple. With the exception of Brahmins, who passively participated in the ceremonies, all other jati groups actively involved themselves. Greater or lesser involvement in mother goddess worship did not correlate with lower or high social/ritual statuses of the non-Brahmin groups. The two most important annual ceremonies, associated with the three goddesses, took place in July/August and in October and were performed to insure prosperity of the village as a whole. Members of different groups contributed to the expenses, although Draupathi-amman had a jati-specific orientation. A Draupathi-amman ceremony referred to in Tamil as *kul uthum vila* (gravy festival) was performed in July/August on five consecutive Sundays. Another ceremony was performed in October in association with the Hindu festival of nine nights (*nava rathri kolu*); propitiatory rites were performed on nine nights, culminating on the tenth day with a ceremonial village parade with the idol of Draupathi-amman. A third annual ceremony, called the fire festival (*agni uthsavam*), was performed in Draupathi-amman temples, but its regularity was related to the availability of funds, and years went by without the ceremony if the expenses could not be met by the community.

In the gravy festival, the most significant rituals were the propitiatory purification of the deities through a series of annointings (*abishegam*) that included the use of milk, sesame seed oil, buttermilk, coconut juice, sandal and scented powders mixed in water, and the immersion in the river of the sacred pot (*kalasam*), which the believers perceived as the abode of the goddesses during ritual purifications. The ritual procedures of the immersion varied from temple to temple, but the same principles operated in the general conceptualization of the ritual. As an example, the procedure adopted in the Draupathi-amman temple is cited here.

On the final evening of the festival, a young man carried the sacred pot on his head and a chicken in his left hand to the river. He was accompanied by three shamans, who were possessed by Pothi-raja, Draupathi-amman, and Mukkunth-amman, the priest of Draupathi-amman, and a few other males. On the way to the river, seven special propitiations called *gava* were performed for Draupathi-amman, involving the offering of lemons (to safeguard the carrier from the violence of the goddess). On reaching the river bed, the sacred pot was placed on the ground, and the priest performed the ritual of waving camphor fire (*thipa-arathanai*) and offering a coconut. Following this, the chicken was sacrified, and the contents of the sacred pot, which included cash, rice, lemons, and betal leaves, were taken out and given to the carrier. Then the carrier placed the emptied sacred pot on his head, and, at the command of the shaman possessed by Pothi-raja, entered the river. At waist-deep water, the decorative attachments of the sacred pot, which included neem leaves, were removed and the pot was thrown into the river. When this was done, Pothi-raja and Draupathi-amman left their shamans, but Mukkunth-amman stayed with her shaman until the party returned to the village.

The festival of nine nights involved the Mukkunth-amman temple and the two Draupathi-amman temples. The festival had two aspects: one called lullaby singing (*thalattu-pattu*) which involved all three goddesses, and the other called the village parade (*ur-valam*) which involved Draupathi-amman only. Twenty-seven men bore the expenses related to the singing of lullabies, each man defraying the cost of one night in one temple. As there were three temples and nine nights of ceremonies, there were 27 specific rituals. In the lullaby ceremony, the ritual of waving camphor fire (thipa-arathanai) in front of the goddess was performed ten times. After the completion of this ritual, the decorated idol of the goddess was brought out of the inner sanctum of the temple and placed on a specially built swing (*unjal*). Before the swinging, however, the idol was carried by four men who circled the temple three times. Following two hours of singing to the accompaniment of music, the idol was returned to the inner sanctum. The expenses of this ceremony were borne mainly by the members of the jati who helped to maintain the Draupathi-amman temple, although a subscription from all the villagers was also collected. In another ceremony, the idol of Draupathi-amman was placed on a chariot (*vahanam*) and drawn by two bullocks. Dancing, singing, and acrobatic feats by professionals (*kuthu-karar*) and others were performed on the way. The parade stopped in front of the inmates of homes who offered coconuts, and on every such occasion the priest performed the ritual of waving camphor fire and returned the coconut which was symbolically offered to the deity. On the completion of the parade, the idol was installed back in the inner sanctum of the temple. Contributions were collected from the villagers, but usually particular families bore most of the expenses. The fire festival, when it was performed, was associated with Draupathi-amman. On this occasion, men walked on embers in fulfillment of an oath or vow, but the ceremony was also perceived as contributing to the prosperity of the entire village. A specific ritual of this ceremony was the burying of the ashes after the fire walking. It was believed that if the ash were taken or stolen by members of other villages, nothing good would happen to the host village, and thus the burial ritual was done secretly.

iii. Household Rituals and Religious Integration of the Cultural Self

In descriptions of village religious traditions, it is common to distinguish between Brahmanical-Sanskritic Hindu beliefs and practices and non-Brahmanical/non-Sanskritic beliefs and practices. Such a distinction is often made to show that certain beliefs and practices are part of the all-India, pan-Hindu great tradition, and other beliefs and practices belong only to particular regions and the nonliterate traditions of peasant villages. The most important criterion used in making the distinction is to identify whether or not a Brahmin priest (or the Brahmanical priesthood in general) is associated with religious beliefs and practices. Although this kind of identification has merit in certain areas of intellectual inquiry, it is important to show how villagers integrate the diverse religious beliefs and practices within the framework of the Hindu perspective of a given village.

In the first section of this chapter I described the performance of various rituals that had significance for the maintenance of individual and jati group identity. Most of these rituals affirmed the validity of Brahmanical-Sanskritic religious authority, but they combined with village-specific traditions and non-Hindu religious traditions as well. In the second section of this chapter I focused on shamanistic or non-Brahmanical religiosity of the village tradition and noted that this type of religious beliefs and practices were very important for all the villagers including Brahmin and non-Brahmin Hindus as well as for Christians and Muslims.

In this section I describe the performance of rituals in the household that symbolically connect the Brahmanical-Sanskritic Hindu beliefs and practices with non-Brahmanical/non-Sanskritic beliefs and practices. It will be clear that the performance of Brahmanical-Sanskritic rituals are often a function of economics: Affluent families can perform and do engage in practices that are often identified with the Brahmanical-Sanskritic tradition. For example, only the wealthy can adopt all the food taboos and enact menstruation taboos or dramatize expensive purificatory rituals; the poor who live in a single-room house and depend on women to work and feed the members of the household cannot have all the luxuries of taboos and ceremonial purifications.

In Pulicat, ideally every house was supposed to have a region identified as *nadu veadu*. In a large house, a particular room was designated as nadu veadu, and in a one-room house, a corner of the room was identified as the nadu veadu. The word *nadu* means middle, central, or center, and the word veadu means house or home. Nadu veadu was the term used to identify the place of worship in the home. To the members of a household, their nadu veadu was a sacred symbol which linked them to their ancestors and affirmed the presence and blessing of deities. It was a symbol through which the supernatural power of purity and pollution were comprehended by the child. Also, it was a symbol of great importance in the development of selfhood with reference to social/physical categories that were classified as pure or impure. A child was socialized into accepting certain things and actions as pure or impure. Women had the most important symbolic function in this regard. They socialized the child and performed the rituals in nadu veadu. But a menstruating woman was prohibited from performing rites in nadu veadu, and in some cases the idols and pictures of gods and goddesses were covered by a yellow cloth when a woman in the family was menstruating. Regular purificatory ceremonies were conducted in the nadu veadu; after menstruation, birth, sickness, and death, specific rituals were performed. Many of the beliefs and practices associated with purity and pollution (or impurity) were rooted in nadu veadu and extended to other domains of cultural experience.

In the nadu veadu worship in Pulicat, women took an active role; every evening a lamp which was sometimes referred to as *kamatchi-amman vilakku* (mother goddess Kamatchi's lamp) was lit by the woman of the house and she waved it in front of the deities, symbolically inviting them to be present in the house during the night. Waving the lamp was called *thipa-arathanay* (fire ceremony), and the lamp was usually kept burning until daybreak. When the thipa-arathanay ritual was performed in the nadu veadu, it was common to perform part of this ritual (the waving of burning camphor) in front of the kitchen utensils and grinding stones such as *ammi* and *attukal*.

There was great variation within and among jati groups in terms of the elaborateness of the nadu veadu itself and of the rites performed in the nadu veadu. The variations corresponded to the economic status of individual households. The wealthy generally had the most elaborate paraphrenalia in the nadu veadu and incorporated rituals considered to be prestigious. The poor generally allotted very little space for the nadu veadu, and the taboos associated with the sanctity of the nadu veadu were not strictly adhered to. The elaborateness of the nadu veadu and rituals was to a large extent determined by the economic power of the household, thus separating ritually the households of the same jati groups; the distinctive rites and deities in the nadu veadu provided the household with a measure of religious autonomy and power shared by no other household. (At the jati group level a similar ownership of rituals and deities was claimed.) Puja, or ritual offering, was more elaborate on certain days of the week when nadu veadu was cleaned and members of the household abstained from consuming meat and other elaborately cooked food. Often referred to as *oru poluthu* (one meal day), these days were different for different groups, but Friday, Saturday, Sunday, and Monday were the usual days on which oru poluthu was practiced.

Nadu veadu had great personal significance for every member of the household. All the crises and calendrical ceremonies began and ended in the nadu veadu. Propitiation of the household god and elaborate puja were performed in the nadu veadu during these ceremonies. Calendrical ceremonies such as *Deapavali, Navarathri,* and *Pongal* were made personally relevant in the nadu veadu. Crisis ceremonies such as *punnithanam* (offering milk at the grave and ritual purification of the house), *kariam* (ritual at the cemetery and ritual purification of the members of the household), *valaikappu* (ritual of bangles for the pregnant woman in her ninth month of pregnancy) and *seemantham* (rituals associated with the seventh month of pregnancy) as well as a number of initiation ceremonies were symbolically linked with the nadu veadu. Also spirit exorcism and family shamanistic rituals were located in the nadu veadu.

Thus, nadu veadu represented the religious and moral values of the household, made the woman of the household the medium between the mundane and the sacred, and served as a symbol to unify a number of existential concerns to comprehend one's selfhood or identity.

iv. Pulicat Hindu Religious Tradition, and the All-India Parochial Models of Village Hinduism

The question may be raised whether the Pulicat Hindu tradition is typical of all-India village traditions of Hinduism. The answer is simply that there is no typical all-India village Hinduism, and it should be pointed out that village Hindu traditions resemble and differ from each other in some ways in relation to the diverse, historical experiences of the villages. Thus, our concern should be to investigate how the similarities and differences come about. In order to undertake such an investigation we must conceptualize *village Hinduism as a distinguishable religious system with a set of propositions about ultimate reality and meaning concerning human existence, self, and suffering, and also delineate the historical origins, maintenance, and uses of the particular Hindu symbols that synthesize various existential themes and experiential domains of the village.*

Hindu deities and rituals may be analyzed as parochial models that synthesize various existential concerns, historical themes, and experiential domains of the village. Parochial models of village Hinduism may have their origins in the Brahmanical-Sanskritic literary traditions of Hinduism, in the non-Brahmanical ethnolinguistic literary traditions of Hinduism, or in the village nonliterary traditions of Hinduism. Often, the parochial models merge or blend the characteristics of Brahmanical, ethnolinguistic, and village traditions in such a manner that their origins cannot be ascertained with accuracy. As Cohn (1971:63–64) correctly notes, "Hinduism has displayed a constant dialectic between the thought and practices of specialists and the religious activities of the masses" and any effort to identify which aspect of Hinduism was originally evolved by the literati or the unreflective masses is a futile attempt. Therefore, it is relevant to analyze the village parochial models of Hinduism in terms of how they are structured and in terms of their meanings and uses. The sociological theory of Hindu civilization which identifies the dialectical relationship between the literary and nonliterary traditions and the delineation of historical (all-India processes) of universalization and parochialization have enabled the students of Indian villages to investigate, interpret, and explain the parochial models of Hinduism with reference to the role of village traditions and village Hinduism in the maintenance of the all-India Hindu civilization.

A unique aspect of Hinduism is that it tolerates, and in fact promotes the creation, maintenance, and use of distinctive deities and rituals (parochial models) that have intellectual and emotional significance for particular individuals, groups, regions, and civilizations. Throughout the history of India, the Great God Siva and his complementary counterpart the Great Goddess Sakti have served as the prototypes or metaphors for conceptualizing Hindu spirituality all over India, and a large number of regional and village deities have been created to represent certain manifestations or emanations of Siva and Sakti. And, the Great God Vishnu and his avatars (incarnations) are important Hindu models with moral/ethical/social connotations: They have been represented throughout India to link religion and morality. However, the most important feature of Hinduism is its affirmation of the historical experiences of individuals, groups, and regions in the formulation of the parochial models of Hinduism. As a result we find the existence of hundreds of thousands of regional and civilizational variations and adaptations of Hindu deities and rituals. Historically, the different regions and ethnolinguistic civilizations of India have been linked through religious discourse that has been undertaken by priests and Hindu sectarian leaders (belonging to the different jati groups, different regions, and different village traditions) who often transcended the boundaries of regional and ethnolinguistic civilizations. Such a discourse often resulted in the beliefs and practices of particular village traditions (nonliterary communities or nonliterary traditions) being transmitted to other villages and becoming universalized. The interplay and exchanges between and among the nonliterary traditions and literary traditions of India have been so long and continuous that it is difficult to ascertain when or where a particular Hindu belief, ritual, or deity began. The great Hindu gods and goddesses are universal in India, but they often serve village-specific or region-specific functions (as parochial models) with diverse characteristics that are associated with regional and village cultural traditions. Likewise the great Hindu epics of *Mahabharata* and *Ramayana* are universal in India but they have been adapted in hundreds of different ways so that their uses have specific, particular significance for different ethnolinguistic civilizations as well as for different regions, villages, and jati groups.

The father (at least one of the fathers) of the anthropological study of Indian villages and the dean (at least one of the deans) of the anthropological study of village India, Professor McKim Marriott, noted long ago that we should study the processes that link and relate the various traditions of India as well as study the adaptations and uses of Hinduism in Indian villages in order to understand the nature and function of Hinduism and caste. I quote below his views on the study of village Hinduism which he eloquently presented in an early essay that was included in his edited book *Village India* (1955).

> Seen through its festivals and deities, the religion of the village of Kishan Garhi [of northern India] may be conceived as resulting from continuous processes of communication between a little, local tradition and greater traditions which have their places partly inside and partly outside the village. Only residual fragments of the religion of such a little community can be conceived as distinctive or separable.
>
> Since both great and little traditions exist within the religion of little communities and there communicate, study of the religion of a little community can contribute to understanding of processes of universalization and parochialization which are generally operative in Indian civilization. Preliminary study of the contents of religion in Kishan Garhi indicates, for example, that great and little traditions may remain in equilibrium within the little community, neither tending to exclude the other: elements of the great tradition undergo parochial transformation as they spread, while the great tradition itself, where it originates as a universalization of indigenous materials, lacks authority to replace elements of the little tradition. Communication between indigenous greater and lesser traditions may proceed vertically without necessarily effecting any contiguous lateral enlargement of the community of common culture. A focus upon the small half-world of the village and a perspective upon the universe of Indian civilization thus remain mutually indispensable for whole understanding, whether of Hinduism or of the traditional forms of India's social structure.
>
> —*Marriott (1955:218)*

✒ CONCLUSION

i. The Making of India and Indian Traditions

The political realities of what we identify as India and Indian traditions and our knowledge of India and Indian traditions in general have been shaped by the West despite the fact that the West was intimately involved with the politico-economic affairs of India and with the production of knowledge about Indian and Indian traditions for only about two centuries. The British played a major role in delineating the territorial boundaries of India from the middle of the 18th century and introduced various revenue and legal systems from that time, most of which have survived up to this day. Likewise, British scholarly traditions created various models of understanding India and Indian traditions, and most of these have also survived. As a result, our studies on Indian anthropology, Indian civilization, Indian history, Indian ethnicity, and Indian religion have been filtered through the intellectual and political concerns of the West, and the Western intellectual perspectives such as aryanism, orientalism, and utilitarianism have helped to create or invent conceptions of India and the Indian traditions in images and symbols that have relevance and significance to the West. Western conservative and liberal ideologies as well as Western imperialist and socialist sentiments have also been intimately involved in the British dialectics with India. Britain and India were caught in a politico-economic and intellectual-emotional embrace; only surgery could have separated India from the impact of Western intellectual perspectives.

The government of Jawaharlal Nehru did not seek a surgical separation from the West mainly because Nehru was a product of the Western discourse on India, and thus the British Empire was replaced by the Indian Empire which fostered, with some modifications, the British scholarly traditions and the British-created political configurations.

The post-modernist discourse since the 1960s has challenged the Western cultural-intellectual assumptions of aryanism, orientalism, utilitarianism, and positivism, and there have been studies on India and Indian traditions that seek to present a semiotic understanding within the cultural or symbolic framework of Indian traditions themselves. However, the modernization processes of India have still linked India and the West; thus, discourse on India is still related to validation by the scholarly traditions of the West. This kind of Western validation of knowledge about India and Indian traditions is similar to how certain Indian creations acquire legitimacy in India through their recognition in the West. The Indologist/anthropologist, the late Professor Agehananda Bharati, commented on this process of validation in an insightful paper, "Hinduism and Modernization":

A strange phenomenon pervades the subcontinent [India] in its process of modernization. A somewhat facetious term for this phenomenon might be the "pizza effect." The pizza originated in southern Italy as a humble staple, a bread dish without any of the accouterments which we now associate with the Italo-American pizza. But when the *mafiosi* and other Sicilians and Calabrians brought it to the United States, it became, as it were, affluent in the proportion the settlers became affluent. Since about 1920 this modified pizza has been making its victorious reentry into Italy. At many places, north and south, pizza has become much the same dish as the one available in the United States. Something parallel to this has happened in South Asia. Cultural things formerly looked upon as archaic, "superstitious," and not conducive to the modern spirit, began to be sought out, their importance being positively reassessed on the merit of having been appreciated abroad. Satyajit Ray's Bengali film trilogy, to take an example, was originally a flop in Bengal and elsewhere in India. The average movie-goer preferred to see chintzy stories of papier-mache romance or of mythological royalty and divinity, while the more enlightened favored *samajik*, "social" stories with a message. Neither cared to see chunks out of Indian village, which is poor and uninteresting. But when *Pather Panchali, Aparajita,* and *The World of Apu* received awards at the Venice film festivals and high acclaim in Europe and America, things changed. In the past five years modern sophisticated movie-goers in India have come to praise these productions. The pizza effect benefited not only Satyajit Ray but, to a greater degree, the masters of Indian instrumental music such as Ravi Shankar, Ali Akbar Khan, Bismillah Khan, and Subbulaxmi.

—*Bharati (1971:88–89)*

For heuristic and analytic purposes, it is possible to delineate four periods to describe, discuss, and interpret India and Indian traditions. The period of 1700–700 B.C.E. may be characterized as *the age of Dravidian-Aryan synthesis* when Dravidian and Aryan linguistic/cultural traditions merged; the period 700 B.C.E. to 700 C.E. as *the age of ethnic-caste blending* when ethnic groups such as Scythians, Greeks, and Huns acquired caste identity; the period 700–1700 C.E. as *the age of western and central Asian ethnic identities* when non-Indian group identities became symbols of political/social dominance; and the period 1700–1950 C.E. as *the age of European domination* when the European scholarly traditions preempted the Indian discourse. I have suggested in this book that the Aryan speakers who entered India between 1700 and 1500 B.C.E. had racially blended with the Dravidian speakers over a period of about a thousand years and that the differences that exist in the physical features of the peoples of northern India and southern India stem from the fact that there were waves of immigrants and invaders from west and central Asia entering India between 700 B.C.E. and 700 C.E. The period from about 700 to 1700 C.E. is quite significant for our understanding of India and Indian traditions: Many aspects of modern India and Indian traditions developed during that period. It was during this period that the alien ethnic groups such as the Parsis, Syrian Christians, Arabs, and Coorgs as well as the Islamised Persians, Turks, Afgans, Mongols, and Muslim Arabs established themselves in different parts of India, often in politico-economically dominant positions. The earlier immigrants of the period 700 B.C.E. to 700 C.E. were assimilated into the Hindu civilization and became a part of the caste system. The Scythians, Persians, Greeks, Huns, and others who entered at that time acquired caste status positions in relation to their political-economic power and adopted the Hindu rituals and idioms of caste hierarchy. But, the immigrants and invaders of the period 700 C.E. to 1700 C.E. did not fit in the caste system although some of them had adopted castelike characteristics. They used their alien heritage as symbols of high status, and with this kind of symbolization along with the proselytizing religion of Islam there came into being a new kind of political reality in India.

Western involvement in India began in 1510 with the Portuguese settlement on the west coast of India before the creation of the Mughal Empire in India (by Babur in 1526). However, the West became active in Indian trade only in the 17th century with the English, Dutch, and French trading companies located in different parts of India, and by the middle of the 18th century the British became the dominant European power in India. Although the

British progressively acquired territories all over India and began to control the economic and political fate of many kings, the Mughal emperor was still recognized as the legitimate political authority, and the British paid the Mughal emperor a large sum of money to affirm British acceptance of Mughal authority until 1848. After the revolt of the soldiers and some kings against the British in 1857, the British disowned the political legitimacy of the Mughal emperor, and Queen Victoria was proclaimed the empress of India in 1877.

It is obvious that the Western involvement in India did not last long. However, within a short period, the British succeeded in linking the different parts of India with new types of communication networks (printing press, mail service, and telephone) and transport (railway), and a uniform education system. *With the Western involvement in India, there came into being a cognitive shift, or an intellectual transformation, and new symbols and conceptions of private property, rule of law, class categories, and nationalism emerged.* As Rawlinson pointed out:

> From time to time an Indian Napoleon arose who would temporarily knit this vast congeries of peoples into a coherent whole, and the Mogul Emperors even imposed a single official language, Persian. *But it was reversed for her latest conquerors to introduce, not only a common tongue, but common political aspirations, the growth of which had been immensely facilitated by the opening up of communications, the spread of education, and the diffusion of Western political ideas.* This lack of national consciousness is perhaps the main reason why pre-Muhammadan India had no historians. Her vast literature contains no Herodotus or Rhucydides, no Tacitus or Livy; the very memory of her greatest ruler, the Emperor Asoka, was forgotten, until European scholars at the beginning of the nineteenth century laboriously reconstructed the story by piecing together the fragments which had survived the ravages of time. [emphasis mine]
>
> —*Rawlinson (1964:12)*

As a result of the Western involvement in India, there came into existence an extensive body of literature on "what is India," "what are the Indian traditions," "how did India and the Indian traditions come into being," "what are sources of unity and conflict in India," and so on. As noted earlier, most of this discourse until recently was by Western and Western-educated scholars who directly or indirectly served the intellectual concerns and needs of the Western scholarly traditions. In the following sections I will examine briefly the discourse on India and Indian traditions with reference to some of the epistemological assumptions of the West—and the descriptions and interpretations that I have offered in this book.

ii. India and Discourse on History

It is true that we know much about the prehistory and history of India through the efforts of Western and Western-trained archaeologists and historians. Indeed, had Sir John Marshall not excavated the mounds of Harappa and the Mohenjo-daro in the 1920s, we might still be erroneously attributing the foundations of Hinduism and Indian civilization to the Aryan nomads of central Asia rather than to the Dravidian speakers of the Indus Valley Civilization. Also, we know a lot about the historic migrations of central and west Asians through the archaeological, historical, linguistic, and anthropological studies that were undertaken by Western scholars. While recognizing the importance of these studies, it is also necessary to recognize the fact that such a scholarship has mythological relevance and significance for the Judeo-Christian West in its quest to discover itself in relation to other peoples. The mythological significance of history is widely accepted as an important function of historiography, and the following quote illustrates clearly the mythological function of Western historiography:

> The atmosphere in which the Fathers of History [i.e., the Greeks] set to work was saturated with myth. Without myth, they could never have begun their work. The past is an intractable, incomprehensible mass of uncounted and uncountable data. It can be rendered intelligible only if some selection is made, around some focus or foci. In all the endless debate that has been generated by Ranke's "how things really were," a first question is often neglected: what "things" merit or require consideration in order to establish how they "really were"? Long before anyone dreamed of history, myth gave an answer. That was its function, or rather one of its functions; to make the past intelligible and meaningful by selection, by focusing on a few bits of the past which thereby acquired permanence, relevance, universal significance.
>
> —*Finley (1965:281)*

But it is important to stress the fact that memories of the past exist in the present consciousness (and will continue in the future) only in terms of how the past is used. People everywhere, including historians, use the past selectively, and certain events of the past that have had no relevance or significance at a certain time and in a certain cultural tradition acquire importance at a different time and in other cultural traditions. In other words, the past is a meaningful dimension or component of the present only insofar as it is used, and, from semiotic studies we can say that the use of the past to validate and legitimize the present and future is a mythological aspect of all cultures. As the validity of the mythological dimension or a myth is derived from its providing coherence and meaning for the users rather than from its continuing factual information, the historical facts that have been scientifically verified and empirically tested do not necessarily serve a mythological function in all cultures and they may have no relevance in some cultures. A myth is valid, relevant, and meaningful not because it contains factual information but because it is held to be true by the believers or users. Historians frequently extol their methods of verification and archival research to justify the importance of their scientific discoveries of documents and other artifacts and connect them scientifically to the present. But seldom do the historians note the fact that the documents and other artifacts that they discover are themselves fabrications (literally, human creations for a purpose) and cannot be presented as physical evidence of connecting the past and present without reference to their symbolic connections, meanings, and uses that may have significance to the present.

In other words, whether or not historians consider their research as scientific reconstruction of the past to show how cultural developments occur, all histories have mythological components for them to be significant; historiographies are guided by their mythological function in the present. Thus, it is not accurate to say that Hindus have no sense of history, or that Indians have no historical memory. It is important to point out why Hindus do not have a Judeo-Christian conception of history (or Judeo-Christian assumptions of historical memory). The confusion in what is regarded as history and what is regarded as myth by Western and Western-oriented scholars is clearly evident in the historical/sociological/anthropological studies of caste mobility.

When low-ranking caste groups acquire sufficient politico-economic power to challenge and enhance their low socioreligious status, it is common for them to reconstruct their caste history to show that they had originally occupied a very high socioreligious status and that they had lost that exalted status due to economic misfortunes or political debacles in their recent history. Historians, sociologists, and anthropologists call these reconstructions caste myths and often try to show that these myths are historically inaccurate. Seldom do these scholars realize that caste histories or caste myths (or whatever they are called) are an integral aspect of the structure and function of the caste system which enables (or indeed requires) the mythological reconstruction of caste histories in order to establish a correspondence or congruence between socioreligious status and politico-economic power. Contrary to a long-standing fallacious theory of the caste system as a rigid, unchanging hierarchy of high- and low-ranked status groups, it is evident that caste group mobility is a fundamental mechanism for the survival and maintenance of the caste system. In the Hindu caste system, there is mobility at the group level of caste groups that are ranked between the most ritually pure castes (Brahmins) and the most ritually impure castes (Untouchables); Brahmins and Untouchables are historyless, or people without history, because they cannot participate in the caste mobility processes of the caste system. The castes who are grouped as Kshatriyas (warriors and rulers), Vaisiyas (traders and merchants), and Sudras (artisans and agricultural laborers), who are located in between Brahmins and Untouchables, have histories and are the people with history, and elaborate dynastic histories are usually associated with the politically powerful caste groups (who usually use the labels of Kshatriyas).

At a larger national or state level a similar mythological role is assigned to history, and, as a result histories are lost or re-created in relation to the rise and fall of political dynasties. The significant fact in the use or uses of the past is that historical records about a dynasty's past greatness (by themselves) could not legitimize its present superior socioreligious status. In order for a dynasty to have superior socioreligious status, the dynasty must have politico-economic dominance and support of the Brahmanical priesthood. The role of the Brahmanical priesthood has great significance in legitimizing political authority. The Brahmin priest could reconstruct a mythological history and ritually purify a low-caste king, linking the king to mythical emperors and raising the king's socioreligious status to that of the Kshatriya so long as the king had the necessary politico-economic strength. In this type of sociocultural context, historical memory (of the scientific kind) is totally dysfunctional, and, as a result, Hindus do not make any attempt to keep chronicles and records on dynastic rulers as the Chinese did. Low castes become Kshatriyas and some Kshatriyas become kings, but they also vanish and are lost in the consciousness of succeeding generations unless a continuity in politico-economic dominance and high socioreligious status is maintained. Historiography and the Western type of discourse on history are useless or dysfunctional within the epistemological framework of Hindus. For the Hindus, the significant and useful discourse is on the recurrent forms and principles, and therefore discourse on gods and goddesses who embody these forms and principles is common. As Knipe (1991) points out, Hindus have "selective memory," remembering all the names and details of the gods and goddesses but not in the lineal, nonrecurring, historical framework.

Hinduism as a living tradition today has a long and exacting but quite selective memory. It is a tradition that remembers the cumulative experience of ages rather than specific events of a decade or century. Only the Greeks recalled that Alexander and his armies once invaded South Asia, and it was Chinese travelers who retained important details about early Buddhism in India. *It is a tradition that prefers to live on cosmic time, not human social calendars.* To this day there is often uncertainty about the beginning times of major festivals: the proper moment is eventually divined from the movements of celestial bodies and communicated from the specialists to the public. It is a tradition that seldom remembered the names of its ancient poets and rarely recorded political details, but generated the longest known epic poem about a war that may never have happened. Today many people who routinely recite 108 names of a goddess or a god cannot recall the name of any Hindu ruler before Jawarharlal Nehru became prime minister of India in 1947. [emphasis mine]

—*Knipe (1991:12)*

iii. India and Western Discourse on Civilization

The concept of civilization was formulated in the context of the 18th century Western Enlightenment when the French and to some extent the English viewed civilization as a process through which upward social mobility and rational achievements occurred. Civilization was conceptualized as an achievement of sophistication in intellectual and material pursuits, and the West of the 18th century was identified as the most civilized. In theorizing about progress in human history, a dichotomy between civilized and primitive states of human existence was made, and Western scholars formulated a continuum of developmental stages beginning with the primitive stage and culminating in the civilized stage; different human groups were located on a continuum in terms of their advancement toward civilization. (The German intellectual tradition eschewed the use of the concept of civilization, denoting it as a manifestation of pragmatic technological achievements, and focused on the concept of *kultur* to discuss the spiritual and intellectual achievements of particular groups.) In the 19th and early 20th centuries, progress toward civilization was explained as achieved through higher or lower levels of biological or genetic endowments of particular groups, and the West was considered to have achieved the height of civilization because of its biological and mental superiority. This kind of theorizing about civilization is often identified as the racialization or biologization of human history.

In recent Western scholarship, however, the concept of civilization has been used to describe and discuss complex cultural traditions that have literate learning centers, urban centers, large populations that are divided into various occupational or religious groups, and so on. Another way of conceptualizing civilization that was initiated by the anthropologists Robert Redfield and Milton Singer (of the University of Chicago) and others has borne some valid theoretical and empirical research on the process of civilization. In this research, a civilization is seen as an evolving process engendered by internal and external activities. For analytic purposes, a distinction is made between the existence of a Great Tradition and a Little Tradition in a civilization. The Great Tradition is composed of the literary forms as well as the urban developments and technological achievements. The custodians of the Great Tradition are the educated classes who largely are part of the urban centers. The Little Tradition is composed of the village folk or the peasants who engage in agricultural production and who are less reflective on the literary and philosophical concerns of the civilization. A dialectical relationship exists between the Great and Little Traditions; one cannot exist without the other in that they are interdependent. Those who participate in the Great Tradition systematize the elements within the civilization as well as those that are borrowed from outside the civilization, and in that process they also universalize the elements of that civilization, making them relevant and meaningful to all those within as well as outside the civilization.

In discussing civilizational processes in India, it is often suggested that Hindu civilization has been evolving for over five thousand years, absorbing many external elements, with the literati organizing and refining many internal cultural factors. Many cultural factors are universal throughout India and the literati living in different parts of India are custodians of these universal cultural elements. Folk activities that are part of the Little Traditions of different regions often get universalized, and urban forms often get parochialized in the Little Traditions of different regions.

Prior to the archaeological discovery of the remains of Indus Valley cultures in the late 19th and early 20th centuries, and the subsequent discussion of the discovery's significance for the reconstruction of the cultural and linguistic history of India, Western scholars expounded upon the pristine Aryan or Sanskritic civilization of India. The late 18th- and 19th-century orientalists and philologists studied Hindu law and scriptures written in Sanskrit. They translated many of them, compared Sanskrit and other ancient Indo-European languages, and also gave rise to the myth of the Aryan race, erroneously linking language, culture, and biology.

From the late 19th century to the middle of the 20th century, the British government in India spent large sums of money on the ethnographic and archaeological survey of India, and several multivolume editions describing the castes and tribes of India were published during this period. (See, for example, Risley 1891; Iyer 1909, 1928–1935; Thurston 1909; Ibbetson 1916; Russell 1916; Rose 1919; Enthoven 1920.) Many of the government officials who surveyed India were trained in the British scholarly tradition. Many were affiliated with the British ethnological or anthropological societies. Some of them, such as T.C. Hodson and J.H. Hutton, became professors of anthropology when they returned to England from India (Fortes 1974:427). These British scholars introduced paradigms such as Brahmanization and Hinduization in their interpretation of what they regarded as the civilizing process in India. Their epistemological assumptions were rooted in the Anglo-French notions of civilization and cultural evolution. They saw the West as civilized in contrast with the noncivilized non-West but identified within countries like India the existence of particular types of civilizing processes. Thus, while Western civilization was thought to represent the apex of evolution, these scholars saw within the non-Western countries the existence of certain traditions that were superior. The tribes and low castes of India were located at the bottom of the lineal progression toward civilization, and these groups were thought of as primitive, external social units that were able to participate a little in the civilization only by acquiring customs of the Brahmanical tradition of Hinduism.

The paradigm of civilization became important in the West as the exalted expression of the natural history of humankind. The beliefs and institutions of the West were seen as the most refined and rational of all human beliefs and institutions. Such notions were more than the common expression of ethnocentrism which is present in all human groups. The West saw itself as having acquired a scientific knowledge of humanity; it was assumed that this knowledge was universally valid. What was a cultural-epistemological system (a particular kind of imagery and a particular kind of knowledge validation) was elevated to the status of pan-human imagery and pan-human knowledge. A consequence of universalizing the Western cultural epistemology was to render India intellectually subordinate to the West. The scholars of India had to acquire the cultural, epistemological, and methodological language of the West in order to prove or disprove whether the Western interpretations of themselves were valid or invalid.

A problem in the use of the concept of civilization in general and in the use of the Great/Little Tradition, folk/urban model of civilization in our description and discussion of India is in the fact that India is composed of many regional civilizations, and many non-Hindu groups as well. Each of the regional civilizations and ethnic groups has over a period of hundreds of years developed and systematized distinctive forms of cultural structures, literary forms, and ecological adaptations. Furthermore, the difference between folk and urban masses, the literate and nonliterate peoples, is more marked in some parts of India than in others. A more suitable approach to the study of civilization in India is to delineate the particular cultural traditions that historically have developed diverse approaches to the dominant trends of Hinduism, Islam, or Christianity. Also, it is reasonable to suggest that despite the existence of a similar system of social organization (which we call caste) in most areas of India, this social organization itself is adapted in different ways in the different cultural traditions of India. Thus it is more appropriate to study how the peoples of India use religious, political, economic, and other symbols, and how they have expressed this use in literary forms in both the urban and nonurban centers.

iv. India and Discourse on Ethnicity and Nationalism

The study of ethnicity, or the symbols of group identity that perpetuate group distinctiveness with reference to race, religion, language, or particular cultural tradition, became an important scholarly research concern only during the past three decades. As DeVos (1975:78) points out, "Social science theorists have until recently paid little attention to enduring ethnic or cultural identity as a primary social force comparable to nationalism or class affiliation." And as Gupta (1975:467) notes about the change in the Western political scene in the 1960s, "The explosive demonstration of ethnic politics in the very home of mature modernity shocked those theorists into the recognition that the salience of ethnic action can hardly be inferred from the standard aggregate indices of modernity."

For a very long time, the universalist and rationalist ideals of Western scholarship viewed ethnicity as an expression of irrational, primordial sentiments and hoped that modernization would eventually lead to the elimination of ethnicity. However, there was a curious epistemological double standard: Nationalism was viewed as an important aspect of state formation, glorified as the "will of the people" and represented as a legitimate sociopolitical movement. There were several reasons for the existence of an epistemological language game, viewing ethnicity as irrational and nationalism as rational. I will discuss here a few of these reasons because it should help us clarify some of the distortions and misunderstandings about India and Indian traditions. (1) As almost all the European state boundaries were created (by the 19th century) as nations, either as national monarchies or as national republics, which frequently corresponded with linguistic boundaries, Western scholars accepted such a political form as rational and good and rendered scholarly legitimacy and validation for the nation-state. (2) As there was extensive scholarly discourse on political and legal processes of the nation-states, evaluating the significance and workings of representative democracy, rational bureaucracy, and the rule of law, it was believed that nationalism and national entities operated without the biases and prejudices of kinship, religious, racial, and linguistic loyalties, and such an assumption led to the *denial* of the operation (and the existence) of ethnicity in national affairs. (3) As a result of according positivist rationality and objectivity to nationalism and national socioeconomic and politico-legal processes, ethnicity was conceptualized as the opposite of nationalism in its being rooted in the irrational, subjective orientations of kinship, religious, racial, and linguistic biases and prejudices. (4) As the nation-states were controlled by numerically or economically dominant groups, the actions of dominant groups acquired the significance (in the eyes of scholars) of their being rational and universal, and the actions of numerically or economically subordinate groups acquired the significance (in the eyes of scholars) of their being irrational and parochial, and these subordinate groups were labeled *ethnic groups* and their sentiments and aspirations were labeled *ethnic politics*.

If we applied this analysis of scholarship on ethnicity and nationalism to understand India and Indian traditions, it would be clear that the labeling of ethnicity and the appellations of ethnic group and ethnic politics should identify *only* the caste symbols, caste group, and caste politics. Caste groups have become, in many parts of India, "political" action groups (Rudolph and

Rudolph 1967), and kinship and "communal" loyalties are important components of caste politics. However, distortion and misunderstanding of the Indian sociopolitical reality occur if and when the linguistic-national traditions are identified as ethnic traditions in relation to the all-India (empire) state configuration. Politicians and scholars frequently equate the ethnic politics of castes and those of linguistic-national traditions, thus according positivist, rational, and universal legitimacy for the actions of the all-India federal government only. In Chapters 5 through 10, I discussed in detail the consequences of conceptualizing the legitimacy of certain types of state boundaries in India. In order to analyze the ethnic-linguistic-national-state-level politics, I identified the all-India state boundary as the empire-state boundary and the linguistic state boundary as the national state boundary, viewing the latter as equally rational and universal to the all-India empire-state politics.

We must recognize the fact that symbols of ethnicity and ethnic identity systems have been core features of India from ancient times. The Aryan speakers who entered India between 1700 and 1500 B.C.E. and the Scythians, Huns, and others who immigrated during the period from about 700 B.C.E. to 700 C.E. undoubtedly used central and west Asian religious and linguistic symbols of ethnicity, but the fact was that they were incorporated into the Hindu caste system. The caste system of the Indus Valley Dravidian civilization was resilient to the frequent changes in the politico-economic environment and acquired certain cultural characteristics of flexibility in the use of the Hindu principles of religious purity and hierarchy. Thus the ethnic and tribal groups of western and central Asia could easily locate themselves through the adoption of the Hindu principles. Time and again, invading tribal and ethnic groups became caste groups. While this process (of ethnic groups or tribes becoming castes), which has been identified as Hinduization, has been an essential aspect of Indian civilization, another process, which can be identified as sectarianism, was also an important feature of Indian civilization. New caste or ethnic groupings emerged through reformist Hindu leaders seeking to change certain practices such as untouchability and founding a sect; sects of this kind frequently became separate caste groups, and in some instances they became religious-ethnic groups that acquired internal divisions resembling caste groupings; the Jains and Lingayats are the well-known examples of this phenomenon but there have emerged several other religious-ethnic groups as well.

A different kind of ethnic politics began after the 8th century C.E. As pointed out in Chapter 4, the post-8th-century C.E. immigrants retained their alien ethnic identity as symbols of political or social dominance, and the ethnic symbols referring to Arab, Persian, Afgan, Turk, and Mongol identities as well as the religious symbols referring to Islam became important and significant all over India after the 11th century C.E. (See Fardi and Siddiqui 1992.) This kind of ethnic politics culminated in the emergence of the *two-nation theory of India* (an Islamic nation and a Hindu nation) which led to the separation of Pakistan (from India) as an Islamic state.

Despite all this interplay of dramatization of caste and ethnic identities in India, there was very little use of ethnicity for attaining national-political autonomy until the 19th century. In other words, ethnicity did not acquire nationalist goals with reference to territorial integrity or political autonomy. Even the Tamil national tradition (discussed in Chapter 9) which had symbols and conceptions of Tamil peoplehood did not develop cultural assumptions of statehood relating such assumptions to Tamil nationality. The deification or apotheosis of Tamil language, and the conception of the land of the Tamils did not acquire significance as symbols of statehood until the 19th century, about the same time that other linguistic traditions such as the Marathas and the Bengalis also manifested nationalist aspirations. The 19th century nationalism or nationalization was essentially an Indian intellectual adaptation of the Western conceptions or models of nationalism that developed in Europe after the 15th century C.E. As a result of such an adaptation, the use of Hindi language acquired all-India nationalist significance during the 20th century as the language to replace English (which had been the national, universal language of India in the 19th century), and other languages of India became *ethnic languages*. I have suggested in this book that it would have served the political and intellectual goals of India better had Sanskrit rather than Hindi been adopted as the official all-India national language of post-British India. In many respects, Sanskrit could legitimately claim to be the only all-India language although it is not spoken as a mother tongue; Hindi, on the other hand, is one of the several regional-national languages of India, functioning until the 19th century as a Persianized Indian dialect of northern India. As noted in Chapter 1, the ancient Dravidian-Aryan linguistic/cultural synthesis produced Sanskrit (or the perfected literary language of Hindu scriptures), and at a later date Sanskrit influenced all the other Aryan languages as well as the Dravidian languages, thus contributing to the emergence of common vocabularies and similar religious and caste concepts all over India. The adoption of the Persianized northern Indian dialect (Hindi) as the all-India nationalist language in the 20th century essentially created a major cultural-linguistic separation between northern and southern India and between the Hindi-speaking and non-Hindi-speaking regions of northern India. The Tamils were in the forefront, opposing what they called Hindi imperialism, and the Tamil quest to create a separate nation-state for the Tamils acquired momentum in the 20th century. Although opposition to Hindi has not been so vocal in other linguistic states, it is likely that peoples of most of the linguistic states of India would favor national political autonomy; also, there is the possibility that smaller divisions of the linguistic states will emerge in relation to the emergence of regional dialectical or religious differences within the existing linguistic states of India.

In recent times, largely in reaction to Islam, Hindu fundamentalism acquired political significance, and many Hindu leaders have used Hinduism, Hindu nationalism, and Indian nationalism interchangeably to connote that the Indian nation belongs to Hindus and that Hinduism would be in great danger unless the unity of India as a Hindu nation is protected. This kind of correspondence between Hinduism and Indian territory has no empirical validity although it has the potential to become a sociopolitical reality. As Worsley (1964:32) pointed out long ago, "The Muslim conquest, which produced the Mogul Empire, demonstrates how a political system might develop over the major part of geographical India without any foundation in Hinduism at all. *The linking of nationhood to Hinduism was a post-European development.*" [emphasis mine]

In his insightful analysis of nationalism, Ernest Gellner has correctly drawn our attention to the fact that there is no intrinsic or natural affinity between nationalism and any particular religious, racial, or linguistic "reality." Religious, racial, or linguistic realities become national symbols of boundary and become political realities.

> Nationalism—the principle of homogenous cultural units as the foundations of political life, and of the obligatory cultural unity of rules and ruled—is indeed inscribed neither in the nature of things, nor in the hearts of men, nor in the preconditions of social life in general, and the contention that it is so inscribed is a falsehood which nationalist doctrine has succeeded in presenting as self-evident. But nationalism as a phenomenon, not as a doctrine presented by nationalists, is inherent in a certain set of social conditions; and those conditions, it so happens, are the conditions of our time.
>
> —*Gellner (1983:125)*

It must also be pointed out that the same process which shapes national consciousness operates in shaping the ethnic consciousness as well. As a result, both national and ethnic politics can be irrational and primordial and both can also be rational and universal. In recent times, India has been witnessing a particular type of political development that involves the creation of a new sense of ethnic identity among the untouchable caste groups of India. In some ways, this sociopolitical movement in India, called the *Dalit* movement, is comparable to the Black Power movement among African Americans of the United States. The word Dalit is derived from the Hebrew root word for broken (*dal*), to signify the broken soul of the untouchable peoples of India, and leaders of the Dalit movement refer to the untouchable peoples as *Black Untouchables of India* and seek to establish a separate nation-state called *Dalistastan*. V.T. Rajshekar, a leader of the Dalit movement, has stated the goals as follows:

> The right of Black Untouchables to quota jobs should not be tied to their declaring themselves to be Hindus. Blacks should have the freedom to create a new cultural system which can promote and sustain

their struggle for justice and human dignity. While preserving the right to quotas, they should have the cultural freedom to transform their society, to create and live in a society where the notions of Black untouchability and caste discrimination are non-existent. The present arrangement of tying their economic rights to their participation in the old cultural system is a cruel denial of their full range of human rights. It is for these many reasons that the Black Untouchables of India are fighting for a homeland, *Dalitastan*.

—Rajshekar (1987:74)

About three decades ago, an American sociologist used the concept of *ethnogenesis* to identify the transformation of social aggregates from social categories to ethnic groups. In this view (Singer 1962:419–32), African Americans became an ethnic group recently through a transformation from a loose conglomeration of subordinate peoples into a distinctive social entity, a people. The ethnic identity of African Americans developed through the cultivation of norms for a united expression in the political arena. Ethnogenesis, in Singer's analysis, is characterized by the existence of a group's awareness as a corporate body, with its having a distinctive self-image. The Dalit movement in India seeks to achieve an awareness among the untouchables as a corporate body with a particular self-image, and this ethnic awareness is believed to be a prerequisite for achieving the political goal of creating a separate nation-state called Dalitastan. It can be argued from a general theoretical perspective that ethnicity is a political phenomenon. Abner Cohen (1976) has eloquently put forward this idea.

Ethnicity is fundamentally a political phenomenon, as the symbols of the traditional culture are used as mechanisms for the articulation of political alignments. It is a type of informal interest grouping. It does not form part of the formal structure of the state. If an ethnic group is formally recognized by a state, for example within a federation, then it is no longer an ethnic group, but a province or a region. Ethnicity differs, on the other hand, from formal associations in that an ethnic group has no explicitly stated aims and is not rationally and bureaucratically organized. An ethnic group is thus sociologically different from an ethnic association, just as caste is different from caste association.

—Cohen (1976:97)

Most of what I have said in the foregoing paragraphs deals with the ethnic or national status of the religious minorities, castes, and linguistic nationalities. Before we close our discourse on this subject, it is necessary to discuss the structure of ethnicity and nationalism as it refers to the tribal populations of India. The tribal situation is complicated by the fact that some of the populations located within the linguistic states aspire to create their own separate states, and some of the tribal populations that have their own states aspire to create separate nation-states. The tribal populations are not a linguistically or culturally homogeneous group. The tribal populations in south-central India speak Dravidian languages, and those in eastern and northeastern India speak Austro-Asiatic and Tibeto-Burman languages. Most of the tribal populations of northeast India have separate states within the political state boundary of India, and some of them are in the Assam (linguistic) state of India. During the British rule, the tribes were politically semiautonomous because they were not brought within the political and legal framework of the British Empire. The Indian Empire, on the other hand, had attempted to enforce its political and legal institutions, and for well over two decades the Indian army fought the Naga tribes (many of whom had become Christians in the early 20th century) to bring them under Indian political control. A compromise solution was made by providing the tribes of northeastern India with separate states, but there still are unresolved political problems. Also, some tribes such as the Bodo tribe in Assam have been waging guerrilla warfare, seeking independence.

On the other hand, the following quote from a book by a tribal leader of Nagaland indicates that there are tribal minorities in India who seek to integrate their territories within the national boundary of India, and participate fully in the sociopolitical-economic institutions of India.

> As we look ahead to the future of Nagaland we see that now there is no place or scope for insurgencies in its life. An era of productive peace has to be ushered in so that the fruits of economic planning and development can be shared by all its people. They have missed the fruits of many years of economic planning and development. Nagas must now take active part in the national mainstream. They should no longer entertain the idea of keeping themselves isolated from the mainstream of national life. The new generation of Nagaland should think in terms of what they can give to their country and not what they can get. Today, under the fresh perspectives into national unity offered by the dynamic leadership of Shri Rajib Gandhi, the Nagas can look forward to better opportunities in all spheres of life and Nagaland looks ahead with confidence, faith and optimism.

> —*Sema (1986:192)*

v. Some Final Thoughts

In concluding this book I would like to reflect upon the significance and relevance of communicating ideas and facts about sociocultural reality to the insiders and outsiders, or (stated in a semiotic framework), to those who experience that reality (in a number of different ways and in different contexts) and to those who use the reality to encounter the range of multiple creations of the human others. In the scholarly commentaries on India and Hinduism, I have found the writings of Professors Wendy Doniger and Milton Singer (both of the University of Chicago) most illuminating for acquiring an appreciation of the historical creations of symbols, the cultural performances of the symbols, and the *hermeneutic documentation of the symbols in the dialogue between the self and the other.* I will comment briefly on their writings that relate to my reflections.

The late Professor Joseph Campbell was probably the most popular 20th-century American interpreter of Hinduism. He edited Heinrich Zimmer's *Philosophies of India* in 1950, and during the next four decades he was a much sought after speaker on India and Hinduism for television and college audiences. His interpretations troubled a few thoughtful religious scholars such as Wendy Doniger (O'Flaherty) who wondered whether Campbell was creating or inventing a form or version of India and Hinduism to relate to (and connect with) his audiences, or whether he was committed to intellectual honesty and remained true to the facts about India and Hinduism. In a review article published in the *New York Times Book Review* in 1992, Professor Doniger pointed out that there was a big difference between how India and Hinduism were experienced and used by those who were culturally Hindus and by those who selected certain aspects or bits and pieces of India and Hinduism to create or invent personal and philosophical treatises on humankind. She noted that although Campbell never fully understood or comprehended Hinduism, he was a very effective popularizer of his version of Hinduism and presented it with charm and clarity to his Western audience. What bothered Doniger came from the questions she repeatedly asked of herself about whether we can condone Campbell's behavior and accept his version of Hinduism and India to be valid because it served an important function of communicating religious beliefs of another country, or whether we should insist on scholarly responsibility and intellectual honesty for facts and truth. Doniger opted for the latter:

> In the 60's, years before Bill Moyers made "Campbell" a household word for something more than soup, Campbell had a cult following: he was the hippie hero (though his own self-discipline kept him from indulging in drugs or free love). He brought much joy into the world by making accessible to many people the ideas contained in books they did not know about or have the patience to read. This is no small thing. When thousands of people are walking around happy in their understandings of Hinduism or the Navajos because of Joseph Campbell, who am I to point out that they don't understand Hinduism or the Navajos, because Campbell didn't understand them? Does it matter?
>
> I think it does. It matters not just for the record—what else is scholarship?—but, more important, for the sake of the Hindus and

Navajos, who deserve to have their stories truly known. Out of respect for them, we must take the trouble to get the stories right. Buddhists did not struggle through two and a half millenniums in India, Japan and China just so people in California could feel better about themselves. The myths have other goals, and we must know and respect those goals, even if we do not choose to follow them.

—*Doniger (1992:8)*

The questions raised by Doniger can be rephrased: When we visit a museum, should we ask only "what the artifacts meant to the people who made them" and strive for an understanding from the native cultural perspective, or should we ask only "what the artifacts mean aesthetically for revealing certain universal truths and principles"? In her study of Siva myths of Hinduism, Doniger (1973) addressed this issue and created (wrote) one of the best books on Hinduism; she showed why it was absolutely essential to comprehend how the users of Siva myths experienced the myths to cope with cultural paradoxes before the scholar offered interpretations about why different versions of Siva myths existed and why Freudian and structural theories might have validity for understanding the nature and role of myths. In her study of Siva myths, Doniger shows that the myths make sense only when we relate them to Hindu cultural orientations of pollution/purity, hierarchy, and spiritual power. In the Hindu tradition, spiritual power can be gained in several ways, including the opening of the psychic centers through the flow of sexual energy as well as through chastity or celibacy. Siva is an ascetic god but is also the god of virile sexuality; he has a permanently erect penis (ithyphallic) but he is eternally chaste; Siva, the ascetic god, conserves semen on the one hand and spills it on the other, but the spilling of semen is for creative regeneration of spiritual power. Doniger applies Freudian and structuralist theories to understand or show how Siva myths defy meaninglessness and chaos, and notes that myths "express unconscious wishes in the context of culturally stipulated paradoxes."

If Doniger's discourse is held as the ideal model of scholarship on Hinduism, most studies do not even come close to that ideal. But we can say that Western Orientalists-Indologists, missionaries, administrator-scholars, historians, sociologists, and anthropologists have produced tomes of books and essays on Hinduism and India and have contributed equally to our understanding and misunderstanding of Hinduism and India. Orientalists and Indologists have contributed to the fallacy of aryanism, interpreting Hinduism as an Aryan religion, and Orientalists theorized on the similarities between Hindu polytheism and Greek polytheism through the application of a fallacious comparative method; however, Max Muller's monumental and epoch-making multivolume translation of "the sacred scriptures of the east" created a lasting understanding of India's past. Likewise, despite their antipathy toward Hinduism, many missionaries produced relatively accurate accounts of caste and village life as well as of Hindu cults, sects, and religious movements. Although the studies by professional historians have often been tendentious, the two prototypic contentious models of Indian history that emerged in the form of *Cambridge History of India* and *Oxford History of India* helped to bring the historiography and historical understanding of India on the world stage, and there have been excellent histories of India such as Basham's *The Wonder That Was India.* Recently, the historical scholarship of Professor Stanley Wolpert has greatly enhanced our interpretive understanding of India's past; I have incorporated many of his interpretations in this book.

A curious fact about sociological studies of India is that such studies are frequently labeled "anthropological" studies by Western scholars, and sociologists from India may acquire the designation of "anthropologist" in the West. The epistemological foundations of this practice of viewing Indian sociologists as anthropologists in the West is rooted in signifying native scholars as cultural informants and in using data on non-Western cultures as anthropological data. Among recent sociological/anthropological publications, the book *Religion and Society Among the Coorgs of South India* (1952) by the Indian sociologist/anthropologist M.N. Srinivas and the book *Homo Hierarchicus* (1970) by the French sociologist/anthropologist Louis Dumont have been rightfully regarded as classics. I regard Milton Singer's *When a Great Tradition Modernizes: An Anthropological Approach to Indian Civilization* (1972) to be one of the most important scholarly contributions to foster an understanding of how the documented sociocultural reality is experienced and dramatized in the contexts in which it has significance and how such a reality reveals significant facts about a culture and about the nature of culture in general.

Singer rightly emphasizes that humanistic and anthropological scholarship must go together in the study of civilizations and that the anthropologist must study the contextual use of text. Through the study of the Hindu texts and their use, Singer demonstrates how the social structure and organization of the "great tradition" of a civilization can be inferred. There are three methods through which we could identify the great tradition of Indian civilization: (1) through a study of Sanskritic sacred geography (temple, pilgrimage centers, etc.); (2) through a study of Sanskritic professional representatives and their social organization (learned specialists of myth and ritual); and (3) through a study of the cultural performance (rituals) in the context of the cultural stage (home, temples, pilgrimage centers, etc.). The anthropological data thus acquired cannot be presented with inferences and conclusions. Singer presents the data in detail, "making use of actual field notes," and asks the reader to apprehend the existence of the cultural pattern. He states: "By retracing the order of discovery of the structure in the field, this procedure will enable the reader to check the author's inferences and will also furnish insight into the existential and functional interrelations among the different structural components of the Great Tradition in the context of daily life" (Singer 1972:86).

Beyond the above-stated commitment to intellectual honesty which characterizes Singer's work, he has taken pains to comprehend the nature of the relationship between the tale and teller of the tale, the studier and studied, the signifier and signified, and the image and reality in our discourse on India. In an essay entitled "Passage to More Than India: A Sketch of Changing European and American Images," which is included in the book *When a Great Tradition Modernizes,* Singer presents an illuminating discussion of why and how certain images and symbols of Indians and India were created. Indians and India were known to the Persians and Greeks of the 6th–5th century B.C.E. in a number of ways with exotic representations; at a later period, teratological representations of Indians and Indian customs became popular in the Greco-Roman world; medieval Christians of Europe derived their images from Marco Polo's writings and from Arabs; the direct contact between Europeans and Indians, beginning with the Portuguese settlements on the west coast of India had unforeseen consequences for both India and Britain, and British attitudes toward India from the middle of the 18th century, when the British succeeded in establishing politicoeconomic dominance in India, were shaped by both positive and negative images. I give below a few excerpts from Singer's "Passage to More Than India":

> The foundation for the image of India as a land of dark-skinned, benighted heathen who need the blessings of Christianity and European civilization was laid several hundred years before England's industrial revolution and the establishment of the British Raj in India. It goes back to the conflict of Christian Europe with Islam. The Portuguese and other early explorers looked upon the Muslims as their hated enemies and rivals. They expected to find in India the Nestorian Christians and the fabled Christian monarch Prester John, about whom Marco Polo and other medieval travelers wrote. When Vasco da Gama was asked at Calicut what he had come for, he replied, "Christians and spices." He found the spices, but many more Hindus and Muslims than Christians.
>
> In retrospect, the exaggerated modern contrast of Eastern spirituality with Western materialism recalls the fanciful ideas of the ancient and medieval images, but with one important difference. The splendor of the ancient and medieval images was as much material as spiritual—deriving from the gems, spices, and silks of the luxury trade. No attempt was made to segregate in moral or intellectual principle these "material treasures" from the "spiritual treasures" of Indian civilization. Such segregation is a legacy of European colonial rule and attitudes. As an object of the "white man's burden," India was stripped, at least in image, of both material and spiritual treasures, and was left as the land of naked

and benighted heathen. As if to compensate for such an uncharitable view and for the activities with which they were associated, the orientalists rediscovered the ancient spiritual wisdom. This inspired a romantic enthusiasm for Indian philosophy and religion in the West and a new-found pride among Indians in their spirituality. Unfortunately, this compensatory movement did little to restore respect for the material arts and achievements of Indian civilization. At best, "material India" came to be considered a field for Western improvements and for humanitarian endeavor. This cleavage between a "spiritual" and "material" India has been of the greatest consequence, not only for Western understanding but India's self-understanding as well. For Indians, too, were lulled by this half-flattering Western attitude to develop a one-sided image of their civilization.

—Singer (1972:17, 35–36)

As I reflect upon the data that I have used in writing this book, I wonder about the image of India that I have created for the reader. The image of India that most Western readers have comes from the writings of Mahatma Gandhi and Jawaharlal Nehru, and it is reasonable to ask what relationship or correspondence exists between my creation and the imaginations of Gandhi and Nehru.

Gandhi and Nehru imagined India through the filters of their cultural experiences of being Indian and through the paradigms of Hindu universalism and scientific humanism. Both played major roles in the shaping of the modern political configurations of India, and were thus proponents of certain ideas and images of India. Gandhi became the cultural archetype of Hindu spirituality and Nehru became the cultural archetype of Indian secularism. Gandhi synthesized and mediated several cultural, social, and political aspects of India within a framework of Hindu universalism. Nehru sought to modernize India within a framework of scientific humanism, while at the same time affirming the greatness of Indian civilizations. Gandhi's Hindu universalism was rooted in introspective self-reflection; Nehru's scientific humanism was based on the ideals of Western Enlightenment and historical scholarship.

I have also imagined India through the cultural filters of being an Indian, and I have used a semiotic perspective for analyzing and interpreting certain significant symbols and traditions of India. But as someone who became a teacher of anthropology in California, I have no political or religious affiliation with the present India. Thus, my perception and analysis of India differs from those of Gandhi and Nehru.

Perhaps the paradigms of Hindu universalism and scientific humanism that Gandhi and Nehru used in their quest to understand India and humanity will endure, and perhaps these paradigms can be used by us in our efforts to understand India. However, we must also recognize the fact that such paradigms acquire significance only when we have in our possession some basic understanding of the anthropological, historical, and sociological factors that constitute what we identify as traditions. It is my hope that I have provided some basic anthropological, historical, and sociological facts and interpretations of the various traditions of India. I urge the reader to reflect upon the musings of Gandhi and Nehru cited below because they reveal the workings of Hindu universalism and scientific humanism in the making of India.

What I want to achieve,—what I have been striving and pining to achieve these thirty years,—is self-realization, to see God face to face, to attain *Moksha*. I live and move and have my being in pursuit of this goal. All that I do by way of speaking and writing, and all my ventures in the political field, are directed to this same end. But as I have all along believed that what is possible for one is possible for all, my experiments have not been conducted in the closet, but in the open; and I do not think that this fact detracts from their spiritual value. There are some things which are known only to oneself and one's Maker. These are clearly incommunicable. The experiments I am about to relate are not such. But they are spiritual, or rather moral; for the essence of religion is morality.

—*Gandhi (1957:xii–xii)*

The discovery of India—what have I discovered? It was presumptuous of me to imagine that I could unveil her and find out what she is today and what she was in the long past. Today she is four hundred million separate individual men and women, each differing from the other, each living in a private universe of thought and feeling. If this is so in the present, how much more difficult is it to grasp that multitudinous past of innumerable successions of human beings. Yet something has bound them together and binds them still. India is a geographical and economic entity, a cultural unity amidst diversity, a bundle of contradictions held together by strong but invisible threads. Overwhelmed again and again, her spirit was never conquered, and today when she appears to be the plaything of a proud conqueror, she remains unsubdued and unconquered. About her there is the elusive quality of a legend of long ago; some enchantment seems to have held her mind. She is a myth and an idea, a dream and a vision, and yet very real and present and pervasive. There are terrifying glimpses of dark corridors which seem to lead back to primeval night, but also there is the fullness and warmth of the day about her. Shameful and repellent she is occasionally, perverse and obstinate, sometimes even a little hysteric, this lady with a past. But she is very lovable and none of her children can forget her wherever they go or whatever strange fate befalls them. For she is part of them in her greatness as well as her failings, and they are mirrored in those deep eyes of hers that have seen so much of life's passion and joy and folly and looked down into wisdom's well. Each one of them is drawn to her, though perhaps each has a different reason for that attraction or can point to no reason at all, and each sees some different aspect of her many-sided personality.

—Nehru (1946:575–76)

✤ BIBLIOGRAPHY

ABEL, E. *The Anglo-Indian Community.* Delhi: Chanakya Publications, 1988.

ADINARAYAN, S.P. *The Case for Colour.* Bombay: Asia Publishing House, 1964.

AGGARWAL, P.C. "A Muslim Sub-Caste of North India," *Economic and Political Weekly* 1 (1966).

AHMAD, I., ed. *Caste and Social Stratification Among the Muslims.* Delhi: Manohar Book Service, 1973.

AHMAD, I. "For a Sociology of India," *Contributions to Indian Sociology* 4 (1972).

AINAPUR, L.S. *The Dynamics of Caste Relations in Rural India.* Jaipur: Rawat Publications, 1986.

ALLCHIN, R., and B. ALLCHIN. *The Rise of Civilization in India.* Cambridge: Cambridge University Press, 1982.

ANONYMOUS. "India," *Los Angeles Times* (October 31, 1990).

ANSARI, G. "Muslims in Uttar Pradesh," *Eastern Anthropologist* 13 (1959).

ANSARI, I.A. *The Muslim Situation in India.* London: Oriental University Press, 1989.

ANTHONY, F. *Britain's Betrayal in India.* New Delhi: Allied Publishers, 1969.

ARCHER, J.C. *The Sikhs.* Princeton, NJ: Princeton University Press, 1971.

AROKIASWAMI, M. *The Kongu Country.* Madras: University of Madras, 1956.

ARRIAN. *The Campaigns of Alexander.* New York: Penguin Books, 1971.

ARUNACHALAM, M. *An Introduction to the History of Tamil Literature.* Tiruchi: Gandhiridyalam, 1974.

BABB, L.A. *The Divine Hierarchy: Popular Hinduism in Central India*. New York: Columbia University Press, 1975.

———. *Redemptive Encounters: Three Modern Styles in the Hindu Tradition*. Berkeley: University of California Press, 1986.

BADEN-POWELL, B.H. *The Village Community*. London: Longmans, Green and Co., 1896.

BALY, S. *Saints, Goddesses and Kings: Muslims and Christians in South Indian Society, 1700–1900*. Cambridge: Cambridge University Press, 1989.

BALYUZI, H.M. *Bahaullah*. Oxford: George Ronald, 1963.

BARBER, B. "Social Mobility in Hindu India," in J. Silverberg, ed., *Social Mobility in the Caste System*. The Hague: Mouton, 1968.

BARNETT, M.R. *The Politics of Cultural Nationalism in South India*. Princeton, NJ: Princeton University Press, 1976.

BARTH, F. *Ethnic Groups and Boundaries*. Boston: Little, Brown, 1969.

BASHAM, A.L. *The Wonder That Was India*. New York: Grove Press, 1959.

BEALS, A.R. *Gopalpur: A South Indian Village*. New York: Holt, Rinehart and Winston, 1962.

BECK, B.E.F. *Peasant Society in Konku: A Study of Right and Left Subcastes in South India*. Vancouver: University of British Columbia Press, 1972.

———. "Centers and Boundaries of Regional Caste Systems: Toward a General Model," in Carol Smith, ed., *Regional Analysis*, vol. 2. New York: Academic Press, 1976.

BERGER, A.A. *Signs in Contemporary Culture: An Introduction to Semiotics*. Salem, MA: Sheffield Publishing Co., 1984.

BERREMAN, G.D. "The Concept of Caste," *International Encyclopedia of the Social Sciences* 3 (1968).

BETEILLE, A. *Caste, Class and Power: Changing Patterns of Stratification in Tanjore Village*. Berkeley: University of California Press, 1965.

———. *Castes: Old and New*. New York: Asia Publishing House, 1969.

———. "Race and Descent as Social Categories in India," in J.H. Franklin, ed., *Color and Race*. Boston: Beacon Press, 1968.

BHARATI, A. "Hinduism and Modernization," in R. Spencer, ed., *Religion and Change in Contemporary Asia*. Minneapolis: University of Minnesota, 1971.

BROWN, J.M. *Modern India: The Origins of an Asian Democracy*. Oxford: Oxford University Press, 1985.

BURGESS, J. *The Chronology of Modern India (1494–1894)*. Edinburgh: John Grant, 1913.

CALMAN, L.J. *Protest in Democratic India*. Boulder, CO: Westview Press, 1985.

CANTLIE, A. *The Assamese: Religion, Caste and Sect in an Indian Village*. London: Curzon Press, 1984.

CARSTAIRS, G.M. *The Twice-Born: A Study of a High-Caste Hindu*. Bloomington, IN: University Press, 1967.

CHATTERJI, S.K. *Dravidian*. Annamalainar: Annamalai University, 1965.

COHEN, A. *Two-Dimensional Man.* Berkeley: University of California Press, 1976.

COHN, B.S. *India: The Social Anthropology of a Civilization.* Englewood Cliffs, NJ: Prentice Hall, 1971.

COLE, W.O. *The Guru in Sikhism.* London: Darton, Longman and Todd, 1982.

———. *Sikhism and Its Indian Context.* London: Darton, Longman and Todd, 1984.

COON, C.S. *The Living Races of Man.* New York: Alfred A. Knopf, 1965.

COWARD, H. *Pluralism: Challenge to World Religions.* New York: Orbio Press, 1985.

CROLE, C.S. *Manual of Chingleput District.* Madras: Government Press, 1879.

DALE, S.F. *Islamic Society on the South Asian Frontier: The Mappilas of Malabar.* Oxford: Clarendon Press, 1980.

DANIELOU, A. *Gods of Love and Ecstasy: The Tradition of Shiva.* Rochester, NY: Inner Traditions International, 1984.

———. *While the Gods Play: Shaiva Oracles and Prediction.* Rochester, NY: Inner Traditions International, 1987.

———. *Yoga.* Rochester, NY: Inner Traditions International, 1991.

———. *The Myths and Gods of India.* Rochester, NY: Inner Traditions International, 1991.

DAS, V. *Structure and Cognition: Aspects of Caste and Ritual.* Delhi: Oxford University Press, 1990.

DASGUPTA, S. *Caste, Kinship and Community: Social System of a Bengal Caste.* Madras: University Press, 1986.

DEAN, V.M. *New Politics of Democracy in India.* Cambridge, MA: Harvard University Press, 1969.

DE BARY, WILLIAM T., ed. "Ananda Ranga Pillai: Hindu Agent for the French," *Sources of Indian Tradition,* vol. II. New York: Columbia University Press, 1958.

DEELY, J. *Basics of Semiotics.* Bloomington, IN: Indiana University Press, 1990.

DERRETT, J.D.M. "The Reform of Hindu Religious Endowments," in D.E. Smith, ed., *South Asian Politics and Religion.* Princeton, NJ: Princeton University Press, 1966.

DESOUZA, A.A. *Anglo-Indian Education.* Delhi: Oxford University Press, 1976.

DEVOS, G. "Ethnic Pluralism, Conflict and Accommodation," in G. DeVos and L. Romanucci-Ross, eds., *Ethnic Identity,* Palo Alto, CA: Mayfield Publishing Co., 1975.

DIRKO, N.B. "The Pasts of a Palaiyakarar: The Ethnohistory of a South Indian Little King," *The Journal of Asian Studies* 4 (1982).

DONIGER (O'FLAHERTY), W. *Siva: the Erotic Ascetic.* New York: Oxford University Press, 1973.

———. *Women, Androgynes and Other Mythical Beasts.* Chicago: University of Chicago Press, 1980.

———. "Origins of Myth-Making Man," *New York Times Book Review* (December 18, 1983).

———. "A Very Strange Enchanted Boy," *New York Times Book Review* (February 2, 1992).

DREKMEIER, C. *Kingship and Community in Early India.* Stanford, CA: Stanford University Press, 1962.

D'SOUZA, V.S. "Social Organization and Marriage Customs of the Moplahs on the South-West Coast of India," *Anthropos* 54 (1959).

DUBE, S.C. *Indian Village.* New York: Harper & Row, 1967.

DUMONT, L. *Homo Hierarchicus: An Essay on the Caste System.* Chicago: The University of Chicago Press, 1970a.

———. *Religion, Politics and History in India.* The Hague: Mouton, 1970b.

———. "A Structural Definition of a Folk Deity of Tamil Nad: Aiyanar, the Lord," in W.A. Lessa and E.Z. Vogt, eds., *Reader in Comparative Religion.* New York: Harper & Row, 1972.

ECO, U. *A Theory of Semiotics.* Bloomington, IN: Indiana University Press, 1976.

EGNOR, M. "The Sacred Spell and Other Conceptions of Life in Tamil Culture." Ph.D. Dissertation, Department of Anthropology, University of Chicago, 1978.

EMENEAU, M.B. "Dravidian and Indo-Aryan: The Linguistic Area," in A.F. Sjoberg, ed., *Symposium on Dravidian Civilization.* New York: Jenkins Publishing Co., 1971.

ENGLE, J. *Servants of God: Lives of Ten Sikh Gurus.* Franklin, NH: Sant Bani Ashram, 1980.

ENTHOVAN, R.E. *The Tribes and Castes of Bombay* (3 vols.). Bombay: Government of Central Press, 1920.

FAIRSERVIS, W. *The Roots of Ancient India.* Chicago: University of Chicago Press, 1975.

———. "The Script of the Indus Valley Civilization," *Scientific American,* October 1981.

FARDI, F.R. and M.M. SIDDIQUI. *The Social Structure of Indian Muslims.* New Delhi: Institute of Objective Studies, 1992.

FARMER, E.L., et al. *Comparative History of Civilizations in Asia* (2 vols.). Boulder, CO: Westview Press, 1986.

FINLEY, M.I. "Myth, Memory, and History," *History and Theory* 5 (1965).

FORTES, M. "Social Anthropology at Cambridge Since 1900," in R. Darnell, ed., *Readings in the History of Anthropology.* New York: Harper & Row, 1974.

FRANKLIN, J.H., ed. *Color and Race.* Boston: Beacon Press, 1968.

GAIKWAD, V.R. *The Anglo-Indians.* Bombay: Asia Publishing House, 1967.

GANDHI, M.K. *An Autobiography: The Story of My Experiments With Truth.* Boston: Beacon Press, 1957.

GEERTZ, C. *The Interpretation of Cultures: Selected Essays.* New York: Basic Books, Inc., 1973.

GELLNER, E. *Nations and Nationalism.* Ithaca, NY: Cornell University Press, 1983.

GOPAL, R. *Indian Muslims.* Bombay: Asia Publishing House, 1964.

GOUGH, E.K. "Caste in a Tanjore Village," in E.R. Leach, ed., *Aspects of Caste in South India, Ceylon, and North-West Pakistan.* Cambridge: Cambridge University Press, 1960.

————. "The Social Structure of a Tanjore Village," in M. Marriott, ed., *Village India.* Chicago: University of Chicago Press, 1969.

GUHA, B.C. "Negrito Racial Strains in India," Government of India Report, vol. 1, part III, 1935.

GUHA, U. "Caste Among Rural Bengali Muslims," *Man in India* 45 (1965).

GUPTA, A.R. *Caste Hierarchy and Social Change: A Study of Myth and Reality.* New Delhi: Jyotona Prakashan, 1984.

GUPTA, J.D. "Ethnicity, Language Demands and National Development in India," in N. Glazer and D.P. Moynihan, eds., *Ethnicity.* Cambridge, MA: Harvard University Press, 1975.

HARDGRAVE, JR., R.L. *The Dravidian Movement.* Bombay: Popular Prakasam, 1965.

————. *The Nadars of Tamilnad: The Political Culture of a Community in Change.* Berkeley: University of California Press, 1969.

HARRISON, S.S. *India: The Most Dangerous Decades.* Princeton, NJ: Princeton University Press, 1960.

HART III, G.L. "Women and the Sacred in Ancient Tamilnad," *Journal of Asian Studies* 32 (1973).

————. *The Poems of Ancient Tamil.* Berkeley: University of California Press, 1975a.

————. "Ancient Tamil Literature: Its Scholarly Past and Future," in B. Stein, ed., *Essays on South India.* Honolulu, Hawaii: The University Press, 1975b.

————. *The Relation between Tamil and Classical Sanskrit Literature.* Wiesbaden: Otto Harrassowitz, 1976.

HEALY, JOHN F., translator, *Pliny the Elder: Natural History: A Selection.* New York: Penguin Books, 1991.

HERBERT, J. *An Introduction to Asia.* New York: Oxford University Press, 1968.

HERODOTUS. *The Histories.* New York: Penguin Books, 1972.

HOLMES, G. "The First Orientalists," *New York Times Book Review* (September 5, 1993).

HOOTON, E.A. *Up From Ape.* New York: The Macmillan Co., 1946.

HUDSON, T.C. *The Naga Tribes of Manipur.* London: Macmillan and Co., 1911.

HUTTON, J.H. *Caste in India.* Oxford: Oxford University Press, 1961.

————. *The Angami Nagas.* London: Oxford University Press, 1921.

IBBETSON, D. *Panjab Castes.* Lahore: Government Printing Press, 1916.

INDEN, R. *Imagining India.* Oxford: Blackwell Publishers, 1992.

IRSHICK, E.F. *Politics and Social Conflict in South India: The Non-Brahmin Move-*

ment and Tamil Separatism 1916–1929. Berkeley: University of California Press, 1969.

ISHWARAN, K. *Shivapur: A South Indian Village.* London: Routledge and Kegan Paul, 1968.

IYER, L.K.A. *The Cochin Tribes and Castes,* vols. I and II. Madras: Government of Cochin Publications, 1909.

———. *The Mysore Tribes and Castes.* Bangalore: Mysore Government Press, 1928-35.

JAY, E.J. *A Tribal Village of Middle India.* Calcutta: Anthropological Survey of India, 1970.

JOSHI, L.M., ed. *Sikhism.* Patiala: Punjabi University, 1980.

KANAKASABHAI, V. *The Tamils Eighteen Hundred Years Ago.* Tirunelveli: The South India Aiva Siddhanta Pub. Society, 1966.

KAPUR, R.A. *Sikh Separatism: The Politics of Faith.* London: Allen and Unwin, 1980.

KHAN, Z. "Caste and Muslim Peasantry in India and Pakistan," *Man in India* 45 (1968).

KNIPE, D.M. *Hinduism.* New York: Harper Collins Publishers, 1991.

KRISHNAMURTHI, S.R. *A Study of Cultural Development in the Chola Period.* Annamalainagar: Annamali University, 1966.

KRISHNASWAMY, A. *The Tamil Country Under Vijayanagar.* Annamalainagar: Annamalai University, 1964.

LACH, D.F. *India in the Eyes of Europe.* Chicago: University of Chicago Press, 1965.

LAHOVARY, N. *Dravidian Origins and the West.* Bombay: Orient Longmans, 1963.

LALL, A. *The Emergence of Modern India.* New York: Columbia University Press, 1981.

LANNOY, R. *The Speaking Tree: A Study of Indian Culture and Society.* London: Oxford University Press, 1971.

LEACH, E.R. "Review of Caste in Modern India," *British Journal of Sociology* 14 (1963).

———. "Pulleyar and the Lord Buddha: An Aspect of Religious Syncretism in Ceylon," in W.A. Lessa and E.Z. Vogt, eds., *Reader in Comparative Religion: An Anthropological Approach.* New York: Harper & Row, 1972.

LEAF, M.J. *Information and Behavior in a Sikh Village.* Berkeley: University of California Press, 1972.

LEHMANN, W.P. *Descriptive Linguistics: An Introduction.* New York: Random House,

LEWIS, I.M. *Ecstatic Religion.* London: Routledge, 1989.

MALONEY, C. *Peoples of South Asia.* New York: Holt, Rinehart and Winston, 1974.

———. *South Asia: Seven Community Profiles.* New York: Holt, Rinehart and Winston, 1974.

———. "Archaeology in South India: Accomplishments and Prospects," in B. Stein, ed., *Essays in South India*. Honolulu: University Press, 1975.

———. *The Indian Tamils: Identity and Politics*. Indianapolis, IN: Universities Field Staff International, 1986.

———. *Language, Politics, and Modernization in India*. Indianapolis, IN: Universities Field Staff International, 1991.

MANDELBAUM, D.G. *Society in India*, vol. I and II. Berkeley: University of California Press, 1970.

MARRIOTT, M., ed. *Village India: Studies in the Little Community*. Chicago: University of Chicago Press, 1955.

———. "Caste Systems," *The New Encyclopedia Britannica* 3 (1976).

———. *India Through Hindu Eyes*. New Delhi: Sage Publications, 1990.

MAYO, K. *Mother India*. New York: Harcourt Brace, 1927.

MCGRINDLE, J.W. *The Invasion of India by Alexander the Great*. Westminster, England: Archbold Constable, 1893.

———. *Ancient India as Described in Classical Literature*. Westminster, England: Archbold Constable, 1901.

MCLEOD, W.H. *The Evolution of the Sikh Community*. Oxford: Clarendon Press, 1976.

———. *The Sikhs: History, Religion, and Society*. New York: Columbia University Press, 1989.

MEILE, P. "Mythology of the Tamils," in P. Grimal, ed., *World Mythology*. London: Hamlyn Publishing, 1965.

MILLER, P. "Jewel of India's Malabar Coast, *National Geographic*, May 1988.

MILLS, J.P. *The Lhota Nagas*. London: Macmillan and Co., 1922.

———. *The Regma Nagas*. London: Macmillan and Co., 1937.

MINES, M. "Social Stratification Among Muslim Tamils in Tamilnadu, South India," in I. Ahmad, ed., *Caste and Social Stratification Among the Muslims*. New Delhi: Manohar Book Service, 1973.

———. "Islamisation of Muslim Ethnicity in South India," *Man* 10 (1975).

MITRA, S.M. *Anglo-Indian Studies*. London: Longmans, Green and Co., 1913.

MITTER, S. *Dharma's Daughters: Contemporary Indian Women and Hindu Culture*. New Brunswick, NJ: Rutgers University Press, 1991.

MOORE, C.A., ed. *The Indian Mind: Essentials of Indian Philosophy and Culture*. Honolulu: University Press of Hawaii, 1971.

MOSES, S.T. "The Muhammadans of Pulicat: An Ethnical Study," *Man in India* 3 (1923).

MUDALIAR, C. "State and Religious Endowments in Madras." Ph.D. Dissertation, Madras: University of Madras, 1965.

———. *The Secular State and Religious Institutions in India*. Wiesbaden: Franz Steiner, 1974.

MUJEEB, M. *The Indian Muslims*. London: Oxford University Press, 1967.

NADARAJAH, D. *Women in Tamil Society: The Classical Period*. Kuala Lumpur: University of Malaya, 1966.

NAYAGAM, X.S.T. *Tamil Culture and Civilization.* New York: Asia Publishing House, 1973.

NEHRU, J. T*he Discovery of India.* New York: The John Day Co., 1946.

O'CONNELL, J.T., et al., eds. *Sikh History and Religion in the Twentieth Century.* Toronto: University of Toronto, 1988.

———. "Jati-Vaishavas of Bengal: Subcaste (Jati) Without Caste (Varna)," *Journal of Asian and African Studies* 17 (1982).

OLDENBURG, V.T. "Tolerant Hinduism Under Assault," *Los Angeles Times* (November 25, 1990).

ORANS, M. "A Tribe in Search of a Great Tradition," *Man in India* 39 (1959).

———. *The Santal: A Tribe in Search of a Great Tradition.* Detroit, MI: Wayne State University Press, 1965.

PALANI, S.S. "Insight," *Hinduism Today* (February 1991).

PANDARATHAR, S.T.V. *History of the Later Cholas.* Annamalainagar: Annamalai University, 1967.

PANDIAN, J. "The Anthopological Quest for a Sanskritic Civilization of India," *South Asian Anthropologist* 5 (1984).

———. *Anthropology and the Western Tradition.* Prospect Heights, IL: Waveland Press, 1985.

———. *Caste, Nationalism, and Ethnicity.* Bombay: Popular Prakashan, 1987.

———. *Culture, Religion, and the Sacred Self.* Englewood Cliffs, NJ: Prentice Hall, 1991.

PARAMASIVANANDAM, A.M. *Tamilnad Through Ages.* Madras: Tamil Kalai Illam, 1960.

PILLAY, K.K. *A Social History of the Tamils.* Madras: University of Madras, 1969.

POCOCK, D.F. "The Movement of Castes," *Man* 55 (1955).

POLO, M. *The Travels of Marco Polo.* New York: Penguin Books, 1958.

POSSEHL, G.C. *Ancient Cities of the Indus.* Durham, NC: Carolina Academic Press, 1979.

PRESLER, F.A. "Religion Under Bureaucracy," Ph.D. dissertation, Department of Political Science, University of Chicago Press, 1978.

QUIGLEY, D. *The Interpretation of Caste.* New York: Oxford University Press, 1993.

RADHAKRISHNAN, S. and C.A. MOORE, eds. *A Source Book in Indian Philosophy.* Princeton, NJ: Princeton University Press, 1957.

RAHEJA, G. *The Poison in the Gift: Ritual, Prestation, and the Dominant Caste in a North Indian Village.* Chicago: University of Chicago Press, 1988.

RAJSHEKAR, V.T. *Dalit: The Black Untouchables of India.* Atlanta, GA: Clarity Press, 1987.

RAKSHIT, H.K. "The Brahmins of India: An Anthropometric Study," *Man in India* 46 (1966).

RAMANUJAN, A.K. *Speaking of Siva.* New York: Penguin Books, 1973.

RAWLINSON, H.G. "Geography and Prehistory," in O.L. Chavarria-Agilar, ed., *Traditional India.* Englewood Cliffs, NJ: Prentice Hall, 1964.

Report of the Backward Classes Commission of Tamilnadu. Madras: Government of Tamil Nadu Press, 1971.

RISLEY, H. *The People of India.* London: Thacker and Co., 1891.

ROBINSON, F., ed. *The Cambridge Encyclopedia of India.* Cambridge: Cambridge University Press, 1989.

ROCHE, P.A. *Fishermen of the Coromandel: A Social Study of the Paravas of the Coromandel.* New Delhi: Manohar, 1984.

ROSE, H.A. *A Glossary of the Tribes and Castes of the Punjab and North-West Frontier Province* (3 vols.). Lahore: Government Printing, 1919.

ROY, S.C. *The Mundas and Their Country.* New York: Asia Publishing House, 1970.

RUDOLPH, L.I. and S.H. RUDOLPH. *The Modernity of Tradition: Political Development in India.* Chicago: University of Chicago Press, 1967.

RUSSELL, R.V. *The Tribes and Castes of the Central Provinces of India* (4 vols.). London: Macmillan and Co., 1916.

SAHNI, J. "Passover in India," *Los Angeles Times* (March 24, 1991).

SASTRI, K.A.N. *Development of Religion in South India.* Bombay: Orient Longmans, 1963.

———. *The Culture and History of the Tamils.* Calcutta: Mukhopadhayay, 1964.

———. *A History of South India from Prehistoric Times to the Fall of Vijayanagar.* Madras: Oxford University Press, 1960.

SASTRI, R. *The Tamils and Their Culture.* Annamalainagar: Annamalai University, 1967.

SCHIFFMAN, H. "Language, Linguistics, and Politics in Tamilad," in E. Gerow and M.D. Lang, eds., *Studies in the Language and Culture of South Asia.* Seattle: University of Washington Press, 1973.

SCOFIELD, J. "India in Crisis," *National Geographic,* May (1963).

SEMA, H. *The Emergence of Nagaland.* New Delhi: Vikas Publishing House, 1986.

SEN, K.C. *Hinduism.* New York: Penguin Books, 1961.

SEWELL, R. *The Historical Inscriptions of Southern India and Outlines of Political History.* Madras: University of Madras, 1932.

SHARMA, V.M. "The Problem of Village Hinduism: Fragmentation and Integration," *Contributions to Indian Sociology* 4 (1970).

SHEPPHERD, J. *The Elements of Bahai Faith.* Shaftesbury, England: Element Books, Ltd., 1992.

SHULMAN, D.D. *Tamil Temple Myths: Sacrifice and Divine Marriage in South Indian Saiva Tradition.* Princeton, NJ: Princeton University Press, 1980.

SILVERBERG, J., ed. *Social Mobility in the Caste System.* The Hague: Mouton, 1968.

SINGARAVELU, S. *Social Life of the Tamils.* Kuala Lumpur: University of Malaya Press, 1966.

SINGER, L. "Ethnogenesis and the Negro Americans Today," *Social Research* 28 (1962).

SINGER, M. "The Social Organization of Indian Civilization," *Diogenes* 45 (1964).

————. *When a Great Tradition Modernizes: An Anthropological Approach to Indian Civilization.* New York: Praeger Publishers, 1972.

SINGER, M. and B.S. COHN, eds. *Structure and Change in Indian Society.* Chicago: Aldine Publishing Company, 1968.

SINGH, H., ed. *Caste Among Non-Hindus in India.* New Delhi: National Publishing House, 1977.

SINGH, K. *The Sikhs Today.* New Delhi: Orient Longman Limited, 1985.

SINNATAMBY, J.R. "The Pandyans," *Journal of Tamil Studies* 3 (1973).

SIVERTSEN, D. *When Caste Barriers Fall.* New York: Humanities Press, 1963.

SLATER, G. *The Dravidian Elements in Indian Culture.* New Delhi: Ess Ess Publications, 1976.

SMITH, V.A. *Early History of India, From 600 B.C. to the Muhammadan Conquest.* Oxford: Oxford University Press, 1924.

SMITH, W.C. *The Ao Naga Tribe of Assam.* London: Macmillan and Co., 1925.

SPEAR, P. *A History of India,* vol. 2. Baltimore, MD: Penguin Books, 1968.

————. *India, Pakistan and the West.* London: Oxford University Press, 1963.

————. *A History of India,* vol. 2. Baltimore, MD: Penguin Books, 1965.

SPRATT, P. *D.M.K in Power.* Bombay: Nachiketa Publications, 1970.

SRIDHARAN, K. *A Maritime History of India.* New Delhi: Ministry of Information and Broadcasting, 1965.

SRINIVAS, M.N. *Religion and Society Among the Coorgs of South India.* Oxford: Oxford University Press, 1952.

————. *Indian Villages.* Bombay: Asia Publishing House, 1955.

————. "A Note on Sanskritization and Westernization," *Far Eastern Quarterly* 15 (1956).

————. *Caste in Modern India and Other Essays.* London: Asia Publishing House, 1962.

————. *Social Change in Modern India.* Berkeley: University of California Press, 1966.

————. "The Cohesive Role of Sanskritization," in P. Mason, ed., *India and Ceylon.* New York: Oxford University Press, 1967.

————. *The Dominant Caste and Other Essays.* Delhi: Oxford University Press, 1987.

STAAL, J.F. "Sanskrit and Sanskritization," *The Journal of Asian Studies* 22 (1963).

STEIN, B. "Social Mobility and Medieval South Indian Hindu Sects," in J. Silverberg, ed., *Social Mobility in the Caste system in India.* The Hague: Mouton, 1968.

————. "Circulation and Historical Geography of Tamil Country," *Journal of Asian Studies* 37 (1977).

STRIZOWER, S. "News as an Indian Caste," *The Jewish Journal of Sociology* 1 (1959).

SUBRAMANIAM, N. *Sangam Polity: The Administration and Social Life of the Sangam Tamils.* Bombay: Asia Publishing House, 1966.

SUKHWAL, B.L. *Modern Political Geography of India.* New Delhi: Sterling Publishers, 1985.

SULERI, S. *The Rhetoric of English India.* Chicago: University of Chicago Press, 1992.

TARWICK, M. *Notes on Love in a Tamil Family.* Berkeley: University of California Press, 1992.

THAPAR, R. *A History of India.* Middlesex, England: Penguin Books, 1966.

THURSTON, E. *Castes and Tribes of Southern India* (7 vols.). Madras: Government Press, 1909.

TINKER, HUGH. *South Asia: A Short History,* 2nd ed. Honolulu: University of Hawaii Press, 1990.

————. "South Asia at Independence: India, Pakistan and Sri Lanka," in A.J. Wilson and D. Dalton, eds., *The States of South Asia.* Honolulu: University of Hawaii Press, 1989.

TYLER, S.A. *India: An Anthropological View.* Pacific Palisades, CA: Goodyear Publishing House, 1973.

WALLACE, A.F.C. *Culture and Personality.* New York: Random House, 1970.

WALLBANK, T.W. *A Short History of India and Pakistan.* New York: The New American Library, 1965.

WATKINS, F.M. "State: The Concept," *The International Encyclopedia of the Social Sciences* 15 (1968).

WEBER, M. *The Religion of India.* New York: Free Press, 1967.

WILSON, A.J. and D. DALTON. *The States of South Asia: Problems of National Integration.* Honolulu: University of Hawaii Press, 1990.

WINK, A. *Al-Hind: The Making of the Indo-Islamic World.* Leiden: E.J. Brill, 1990.

WINKS, R.W. and J.R. RUSH, eds. *Asia in Western Fiction.* Honolulu: University of Hawaii Press, 1990.

WISER, W.H. *The Hindu Jajmani System.* New Delhi: Munshiram Manoharlal Publishers, 1988.

WOLF, E.R. *Europe and the People Without History.* Berkeley: University of California Press, 1982.

WOLPERT, S. *A New History of India.* New York: Oxford University Press, 1989.

————. *India.* Berkeley: University of California Press, 1991.

WORSLEY, P. *The Third World.* Chicago: University of Chicago Press, 1964.

ZIMMER, H. *Philosophies of India.* Princeton, NJ: Princeton University Press, 1951.

✠ INDEX

A

Abel, E., 101-102
Achaemenid Persian Empire, 6, 7, 24
Adigal, Ilango, 183 (*See also* Kannagi)
Adigal, Maraimalai, 187 (*See also* Swami
    Vedachalam Pillai)
Aggarwal, P.C., 91
Ahmad, I., 91
Aiyar, Swaminatha, 187
Ajlat, 90
Akali Dal movement, 194, 195 (*See also* Sikhism)
Akbar, 109, 140
al-Hind, 23, 25
Alexander the Great, 24, 125
Ali, Hyder, 163
Ambedkar, B.R., 160
amman, 177, 232, 249-254 (*See also* Mother goddess;
    Pulicat village)
Andhra Pradesh, 146, 163-164 (*See also* Telugu)
Anglo-Indian:
    definition, 100-101
    identity, 99-102
    population, 102
Anna DMK, 191
Annadurai, Aringar C.N., 189 (*See also* Dravidastan)
Ansari, G., 91
Ansari, I.A., 92
Anthropological surveys, 35-36, 79
Arab, 35, 84 (*See also* Labbays)
    settlements in southern India, 26, 87-90, 127
Arabi-Malayalam, 87-88 (*See also* Moplahs)
Arabi-Tamil, 87-88 (*See also* Labbays)

Arabization, 87-90, 92
    compared with Persianization, 87
Arabized Muslims, 87 (*See also* Moplahs)
Arokiaswami, M., 173
Arrian, 24 (*See also* Xenophon)
Artha-sastra, 125
Arunachal Pradesh, 162
Arunachalam, M., 173
Arya Samaj movement, 62, 154, 194
Aryan: (*See also* Caste system)
    institution of village communalism, 207
    institution of warrior-king, 60
    meaning of, 25
    and religious practices, 60
    and Sanskritic tradition, 61 (*See also*
        Hinduization)
Aryanism, myth of, 14, 105-106, 110-113, 137-138,
    267
Aryans, 7-8, 28, 35, 57, 60, 112
    color differences between Pakistan and Iran,
        24
    Dravidianized, 7, 30, 35, 261
    Hinduized, 7, 78
    as interpreted in the 19th century, 8
Aryavarta, 23, 25, 112
Ashraf, 90
Asoka, 25, 54, 124, 125, 161 (*See also*
    Buddhism; Indian identity)
Assam, 160, 162, 274
Assamese, 5, 162-163
atman, 57, 58
Aurangzeb, 109, 157, 160
Austro-Asiatic languages, 6, 162

B

Babur, 85, 109, 197, 261
Baden-Powell, B.H., 207-208
Bangladesh, 32, 92, 112
  and Bengali, 92, 160
Barth, F., 92
Basarappa, 163
Basham, A.L., 277
Beals, A.R., 208
Beck, B.E.F., 173, 210
Bengal, 160-161
Bengali language, 5, 32
Beteille, A., 105, 113, 209-210
Bharat, 32
Bharata Natyam, 124, 164
Bharati, Agehananda, 260-261
Bhindranwale, Sant Jarnail Singh, 195-196 (*See also* Khalistan)
Bihar, 154 (*See also* Hindi; Hindistan; Linguistic states)
Bose, Subhas C., 142
Brahman, 57, 58
Brahmanical priesthood, 60 (*See also* Aryan; Caste System; Indus Valley Civilization; Sanskritization)
  and Hindu kingship, 125
  movements against, 62, 76-77
  and state temples, 177
  village rituals, 245-249, 254-258 (*See also* Pulicat village)
Brahmanization, 72, 267 (*See also* Sanskritization)
Brahmins:
  classified by region and dietary prohibitions, 155
  identified as Aryan/Sanskritic, non-Brahmins as Dravidian/Tamil, 187-188
  Nambutri, 165
  Panc Gauda vs. Panc Dravida, 154-155
Brahmo Samaj, 161
British: (*See also* Colonialism; Pulicat village; Racism)
  colonialism in India, three periods, 135-138
  compared with Mughal Empire, 86, 126, 133, 135, 136
  effect on tribal groups, 78-79
  land system, 174-175
  role in creating nationalism, 31-34, 121
  segregation in India, 34-35, 86, 135-138 (*See also* Colorism; Racism)
  and Sikhs, 193-194, 201, 202
  using Indians to fight Indians, 134, 141
  vs. Dutch and French, 126-127
Brown, J.M., 150-151
Buddhism, 7, 52, 54, 62, 160, 179, 181, 185
Burgess, J., 229
Burma, 162

C

Caldwell, Bishop Robert, 74, 111, 187
Campbell, Joseph, 275
Caste: (*See also* Caste groups; Caste system; Jati; Varna)
  definition of, 67, 80
  and ethnic group, 76-77, 261
  and Hindu sectarianism, 75-77
  identity, confusion concerning, 69-71
  and individual identity, 72
  and Islam (*See also* Islamic ethnicity; Islamic identity)
  and Jainism, 52, 77
  names, 211-213, 240-241
  and skin color, 68, 104-105, 112 (*See also* Colorism)
  and social mobility, 61, 71-75 (*See also* Invasions; Nadar caste)
  titles, 70-71, 211-213, 240-241
Caste groups:
  compared to ethnic groups, 81, 269, 270 (*See also* Hinduization)
  emergence of new, 80
Caste system, 35, 66-79 (*See also* Hinduization; Jajmani system; Pulicat village; Sanskritization)
  anthropological studies, 209
  and Aryans, 67, 270
  attacked, 188 (*See also* Dravidastan; Justice Party)
  compared to other systems of stratification, 66, 68
  Hindu and Muslim compared, 90-91
  and history, 264-265 (*See also* Myth and history contrasted)
  legitimizing role of Brahmanical priesthood, 60, 62, 72
  origin of, 67-68, 108
  and Sikhism, 156-158
  and tribal groups, 77-79
  why it continues to survive, 148
Chatterjee, Bakim Chandra, 161
Chatterji, S.K., 111, 173, 187
Chattopadhyay, Sarachandra, 161
Chenthamil, 178-179
Chola Empire, 125, 167
Civilization, concept of, 266-268
  contrasted with *kultur*, 266
Clive, Robert, 127, 129-131
Cohen, A., 273
Cohn, B.S., 228, 257
Cole, W.O., 198-199
Colonialism, 34-35 (*See also* British)
Colorism, 35, 86, 93, 103-115 (*See also* British; Racism)
  definition of, 84
  and status, 107-108
  and varna, 108-109
Company Raj, 129-133, 136, 140 (*See also* British; Crown raj; Empire-state; Robert Clive)
Congress (I) party, 114
Coon, C.S., 40-41
Coorg, 163
Coromandel Coast, 27, 87
Coward, H., 49, 53
Crisis rituals, 246-249
Crole, C.S., 218
Crown Raj, 139-141, 148, 169
Cultural analysis, 4
Culture as a communication system, 12-13 (*See also* Semiotic perspective)

D

Dale, S.F., 91
Dalistastan, 272
Dalit movement, 272
Danielou, A., 52, 55, 107-108
Dasa, 111
Datta, Michael Madhusudan, 161
Dean, V.M., 150
De Bary, William T., 129
Deely, J., 14
Democracy as historical development in Europe
    compared with India, 148-149
Derrett, J.D.M., 177
Deva, 60
Devanagari script, 34, 155 (*See also* Hindi-ization;
    Urdization)
DeVos, G., 268-269
Dharma, 56, 60, 124
Diglossia, 178
Disease and possession, 251
Divinity and kingship, 60
Diwani rights, 135, 206
DMK, 189-191 (*See also Dravida Munnetra Kalagam*)
    political power, 191
Doniger (O'Flaherty), W., 275-276
Dravida Kalagam (Dravidian Association), 189
Dravida Munnetra Kalagam (Dravidian Advance-
    ment Association), 189 (*See also* DMK)
Dravidastan, 169-191
    origin, 188
Dravidian:
    –Aryan synthesis, 261
    as interpreted in the 19th century, 8, 111
    languages, 5, 171-172
    as non-Brahmin, 187-188
    origin of term, 111-112, 187
    purity movement, 62, 187
    settlement in India, 164-165, 171-173
D'Souza, V.S., 90, 91
Dube, S.C., 208
Dumont, L., 69, 70, 90, 91, 277
Dupleix, Francois, 128-129
Dutch, 127 (*See also* Pulicat village)
Dyer, Reginald, 141

E

East India Company, 129
East Pakistan, 160
Eco, U., 14
Egnor, M., 173, 182
Empire concept, 6, 33, 120 (*See also* Empire-state;
    India as nation-state; Nation; Nationalism)
Empire-state, 120-151, 142-145, 169, 270 (*See also*
    Crown Raj; Hindi Raj; Nation)
    colonial, 169-170
    four kinds, 122
    opposed to ethnic "separatism," 170
Engle, J., 199-200
English language, 28, 33, 34, 86, 136, 143 (*See also*
    British; Nationalism)

Enthoven, R.E., 267
Equivalence structure models, 92
Ethnic groups, 76 (*See also* Caste; Caste groups)
    aspirations for national political autonomy,170
    definition of, 81, 269
Ethnic identity, alien, 80-102
Ethnicity: (*See also* Nationalism)
    definition of, 81, 268-274
    and modernization, 269
    non-Hindu, 80-81, 270
Ethnic politics, 269-274
Ethnogenesis, 273

F

Fairservis, W., 171
Fardi, F.R., 270
Farmer, E.L., 83, 86, 109, 134, 197
Finley, M.I., 263
Fishing, organization of rights, 236-240 (*See also*
    Padu muray; Pulicat village)
Fortes, M., 267

G

Gaikwad, V.R., 101
Gandhi, Indira, 115, 150, 195, 202
Gandhi, Mahatma, 33, 102, 125, 142, 159, 279
    origin of name, 159
    plan for India, 143-144
    as symbol of Hindu spirituality, 279-280
Gandhi, Maneka, 115
Gandhi, Priyanka, 115
Gandhi, Rajiv, 6, 11, 100, 114
Gandhi, Sanjay, 115
Gandhi, Sonia, 114
Ganges, 56-57
Geertz, C., 12
Gellner, E., 272
Gopal, R., 91
Gough, E.K., 209
Great Tradition vs. Little Tradition, 266-267, 268
Greeks, 7, 24-25, 35, 106
Guha, B.C., 38
Guha, U., 91
Gujarat, 159-160
Gujarati, 5, 98, 159
Gupta, Chandra, 125
Gupta, J.D., 269
Gurmukhi script, 155
Guru Nanak Panth, 199-200 (*See also* Guru
    Nanak; Sikhism)

H

Hansen, Barbara, 9
Hardgrave, R.L., 73, 74, 191
Harijan, 102
Hart, G.L., 173, 180, 182

Haryana, 154, 194-195 (*See also* Hindi;Hindistan; Linguistic states; Sikhs)
Hastings, Warren, 127, 132-133 (*See also* Company raj)
Healy, J.F., 26
Herbert, Jean, 50
Herodotus, 24
Himachal Pradesh, 154 (*See also* Hindi; Hindistan; Linguistic states)
Hindavi, 30, 31 (*See also* Khari Boli)
Hindi, 5, 28, 34, 142, 143, 153-155, 159
  criticized as a national language, 143-144, 145 (*See also* Hindi Raj; Mahatma Gandhi)
  number of speakers, 34
Hindi Raj, 142-145, 148, 169
Hindi-ization, 33-34, 146, 271 (*See also* Linguistic states; Nationalism)
Hindistan, 153-155, 169
Hindi/Urdu, 33 (*See also* Urdu/Hindi)
Hindu:
  biopsychological system, 57-58
  gods, 55-56
    color of, 107-108
  identity, 63 (*See also* Sanskritization)
  metaphysical system, 57-58
  vs. non-Hindu traditions, 91-92 (*See also* India; Indian identity)
  origin of name, 23, 30
  sectarianism, 75-77
Hinduism: (*See also* Hindu gods; Mother goddess; Pulicat village; Sanskritization)
  absence of heresy in, 51, 53, 65, 75, 257-258
  biopsychological, 58
  and Buddhism, 54
  concept of divinity in, 55
  and conceptions of the self, 57-58
  contrasted with Christianity, 65
  group-specific sacred symbols, 63 (*See also* Mother goddess)
  metaphysical, 58
  origins of, 57-58
  parochial models, 256-258
  personal freedom in, 52
  personal god (*ishta devta*), 56
  pilgrimage centers, 56
  and protest movements, 52
  quotes concerning, 49-50
  ritual traditions, 56
  sant tradition, 198-199
  sectarian traditions, 56, 75-77
  Siva myths, 276
  sociological, 58
  state temples vs. communal temples, 177
  Tantric, 162
Hinduization, 58-61, 78, 197, 267, 270 (*See also* Caste system)
Hindustani, 30, 31, 33, 143 (*See also* Hindi; Hindistan; Khari Boli; Muslims)
Hodson, T.C., 267
Holmes, G., 229
Hooton, E.A., 38-40
Hudson, 79

Huns, 7, 35, 78, 106
Hutton, J.H., 79, 267

I

Ibbetson, D., 267
Ibn Battuta, 27
Inam (gifted) villages, 208
Inden, Ronald B., 66, 138
India:
  anthropological studies, 267, 277-278
  Arab references to, 23, 25-27
  communal villages as evolutionary stage, 206-207
  compared with Britain in the 18th century, 131-132
  ethnic diversity in, 6, 9-10, 27-29, 30, 35, 261 (*See also* Ethnicity; Nationalism)
  and European powers, 127-128, 261
  four periods, 261
  Greek and Persian conceptions of, 24
  as Hindu vs. non-Hindu, 91-92, 271-272 (*See also* Hindi-ization; Linguistic states)
  and independence, 140-141
  influence of Islam, 82, 84 (*See also* Islamization)
  language families, 5-6 (*See also* Assamese; Austro-Asiatic languages; Bengali; Dravidian languages; Gujarati; Hindi; Indo-European languages; Kannada; Kashmiri; Konkani; Malayalam; Marathi; Panjabi; Tamil; Telugu; Tibeto-Burman languages; Urdu; Uriya)
  linguistic diversity in, 143, 145-148, 153-168
  and Mongols, 85 (*See also* Mughal; Turks)
  as nation-state, 6, 32, 33, 120-121, 142-143 (*See also* Empire concept; Hindi Raj; Indian nationality)
  origin of name, 23
  paradoxes, 5, 51
  Persian-Greek invention, 25
  physical features, 112
  population, 5-6
  references to in history, 23-27
  regional variation in village organization, 207-208
  and Sanskrit, 271
  shaped by the West, 259-281
  southern cultural tradition, 26
  survey textbooks, 17-18
  tribes, 18
  and Turks, 84-86
  and Western democracy, 148-151
Indian identity, 6 (*See also* Caste system; Empire concept; India; Indian nationality; Language as unifying)
  anthropometric studies, 36 (*See also* "Races of India"; Scientific racism)
  and Arabs, 25-26, 87 (*See also* Arabization; Persianization)
  and Asoka, 25
  and Brahmanical priesthood, 63

and caste, 61
and colonialism, 35
and food, 9
Gandhi and Nehru's perceptions contrasted,
   143-145
and Hindi, 143-144
and Hinduism, 91-92
of Indus Valley Civilization, 25
and Islam, 30 (*See also* Islamic ethnicity; Islamic
   identity; Islamization; Muslim identity;
   Religion and national identity)
and Persian, 83 (*See also* Persianization)
and Sanskrit, 63 (*See also* Sanskritization)
Western influence, 262, 278-279
Indian nationality: (*See also* British; India; Indian
   identity; Nationalism)
conception of, 31-34
Indianization, 146
Indians:
   early descriptions of, 23-24
Indo-European languages, 5, 159, 162
Indu, 23
Indus cultural pot, 7
Indus Valley Civilization, 25-26, 59
and Brahmanical priesthood, 60
and caste, 67-68
decline of, 164
and Dravidians, 171-172
knowledge of, 137-138, 267
Invasions of India, 7-8, 35, 124, 125
and caste identity, 81
and caste mobility, 72
and colorism, 35, 106, 112
and high status of foreign invaders, 86, 261
less in south than in north, 26 (*See also* Trade)
Iranians, 7 (*See also* Persians)
Ishwaran, K., 208
Islam: (*See also* Pulicat village)
definition, 82
founding principles, 82
schisms, 82
Islamic ethnicity, 81-83
Islamic identity, 81-90
Islamization, 87, 197
Iyer, L.K.A., 79, 267

J

Jajmani system, 68-69
Jainism, 7, 52, 54, 62, 77, 159, 179, 181, 185
Jallianwala Bagh, 141
Jammu and Kashmir, 158
Jati, 58, 67, 68, 109, 176, 209-213, 245-246 (*See also*
   Caste System)
compared with tribe, 79
Jewish identity, 93-96
and colorism, 93-94, 110
Jiva, 57
Juggernaut (*Jagannath*), 162
Justice Party, 188 (*See also* South Indian
   Libertarian Federation)

K

Kailas, 57
Kalaingar, Paritimal, 187 (*See also* Suryanarayan
   Sastri)
Kalinga Empire, 161
Kanakasabhai, V., 173
Kannada, 5, 163
Kannagi, 182, 183-185
Karma, 56, 124
Karnataka, 162-164
Karppu, 181-183
definition, 182
Kashmiri, 5, 155, 158-159
Kerala, 164-168
Khalsa, 192, 194, 200 (*See also* Sikhism)
Panth, 200-201
Khalistan, 11, 158, 192-202 (*See also* Sikhism; Sikhs)
Khan, Z., 91
Khan, Chingiz, 85
Khari Boli, 29-31, 153
Knipe, David M., 50, 265-266
Konkani, 5
Krishnamurthi, S.R., 173
Krishnaswamy, A., 229
Kshatriyas: (*See also* Caste system; Hinduization)
Persian, Greek, Scythian, and Hun origins, 7
Kuppam, 222

L

Labbays, 87, 88-90 (*See also* Pulicat village)
definition of, 88
Ladakh, 158
Language as unifying, 27-28, 34 (*See also* English
   language; Hindi; Hindi-ization; Persian
   language; Sanskrit; Sanskritization; Urdu)
Leach, E.R., 65
Leaf, M.J., 208
Lehmann, W.P., 178
Lingayat movement, 54, 62, 77, 163
Linguistic state, 6-8, 121, 143, 144, 145-148 (*See
   also* Empire-state; India; Nation-state)
Linguistic states:
   six Hindi, 146, 148, 153-155, 169 (*See also* Hindi;
      Hindi Raj; Hindistan; Hindustani)
   Telugu, 146
   Tibeto-Burman, 146, 148

M

Madhya Pradesh, 154 (*See also* Hindi;
   Hindistan; Linguistic states)
Mahabharata, 56, 108, 109, 124, 164, 181, 257
Maharashtra, 160
Maine, Sir Henry, 206-207
Malabar Coast, 26-27, 87, 166
Malayalam, 5, 87, 165
Maloney, Clarence, 6-7, 18, 146-147, 171-173, 180
Mamluk, 84-85 (*See also* Turks)

definition of, 84
dynasties, 85
Mandelbaum, D.G., 76, 79, 90, 94, 228
Manimaekalai, 175
Manipur, 162
Mappilas, 87, 89, 90 (*See also* Moplahs)
Marathi language, 5, 159
Maravar, 74 (*See also* Nadar caste)
Marco Polo, 27, 107-108
Marriott, McKim, 66, 208, 258
Maurya, Chandra Gupta, 125
Mauryan Empire, 25, 125 (*See also* Asoka)
McLeod, W.H., 195-196, 201
Meghalaya, 162
Megasthenes, 24
Meile, P., 173
Migrations (*See also* Invasions of India)
Miller, P., 27
Mills, J.P., 79
Mines, M., 90, 91
Mirasidars (landlords), 208
Mitter, Sara S., 49
Mizoram, 162
Mongols, 29, 30, 34, 35, 85, 106
Moore, C.A., 55
Moplahs, 87-88, 90 (*See also* Mappilas)
   divided into five castes, 90
Moses, S.T., 226, 228, 231
Mother goddess, 63-65 (*See also* Amman; Pulicat
   village)
   and caste conflict, 65
   compared to Christian saints, 65
   and disease, 65, 251
Mudaliar, C., 177
Mughal:
   definition of, 84
   Empire, 29, 85, 86, 126, 130, 136, 163-165, 197
Mujeeb, M., 91
Muller, Max, 137, 276-277
Munivar, Veerama, 187
Muruga worship, 177
Muslim, 33 (*See also* Hindustani; Indian identity;
   Islam; Labbays)
   definition of, 82
   identity, 8, 81-82, 93, 159, 161
Mysore, 163
Myth and history contrasted, 264 (*See also* Caste
   system; Western historiography)

N

Nadan, 73-75 (*See also* Nadar caste)
Nadar caste, 72-75
Nadarajah, D., 173
Nadu veadu, 255-256
Nagaland, 162
Naicker, Periyar E.V. Ramaswamy, 188-189 (*See
   also* Dravidastan)
Naming ceremony, 246 (*See also* Crisis rituals)
Nanak, Guru, 156-157, 192, 198 (*See also* Sikhism)
Nation: (*See also* Empire-state; Linguistic state)
   definition, 120
   -state, 6, 121-122
Nationalism: (*See also* British; Ethnicity; India)
   definition, 272

Hindi, 15 (*See also* Hindi-ization)
linguistic, 33-34, 168, 170-191, 192 (*See also*
   Dravidastan)
religious, 168, 192-202 (*See also* Khalistan)
among tribal groups, 274
Western influence, 262, 269, 271
Nayagam, X.S.T., 173
Nayars, 165
Nehru, Jawaharlal, 15, 114, 142, 154, 202, 279
   dynastic rule, 114-115
   plan for India, 143-145
   as product of Western discourse, 260, 279-281
Nizam of Hyderabad, 164

O

Oldenberg, Veena Talwar, 50
Opium trade, 133 (*See also* Company raj)
Orans, M., 78, 79
Oriya language, 162
Orissa, 160-162

P

Padu muray (area system), 237-240 (*See also*
   Fishing; Pulicat village)
Pakistan:
   Aryan settlers of, 24
   and ethnic-linguistic diversity, 92-93, 155
   migrations into, 24
   as nation-state, 32, 141-142
   and Urdu, 31, 92
Palani, Rev. Swami Siva Siva, 50
Pandarathar, S.T.V., 173
Pandian, Jacob, 57, 61
Pandyas, 167
Panini, 28
Panjab, 194-195 (*See also* Sikhs)
Panjabi language, 5, 32, 92-93, 155 (*See also*
   Pakistan; Sikhs)
Paramahamsa, Ramakrishna, 161
Paramasivanandam, A.M., 173, 174
Parsi identity, 97-99, 115
Patel, Sardar V., 142
Persian language, 28, 29, 33, 34, 83, 86, 164
Persianization, 83-86, 87, 92, 106-107 (*See also*
   Arabization)
   effect on upper-class Indians, 87
Persians, 7, 24-26, 35, 106 (*See also* Invasions;
   Iranians)
Perso-Arabic script, 34, 155
Pillai, Ananda Ranga, 128-129
Pillai, Swami Vedachalam, 187 (*See also* Maraimalai
   Adigal)
Pillay, K.K., 173, 176
"Pizza effect," 260-261
Pliny the Elder, 26, 27
Pluratheism, 55 (*See also* Hinduism)
   vs. polytheism, 55
Portuguese, 127-128, 135
Possehl, G.C., 113
Post-modernist discourse, 260
Presler, F.A., 177
Pulicat village, 215-258

Brahmanic ritual and jati identity, 245-249
Brahmanical/Sanskritic and non-Brahmanical/
    non-Sanskritic beliefs integrated, 254-256
corporate authority, 242-244
description, 217-225
economic and social history, 230-232
European colonization of, 227-229
left-hand and right-hand jatis, 231-232
mother goddess temples, 232, 251-252
non-Brahmanical shamanism, 249-254
origin of name, 226-227
patron-client relationships, 236-240
political history, 226-230
reasons for studying, 217
religious history, 232-235
sociopolitical structure, 240-241

Q

Queen Victoria, 139-140

R

Race, 34-35
    and caste, 68
    and slavery, 111
"Races of India," 36-48
Racism, 35-36, 110, 137-138, 141 (*See also* Aryanism;
    British; Colonialism; Colorism; "Races of
    India"; Scientific racism)
    and slavery, 35
Radcliffe-Brown, A.R., 208
Radhakrishnan, S., 55
Rajasthan, 153-154 (*See also* Hindi; Hindistan;
    Linguistic states)
Rajshekar, V.T., 272
Ramayana, 56, 108, 124-125, 164, 181, 257
Rao, Narashimha, 114
Rawlinson, H.G., 262
Redfield, Robert, 208, 266
Religion: (*See also* Brahmanical priesthood;
    Shamanism)
    and conceptions of the self, 57
Religion
    functions of, 57
    and national identity, 32
Religious:
    conversion from Hinduism, 52
    freedom and religious violence, 51
    syncretism, 197-198 (*See also* Sant tradition)
Risley, H., 267
Robinson, F., 98, 158
Rose, H.A., 267
Roy, Raja Ram Mohan, 161
Roy, S.C., 79
Rudolph, L.I., 73, 74, 269-270
Rudolph, S.H., 73, 74, 269-270
Rushdie, Salman, 6
Russell, R.V., 267
Ryotwari system, 174, 207-208

S

Sacred cow, 108
Sah, Julie, 96
Sanskrit, 28, 29, 34
    compared with Latin, 28
    self as male, 182
Sanskritization, 34, 61-63, 72, 159, 164, 166 (*See
    also* Brahmanization)
    compared with Latinization in Europe, 62-63
    in Southeast Asia, 63
Sant tradition, 198-201
Sastri, R., 173
Sastri, Suryanarayan, 187 (*See also* Paritimal
    Kalaingar)
Satya Shodak Samaj, 160
Schiffman, H., 173, 178
Scientific racism, 35-36 (*See also* "Races of India")
Scythians, 7, 35, 78, 106
Sea trade, 26-27
Sectarianism, 56, 75-77, 270 (*See also* Hinduism)
Seleucid dynasty, 24
Seleucus, 24
Sema, H., 274
Semiotic perspective, 11-15, 274-281
Sen, Keshab Chandra, 161
Sepoy mutiny, 134, 139
Sewell, R., 228, 229
Shamanism, 60, 249-254 (*See also* Aryan;
    Brahmanical priesthood; Pulicat village)
Shanar, 73-74 (*See also* Nadar caste)
Shia, 82 (*See also* Islam)
Shivaji, 160
Shulman, D.D., 173
Siddiqui, M.M., 270
Sikh Panth, 199-200
Sikhism, 77, 155-158, 192 (*See also* Nationalism)
    compared with other religious identities, 156,
    193
Sikhs, 10-11, 192-193
    two categories of castes, 77
Silapathikaram, 175, 182, 183
Silverberg, J., 72
Sindhavan, 23
Singaravelu, S., 173
Singer, L., 273
Singer, Milton, 228, 266, 275, 277-279
Singh, H., 91
Singh, Guru Gobind, 157, 200-201
Singh, Maharaja Ranjit, 158
Sinnatamby, J.R., 180
Sivertsen, D., 209
Slater, G., 110
Slavery (*See also* Mamluk)
    European vs. Muslim conceptions, 35
Smith, Vincent A., 138
Social science as interpretive discourse rather
    than falsifiable, 16
Soma, 60
Southern India:
    history of sea trade, 26 (*See also* Coromandel
    Coast; Malabar Coast)
South Indian Libertarian Federation, 188 (*See also*
    Justice Party)
Spear, P., 140

Spratt, P., 187, 191
Sridharan, K., 229
Srinivas, M.N., 61, 208, 277 (*See also* Sanskritization)
State, 120-121
Stein, Burton, 71, 173, 174, 176, 185, 186
Strizower, S., 93
Subramaniam, N., 173
Sultan, Tippu, 163
Sunni, 82 (*See also* Islam)
Suya Mariyathai Iykkam (Self-Respect Union), 189 (*See also* Dravidastan)
Swarajya, 33
Syrian-Christian identity, 96-97

T

Tagore, Rabindranath, 161
Taittriya Upanisad, 55
Taj Mahal, symbol of Persian influence, 84, 109
Tamil:
   history, 171-191
   identity, 177, 178
      concepts of chastity, 181-185
      self as female, 182
   language, 5, 87, 178-180
      academies, 180
      compared with Latin and Sanskrit, 178
      and Muslims in southern India, 88-89
      platform speech, 190
   literature, 172-173, 175, 176, 179-191
      myth of homeland, 180
   religion, 177
Tamil Nadu, 164-168 (*See also* Dravidastan; Nationalism)
   kingdoms, 173-174
   origin of linguistic state, 175
   political organization, 174-175
Tamilakam, 175, 185-186
   definition, 185
   five ecological/cultural zones, 175-176
Tamils, 11
Telugu, 5, 146, 163-164
Textbooks:
   as paradigmatic, 16
   survey, 17
Thirukkural, 175, 180-181
Tholkappiam, 175
Thurston, E., 73, 74, 79, 210-211, 267
Tibeto-Burman languages, 6, 162
Tinker, Hugh, 93, 145
Tirupura, 162
Trade:
   Arab, 87 (*See also* Arabization)
Tribal groups, 77-79 (*See also* Hinduization)
   anthropological surveys of, 79
   influence of Christianity and Westernization on, 79
   and nationalism, 274

Tribe:
   compared with jati, 79
   definition of, 78
Two-nation theory, 8, 270
Turkish Muslims, 29, 84, 86, 106 (*See also* Persian language)
Turks, 29, 31, 34-35, 84-86, 136, 163, 196-197 (*See also* Persianization)
Tyler, S.A., 18, 23, 29-30, 59, 70, 155, 176, 182, 213

U

Untouchables, 272-273 (*See also* Dalistastan)
Urdization, 34 (*See also* Hindi-ization)
Urdu, 8, 30-31, 32, 83, 92, 164
   meaning of, 31
   Muslims in southern India, 88, 90
Urdu/Hindi, 29-31, 33 (*See also* Persianization)
Uriya, 5
Utar Pradesh, 154 (*See also* Hindi; Hindistan; Linguistic states)

V

Varna, 67, 91, 109, 212-213, 240-241 (*See also* Caste system)
Varna sankara, 109
Varnashrama-dharma, 57, 67
Vasco de Gama, 127
Vedas, 53, 55
Village types, 208, 215-216
   anthropological studies, 208-214
   caste operation in, 209
   ecological adaptations and social structure, 216

W

Wallace, A.F.C., 92
Watkins, F.M., 121
Weber, Max, 60, 76
West Pakistan, 161
Western historiography, 262-266 (*See also* Myth and history contrasted)
Wink, A., 25
Wolpert, S., 99, 139, 197, 198, 202
Worsley, P., 272

X

Xenophon, Flavius Arrianus, 24 (*See also* Arrian)

Z

Zamindari system, 174, 208
Zoroastrians (*See also* Parsi identity)